M359 Block 4
UNDERGRADUATE COMPUTING

Relational databases: theory and practice

Database life cycle

Block 4

This publication forms part of an Open University course M359 *Relational databases: theory and practice.* Details of this and other Open University courses can be obtained from the Student Registration and Enquiry Service, The Open University, PO Box 197, Milton Keynes MK7 6BJ, United Kingdom: tel. +44 (0)845 300 60 90, email general-enquiries@open.ac.uk

Alternatively, you may visit the Open University website at http://www.open.ac.uk where you can learn more about the wide range of courses and packs offered at all levels by The Open University.

To purchase a selection of Open University course materials visit http://www.ouw.co.uk, or contact Open University Worldwide, Michael Young Building, Walton Hall, Milton Keynes MK7 6AA, United Kingdom for a brochure: tel. +44 (0)1908 858793; fax +44 (0)1908 858787; email ouw-customer-services@open.ac.uk

The Open University
Walton Hall, Milton Keynes
MK7 6AA

First published 2007, second edition 2009.

Edited and designed by The Open University.

Typeset by S&P Enterprises (rfod) Limited, Glos.

Printed and bound in the United Kingdom by Hobbs the Printers Ltd, Totton, Hampshire.

ISBN 978 0 7492 5490 2

2.1

Contents

1 Introduction   **6**

  1.1 Case study   9

  1.2 Establishing requirements   10

  1.3 Data analysis   10

  1.4 Database design   11

  1.5 Implementation   12

  1.6 Maintenance   12

  1.7 Distributed data management   13

  1.8 Data warehousing   13

  1.9 Summary   14

2 Walton Stores: the supermarket case study   **15**

  2.1 Walton Stores   15

  2.2 Specification of requirements   24

  2.3 Summary   24

3 Data analysis   **25**

  3.1 Overview of the data analysis task   27

  3.2 Entity–relationship model   28

  3.3 Analysing text   58

  3.4 Analysing documents   90

  3.5 Validating an entity–relationship model   137

  3.6 Summary   139

4 Database design   **141**

  4.1 Representing entity types   144

  4.2 Representing relationships   151

  4.3 Representing complex data   168

  4.4 Representing constraints   171

  4.5 Representing entity subtypes   179

  4.6 Summary   187

5 Implementation   **188**

  5.1 Implementing a database schema   189

  5.2 Populating a database with data   193

  5.3 Developing and testing application software   196

  5.4 Summary   199

6	Database maintenance		200
	6.1	Denormalisation	201
	6.2	Database restructuring	205
	6.3	Summary	208
7	Distributed data management		209
	7.1	Client–multiserver systems	209
	7.2	Distributed databases	215
	7.3	Replication systems	225
	7.4	Summary	230
8	Data warehousing		231
	8.1	Decision support systems	232
	8.2	Multidimensional data model	234
	8.3	Data warehouses	250
	8.4	Summary	263
Block summary			265
Solutions to Exercises			266
Index			318

M359 COURSE TEAM

This course was produced by the following team (affiliated to The Open University, unless otherwise stated):

Course team

Kevin Waugh   Course Team Chair and Author
Ian Cooke   Author
Mike Newton   Author
Judith Segal   Author
Steven Self   Author
Alistair Willis   Author
Kay Bromley   Academic Editor
Ralph Greenwell   Course Manager and Accessibility Consultant

External assessor

Barry Lowden   University of Essex

Critical readers

Sue Barrass
Peter Blachford
Terry Burbidge
Pauline Butcher
Pauline Curtis
Hugh Darwen
Ivan Dunn
Gillian Mills
Ron Rogerson

LTS Media team

Andrew Seddon   Media Project Manager
Steve Rycroft   Editor
Andrew Whitehead   Designer and Graphic Artist
Pam Callow   Compositor
Kamy Yazdanjoo   Software Developer
Sue Stavert   Technical Testing Team

Thanks are due to the Desktop Publishing Unit of the Faculty of Mathematics and Computing.

1 Introduction

This block is concerned with the **database life cycle**, which describes the stages a database goes through, from the time the need for a database is established until it is withdrawn from use. The database life cycle has two main phases – **database development** and **database maintenance**. Database development concerns the tasks associated with those stages a database goes through during the building and installation of a new database that satisfies the information requirements of an enterprise. Database maintenance involves the tasks which ensure that the database continues to satisfy those requirements after it has been installed, and adapting the database to meet new and changing requirements.

The aim of this block is to enable you to develop the practical skills you will need to undertake the development of a database, from the analysis of the information requirements of some enterprise through to the implementation of a database that satisfies those requirements, using the database management system (DBMS) supplied with the course, SQL Anywhere.

This introductory section has two aims. First, to provide you with an opportunity to review your understanding of the model of database development presented in Section 4 of *Block 1*. Second, to provide an overview of the aims and content of the following sections of this block, which in turn focus on the tasks that must be completed before the database can move to the next stage of its life cycle – establishing requirements, data analysis, database design, implementation, testing and maintenance.

EXERCISE 1.1

Why do we need to take a formal approach to database development? Why should users not simply use SQL or the facilities provided by a database tool to develop their databases?

EXERCISE 1.2

(a) What are the desirable properties of a database?

(b) What would be the consequences if a database did not have these properties?

(c) What is the key task in database development that avoids these problems?

There are two important points related to system development in general, and database development in particular, which we raised in Section 4 of *Block 1* and need to review.

The first point is that our model of database development (see *Block 1*, Figure 4.5) is derived from the general model of system development (see *Block 1*, Figure 4.4) by incorporating the following three assumptions:

▶ we can separate development of a database – that is, specification and creation of a schema to define data in a database – from user processes that make use of the database;

▶ we can use the three-schema architecture (see *Block 1*, Figure 3.2) as a basis for distinguishing the activities associated with a schema;

▶ we can represent the constraints to enforce the semantics of data once, within a database, rather than within every user process that uses the data.

The aim of database development is to satisfy the **information requirements** of some enterprise that are expressed as a **statement of requirements**. Information requirements have two components – **data requirements** and **operational requirements**. Data requirements describe the data items, and the relationships *between* those data items, that need to be recorded by the database. Operational requirements describe how these data items, and the relationships between them, need to be processed.

EXERCISE 1.3

Which components of the three-schema architecture:

(a) represent the data requirements, and

(b) represent the operational requirements?

logical schema

storage schema   external schema

The first assumption, as stated above, enables us to postpone consideration of the operational requirements until the implementation stage when the user processes (application software) and associated external schemas are developed.

The second point that we raised in Section 4 of *Block 1*, which we need to review, is that we do not describe a particular database development method, but aim to present database development principles and techniques that are common to many system development methods. Our model of database development (see *Block 1*, Figure 4.5), based on the waterfall model (see *Block 1*, Figure 4.4), provides a framework for developing databases.

> The complete separation of the development of a database from the user processes is an ideal. In reality, there are often situations where, at the database design stage, how we represent certain data is dependent on how it is to be processed. These situations will be described in Section 4 of this block.

EXERCISE 1.4

The waterfall model follows a strict sequence of tasks – establishing requirements, data analysis, database design, implementation, testing and maintenance – where the output of one task is the input to the next, and all of one task has to be completed before tackling the next. As each task is completed, the database moves to the next stage of its life cycle. Describe the purpose and output of each task of the waterfall model as applied to our model of database development.

We refer to each stage of the database life cycle by the name of the output that the associated task produces. For example, the data analysis task represents the data requirements component of the information requirements of an enterprise as a conceptual data model. So we say that the data analysis task entails all of the activities that need to be completed before a database development can move from the information requirements stage to the next stage of its life cycle, the conceptual data model stage.

The database development phase involves the tasks that are associated with the building and installation of a new database that satisfies the information requirements of an enterprise – establishing requirements, data analysis, database design, implementation and testing.

The database maintenance phase primarily involves the maintenance task, which ensures that a database continues to satisfy information requirements after it has been installed. However, to adapt the database to meet new and changing requirements will usually involve revisiting the tasks associated with the database development phase.

EXERCISE 1.5

Testing is usually considered to involve two main tasks – validation and verification. What does each of these tasks attempt to confirm?

In our model of database development, testing is shown to occur between the 'initial schema and database' and 'released schema and database' stages, where the developer demonstrates to the client that the database developed satisfies the information requirements of the enterprise. This is known as **acceptance testing**. However, testing is a continuous process through each stage of the database life cycle. That is, the developer should validate and verify the output of each task (see the solution to Exercise 1.4) by checking that the output meets the requirements and that the requirements meet the needs of the client. Acceptance testing is just the final stage in the testing process before the database is accepted for operational use.

The extent to which a formal approach to database development is adopted, or a particular database development technique is employed, or whether the development follows a strict sequence of tasks as dictated by the waterfall method, depends on the nature of the database being developed.

It will be useful here to consider briefly the range of different types of database which individuals and organisations may require to develop. At one end of the spectrum we could have an OU student who, having successfully completed M359, wishes to develop a database to support their hobby of bird-watching. The database would record details of the birds that the student has observed on particular days. At the other end of the spectrum, we could have a nationwide retailer which requires a database to facilitate the day-to-day running of its operations. The database would record details of the retailer's products, sales and customers. The retailer contracts an IT company which employs specialist IT staff to build and install the database.

The importance of following a formal approach to database development to ensure that the database satisfies the information requirements of an enterprise has already been expounded in the solution to Exercise 1.1. For large and complex database developments involving many people – the client and their staff, the developer and their staff, and the end-users (including customers) – a formal approach also serves to coordinate tasks and responsibilities. From a developer's viewpoint, it is crucial to have well-defined tasks that make it possible to estimate when the database will be completed and the human and financial resources required. From the developer's staff's viewpoint, it is important to have well-defined tasks and clear outcomes, and to know which documents and artefacts should be produced by each of these tasks. From a client's viewpoint, it is fundamental to be reassured that the required database is the one being built and that it will be delivered on time and within budget.

EXERCISE 1.6

Although it is clear from the above text that the nationwide retailer should employ a formal approach to the development of its database, should the M359 student also employ a formal approach?

EXERCISE 1.7

In reality, database development does not always proceed strictly according to the waterfall model: usually, there is some degree of refinement and feedback as the database proceeds. Between which stages of a database development would you expect most refinement and feedback to occur?

In the remainder of this section, we provide an overview of the aims and content of the following sections of this block, starting with the case study, and followed by the tasks associated with each stage of the database life cycle – establishing requirements, data analysis, database design, implementation, testing and maintenance. Finally, we consider how data may be distributed and managed across several databases, and how the distributed data may be integrated to create a data warehouse to support strategic decision making.

1.1　Case study

In order to illustrate database development and maintenance, we have chosen as our case study a particular business environment that we are all probably familiar with – the supermarket chain. Here we describe how supermarket chains use databases to facilitate the day-to-day running of their businesses and the marketing of their products and services. In Section 2 of this block, we provide a description of Walton Stores, a fictional supermarket chain, and specify the data and operational requirements of the business enterprise.

Prior to the late 1990s, supermarket chains primarily used their database systems for stock control to manage the supply of products to their branches. The database would record details of the quantity of each product supplied to the branches, who would order new supplies when stocks of a product were low. It was not possible to record sales of products at a particular branch other than by monitoring the stock level on the shelves and in the warehouse.

With the universal adoption of barcoding of retail products and the introduction of barcode scanners at supermarket checkout tills, a supermarket chain can now monitor sales of products and thereby manage the supply of products to their branches more effectively. The data gathered facilitate the daily operations of the business, ensuring that stock sold is replaced promptly. Since the database can now additionally store a detailed record of the products purchased by a customer on each visit to a supermarket, it also has the potential to enable the supermarket chain to identify patterns of purchasing behaviour within its customer base. With this knowledge, a supermarket chain will be able to not only manage its business more effectively but also make informed business decisions to sustain its position in the marketplace.

The supermarket chain can manage its business more effectively because knowledge of patterns of purchasing behaviour will enable it to predict the demand for products by its customers, so that it can ensure that its branches are always sufficiently stocked with products to meet the demand. It is particularly important that supply meets demand in the case of perishable goods with a short shelf-life, especially if they are in demand only at certain times. This will promote customer satisfaction and ensure reduction in the wastage of unsold goods that have passed their sell-by date.

In order to exploit fully the data captured by the barcode scanners, supermarket chains need to associate the data with, and gather data about, individual purchasers and households. Supermarket chains have obtained addresses and demographic data from their customers by offering them discounts on their purchases in return for using the supermarket's loyalty (or discount) card when they make their purchases. Each time the customer presents their loyalty card, their transaction history is updated in the database and a profile of the customer's or a household's purchasing habits becomes established.

Knowledge of patterns of purchasing behaviour can assist the supermarket chain to maintain its customer base by enabling it to provide a more personalised service to its customers – making shopping a more pleasant experience. It can also use this knowledge to select customers who will be targeted by each of the marketing strategies that the supermarket may employ to promote product lines. A marketing strategy could be a special promotional offer where a coupon is sent to a customer who, based on their known buying habits and the data they supplied with their loyalty card application, is a likely prospect for a particular supplier's product. Since the coupon will have a barcode, its redemption also becomes an entry in the customer's purchase history held by the database, and so the supermarket can assess the success of a particular promotion.

EXERCISE 1.8

What specialist data processing system could a supermarket chain employ to facilitate its marketing strategy and support decision making in general?

Walton Stores will need many different databases to facilitate the day-to-day running of its business operations. We will initially focus on the development and maintenance of a database that would need to be installed at an individual store, which would record details of products sold at such a store and their purchase by customers.

1.2   Establishing requirements

As requirements gathering and analysis are activities common to software development in general, we will not cover this task in any detail. Our description of database development will start at the point where the information requirements of an enterprise have been established, and a statement of requirements has been agreed between the client and developer. However, we provide the following list of techniques that are commonly used to elicit requirements:

▶ examining documents created or used by the enterprise, in particular those used to record or display information;

▶ using questionnaires to gather information from a wide number of users;

▶ observing the enterprise in operation;

▶ interviewing individuals within the enterprise, particularly those who are regarded as experts within a specific area of interest.

EXERCISE 1.9

Using your knowledge of retail shopping in general, how would you elicit the information requirements for a supermarket chain like Walton Stores?

1.3   Data analysis

The data analysis task entails all of the activities that need to be completed before a database development can move from the information requirements stage to the next stage of its life cycle, the conceptual data model stage. Data analysis is the key task in database development as it results in a detailed understanding of the meaning of the data and the relationships between the data.

EXERCISE 1.10

What is the role of the conceptual data model in database development?

Section 3, which relates to data analysis, has the following two aims.

1   To provide you with an opportunity to review your understanding of conceptual data models, in particular the entity–relationship model as presented in Section 5 of *Block 1*.

2   To enable you to acquire the practical skills you need in order to develop, refine and validate a conceptual data model that represents the data requirements of some enterprise.

As data analysis is a subjective rather than an objective task, we will present you with guidelines to help you develop and refine conceptual data models, rather than a formal methodology. Because of the subjective nature of the data analysis task, you may find it initially difficult to acquire the necessary practical skills. Like all creative activity, competence in data analysis will develop through practice.

This section on the data analysis task is a substantial part of *Block 4*, covering the following topics:

▶   a review and extension of the entity–relationship model presented in Section 5 of *Block 1*;

▶   the analysis of textual descriptions of an enterprise either provided by the client or produced as a result of the requirements gathering and analysis activity;

▶   the analysis of the various documents created and used by an enterprise to facilitate its day-to-day operations;

▶   how we can demonstrate that an entity–relationship model is an accurate representation of the data requirements of an enterprise.

1.4   Database design

The database design task entails all of the activities that need to be completed before a database development can move from the conceptual data model stage to the next stage of its life cycle, the specification of the logical (database) schema. The aim of the database design task in this course is to develop a first-cut design of the entity–relationship model, where the logical (database) schema is specified by SQL data definition language (DDL) statements and where the database tables are normalised, that is, they do not include any redundant duplication. The database design task will concern primarily the direct transformation of an entity–relationship model into a relational representation expressed by the SQL DDL statements required to define the logical (database) schema.

EXERCISE 1.11

Why is it important that the database tables are normalised?

Section 4, which relates to database design, has the following two aims.

1   To provide you with a review of the transformation of an entity–relationship model into a relational representation as described first in *Block 2*, from the viewpoint of relational theory, then in *Block 3*, from the viewpoint of the practical realisation of relational theory by SQL.

2   To provide you with a detailed overview of the choices available when transforming an entity–relationship model into a logical (database) schema for a first-cut design.

In this section we describe the options available for representing relationships, complex and missing data, constraints and those elements of the entity–relationship model that have no direct equivalent in relational theory.

1.5   Implementation

The database implementation task entails all of the activities that need to be completed before a database development can move from the logical (database) schema stage to the next stage of its life cycle, a database that satisfies all of the information requirements of an enterprise and which is acceptable to the client who commissioned the database development. In this course, we have incorporated acceptance testing into the implementation task.

EXERCISE 1.12

What tasks do you think will need to be accomplished during implementation to produce an operational database that satisfies the information requirements of the enterprise?

As the solution to Exercise 1.12 implies, implementation is about not just developing and testing a database system, but also integrating the database system into a client's existing hardware and software systems, and providing the client with adequate documentation and training for their staff and users.

Section 5 aims to provide you with some basic guidelines for implementing databases using SQL Anywhere. We will discuss implementing an SQL database definition, populating a database with data, and the development of application software. A detailed description of the design and implementation of application software is beyond the scope of this course, but in *Block 5* we will describe how software written using programming languages such as Java can interface with a relational DBMS such as SQL Anywhere. However, as application software will need to use SQL statements to query and modify a relational database, in Section 5 we will provide a framework for developing application software using SQL statements. This framework can also be used as the basis for testing a database system to ensure that it satisfies the information requirements of an enterprise.

1.6   Database maintenance

Database maintenance starts when the database development completes, when the database is accepted by the client and it becomes operational. The database maintenance phase continues until the database system is withdrawn from use, and this phase is usually much longer than the database development phase.

There are two main forms of maintenance – operational and adaptive. **Operational maintenance** ensures that the database continues to satisfy the information requirements after it has been installed, by monitoring its performance and undertaking a database restructuring or database reorganisation when necessary. **Adaptive maintenance** concerns restructuring the database to meet new and changing requirements.

EXERCISE 1.13

How do (a) database reorganisation and (b) database restructuring relate to the three-schema architecture and database development tasks?

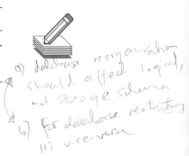

Section 6, which relates to maintenance, has the following two aims.

1   To illustrate how we can restructure an SQL Anywhere database to optimise the performance of data retrieval by relaxing the requirement that database tables should be normalised.

2   To describe how we can restructure an SQL Anywhere database in order to ensure that it continues to satisfy the information requirements after it has been installed, and/or to meet new and changing requirements.

In the preceding sections, our focus has been on the development of a database to facilitate the day-to-day running of an enterprise where the data is located on a single computer system shared by its many users. In the concluding sections of *Block 4*, we consider:

▶   the requirement to distribute and manage data over several computer systems – **distributed data management**;

▶   the requirement to integrate this distributed data to maintain summarised historical data for strategic decision making – **data warehousing**.

1.7 Distributed data management

The need to manage distributed data commonly arises in organisations such as supermarket chains that collect and process data in a number of geographical locations. The advantage of distributing data is that it is often possible to put the data close to the most frequent users of that data, while at the same time making it accessible to other users who may be more remote.

Section 7, which relates to distributed data management, considers three distinct approaches to managing distributed data that were introduced in *Block 1*, Subsection 3.5: client–multiserver, distributed database and replicated systems.

1.8 Data warehousing

Data warehousing concerns the integration of large quantities of historical data from many different operational databases into a data warehouse for the purpose of facilitating strategic decision-making activities within an organisation.

Section 8, which relates to data warehousing, has the following two aims.

1   To provide you with an introduction to decision support systems, the multidimensional data model, data warehouses and data warehousing.

2   To enable you to acquire practical skills that you will need to develop a simple design for a data warehouse using a relational database that facilitates strategic decision making.

Decision support systems (DSS) are computer-based systems that incorporate data warehouses and employ data mining techniques to facilitate and improve strategic decision making by providing decision makers with relevant information.

The **multidimensional data model** is a conceptual data model that enables decision makers to view data from different, and multiple, perspectives. A multidimensional view of data allows decision makers to consolidate or aggregate the data collected from operational databases at different levels of detail.

A data warehouse is a repository of an organisation's operational data where the data is organised around the subjects of interest to the organisation, such as customers, products, locations and sales. It focuses on the modelling and analysis of data for decision makers. Data warehousing is the process of building, managing and using data warehouses.

1.9 | Summary

The aim of this block is to enable you to develop the practical skills that you will need to undertake the development of a database, from the analysis of the information requirements of some enterprise through to the implementation of a database that satisfies those requirements, using the DBMS supplied with the course.

In this introductory section, we have:

▶ Reviewed the base development model presented in Section 4 of *Block 1*.

▶ Provided an overview of the aims and content of the sections of this block, starting with the case study, and followed by the tasks associated with each stage of the database life cycle – establishing requirements, data analysis, database design, implementation, testing and maintenance. Finally, we considered how data may be distributed and managed across several databases, and how the distributed data may be integrated to create a data warehouse to support strategic decision making.

LEARNING OUTCOMES

Having completed your study of this section of the course, you will:

▶ Be able to describe the key points of the waterfall model that are applied to database development.

▶ Appreciate the role of various development artefacts used to communicate between activities in the database development life cycle.

▶ Be able to communicate effectively about aspects of the development of databases.

2 Walton Stores: the supermarket case study

This section introduces the case study that we will use to illustrate database development and maintenance. It provides a description of Walton Stores, which is a fictional supermarket chain that has a requirement for new databases to facilitate the day-to-day operations at its stores and distribution centres (warehouses). The description includes some of the results of the requirements gathering activity of the establishing requirements task – documents created and used by the stores and distribution centres, and a brief specification of the information requirements of the enterprise.

Walton Stores will need to develop and install many databases at different locations within the organisation to facilitate the day-to-day running of its business operations. As a supermarket chain is a complex business with a wide variety of information requirements, we will not have time to undertake a comprehensive development of any of these databases. We will focus primarily on the development and maintenance of a database that will need to be installed at an individual store. The database will record details relating to the products stocked at the store and the purchase of these products by customers. Being able to focus on a particular set of requirements (i.e. those of an individual store) within a wider set (i.e. those of Walton Stores as a whole) is an important skill that data analysts have to develop in order to establish the boundaries of a system. That is, in the context of a database development, being able to determine which information requirements should be satisfied by a particular database.

2.1 Walton Stores

In this section, we provide a brief description of Walton Stores provided by the client together with some of the documents created and used by this enterprise.

Walton Stores is a supermarket chain selling an extensive range of foodstuffs and household goods from stores located in many towns throughout England. The company plans to establish itself as a leading food retailer in a very competitive marketplace by meeting the demands of both its customers and its suppliers. For its customers, the company aims to make shopping a more pleasant experience by stocking the products they require, offering them a range of alternatives and discounts, and arranging the layout of products on the shelves in its stores to make shopping easier by locating those products that are commonly purchased on the same shopping trip close together. For its suppliers, who provide all the products that Walton Stores sells at its stores, the company aims to provide them with profiles of the kinds of customers who purchase their products. The suppliers can then select households to be targeted by their promotional and marketing strategies.

Walton Stores has divided its operation in England into four geographical regions covering the north-east (NE), south-east (SE), south-west (SW) and north-west (NW) quadrants of the country. Each region has a large distribution centre where packs of products from the suppliers are held until they are delivered to individual stores that the region is responsible for. Although a distribution centre can dispatch goods to a particular store within 24 hours, it may take several days for goods to be received from the suppliers. Therefore, a distribution centre has to ensure that it has adequate stock to meet all the demands from the stores within its region. In particular, it needs to monitor carefully stocks of perishable goods, such as fresh fruit and vegetables, which can be held for only a limited period before they need to be on the shelves of the stores.

A store can request deliveries of goods from its distribution centre in two different ways: by a *standing order*, where the goods requested are required at regular intervals throughout the year (see Figure 2.1); and by a *special order*, where the goods requested are in demand only at certain times of the year (see Figure 2.2). A store may need to revise standing orders to meet seasonal fluctuations in the demand for certain products.

Walton Stores operates a regional pricing policy where prices of goods at the stores may vary from region to region, but are the same at all the stores within a region. Prices are reviewed daily and are revised to take account of changes in the purchase cost, customer demand and product promotions. The stores receive current prices from their distribution centre on a daily basis.

Individual stores have a limited warehousing capacity for storing goods before they are put on the shelves, or in the compartments of refrigerators and freezers, as appropriate. Stores need to monitor carefully the stocks of each product and when necessary adjust the appropriate standing order to ensure that supply meets demand. Foodstuffs with a short shelf-life – perishable goods – will have a 'display until' date and it is important that such items that are not sold on or before this date are removed from the shelves, or the compartments of refrigerators and freezers. Other foodstuffs will have a 'use by' date. With both types of foodstuffs a sensible shelf and compartment stocking policy will be to minimise the incidence of the shelves and compartments being stocked with the same product with different 'display until' dates or 'use by' dates, because customers have a tendency to choose items with a later date, which can result in wastage.

Each product line is classified by the type of product, such as fresh vegetables, and lines are typically grouped on the shelves by product type (see Figure 2.3). Each product line sold by Walton Stores has a unique product code (see Figure 2.4). With the exception of unpackaged goods, such as some fresh fruit and vegetables that customers select and package themselves, the product code is found on each item in the form of a barcode. The cost of each item is usually only found on prepacked goods that are sold by varying weights, such as meat, fish and cheese (see Figure 2.5, label 1). The cost of an item, however, will be displayed on a label by the shelf or the compartment of a refrigerator or freezer where the item is found. The database will need to hold the current price of each item and be able to produce product and shelf/compartment labels.

The checkout tills at every store will be equipped with barcode scanners that are linked to the database system to enable the total cost of the customers' purchases to be calculated and recorded (see Figure 2.6). For items without barcodes, which are packaged by the customers themselves, the checkout operator will need to weigh each product and enter the product code manually to calculate and record the cost.

A customer may apply for a loyalty (or reward) card – Walton Stores' *Frequent Shopper Card* – which gives points on all purchases. The customer's details are held only by the store where they applied for their Frequent Shopper Card (see Figure 2.8). Holders of the Frequent Shopper

Card, selected by their known purchasing habits and/or the data they supplied on their card application form (see Figure 2.7), may be sent coupons to promote a product. Since a coupon will have a barcode, its redemption also becomes an entry on the customer's purchase history held by the database system, and so the supermarket chain can assess the success of a particular promotion.

1

WALTON STORES

Standing Order

| Store: | Ramsgard | Distribution centre: | South-West |
| Order number: | 0014588 | Date: | 13-May-2006 |

Item No.	Product code	Description/pack size	Number of packs	Delivery day(s)	Frequency
1	01015277	Pasteurised skimmed milk (72 x 568ml)	5000	Monday-Friday	Weekly
2	01015277	Pasteurised skimmed milk (72 x 568ml)	8000	Saturday	Weekly
3	01015279	Pasteurised skimmed milk (72 x 1.136 litres)	5000	Monday-Friday	Weekly
4	01015279	Pasteurised skimmed milk (72 x 1.136 litres)	8000	Saturday	Weekly
5	04789217	Goats' milk yoghurt (36 x 250g)	1000	Monday, Wednesday, Friday	Weekly
6	08562411	Vegetable fat spread (144 x 250g)	1000	Tuesday, Thursday, Saturday	Weekly
7	06002669	Gorgonzola (10 x 10kg)	50	Monday	Monthly

2

WALTON STORES

Standing Order

| Store: | Ramsgard | Distribution centre: | South-West |
| Order number: | 0014589 | Date: | 13-May-2006 |

Item No.	Product code	Description/pack size	Number of packs	Delivery day(s)	Frequency
1	02348126	Prunes in syrup (48 x 420g)	1000	Tuesday	Monthly
2	02348187	Prunes in apple juice (48 x 410g)	2000	Tuesday	Monthly
3	02524730	Carrots (Class 1) (1 x 50kg)	10	Monday-Friday	Weekly
4	02524730	Carrots (Class 1) (1 x 50kg)	20	Saturday	Weekly

Figure 2.1   Examples of standing orders

1

WALTON STORES				
Special Order				
Store: Ramsgard		Distribution centre: South-West		
Order number: 0014590		Date: 13-May-2006		
Item No.	**Product code**	**Description/pack size**	**Number of packs**	**Delivery date**
1	03214560	Strawberries (48 x 250g)	1000	2-Jun-2006
2	01015255	Clotted cream (24 x 250ml)	500	2-Jun-2006
3	03214560	Strawberries (48 x 250g)	1000	9-Jun-2006
4	01015255	Clotted cream (24 x 250ml)	500	9-Jun-2006

2

WALTON STORES				
Special Order				
Store: Ramsgard		Distribution centre: South-West		
Order number: 0014591		Date: 13-May-2006		
Item No.	**Product code**	**Description/pack size**	**Number of packs**	**Delivery date**
1	08881245	Christmas pudding (48 x 1kg)	1000	1-Dec-2006
2	08881246	Christmas pudding (36 x 1.5kg)	500	1-Dec-2006
3	08881248	Luxury Christmas pudding (48 x 1kg)	700	1-Dec-2006
4	07214781	Château Haut d'Allard 1996 (6 x 75cl)	100	7-Dec-2006
5	07214781	Château Haut d'Allard 1996 (6 x 75cl)	100	14-Dec-2006

Figure 2.2   Examples of special orders

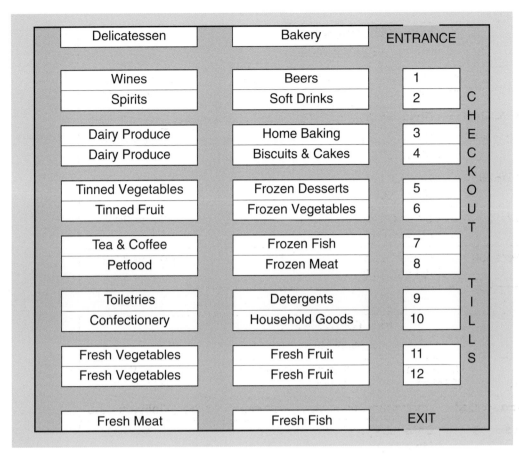

Figure 2.3   The floor plan of a typical store

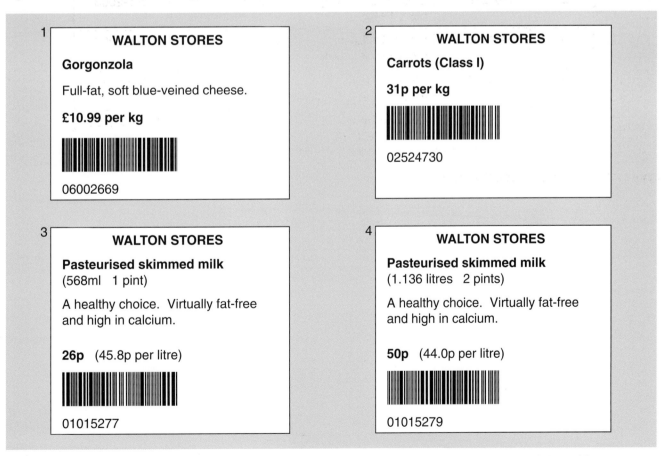

Figure 2.4   Examples of product labels that are displayed on the shelf or the compartment of the refrigerator or freezer where the product is found (*continued overleaf*)

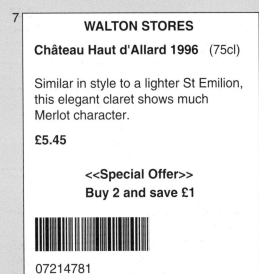

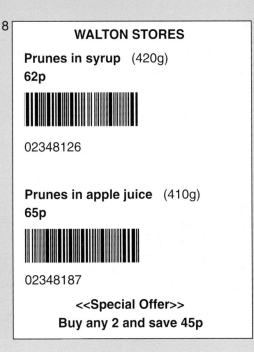

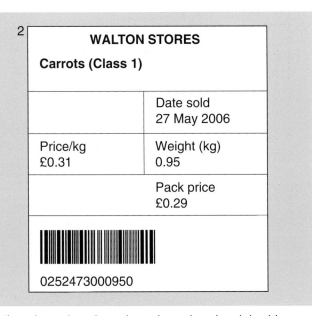

Figure 2.4   *continued*

Figure 2.5   Examples of labels on prepacked goods (label 1) and goods selected, packaged and weighed by customers themselves (label 2)

1

WALTON STORES

Ramsgard

Your checkout operator today was
JASON

	£
Pasteurised skimmed milk 1.136 litres	0.50
Pasteurised skimmed milk 1.136 litres	0.50
Prunes in apple juice 410g	0.65
Vegetable fat spread 250g	2.49
Total	**4.14**
Debit card	4.14

25-May-2006 15:43

2

WALTON STORES

Ramsgard

Your checkout operator today was
SELENA

	£
Pasteurised skimmed milk 568ml	0.26
Château Haut d'Allard 1996 75cl	5.45
Château Haut d'Allard 1996 75cl	5.45
*** Buy 2 and save £1	- 1.00
Total	**10.16**
Cheque	10.16

25-May-2006 16:04

3

WALTON STORES

Ramsgard

Your checkout operator today was
GERDA

	£
Pasteurised skimmed milk 1.136 litres	0.50
Prunes in syrup 420g	0.62
Prunes in syrup 420g	0.62
*** Buy any 2 and save 45p	- 0.45
Château Haut d'Allard 1996 75cl	5.45
Vegetable fat spread 250g	2.49
Vegetable fat spread 250g	2.49
*** Buy 2 and save £1	- 1.00
Total	**10.72**
Frequent Shopper Card	10.72

Frequent Shopper Card	1567-2711-5223
Points earned this visit	10
Total points earned	345

25-May-2006 16:04

4

WALTON STORES

Oxford

Your checkout operator today was
ANNE

	£
Carrots (Class 1)	
0.95kg @ £0.31/kg	0.29
Gorgonzola	
0.242kg @ £10.99/kg	2.66
Goats' milk yoghurt 250g	0.89
Goats' milk yoghurt 250g	0.89
*** Buy 2 and receive 2 extra points	
Total	**4.73**
Cash	10.00
Change	5.27

Frequent Shopper Card	1567-2711-5223
Points earned this visit	6

These points will be added to your
home store total within 2 days

27-May-2006 11:24

Figure 2.6   Examples of checkout till receipts

WALTON STORES
Frequent Shopper Card

The Walton Stores *Frequent Shopper Card* is one more way we can offer you better value, both in everyday shopping and in a choice of how to pay.

By presenting your *Frequent Shopper Card* to the checkout operator before you pay for the goods you have selected, you will receive 1 point for each £1 spent. Extra points may also be awarded for the purchase of certain goods subject to special promotional offers. You can get £1 off your shopping bill for every 100 points you have earned. If you would like money off your shopping, you just request the amount you want off your bill, in multiples of 100 points, when paying. You can only redeem your points at your home store, that is, the store named on your card.

Your *Frequent Shopper Card* is also a credit card for purchases made at Walton Stores supermarkets. It allows you to enjoy a Monthly Interest Rate of only 1.25% (Annual Percentage Rate of 16% variable) and no annual fee. We will agree a personal credit limit with you based on the information you provide on your application form. Each month you will receive a detailed statement showing your balance. You then have the option of making a minimum payment of 10% of the outstanding balance, or you may choose to pay the whole amount and enjoy up to 56 days interest-free credit. There is an interest-free period on all additional purchases, even when the balance exists from the previous month.

Please complete this application form in order to receive your *Frequent Shopper Card*.

Title:

Forename:

Family Name:

Address:

Postcode:

Date of birth: ☐☐ / ☐☐ / 1 9 ☐☐

Gender: Male ☐   Female ☐

Occupation: Professional ☐   Managerial ☐   Clerical ☐
                Skilled ☐   Unskilled ☐   Unemployed ☐

Annual income: < £10k ☐   £10k – £20k ☐   £20k – £30k ☐
                £30k – £40k ☐   £40k – £50k ☐   > £50k ☐

Residence: Owner ☐   Tenant ☐   Other ☐

By signing this form, you confirm that you have read and agree to the Walton Stores *Frequent Shopper Card* Terms and Conditions as specified on the reverse of this application form. You also agree that we may keep and use the information you provide along with your purchase history for the purposes of administering your account and understanding your shopping preferences better. We guarantee never to pass your personal details to another company for their own use.

If we find information or offers that we believe will be of genuine interest to you, from ourselves or our suppliers, we would like to tell you about them. If you do not want us to do this, please tick this box. ☐

Signed [＿＿＿＿＿＿]   Date [＿＿＿＿＿]
(I am over 18)

Figure 2.7   The application form for a Frequent Shopper Card

WALTON STORES

Frequent Shopper Card

Customer: **Miss Christine Malakite**
Home store: **Ramsgard**
Card number: 1567-2711-5223

Figure 2.8   An example of a Frequent Shopper Card

Interviewer: Gerda, can you tell me what you have to do when you start your shift as a checkout operator?

Gerda: When I get to the checkout desk, the operator's screen will be displaying the logon page. I type in my staff number and password, and then press the Logon button.

Interviewer: You are now ready to checkout the customers' purchases?

Gerda: Yes, I just press the Next Customer button and start scanning the items on the conveyer belt. I have to weigh items of fresh fruit and vegetables that the customers have selected and packaged themselves, and I obtain the product codes from a chart showing pictures of these items. If a customer has a 'Frequent Shopper Card', I have to scan their card before I finalise the purchases. When I have scanned all the items, I press the Total button and the total cost is displayed to the customer. The customer then pays for the goods by cash, cheque, Frequent Shopper Card, credit or debit card. Once I have checked and accepted the customer's payment, I just press the Next Customer button.

Interviewer: The procedure seems to be straightforward enough, but surely there must be occasions when things don't go so smoothly?

Gerda: Yes, quite often! Sometimes I pass an item across the barcode scanner too slowly and it gets recorded twice. I then have to scan the item again and press the Cancel button to remove the duplicate entry from the total cost. My error and correction are both recorded on the till receipt. Sometimes customers are unable to pay for the items they have selected because they have brought insufficient cash with them, and I have to cancel a number of items. Sometimes I am unable to obtain authorisation for payment by their credit or debit cards for various reasons. On these occasions, I have to get the checkout tills supervisor to intervene, and if the problem cannot be resolved, the customer may not be able to purchase any of the items they have selected.

Interviewer: Thank you for your time.

Figure 2.9   A transcript of the interview with the checkout operator Gerda

2.2 Specification of requirements

In this subsection, we provide a brief specification of the information requirements of the Walton Stores enterprise. To facilitate the day-to-day running of the enterprise, Walton Stores will need to employ a distributed database system so that the data is held close to the location where it is collected and most frequently used. This will be accommodated by maintaining operational databases at each store and at the distribution centre of each region, and a data warehouse at headquarters. In Table 2.1, we have listed some of the data that needs to be recorded (data requirements) and some of the day-to-day operations that need to be facilitated (operational requirements) by the databases which are located at stores and distribution centres.

Location	Data requirements i.e. recording:	Operational requirements i.e. processing:

Store	products stocked
	products sold
	products ordered from the
	    distribution centre
	customer (holder of a Frequent
	    Shopper Card) details
		customer purchases
		standing orders
		special orders
		Frequent Shopper Card
		    applications

Distribution centre	products stocked products ordered from the suppliers products dispatched to stores supplier details	standing orders special orders supplier orders

Table 2.1 A list of some of the information requirements of Walton Stores

2.3 Summary

This section has introduced the case study that we will use to illustrate database development and maintenance. It provides a description of Walton Stores, a fictional supermarket chain that has a requirement for new databases to facilitate the day-to-day operations at its stores and distribution centres (warehouses). The description of the enterprise includes some of the results of the requirements gathering activity of the establishing requirements task – documents created and used by the stores and distribution centres – and a brief specification of the information requirements of the enterprise.

3 Data analysis

This section focuses on the data analysis task, which entails all of the activities that need to be completed before a database development can move from the information requirements stage to the next stage of its life cycle, the conceptual data model stage. Data analysis is the key task in database development as it results in a detailed understanding of the meaning of the data items and the relationships between those data items, which are expressed in the form of a conceptual data model.

This section has two aims. First, to provide you with an opportunity to review your understanding of conceptual data models, in particular the entity–relationship model as presented in Section 5 of *Block 1*. Second, to enable you to acquire the practical skills you need to develop, refine and validate a conceptual data model that represents the data requirements of some enterprise. As data analysis is a subjective rather than an objective task, we will present you with guidelines to help you develop and refine conceptual data models, rather than a methodology. Because of the subjective nature of the data analysis task, you may find it initially difficult to acquire the necessary practical skills. Like all creative activity, competence in data analysis will develop through practice.

The data analysis task involves answering some key questions about the database we intend to develop:

▶ What is the scope of the system that we intend to develop?

▶ What data is important to support the user requirements?

▶ What does that data mean, how is the data talked about by the users, and what representations are used by the users?

▶ What level of detail is required to adequately model the reality this data represents?

▶ How do the pieces of data relate to each other?

▶ What constraints are necessary to maintain the quality of the data?

A conceptual data model is developed in response to these questions and describes the data, relationships between the data and constraints on the data.

EXERCISE 3.1

In the context of the case study, why is it important to answer the first question, 'What is the scope of the system that we intend to develop?'

Being able to focus on a particular set of requirements within a wider set is an important skill, which data analysts have to develop in order to establish the boundaries of a database development.

EXERCISE 3.2

Explain what a conceptual data model represents and what it does not represent.

A conceptual data model should be a complete, accurate representation of the data requirements of an organisation (or an area of interest within an organisation). It

describes the structure and properties of the data, but not how and when individual occurrences of the data are created or destroyed, or how and when their properties may change.

EXERCISE 3.3

What is the principal difference between a conceptual data model and the relational representation of the conceptual data model?

A conceptual data model provides a shared, formal, representation of what is being communicated between clients and developers during database development – it is focused on the data in a database irrespective of the eventual use of that data in user processes or implementation of the data in specific computer environments. That is, a conceptual data model is concerned with the meaning and structure of data, but not with the details affecting how it is implemented. The conceptual data model describes *what* the data requirements are, not *how* these requirements are to be implemented by any particular database approach.

EXERCISE 3.4

Explain why the data requirements of an enterprise cannot be simply expressed in natural language but need to involve the formal representation of a conceptual data model.

The conceptual data model is a working document that develops during the data analysis task. It usually represents a document that evolves as aspects of the meaning of the data are uncovered and need documenting, or as the scope of the data requirements grows. When an analyst begins collating the data requirements and identifying the data of interest, they will make some working assumptions about the data that will need to be clarified with the clients. The conceptual data model will be developed and refined as the data analyst meets with the clients and data users to refine the domain of discourse to determine the appropriate scope for the data. Gradually, the assumptions will be replaced with concrete decisions about the model or the limitations of the model. By the end of the data analysis task, the conceptual data model will include all the data relevant to the user requirements and describe the domain of discourse without any further need for clarification or ambiguity resolution.

EXERCISE 3.5

Why is establishing a domain of discourse particularly important to those database developments where an enterprise contracts an IT company to build and install the database?

The conceptual data model should be accompanied by additional documents to support the domain of discourse, which typically would include examples of the various documents created and used by the enterprise, and a data dictionary that provides brief descriptions and examples of the data items, and relationships between those data items.

3.1 Overview of the data analysis task

This section on the data analysis task is a substantial part of *Block 4*, therefore before we start our review of the particular conceptual data model that we use in this course, the entity–relationship model, we provide the following detailed outline of the topics that will be covered.

Subsection 3.2   Entity–relationship model

In this subsection, we review and extend the entity–relationship model. This conceptual data model expresses the data requirements in terms of entity types, and the properties of those entity types. These properties are conveyed either by their attributes or by relationships with other (or the same) entity types. We also outline the steps that we need to undertake to analyse the data requirements of an enterprise in order to develop an entity–relationship model that represents those requirements formally.

We use the Hospital case study in our review of the entity–relationship model to illustrate how the *Hospital conceptual data model* represents the data requirements of this enterprise as presented in the *Hospital scenario*. See the laminated cards entitled *Hospital conceptual data model* and *Scenarios*.

We have chosen to use the Hospital case study initially because the *Hospital scenario* describes the data requirements unambiguously and completely. Hence it is easier to illustrate the steps that we need to undertake to analyse the data requirements of an enterprise.

The aim of this subsection is to develop guidelines for how we might analyse the data requirements of an enterprise in order to develop an entity–relationship model.

Subsection 3.3   Analysing text

In this subsection, we describe an approach to analysing textual descriptions of an enterprise in order to develop an entity–relationship model that represents the data requirements of that enterprise. Such descriptions could be either provided by the client or produced as a result of the requirements gathering and analysis activities. With this approach, we perform a grammatical analysis or parse of the text to identify entity types and their properties, and the relationships between those entity types and the properties of those relationships.

We illustrate this approach initially by analysing the *Hospital scenario* and demonstrating that it can be used to develop an entity–relationship model that is comparable to the *Hospital conceptual data model* provided on the laminated card. We then consider how the approach can be used to analyse the textual description of Walton Stores as discussed in Subsection 2.1.

Subsection 3.4   Analysing documents

In this subsection, we describe an approach to analysing the various documents created and used by an enterprise to facilitate its day-to-day operations, in order to develop an entity–relationship model that represents the data requirements of that enterprise, using the guidelines developed in Subsection 3.2. With this approach, we start with the premise that a document will be represented by an entity type in the entity–relationship model, and the contents of the document describe the properties of, or facts about, that entity type. Analysing several documents of the same type, i.e. different occurrences of the corresponding entity type, will enable us to gain a good understanding of the meaning and nature of the data associated with that entity type. The results of analysing several different documents can be pieced together, like a jigsaw, to develop an entity–relationship model that represents the data requirements of the enterprise.

We illustrate this approach by analysing the various documents created and used by Walton Stores, the supermarket case study we described in Section 2, to facilitate its day-to-day operations.

Subsection 3.5   Validating an entity–relationship model

In this concluding subsection on the data analysis activity, we consider briefly how we can demonstrate that an entity–relationship model is an accurate representation of the data requirements of an enterprise.

3.2   Entity–relationship model

The entity–relationship model comprises five sections: *Entity–relationship diagram*, *Entity types*, *Additional constraints*, *Assumptions* and *Limitations*. The *Entity–relationship diagram* shows the relationships between the entity types and the properties of those relationships – name, degree and participation conditions. The *Entity types* section defines the entity types and their properties: entity type name, and the identifying and non-identifying attributes.

EXERCISE 3.6

What do the *Additional constraints*, *Assumptions* and *Limitations* sections of an entity–relationship model record?

In this course, to avoid any misunderstanding in the meaning of the data requirements as expressed by an entity–relationship model, it is accompanied by a domain of discourse summary. This document includes an *Entity type catalogue*, which provides a description of each entity type, its attributes and sample data, and a *Relationship catalogue*, which provides a description of each relationship, its properties and sample occurrences.

Entity types

We have defined an entity as a real or abstract thing that is relevant in a given context and about which there is a need to record data. Entity types are collections of entities with properties in common. The initial step in data analysis is to identify the relevant entity types. The identification of entity types in the data requirements is not an easy task. We will consider different techniques for identifying entity types in Subsections 3.2 and 3.3. However, none of these techniques should be applied mechanically. In the end, it is a good understanding of the enterprise and its data that will help you decide what does or does not constitute an entity type that should be included in the entity–relationship model to represent the data requirements of that enterprise.

Properties of entity types

Each property of, or fact about, an entity type is conveyed either by an attribute of that entity type, or by a relationship with another (or the same) entity type. When analysing the data requirements of an enterprise in order to establish the properties of, or facts about, each entity type, it is necessary to distinguish between those properties that are single-valued and those that are multi-valued.

In Section 5 of *Block 2*, we introduced the concept of a **single-valued fact** (**SVF**), which we defined as a statement (fact) identifying a property of an entity type which can only take a single value for each occurrence of that entity type. In that section of *Block 2*, we noted that identifying the single-valued facts in a requirements specification helps the data analyst identify attributes when developing an entity–relationship model that represents those requirements formally.

An allied concept is a **multi-valued fact** (**MVF**), which is defined as a statement (fact) identifying a property of an entity type which can take several values for each occurrence of that entity type.

The reason we need to distinguish between single-valued properties, or facts (SVFs), and multi-valued properties, or facts (MVFs), is because they are represented in different ways by the entity–relationship model. We can illustrate these different representations by considering the properties of, or facts about, wards, nurses and patients as described in the *Hospital scenario*, and as they are represented by the corresponding **Ward**, **Nurse** and **Patient** entity types of the *Hospital conceptual data model*. For each entity type, we will give the relevant extract from the *Hospital scenario*, and then tabulate its properties, denoting whether they are single-valued or multi-valued, and describe how they are represented by the *Hospital conceptual data model*.

Wards

The hospital is organised into a number of wards, each of which may be empty or may be occupied by one or more patients. Each ward is identified by a ward number; it has a name and contains a fixed number of beds. Each ward is staffed by one or more nurses.

Property	SVF/MVF	Represented by
The ... wards ... may be empty or ... occupied by one or more patients.	MVF	**OccupiedBy** relationship where the **Patient** end is :*n*
Each ward is identified by a ward number ...	SVF	**WardNo** attribute
Each ward ... has a name ...	SVF	**WardName** attribute
Each ward ... contains a fixed number of beds.	SVF	**NumberOfBeds** attribute
Each ward is staffed by one or more nurses.	MVF	**StaffedBy** relationship where the **Nurse** end is :*n*

Table 3.1   Properties of the **Ward** entity type

Nurses

Each nurse is identified by a staff number and has a name. A nurse is assigned to a single ward. Some nurses are designated to supervise one or more other nurses on the same ward. A nurse has at most one supervisor.

Property	SVF/MVF	Represented by
Each nurse is identified by a staff number ...	SVF	**StaffNo** attribute
Each nurse ... has a name.	SVF	**NurseName** attribute
A nurse is assigned to a single ward.	SVF	**StaffedBy** relationship where the **Ward** end is :1
Some nurses are designated to supervise one or more other nurses ...	MVF	**Supervises** relationship where one **Nurse** end is :*n*
A nurse has at most one supervisor.	SVF	**Supervises** relationship where the other **Nurse** end is :1

Table 3.2   Properties of the Nurse entity type

Patients

Each patient in the hospital has a patient identification number and name recorded, their gender, height and weight is kept on record. Each patient is assigned to a single ward and is under the care of (is the responsibility of) a single doctor who must have a position of consultant ... A patient may receive more than one treatment from each doctor ...

Property	SVF/MVF	Represented by
Each patient ... has a patient identification number ...	SVF	**PatientId** attribute
Each patient ... has a ... name recorded ...	SVF	**PatientName** attribute
Each patient ... has ... gender ...	SVF	**Gender** attribute
Each patient ... has ... height ...	SVF	**Height** attribute
Each patient ... has ... weight ...	SVF	**Weight** attribute
Each patient is assigned to a single ward ...	SVF	**OccupiedBy** relationship where the **Ward** end is :1
Each patient ... is under the care of ... a single doctor ...	SVF	**IsResponsibleFor** relationship where the **Doctor** end is :1
A patient may receive more than one treatment from each doctor ...	MVF	**Receives** relationship where the **Treatment** end is :*n*

Table 3.3   Properties of the Patient entity type

From the above text, you should be able to deduce that single-valued properties of, or facts about, an entity type are represented in the entity–relationship model by:

▶ either an attribute of that entity type

▶ or a :1 relationship with another (or the same) entity type.

And multi-valued properties of, or facts about, an entity type are represented by:

▶ a :*n* relationship with another (or the same) entity type.

EXERCISE 3.7

Explain why in the entity–relationship model we cannot simply employ an attribute to represent a multi-valued property of its entity type.

From the above analysis of single-valued and multi-valued properties of wards, nurses and patients, we can also conclude that when a property relates to occurrences of another (or the same) entity type, it is represented in the entity–relationship model by a relationship with that entity type where the degree of this relationship is determined by whether the property is single-valued or multi-valued. If the property is conveyed by a single occurrence of another (or the same) entity type – a single-valued property – then the end of the relationship with this entity type will be :1 (to one). Whereas if the property is conveyed by several occurrences – a multi-valued property – then the end of the relationship with this entity type will be :*n* (to many).

EXERCISE 3.8

The *Hospital scenario* describes the properties of doctors (consultants and junior doctors) as follows:

> Each consultant is responsible for a number of patients. Details of the junior doctors in the hospital, who have a position of either registrar or house officer, are also recorded. Consultants must have a specialism, but registrars and house officers are not specialists and do not have a specialism. All specialists are consultants. Each doctor (whether consultant or junior doctor) in the hospital has a staff number and name recorded. Each consultant must head a single group, known as a team, consisting of one or more house officers and registrars. A team must be headed by a consultant. A house officer or registrar cannot head a team, but must be a member of one team, and consultants cannot be members of a team. ...

> Each doctor may provide treatment for several patients, and each patient may receive treatment from a number of doctors. Any doctor treating a patient must be a member of the same team as the consultant responsible for that patient. ...

Tabulate the properties of doctors, denote whether they represent single-valued or multi-valued properties, and describe how they are represented by the *Hospital conceptual data model*.

We said earlier that single-valued properties of an entity type may be represented either by an attribute of that entity type, or by a :1 relationship with another (or the same) entity type. So how do we decide on which approach to employ when representing a single-valued property of an entity type?

If a single-valued property of an entity type relates to an occurrence of another (or the same) entity type, then we simply draw a relationship between that entity type and the other (or the same) entity type on the entity–relationship diagram, where the end of the relationship with the other (or the same) entity type is :1. Whether the other end of the relationship is :1 or :*n* will be determined by considering the corresponding property of the other (or the same) entity type. Let us illustrate the approach by considering the properties of nurses and wards described in Tables 3.1 and 3.2. One particular single-valued property of nurses is 'A nurse is assigned to a single ward', which is represented by the **StaffedBy** relationship where the **Ward** end is :1 (Table 3.2). The corresponding property of wards is 'Each ward is staffed by one or more nurses'. This is a multi-valued property and is represented by the **StaffedBy** relationship where the **Nurse** end is :*n* (Table 3.1).

Optional properties

Another factor we need to consider when deciding how to represent single-valued properties and, as we shall describe later, multi-valued properties, is whether they are optional properties. That is, whether the property of an entity type is only applicable or relevant to certain occurrences of that entity type. If a single-valued property is optional, we cannot use an attribute to represent the property because for each occurrence of an entity type, every attribute has a value; that is, an occurrence is a complete set of data values. So, instead, we represent the property by introducing a new entity type connected by a relationship with properties as described above but where the entity type whose single-valued property we are representing has optional participation with respect to this relationship. We can illustrate the approach by considering the properties of doctors, in particular consultants, who unlike junior doctors are specialists. In the *Hospital conceptual data model* we represent the single-valued property that 'Consultants must have a specialism, but registrars and house officers are not specialists and do not have a specialism' by introducing the **Specialist** entity type to record the specialisms of consultants. The 1:1 relationship **IsA** between **Doctor** and **Specialist** has optional participation with respect to **Doctor**, denoting that not every doctor will be a specialist.

You may have questioned whether we really need to introduce a new entity type just to represent the fact that consultants have a specialism. Why not simply define an attribute in the **Doctor** entity type named, say **Specialism**, that records the specialisms for those occurrences of the **Doctor** entity type that represent consultants, and a value of 'not applicable' for those occurrences that represent junior doctors? The answer to this question lies in the understanding of the function of a conceptual data model in a database development. We have stated that a conceptual data model provides a shared, formal representation of what is being communicated between clients and developers during database development – it is concerned with the meaning and structure of the data, but not with the details affecting how it is implemented. Although we might decide to represent this single-valued property in the database design using the **Specialism** attribute, for whatever reason, we prefer to use the **Specialist** entity type in the entity–relationship model for reasons of clarity. The *Hospital entity–relationship diagram* effectively communicates to the reader the fact that some doctors are specialists, whereas with the alternative representation using the **Specialism** attribute, the fact would be concealed in the *Additional constraints* section of the *Hospital conceptual data model*. Later in this section, we will describe an extension to the entity–relationship model notation that will allow the entity–relationship diagram to communicate effectively the distinction between different properties associated with the different types of doctors – consultants and junior doctors.

When employing a relationship to represent both single-valued and multi-valued properties of entity types, the participation condition of the entity type with respect to the relationship is determined simply by whether the property is optional or mandatory for the entity type. We can illustrate this by considering the following two multi-valued properties of wards:

> The hospital is organised into a number of wards, each of which may be empty or may be occupied by one or more patients.
>
> Each ward is staffed by one or more nurses.

The first property, patients occupying a ward, is optional: a ward may be empty. The second, nurses staffing a ward, is mandatory: every ward is staffed by at least one nurse. These properties are represented by the **OccupiedBy** and **StaffedBy** relationships, respectively, where the **Ward** entity type has optional participation with respect to the **OccupiedBy** relationship, and mandatory participation with respect to the **StaffedBy** relationship.

Now that we have made the distinction between optional and mandatory properties of entity types, we can revise the guidelines we gave earlier for representing single-valued properties and multi-valued properties of entity types in the entity–relationship model as follows:

▶ A single-valued property of, or fact about, an entity type that relates to occurrences of another (or the same) entity type is represented by a :1 relationship with the other (or the same) entity type, where the participation condition of the entity type with respect to the relationship is determined by whether the property is optional or mandatory for occurrences of the entity type.

▶ A single-valued property of, or fact about, an entity type that is not related to any occurrences of another (or the same) entity type is represented by an attribute if the property is mandatory for occurrences of the entity type, or if the property is optional, by a :1 relationship with a new entity type, where the participation condition of the entity type with respect to the relationship is optional.

▶ A multi-valued property of, or fact about, an entity type is represented by a :n relationship with the other (or the same) entity type, where the participation condition of the entity type with respect to the relationship is determined by whether the property is optional or mandatory for occurrences of the entity type.

EXERCISE 3.9

The *Hospital scenario* describes the properties of teams as follows:

> Each consultant must head a single group, known as a team, consisting of one or more house officers and registrars. A team must be headed by a consultant. A house officer or registrar cannot head a team, but must be a member of one team, and consultants cannot be members of a team. Each team has a team code and a telephone number that people can use to leave messages for the team.

Tabulate the properties of teams, denote whether they are single-valued or multi-valued, optional or mandatory, and describe how they are represented by the *Hospital conceptual data model*.

EXERCISE 3.10

The *Hospital scenario* describes the properties of treatments as follows:

> Each doctor may provide treatment for several patients and each patient may receive treatment from a number of doctors. ... A patient may receive more than one treatment from each doctor, for which the start date and the reason (e.g. a chest infection) for the treatment are recorded. Such a treatment may require several prescriptions,

each of which has a prescription number and specifies a total quantity and daily dosage of some drug.

Tabulate the properties of treatments, denote whether they are single-valued or multi-valued, optional or mandatory, and describe how they are represented by the *Hospital conceptual data model*.

Identifiers of entity types

A key single-valued property of an entity type that must be determined during data analysis is its identity. That is, the property that distinguishes occurrences of the same entity type, one from another.

EXERCISE 3.11

In the entity–relationship model, how is this uniqueness property conveyed?

When developing an entity–relationship model, we need to determine for each entity type which attribute, or combination of attributes, will form the identifier for that entity type. We can do this for a particular entity type once we have established all of its properties. We then look for a single-valued property, or combination of single-valued properties, that performs the following three roles: an assertion of existence, a reference, and a uniqueness constraint. For example, in the solution to Exercise 3.8 we identified 'Each doctor ... has a staff number ...' as a single-valued property of doctors, which is represented in the *Hospital conceptual data model* by the **StaffNo** attribute of the **Doctor** entity type. The **StaffNo** attribute is the identifier of the **Doctor** entity type because it performs those three roles: an occurrence of **Doctor** with a particular value for the identifier, **StaffNo**, is an assertion that a doctor exists who is employed by the hospital with that staff identification number. If we know a value for the identifier **StaffNo**, we can use it to refer uniquely to that doctor and thereby access his or her properties. Finally, specifying that **StaffNo** constrains the **Doctor** occurrences to those where the values of the **StaffNo** attribute are different, that is, no two doctors can have the same staff identification number.

For a particular single-valued property, or combination of single-valued properties, these roles may be stated explicitly in, or implied by, the description of the enterprise. We may have to analyse the sample occurrences of the entity type to determine which single-valued property, or combination of single-valued properties, performs these roles in order to establish which attribute, or combination of attributes, will form the identifier for that entity type. We should always analyse the sample occurrences anyway, to confirm our choice of identifier.

The *Hospital scenario* states, for example, that:

> Each patient in the hospital has a patient identification number ...

This implies that patients will be distinguished by their patient identification numbers. We can confirm this by analysing the patient data shown in the *Hospital domain of discourse summary*, which states that no two patients share the same patient identification number.

The *Hospital scenario* also states that:

> Each doctor may provide treatment for several patients and each patient may receive treatment from a number of doctors. ... A patient may receive more than one treatment from each doctor, for which the start date and the reason (e.g. a chest infection) for the treatment

> are recorded. Such a treatment may require several prescriptions, each of which has a prescription number and specifies a total quantity and daily dosage of a drug.

In the solution to Exercise 3.10, we identified the following single-valued properties of treatments:

> Each treatment is provided by a particular doctor ...
> ... to a particular patient ...
> ... on a particular start date ...
> ... for a particular reason.

Which single-valued property, or combination of single-valued properties, performs the three roles described above, and thereby will become the identifier for the **Treatment** entity type? The existence of a treatment is defined by:

> Each treatment is provided by a particular doctor ...
> ... to a particular patient ...
> ... on a particular start date ...

This combination of single-valued properties also acts as a reference since if we know the identities of the doctor and patient involved in a particular treatment, together with the start date of that treatment, we also know the reason for giving the treatment (and any prescriptions that are dispensed). We can confirm our choice of identifier by analysing the treatment data shown in the *Hospital domain of discourse summary*, which shows no two treatments with the same combination of doctor staff number, patient identification number and start date.

Occasionally, we may identify more than one single-valued property, or combination of single-valued properties, for a particular entity type that could potentially form the identifier of that entity type, and will need to choose one of them. We will illustrate this in Subsection 3.4.

EXERCISE 3.12

When we do identify more than one single-valued property, or combination of single-valued properties, that could potentially form the identifier, what else needs to be included in the entity-relationship model for those single-valued properties, or combination of single-valued properties, that are not chosen to be the identifier?

Since every entity type in an entity–relationship model must have an identifier, we may occasionally have to invent a single-valued property for a particular entity type that will take on the three roles if one is not described in the data requirements. We will illustrate this in Subsection 3.4.

Weak entity types

In Section 5 of *Block 1*, we defined weak entity type as one where occurrences of that entity type cannot exist without there being occurrences of other related entity types. Weak entity types are those entity types that have a mandatory relationship with another entity type where the identifier of that entity type is the same as, or a subset of, the weak entity type, and that entity type is at the :1 end of this relationship.

In the *Hospital conceptual data model*, **Specialist** is a weak entity type since it has mandatory participation with respect to the 1:1 relationship **IsA** with the **Doctor** entity type, and it has the same identifier as the **Doctor** entity type.

(handwritten margin notes)

EXERCISE 3.13

Why is **Treatment** a weak entity type?

When developing an entity–relationship model, we need to identify weak entity types, and those other entity types which they are dependent on, in order to ensure that the necessary additional constraints are included in the entity–relationship model.

EXERCISE 3.14

What additional constraints need to be included in the entity–relationship model for weak entity types?

Generic and specific entity types

The *Hospital scenario* describes different types of doctor, consultants and junior doctors, where the latter may be either registrars or house officers. When you identified the properties of doctors in Exercise 3.8 you might have noticed that some of these properties were associated only with consultants, some only with junior doctors, and others with both types. That is, the *Hospital scenario* describes both the properties associated with doctors in general and those specific to consultants or junior doctors.

Later we will introduce an extension to the notation for the entity–relationship model to allow us to represent explicitly these generic and specific forms of an entity type – entity subtypes. First, however, to help us to consider these extensions to the model, Figure 3.1 shows a subset of the *Hospital conceptual data model* that just represents those properties of doctors identified in the solution to Exercise 3.8.

Entity–relationship diagram

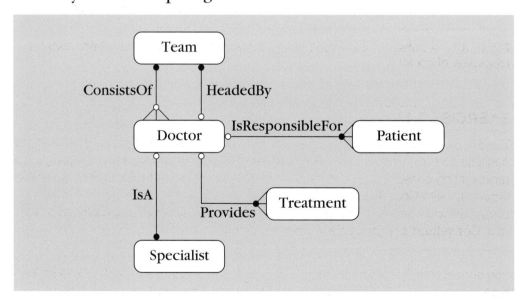

Entity types

Team (<u>TeamCode</u>, TelephoneNo)
Doctor (<u>StaffNo</u>, DoctorName, Position)
Patient (<u>PatientId</u>, PatientName, Gender, Height, Weight)
Specialist (<u>StaffNo</u>, Specialism)
Treatment (<u>StaffNo</u>, <u>PatientId</u>, <u>StartDate</u>, Reason)

Additional constraints

c.1   Each doctor who is responsible for a patient must be a consultant. That is, an instance of the entity type Doctor that is involved in the relationship IsResponsibleFor must have a position of consultant.

c.2   A doctor who is the head of a team must be a consultant. That is, an instance of the entity type Doctor that is involved in the relationship HeadedBy must have a position of consultant.

c.3   A consultant must head a team. Doctors who are not consultants must be members of a team. That is, an instance of the entity type Doctor whose position is that of a consultant belongs to a team via the HeadedBy relationship, whereas other doctors belong to a team via the ConsistsOf relationship.

c.6   Doctors can be consultants, registrars or house officers. That is, the attribute Position (of entity type Doctor) may have a value of Consultant, Registrar or House Officer.

c.7   Only consultants can have specialisms. That is, an instance of the entity type Doctor can only be involved in the IsA relationship if the value of the Position attribute is Consultant.

c.8   Treatment is a weak entity type dependent on Doctor. So, each value of the StaffNo attribute in entity type Treatment must be the same value as the StaffNo attribute of the Doctor instance to which the Treatment is related by the relationship Provides (a consequence of weak–strong entity types).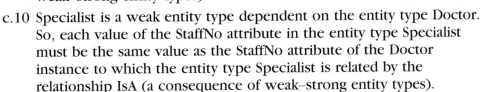

c.10 Specialist is a weak entity type dependent on the entity type Doctor. So, each value of the StaffNo attribute in the entity type Specialist must be the same value as the StaffNo attribute of the Doctor instance to which the entity type Specialist is related by the relationship IsA (a consequence of weak–strong entity types).

Figure 3.1   A subset of the *Hospital conceptual data model* that represents only the properties of doctors

EXERCISE 3.15

The *Hospital conceptual data model* employs the **Doctor** entity type to represent both consultants and junior doctors. We could have chosen to employ separate entity types representing consultant and junior doctors instead. Replace the **Doctor** entity type in Figure 3.1 with **Consultant** and **JuniorDoctor** entity types. Make sure that all properties identified in the solution to Exercise 3.8 are assigned appropriately to the new **Consultant** and **JuniorDoctor** entity types.

You should note from the solution to Exercise 3.15 that by replacing the **Doctor** entity type in Figure 3.1 with **Consultant** and **JuniorDoctor** entity types, the model now represents the properties of consultants and junior doctors explicitly. From the entity–relationship diagram we can see clearly, for example, that consultants head teams, are specialists and are responsible for patients. (Although precisely what this means, of course, requires us to consult the *Hospital domain of discourse summary*.) However, the entity–relationship diagram does not clearly show us that a treatment is provided either by a consultant or by a junior doctor, but not both, which requires the additional constraint c.15. So the revised model, unlike Figure 3.1, no longer represents the properties common to both consultants and junior doctors explicitly.

Before we describe the extensions to the notation for an entity–relationship diagram and the entity type definitions that will enable us to represent both generic and specific forms of doctors explicitly, we need first to consider a necessary simplification of the model. If you look at the entity–relationship diagram given as part of the solution to Exercise 3.15, you will see that the **IsA** relationship between the **Consultant** and **Specialist** entity types has mandatory participation at both ends, and the identifiers of the **Consultant** and **Specialist** entity types are the same, namely **StaffNo**. Since a specialism is a mandatory property of consultants and we now have a **Consultant** entity type, according to our guidelines for representing the properties of an entity type by the entity–relationship model, this property should be conveyed by an attribute. Figure 3.2 shows a revised entity–relationship model where the **Specialist** entity type and associated **IsA** relationship have been deleted, and as **Specialist** is a weak entity type, the associated constraint, c.10, has also been deleted. A consultant's specialism is represented by the **Specialism** attribute of the **Consultant** entity type.

Entity–relationship diagram

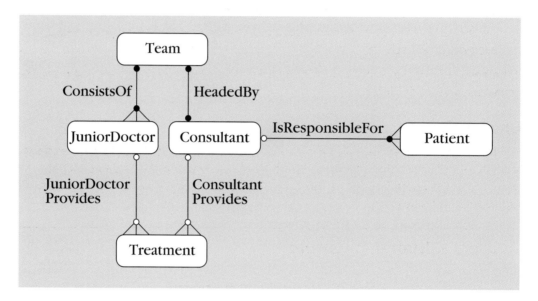

Entity types

Team (<u>TeamCode</u>, TelephoneNo)
JuniorDoctor (<u>StaffNo</u>, DoctorName, Position)
Consultant (<u>StaffNo</u>, DoctorName, Specialism)
Patient (<u>PatientId</u>, PatientName, Gender, Height, Weight)
Treatment (<u>StaffNo</u>, <u>PatientId</u>, <u>StartDate</u>, Reason)

Additional constraints

c.6   Junior doctors can be either registrars or house officers. That is, the attribute Position (of entity type JuniorDoctor) may have a value of Registrar or House Officer.

c.8   Treatment is a weak entity type dependent on JuniorDoctor or Consultant. So, each value of StaffNo in the entity type Treatment must be the same value as the StaffNo of the JuniorDoctor or Consultant instance to which the Treatment is related by the relationship JuniorDoctorProvides or ConsultantProvides (a consequence of weak–strong entity types).

c.14 A consultant cannot have the same staff number as a junior doctor. That is, the value of the StaffNo attribute for each occurrence of the Consultant entity type cannot be the same as the value of the StaffNo attribute for any occurrence of the JuniorDoctor entity type.

c.15 An occurrence of Treatment is either associated with an occurrence of JuniorDoctor via the JuniorDoctorProvides relationship, or with an occurrence of Consultant via the ConsultantProvides relationship, but not both.

Figure 3.2   A subset of the *Hospital conceptual data model* that represents only the properties of doctors generally and those of consultants and junior doctors specifically

Generally, whenever a data analysis results in an entity–relationship model where there are 1:1 relationships between entity types with the same identifiers and where they both have mandatory participation with respect to this relationship, the analyst should review the model by asking the following questions.

▶ Are they the same entity? That is, are they simply different names for the same real or abstract thing associated with the enterprise?

▶ Does one entity simply convey mandatory properties of the other (as in the example of the specialisms of consultants described above)?

If the answer is 'yes' to either question, then the analyst should consider combining the entity types as appropriate.

Entity subtypes

Figure 3.3 shows extensions to the notation for an entity–relationship diagram and the entity type definitions that enable us to represent generic and specific forms of an entity type. The figure just shows those single-valued properties of doctors that are represented by attributes.

Entity–relationship diagram

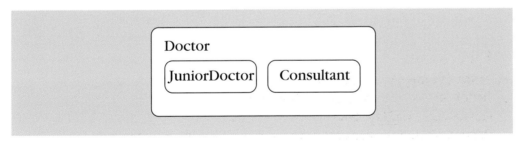

Entity types
Doctor (StaffNo, DoctorName)
    JuniorDoctor (Position)
    Consultant (Specialism)

Additional constraint

c.6   Junior doctors can be either registrars or house officers. That is, the attribute Position (of entity type JuniorDoctor) may have a value of Registrar or House Officer.

Figure 3.3   An entity–relationship model that just represents those single-valued properties of doctors that are represented by attributes

In Figure 3.3, **Doctor** is referred to as an **entity supertype**, and **JuniorDoctor** and **Consultant** as **entity subtypes** (of the supertype). Entity supertypes are abstract concepts in that they have no occurrences and serve solely to define the properties common to all of their subtypes. The properties of a supertype are inherited by all of its subtypes. Entity subtypes, of which there must be at least two, are concrete concepts in that they may have occurrences and define the properties specific to that particular entity subtype. By convention, in the *Entity types* section of an entity–relationship model we indent the subtypes.

As the identifier is defined in the supertype, occurrences of all of the subtypes are mutually exclusive. That is, there cannot be an occurrence of one subtype with the same identifier as occurrences of any of the other subtypes. In Figure 3.3, occurrences of **JuniorDoctor** and **Consultant** will be mutually exclusive and there cannot be an occurrence of **JuniorDoctor** with the same identifier as an occurrence of **Consultant**. In other words, a doctor cannot be both a junior doctor and a consultant simultaneously.

The **Position** attribute of the **JuniorDoctor** entity subtype takes only two values – registrar or house officer – as all instances of the **Consultant** entity subtype represent consultants, and each instance of the **JuniorDoctor** entity subtype represents either a registrar or house officer according to the value of the **Position** attribute.

The *Hospital scenario* says that '... junior doctors ... have a position of either registrar or house officer ...'. Figure 3.4 shows how Figure 3.3 can be extended to represent explicitly the positions held by junior doctors.

Entity–relationship diagram

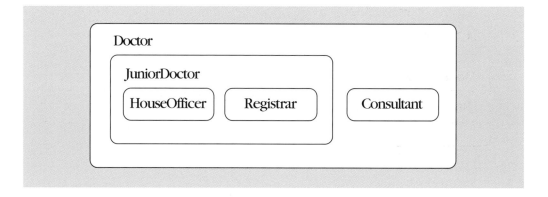

Entity types
Doctor (<u>StaffNo</u>, DoctorName)
      JuniorDoctor ( )
           HouseOfficer ( )
           Registrar ( )
      Consultant (Specialism)

Figure 3.4   An entity–relationship model that represents only those single-valued properties of doctors that are represented by attributes

In Figure 3.4, **Doctor** and **JuniorDoctor** are entity supertypes. Hence they do not have occurrences. **HouseOfficer**, **Registrar** and **Consultant** are mutually exclusive entity subtypes that may have occurrences, and represent the fact that doctors may be house officers, registrars or consultants. The **Position** attribute is no longer required since the property it conveys is implied by respective occurrences of the **HouseOfficer**, **Registrar** and **Consultant** entity subtypes. Note in Figure 3.4 how the indentation of the entity supertypes and subtypes in the *Entity types* section of the entity–relationship model reflects their hierarchical structure.

EXERCISE 3.16

As both doctors and nurses can be considered as medical staff working in the hospital, revise Figure 3.4 by introducing a new supertype named, say, **MedicalStaff**, to represent the staff structure.

Figure 3.5 shows a revised version of Figure 3.1, a subset of the *Hospital conceptual data model* that represents only those properties of doctors identified in the solution to Exercise 3.8, where the **Doctor** entity type has been replaced by the **Doctor** entity supertype as shown in Figure 3.3. Compare the different entity–relationship models that are shown in Figure 3.1, the solution to Exercise 3.15 and Figure 3.5, which represent the properties of doctors. We hope that you will agree that use of entity supertypes/subtypes enables us to represent these properties more explicitly. Note that, in particular, Figure 3.5 requires fewer additional constraints than either Figure 3.1 or the solution to Exercise 3.15.

Entity–relationship diagram

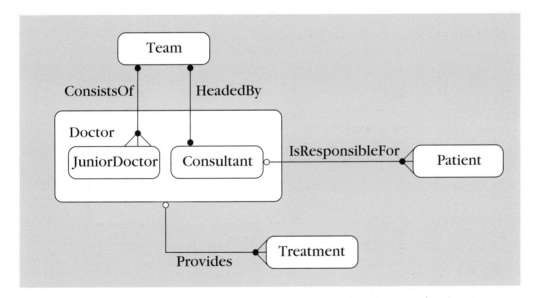

Entity types
Team (<u>TeamCode</u>, TelephoneNo)

Doctor (<u>StaffNo</u>, DoctorName)
   JuniorDoctor (Position)
   Consultant (Specialism)

Patient (<u>PatientId</u>, PatientName, Gender, Height, Weight)

Treatment (<u>StaffNo</u>, <u>PatientId</u>, <u>StartDate</u>, Reason)

Additional constraints

c.4   A doctor who treats a patient must be in the same team as the consultant who is responsible for that patient. That is, an instance of the entity subtype Doctor or Consultant that provides treatment for a patient must be from the same team as the consultant who is responsible for that patient.

c.6   Junior doctors can be either registrars or house officers. That is, the attribute Position (of entity subtype JuniorDoctor) may have a value of Registrar or House Officer.

c.8   Treatment is a weak entity type dependent on Doctor. So, each value of StaffNo in the entity type Treatment must be the same value as the StaffNo of the Doctor subtype instance to which the Treatment is related by the relationship Provides (a consequence of weak–strong entity types).

Figure 3.5   A subset of the *Hospital conceptual data model* that represents only the properties of doctors using entity supertypes/subtypes

Relationships

In Section 5 of *Block 1*, we said that a relationship between two entity types could have the following properties:

►   it has a name;

►   it may have role descriptions;

►   it is of a certain degree – 1:1 (one-to-one), 1:*n* (one-to-many), or *m*:*n* (many-to-many);

►   it has a participation condition for the entity type at each end of the relationship – optional or mandatory;

►   it may be dependent on other relationships – exclusive and inclusive relationships.

EXERCISE 3.17

What are role descriptions?

Exclusive and inclusive relationships

Here we will review dependent relationships: exclusive and inclusive relationships.

EXERCISE 3.18

What are exclusive and inclusive relationships?

In this course we have chosen to represent exclusive and inclusive relationships by conditions in the additional constraints section of the entity–relationship model, rather than employ additional notation on the entity–relationship diagram to convey exclusivity and inclusivity of relationships with respect to a particular entity type. Let us consider what additional constraints are needed to represent exclusive and inclusive relationships when just two relationships are involved.

In the entity–relationship diagram shown in Figure 3.6, the relationships **R1** and **R2** could have a degree of 1:1, 1:*n* or *m*:*n*, and the participation conditions of **B1** and **B2** with respect to **R1** and **R2** could be either optional or mandatory.

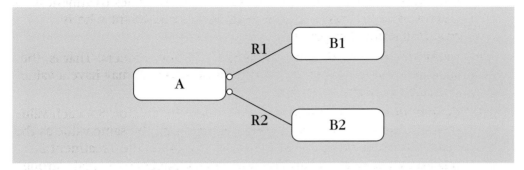

Figure 3.6 An entity–relationship model to illustrate exclusive and inclusive relationships

Exclusive and inclusive relationships can be either optional or mandatory. In Figure 3.6, if relationships **R1** and **R2** are optional exclusive or optional inclusive relationships, an occurrence of the **A** entity type can exist without participating in the exclusive or inclusive relationships. If relationships **R1** and **R2** are mandatory exclusive or mandatory inclusive relationships, then every occurrence of the **A** entity type must participate with the exclusive or inclusive relationships. The additional constraints needed to represent the combinations of optional or mandatory, exclusive or inclusive relationships are as follows.

If **R1** and **R2** are optional exclusive relationships with respect to the **A** entity type, then each occurrence of **A** participates in *none* or *exactly one* of the relationships **R1** and **R2**. This can be expressed by the following additional constraint:

> An occurrence of A is associated *either* with an occurrence of B1 via the R1 relationship *or* with an occurrence of B2 via the R2 relationship, *or with neither, but not with both*.

If **R1** and **R2** are mandatory exclusive relationships with respect to the **A** entity type, then each occurrence of **A** participates in *exactly one* of the relationships **R1** and **R2**. This can be expressed by the following additional constraint:

> An occurrence of A is associated *either* with an occurrence of B1 via the R1 relationship *or* with an occurrence of B2 via the R2 relationship, *but not with both*.

If **R1** and **R2** are optional inclusive relationships with respect to the **A** entity type, then each occurrence of **A** participates in *none* or *both* of the relationships **R1** and **R2**. This can be expressed by the following additional constraint:

> An occurrence of A is associated with *both* an occurrence of B1 via the R1 relationship *and* an occurrence of B2 via the R2 relationship, *or with neither*.

If **R1** and **R2** are mandatory inclusive relationships with respect to the **A** entity type, then each occurrence of **A** participates in *both* of the relationships **R1** and **R2**. This can be expressed without an additional constraint by simply changing the participation conditions of the **A** entity type to mandatory as shown in Figure 3.7.

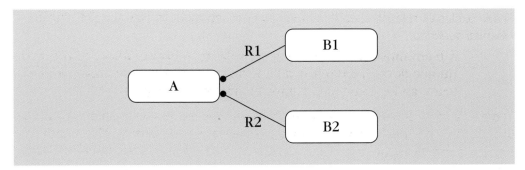

Figure 3.7   An entity–relationship model to illustrate mandatory inclusive relationships

Exclusivity and inclusivity are properties of the roles that the single entity type plays in the two or more relationships with the other entity types. That is, exclusive and inclusive relationships are with respect to this single entity type.

If, in Figures 3.6 and 3.7, **B1** and **B2** were the same entity type, then we would have two relationships between the same two entity types. In this situation, we must be clear about which end is the 'single entity type' when describing these two relationships as either exclusive or inclusive. We can illustrate this by considering the **ConsistsOf** and **HeadedBy** relationships between the **Team** and **Doctor** entity types in the *Hospital conceptual data model*, as shown in Figure 3.8.

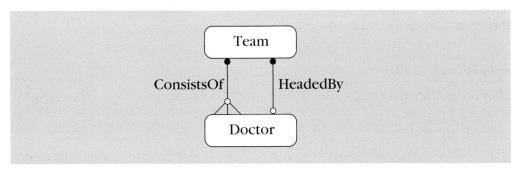

Figure 3.8   An entity–relationship model to illustrate exclusive and inclusive relationships between two entity types

ConsistsOf and **HeadedBy** are mandatory inclusive relationships with respect to the **Team** entity type because **Team** has mandatory participation with respect to both relationships. These inclusive relationships represent the following requirements specified in the *Hospital scenario*:

> Each consultant must head a single group, known as a team, consisting of one or more house officers and registrars. A team must be headed by a consultant.

ConsistsOf and **HeadedBy** are mandatory exclusive relationships with respect to the **Doctor** entity type because of the following condition that is specified in the additional constraints section of the *Hospital conceptual data model*:

> c.3   A consultant must head a team. Doctors who are not consultants must be members of a team. That is, an instance of the entity type Doctor whose position is that of a consultant belongs to a team via the HeadedBy relationship, whereas other doctors [junior doctors] belong to a team via the ConsistsOf relationship.

These exclusive relationships represent the following requirements specified in the *Hospital scenario*:

> **A team must be headed by a consultant. A house officer or registrar [junior doctor] cannot head a team, but must be a member of one team, and consultants cannot be members of a team.**

There is another dependent relationship that we need to consider before completing this section. This dependent relationship is essentially a combination of inclusivity and exclusivity, which we will call inclusive/exclusive relationships, and may be defined as follows:

> Inclusive/exclusive relationships are two or more relationships connecting a single entity type with two or more other (possibly the same) entity types where each occurrence of the single entity type participates in *at least one* of the relationships.

You will encounter later examples of inclusive/exclusive relationships when we consider how time-dependent (temporal) properties can be represented by an entity–relationship model.

Properties of relationships

Here we will consider other single-valued and multi-valued properties of relationships by looking at the **StaffedBy** relationship between the **Ward** and **Nurse** entity types of the *Hospital conceptual data model*.

EXERCISE 3.19

How do we distinguish between occurrences of the **StaffedBy** relationship, one from another?

Each occurrence of a relationship is identified by the combination of the identifiers of the occurrences of the entity types at each end of the relationship involved in that occurrence of the relationship. This combination of the identifiers is a single-valued property of the relationship. For example, in Figure 3.1 each occurrence of the **IsResponsibleFor** relationship is identified by the combination of **StaffNo** and **PatientId** values of the corresponding occurrences of the **Doctor** and **Patient** entity types involved in that occurrence of the **IsResponsibleFor** relationship.

Relationships, like entity types, may have other single-valued and multi-valued properties, or facts about them, that need to be represented by an entity–relationship model. Suppose, for example, that there is a requirement to record the date that a particular nurse was assigned to a particular ward. This is a single-valued property of the **StaffedBy** relationship since it is associated with a particular nurse on a particular ward – the identifier of the **StaffedBy** relationship.

As **StaffedBy** is a 1:*n* relationship, there are two possible approaches that we could employ. One approach would be simply to add an attribute, say **StartDate**, to the entity type **Nurse** at the :*n* end of the **StaffedBy** relationship;

> Nurse (<u>StaffNo</u>, NurseName, StartDate)

The alternative approach is to represent the **StaffedBy** relationship by an intersection entity type, say **WardStaff**, and record the date by a non-identifying attribute, say **StartDate**, of this intersection entity type. The entity–relationship model is shown in Figure 3.9.

Entity–relationship diagram

Entity types
Ward (<u>WardNo</u>, WardName, NumberOfBeds)
WardStaff (<u>StaffNo</u>, StartDate)
Nurse (<u>StaffNo</u>, NurseName)

Additional constraint
c.16 WardStaff is a weak entity type dependent on Nurse. So, each value of StaffNo in the entity type WardStaff must be the same value as the StaffNo of the Nurse instance to which the WardStaff entity type is related by the relationship IsA (a consequence of weak–strong entity types).

Figure 3.9   An entity–relationship model representing the date that a particular nurse was assigned to a particular ward

In Figure 3.9, each occurrence of the **WardStaff** entity type represents an occurrence of the **StaffedBy** relationship where the non-identifying attribute **StartDate** records the date that a particular nurse was assigned to a particular ward. Note that the identifier of the **Ward** entity type, **WardNo**, is not included in the definition of the **WardStaff** entity type as this single-valued property is conveyed by the **StaffedBy** relationship with **Ward**.

Although either approach can be employed to represent single-valued properties of 1:1 relationships, the latter approach that uses an intersection entity type is preferred since it explicitly records the fact that a particular nurse was assigned to a specific ward on a particular date, a property of the relationship between wards and nurses.

This preferred approach is analogous to that described in Subsection 2.6 of *Block 2*, where occurrences of relationships are recorded by tuples of a relation representing that relationship.

EXERCISE 3.20

Let us assume for a moment that a change has been made to the *Hospital scenario* whereby nurses could be assigned to more than one ward, and that there is a requirement to record the date that a particular nurse was assigned to a particular ward. How would you revise the *Hospital conceptual data model* to accommodate these new requirements?

We will conclude this section on the properties of relationships by considering how we can represent a multi-valued property of the **StaffedBy** relationship. Suppose that each nurse works to a weekly rota where, for each day of the week (Monday, Tuesday, etc.), the nurse is assigned to work the morning, afternoon or night shift, or is off duty for that day. The work rota is a multi-valued property of the **StaffedBy** relationship since it is associated with a particular nurse on a particular ward – the identifier of the **StaffedBy** relationship. Figure 3.10 shows how such a work rota can be represented by extending the entity–relationship model shown in Figure 3.9.

Entity–relationship diagram

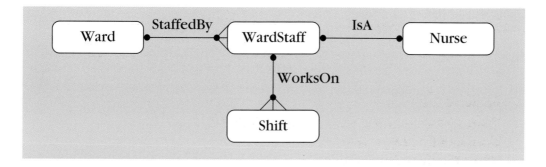

Entity types

Ward (<u>WardNo</u>, WardName, NumberOfBeds)
WardStaff (<u>StaffNo</u>, StartDate)
Shift (<u>StaffNo</u>, <u>WeekDay</u>, ShiftTime)
Nurse (<u>StaffNo</u>, NurseName)

Additional constraints

c.16 WardStaff is a weak entity type dependent on Nurse. So, each value of StaffNo in the entity type WardStaff must be the same value as the StaffNo of the Nurse instance to which the WardStaff entity type is related by the relationship IsA (a consequence of weak–strong entity types).

c.17 Nurses are assigned to work the morning, afternoon or night shift for a particular day of the week. That is, the attribute ShiftTime (of entity type Shift) may have a value of morning, afternoon or night.

c.18 Shift is a weak entity type dependent on WardStaff. So, each value of StaffNo in the entity type Shift must be the same value as the StaffNo of the WardStaff instance to which the Shift entity type is related by the relationship WorksOn (a consequence of weak–strong entity types).

Figure 3.10   An entity–relationship model representing the nurses' work rotas

The solution given in Figure 3.10 complies with our guidelines for representing multi-valued properties as a nurse's work rota is conveyed by a :*n* relationship with another entity type (**Shift**).

EXERCISE 3.21

In Exercise 3.20 we revised the *Hospital conceptual data model* to accommodate a new requirement whereby nurses could be assigned to more than one ward. Extend the solution to Exercise 3.20 to include the nurses' work rotas. You should assume that on each day a nurse can only work on a single ward.

In the solution to Exercise 3.10, we described how the properties of treatment were represented by the *Hospital conceptual data model*. Look at this solution again, in particular at how the following multi-valued property of treatment is represented:

> Such a treatment may require several prescriptions, each of which has a prescription number and specifies a total quantity and daily dosage of some drug.

You should see that the approach taken here to represent this multi-valued property is identical to that given in the solution to Exercise 3.21.

In this section on the properties of relationships, we have developed the following guidelines for representing these properties by an entity–relationship model:

▶ A mandatory single-valued property of, or fact about, a relationship is recorded by an attribute of an intersection entity type that represents the relationship.

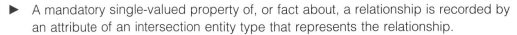

▶ An optional single-valued property of, or fact about, a relationship is represented by a 1:1 relationship between an intersection entity type representing the relationship and another entity type recording the property or fact. The participation condition of the intersection entity type with respect to this 1:1 relationship is optional.

▶ A multi-valued property of, or fact about, a relationship is represented by a 1:*n* relationship between an intersection entity type representing the relationship and another entity type recording the property or fact. The participation condition of the intersection entity type with respect to this 1:*n* relationship is determined by whether the property is optional or mandatory for occurrences of the relationship.

Temporal properties

Temporal properties are those multi-valued properties of entity types where each value is dependent on time. For example, in the *Hospital scenario* the treatment given to a patient is a multi-valued property of **Patient**:

> A patient may receive more than one treatment from each doctor, for which the start date and the reason for the treatment ... are recorded.

It is also a temporal property because each treatment provided by a particular doctor starts on a specified date.

According to our guidelines, a multi-valued property of an entity type is represented by a :*n* relationship with another entity type, whose occurrences record the values. If the property is temporal, then these occurrences are time-dependent, and so the identifier of this entity type will include an attribute that specifies the time. For example, the identifier of the **Treatment** entity type, which represents the multi-valued property of **Patient** as described above, includes the **StartDate** attribute to record the specified start date of the treatment provided by a particular doctor.

In the solution to Exercise 3.6 we noted, when describing the function of the *Limitations* section of an entity–relationship model, that a common limitation of an entity–relationship model is that it may only represent the current situation and does not record historical data, and historical relationships between the data. Here we will consider how we can represent historical situations by an entity–relationship model where historical data and historical relationships are recorded.

The *Limitations* section of the *Hospital conceptual data model* includes the following statement:

1.1   Only the details of a patient's current stay in hospital are recorded (i.e. only as an in-patient with no patient history of previous stays in the hospital).

Let us remove this limitation and decide how the *Hospital conceptual data model* needs to be revised so that the details of previous stays in the hospital by patients can be recorded. Our approach will be to consider each property of **Patient** to determine whether or not it is a temporal property; that is, we consider the likelihood of its value(s) changing over time. If it is a temporal property, then we will consider how it can be represented by revising the *Hospital conceptual data model*.

EXERCISE 3.22

Consider the single-valued properties of **Patient** that are represented by the attributes of the **Patient** entity type. Which of these properties could be temporal, that is, their values are *likely* to change over time?

The single-valued property, or the combination of single-valued properties, that conveys the identity of an entity occurrence should not normally have values that change over time. A unique value should be assigned to the identifier for a particular entity type when each occurrence of that entity type is created and should remain unchanged. Exceptions to this good practice arise if the value of an identifier is dependent on some other property of that entity type which is temporal. For example, let us assume for a moment that in the *Hospital scenario* the staff numbers of the doctors have different ranges of values depending on their positions: consultant, registrar or house officer. For example, if a particular junior doctor who has a position of registrar becomes a house officer, then their staff number will have to change.

Having identified some single-valued properties of **Patient** that are temporal, we will now need to determine how we might represent a history of the changes to the values of each single-valued property. The first thing to note is that as we are now representing a series of historical values, the single-valued property becomes a multi-valued property.

EXERCISE 3.23

Assuming that a patient's height and weight are always both measured on the same day, how should we modify the *Hospital conceptual data model* to record a history of changes to a patient's height and weight?

One decision that needs to be made when representing historical data, and historical relationships between data, is whether there is a need to distinguish between current and historical values. The first solution to Exercise 3.23 makes no distinction in its representation between a patient's current height and weight, and the history of earlier heights and weights. The second solution makes this distinction.

It is not possible, however, at this stage in the database development to choose between the alternative solutions to Exercise 3.23 until the operational requirements have been considered, at which time the need whether or not to distinguish between current and historical values will have been established. This is because the operational requirements are not the concern of the data analysis task, so it may be necessary to carry through both alternative representations (entity–relationship models) until the stage of the database development when the operational requirements are considered.

The approaches described in the solution to Exercise 3.23 could also be used to represent a history of a patient's names.

We will now consider the single-valued properties of the **Patient** entity type that are represented by a :1 relationship with other entity types. The following single-valued property of **Patient** is represented by a :1 relationship **OccupiedBy** with the **Ward** entity type:

> ### Each patient is assigned to a single ward.

It is also a temporal property because each time a patient is admitted to the hospital they may be assigned to a different ward (depending on their illnesses). Patients may also be assigned to different wards during a prolonged stay in hospital. If we are required to represent a history of the wards that patients have been assigned to, then this single-valued property of **Patient** becomes multi-valued. According to our guidelines for representing multi-valued properties, the **Ward** end of the **OccupiedBy** relationship becomes :*n* (to many).

EXERCISE 3.24

If the **Ward** end of the **OccupiedBy** relationship becomes :*n* (to many), then the relationship itself will become *m*:*n* (many-to-many). If we simply redraw the **OccupiedBy** relationship on the entity–relationship diagram as an *m*:*n* relationship (see below), why will this diagram not represent the actual semantics of the relationships between wards and patients?

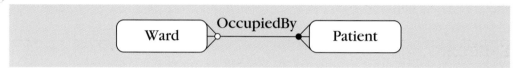

Since the period that a particular patient occupies a bed on a particular ward is a property of the current *m*:*n* **OccupiedBy** relationship, according to our guidelines this property has to be recorded by an intersection entity type representing the relationship. But, as the solution to Exercise 3.24 demonstrates, we cannot simply decompose the **OccupiedBy** relationship as we did with the *m*:*n* **StaffedBy** relationship in the previous section. The identifier of the intersection entity type representing the decomposed *m*:*n* **OccupiedBy** relationship would be (**WardNo, PatientId**), which would allow a particular patient to occupy two or more wards simultaneously, and would disallow a patient to occupy the same ward at different times. Furthermore, since we are representing a temporal property, each occurrence of this intersection entity type is dependent on time – that is, the date a particular patient starts a particular occupancy of a bed on a particular ward – and so the date must be part of its identifier.

The appropriate decomposition of the *m*:*n* **OccupiedBy** relationship is shown in Figure 3.11.

Entity–relationship diagram

Entity types
Ward (<u>WardNo</u>, WardName, NumberOfBeds)
WardPatient (<u>PatientId</u>, <u>StartDate</u>, EndDate)
Patient (<u>PatientId</u>, PatientName, Gender, Height, Weight)

Additional constraints

c.22 WardPatient is a weak entity type dependent on Patient. So, each value of PatientId in the entity type WardPatient must be the same value as the PatientId of the Patient instance to which the

WardPatient entity type is related by the relationship IsA (a consequence of weak–strong entity types).

c.23 For each instance of the WardPatient intersection entity type, the value of StartDate should be less than or equal to (<=) the value of EndDate.

Figure 3.11   An entity–relationship model representing a history of patient admissions

---

In Figure 3.11, each occurrence of the **WardPatient** intersection entity type records the period that a particular patient occupies a bed on a particular ward. Note that the identifier of the **Ward** entity type, **WardNo**, is not included in the definition of the **WardPatient** entity type as this single-valued property is conveyed by the IsOccupiedBy relationship with **Ward**.

EXERCISE 3.25

Although the identifier of the **WardPatient** intersection entity type in Figure 3.11 allows a patient to occupy the same ward at different times, what additional constraint is needed to ensure that a patient cannot occupy beds on two or more wards simultaneously?

Figure 3.11 does not distinguish between current and historical occupancy of beds on wards. This is accomplished by the entity–relationship model shown in Figure 3.12.

Entity–relationship diagram

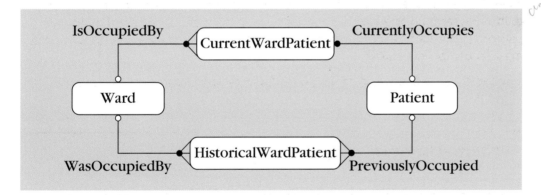

Entity types
Ward (<u>WardNo</u>, WardName, NumberOfBeds)
CurrentWardPatient (<u>PatientId</u>, StartDate, EndDate)
HistoricalWardPatient (<u>PatientId</u>, <u>StartDate</u>, EndDate)
Patient (<u>PatientId</u>, PatientName, Gender, Height, Weight)

Additional constraints

c.25 CurrentWardPatient is a weak entity type dependent on Patient. So, each value of PatientId in the entity type CurrentWardPatient must be the same value as the PatientId of the Patient instance to which the CurrentWardPatient entity type is related by the relationship CurrentlyOccupies (a consequence of weak–strong entity types).

c.26 HistoricalWardPatient is a weak entity type dependent on Patient. So, each value of PatientId in the entity type HistoricalWardPatient must be the same value as the PatientId of the Patient instance to which the HistoricalWardPatient entity type is related by the relationship PreviouslyOccupied (a consequence of weak–strong entity types).

c.27 For each instance of the CurrentWardPatient intersection entity type, the value of StartDate should be less than or equal to (<=) the value of EndDate.

c.28 For each instance of the HistoricalWardPatient intersection entity type, the value of StartDate should be less than or equal to (<=) the value of EndDate.

c.29 When instances of the HistoricalWardPatient intersection entity type for each value of PatientId are ordered chronologically by the values of StartDate, the value of EndDate for each instance should be less than or equal to (<=) the value of StartDate of the succeeding instance.

c.30 Each instance of Patient must participate in the CurrentlyOccupies relationship, or the PreviouslyOccupied relationship, or both.

Figure 3.12   An entity–relationship model representing a history of patient admissions that distinguishes between current and historical occupancy of beds on wards

The final condition in the additional constraints section of the entity–relationship model shown in Figure 3.12 (c.30) describes **CurrentlyOccupies** and **PreviouslyOccupied** as mandatory inclusive/exclusive relationships with respect to the **Patient** entity type. This constraint is required because the **Patient** entity type has mandatory participation with respect to the original **OcccupiedBy** relationship – that is, every patient currently occupies, or has previously occupied, a ward.

EXERCISE 3.26

Consider the following single-valued property of the **Patient** entity type that is represented by a :1 relationship **IsResponsibleFor** with the **Doctor** entity type:

Each patient is under the care of a single doctor.

This is a temporal property because each time a patient is admitted to hospital they may be under the care of different doctors (depending on their illnesses). They may also be under the care of different doctors during a prolonged stay in hospital, or if their doctor leaves the hospital after they have been admitted.

Give an entity–relationship model that represents a history of the doctors' responsibilities to their patients where the current responsibilities are distinguished from the historical ones.

We hope that you appreciate that representing historical data and historical relationships between data by an entity–relationship model is complex. However, historical data is an important and essential asset to almost all organisations. It would be unimaginable, for example, if a real hospital administration system did not record historical data about patients and their treatments, or a real university system did not record historical data about students, the courses they studied, and the grades they achieved.

In Subsection 3.4, we will analyse the data requirements of the supermarket case study. Since the intention is to model a real system, representing historical data will be an important aspect of the data analysis task.

Derivable properties

Derivable properties are those properties where the associated data values can be obtained from the data values of one or more other properties. Data values that are derived (secondary data) from other data collected and/or generated by an enterprise (primary data) are not usually included in an entity–relationship model, as their inclusion results in redundancy in the model because of the duplication of the information. Such duplication is a source of inconsistency and should be avoided.

Suppose the *Hospital scenario* included the requirement for doctors to have knowledge of the body mass index (BMI) of every patient. Although the BMI is a single-valued property of the **Patient** entity type, we will not include an attribute in the definition of that entity type to record the BMI because it is calculated from a patient's height and weight, which are recorded respectively by the **Height** and **Weight** attributes.

Whether or not the derived data needs to be stored in the relational database that implements an entity–relationship model for reasons of usability and/or efficiency, this will be decided upon at a later stage of the database development when the operational requirements are considered.

Data values

We conclude Subsection 3.2 on the entity–relationship model by considering how we should characterise the data values associated with each attribute of the entity types that comprise a model. That is, for each single-valued property of, or fact about, an entity type that is represented by an attribute of that entity type, how do we describe the nature of the data values that need to be recorded in order to satisfy the data requirements of an enterprise?

EXERCISE 3.27

Why is it important to characterise the data values associated with the attributes of the entity types during the data analysis stage of a database development? How is this information used in the subsequent stages of the development?

For each attribute, we need to establish the **value set** – that is, the set of permissible data values that the attribute may hold. A value set may be infinite or finite; that is, it may comprise an unrestricted or a restricted number of values, respectively. An example of an unrestricted value set is {character strings}, which comprises all permutations of strings of characters – letters, numbers and punctuation marks. Other examples are {alphabetic strings}, {integers}, {numbers}, {dates} and {times}, which respectively comprise all permutations of strings of letters and punctuation marks, all possible positive and negative whole numbers, positive and negative real numbers, calendar dates and clock times.

A value set is usually restricted to a number of discrete values or a continuous range of values. Examples of discrete value sets are {1, 6, 7}, {1.1, 6.2, 7.3}, {a, q, z} and {Mr, Miss, Mrs, Ms}. Examples of continuous ranges of values are {1...9}, {0.1...9.9}, {a...z}, {a0...a9} and {a0...z9}, which enumerate respectively as {1, 2, 3, 4, ..., 9}, {0.1, 0.2, 0.3, 0.4, ..., 9.9}, {a, b, c, d, ..., z}, {a0, a1, a2, a3, ..., a9} and {a0, a1, ..., b0, b1, ..., z0, z1, ..., z9}.

When specifying numerical value sets, it is sometimes convenient to use initially, for example, the forms {dddd} and {ddd.d}, where 'd' is a digit, to denote a continuous range of numbers such that the number of digits is known but not the upper and lower bounds. In these examples, the value sets {dddd} and {ddd.d} are equivalent to

{0...9999} and {0.0...999.9}, respectively, therefore to prevent the existence of erroneous data the upper and lower bounds will need to be determined before the data analysis activity is completed. If the upper and lower bounds of a numerical value set are not specified by the enterprise scenario, then they will have to be determined by inspecting the available sample data.

In this block, we will use the forms {n} and {n.n} to denote positive integers and real numbers, respectively, and {1...n} for the continuous unbounded sequence {1, 2, 3, 4, ...}.

Note the distinction between the forms {1...999} and {001...999}, for example. The former defines a numerical value set, the latter a value set that comprises all permutations of strings of three digits where the leading zeros (00) are significant.

The value set should reflect any restrictions, either explicit or implicit, imposed by the context of the enterprise. For example, if people's ages are measured in years, then the value set of an attribute that concerns adults might be {18...120}, whereas a value set that concerns children might be {0...17}.

We also need to answer the following questions in order to characterise the data values.

▶ Are the data values simple or complex?

A simple data value comprises a single data field, whereas a complex data value has two or more fields. Examples of simple data values are those associated with people's ages. Examples of complex data values are those associated with people's names where each name is subdivided into title, forename(s) and family name fields.

How we ultimately represent complex data values in the relational database that implements an entity–relationship model is dependent on how the data needs to be processed in order to meet the operational requirements of the enterprise. As the operational requirements are not considered by the data analysis stage of a database development, complex data values are typically represented by single attributes in an entity–relationship model. How the complex data values are implemented will be decided upon at a later stage of the database development, when the operational requirements are considered.

▶ Are the data values dependent on the values of other attributes of the same or different entity type?

The values that can be assigned to an attribute from its value set may depend on the values that are assigned to other related attributes of the same or a different entity type. For example, the title fields of people's names may be dependent on their gender. If the value set for the title fields of people's names was {Mr, Miss, Mrs, Ms, Dr, Prof} then we would naturally expect the value 'Mr' to be associated with males, 'Miss', 'Mrs' and 'Ms' with females, and 'Dr' and 'Prof' with either gender. In order to prevent the existence of inconsistent data, an appropriate condition may need to be included in the *Additional constraints* section of the entity–relationship model for each data dependency.

The value set for each attribute of the entity types of an entity–relationship model is recorded in the accompanying domain of discourse summary, together with any other characteristics of the data values described above.

Table 3.4 shows the value set and other characteristics of the data values for each attribute of the **Doctor** entity type taken from the *Hospital domain of discourse summary.*

Doctor entity type

Attribute	Value set	Characteristics
StaffNo	{001...999}	Dependency: no doctor has the same staff number as any nurse.
DoctorName	{family names}	
Position	{Consultant, Registrar, House Officer}	

Table 3.4   The value set and other characteristics of the data values for each attribute of the Doctor entity type

The **StaffNo** attribute takes a continuous range of values, 001...999, but as the *Hospital domain of discourse summary* states that

> **No doctor has the same staff number as any of the nurses.**

the data values are dependent on the values that are assigned to the **StaffNo** attribute of occurrences of the **Nurse** entity type. This dependency is expressed by the following condition in the *Additional constraints* section of the *Hospital conceptual data model*:

> **c.13 A nurse cannot have the same staff number as a doctor. That is, the value of the StaffNo attribute for each occurrence of the Nurse entity type cannot be the same as the value of the StaffNo attribute for any occurrence of the Doctor entity type.**

The **DoctorName** attribute takes values that correspond to those of family names. We have chosen to introduce a specific value set, {family names}, rather than use the generic {alphabetic strings} because family names include only a limited number of punctuation marks. Although we would expect to encounter apostrophes (') and hyphens (-) in family names, for example O'Connor and Fox-Pitt, certain punctuation marks, such as the exclamation mark (!) and the question mark (?), would be unexpected.

The **Position** attribute takes a discrete set of values, Consultant, Registrar or House Officer, which is expressed by the following condition in the *Additional constraints* section of the *Hospital conceptual data model*:

> **c.6   Doctors can be consultants, registrars or house officers. That is, the attribute Position (of entity type Doctor) may have a value of Consultant, Registrar or House Officer.**

Table 3.5 shows the value set and other characteristics of the data values for each attribute of the **Specialism** entity type taken from the *Hospital domain of discourse summary*.

Specialism entity type

Attribute	Value set	Characteristics
StaffNo	{001...999}	Dependency: those doctors who have specialisms must be known doctors who are consultants.
Specialism	{medical specialisms}	

Table 3.5   The value set and other characteristics of the data values for each attribute of the Specialism entity type

As with the **Doctor** entity type, the **StaffNo** attribute takes a continuous range of values, 001...999, but the values must correspond to known doctors. That is, the values must be the same as the values assigned to the **StaffNo** attribute of occurrences of the **Doctor** entity type. This dependency is expressed by the following condition in the *Additional constraints* section of the *Hospital conceptual data model*:

> c.10 Specialist is a weak entity type dependent on the entity type Doctor. So, each value of the StaffNo attribute in the entity type Specialist must be the same value as the StaffNo attribute of the Doctor instance to which the entity type Specialist is related by the relationship IsA (a consequence of weak–strong entity types).

Values of the **StaffNo** attribute are restricted further because as the *Hospital scenario* states that

> Consultants must have a specialism, but registrars and house officers are not specialists and do not have a specialism. All specialists are consultants.

the data values are dependent on the value assigned to the **Position** attribute of occurrences of the **Doctor** entity type. This dependency is expressed by the following condition in the *Additional constraints* section of the *Hospital conceptual data model*:

> c.7 Only consultants can have specialisms. That is, an instance of the entity type Doctor can only be involved in the IsA relationship if the value of the Position attribute is Consultant.

The **Specialism** attribute takes values that correspond to medical specialisms, currently Cardiac, Paediatric and Orthopaedic.

Table 3.6 shows the value set and other characteristics of the data values for each attribute of the **Ward** entity type taken from the *Hospital domain of discourse summary*.

Ward entity type

Attribute	Value set
WardNo	{w1...w9}
WardName	{character strings}
NumberOfBeds	{1...50}

Table 3.6   The value set and other characteristics of the data values for each attribute of the **Ward** entity type

The **WardNo** attribute takes a continuous range of values, w1...w9. The **WardName** attribute takes values that are alphabetic strings, currently corresponding to regions of the British Isles. The **NumberOfBeds** attribute takes a continuous range of values, 1...50, because every ward has at least one bed and the hospital never has wards with more than 50 beds.

EXERCISE 3.28

Using the *Hospital scenario* and *Hospital domain of discourse summary*, determine the value set and other characteristics of the data values for each attribute of the **Patient**, **Team** and **Treatment** entity types. For each data dependency, give the associated condition from the *Additional constraints* section of the *Hospital conceptual data model*.

You should note that when describing value sets of attributes of entity types in an entity–relationship model, we use everyday descriptions of the data and not the terminology of SQL data types or that of other programming languages. This is because an entity–relationship model is concerned with the meaning and structure of data, but not with the details affecting how it is implemented.

Summary of Subsection 3.2

In this subsection we have developed the following guidelines for representing the properties of entity types by an entity–relationship model:

▶ A single-valued property of, or fact about (SVF), an entity type that relates to occurrences of another (or the same) entity type is represented by a :1 relationship with the other (or the same) entity type, where the participation condition of the entity type with respect to the relationship is determined by whether the property is optional or mandatory for occurrences of the entity type.

▶ A single-valued property of, or fact about (SVF), an entity type that is not related to any occurrences of another (or the same) entity type is represented by an attribute if the property is mandatory for occurrences of the entity type, or if the property is optional, by a :1 relationship with a new entity type, where the participation condition of the entity type with respect to the relationship is optional.

▶ A multi-valued property of, or fact about (MVF), an entity type is represented by a :n relationship with another (or the same) entity type, where the participation condition of the entity type with respect to the relationship is determined by whether the property is optional or mandatory for occurrences of the entity type.

In Subsections 3.3 and 3.4, we will look in detail at two aspects of analysing the data requirements of an enterprise to identify entity types and the properties of those entity types, in order to develop an entity–relationship model that represents those requirements. The first concerns the analysis of textual descriptions of the enterprise provided by the client or produced as a result of the establishing requirements activity. The second concerns the analysis of the various documents created and used by the enterprise to record or display information that was collected during the establishing requirements task. Such documents will be structured, typically in the form of lists, tables and figures rather than free text, and may include orders, invoices and receipts.

The aim of the remaining subsections is to illustrate not only the process of analysing the data requirements of an enterprise, but also the development of the entity–relationship model that represents these requirements. An entity–relationship model is a working document that evolves as the data analysis task proceeds, and as the meaning of the data is uncovered and needs documenting. That is, the data analysis task and the development of the entity–relationship model proceed incrementally. They also proceed iteratively because, in reality, the data analysis task cannot be done in isolation; it often requires feedback from the client throughout the process. When an analyst begins collating the data requirements and identifying the data of interest, they will make some working assumptions about the data that will need to be clarified with the clients. The conceptual data model will be developed and refined when the data analyst meets with the clients and data users to refine the domain of discourse to determine the appropriate scope for the data. Gradually, the assumptions will be replaced with concrete decisions about the model or the limitations of the model.

The aim of the data analysis task should be to produce a final entity–relationship model that can be passed to the database designers, who will move the database development on to the next stage of its life cycle, the logical schema stage, without the need to consult the clients about the meaning of the data.

3.3 Analysing text

In this subsection, we describe an approach to analysing textual descriptions of an enterprise, in order to develop an entity–relationship model that represents the data requirements of that enterprise. Such textual descriptions would have been provided either by the client or produced as a result of the establishing requirements task. With this approach, we identify entity types and their properties, and the relationships between those entity types and the properties of those relationships, by performing a **grammatical analysis** or **grammatical parse** of the text. If several texts have been acquired during the establishing requirements task, the results of analysing these texts are combined and any differences between them reconciled.

This approach will yield an entity–relationship model that represents all the data requirements of the enterprise only if the texts associated with that enterprise which are made available for analysis are a comprehensive (complete) description. In this subsection, we shall demonstrate that this approach works well for the *Hospital scenario*, which is the sole description of the hospital enterprise provided to you. However, when applied to the description of Walton Stores in Subsection 2.1, only an outline entity–relationship model results because the description only provides an overview of the supermarket enterprise. The approach could be used in combination with the approach described later in Subsection 3.4.

The foundation of this approach is that entity types and their properties often correspond to nouns and noun phrases in a written description of an enterprise, and relationships between those entity types and their properties often correspond to sentences that associate these entity types with each other by a verb or verb phrase. Using this approach to analyse textual descriptions of an enterprise, we:

- ▶ scan the text to identify all the nouns and noun phrases;
- ▶ determine which of these nouns and noun phrases correspond to entity types and properties of these entity types that are relevant to the data requirements of that enterprise;
- ▶ rescan the text to identify those sentences that associate these entity types with each other by verbs or verb phrases that correspond to the relationships between the entity types that are identified;
- ▶ rescan the text again to identify any constraints on the entity–relationship model.

This approach works because nouns and entities are similarly defined, verbs and relationships likewise. The *Oxford Dictionary of English* (2nd edition) defines a noun as 'a word used to identify any of a class of people, places, or things, or to name a particular one of these'. In *Block 1*, Section 5, we defined an entity as 'a thing that has meaning in a given context and about which there is a need to record data'. A noun phrase is a phrase where a noun is preceded by an adjective, an article (the, a), a demonstrative (this, that), a possessive (my, their, etc.), or a numeral (one, two, etc.). Although nouns and noun phrases often correspond to entities in a written description of an enterprise, from the definition of a noun you can probably deduce that they can also correspond to the properties of those entity types, or the values associated with those properties, as well as things that are irrelevant to the model.

If we take the traditional view of a sentence as being regarded as having a subject and an object that are associated by a verb, where the subject and the object of a sentence are both nouns or noun phrases, then this is comparable with the definition of a relationship we gave in *Block 1*, Section 5 as 'an association between entities that has meaning in a given context and which needs to be recorded'. For example, the *Hospital scenario* states

> The hospital is organised into <u>a number of wards</u> [noun phrase], each of which <u>may be empty or may be occupied by</u> [verb phrase] <u>one or more patients</u> [noun phrase].

which describes an association between entities that has meaning in the context of the hospital enterprise that is represented in the *Hospital conceptual data model* by the **OccupiedBy** relationship between the **Ward** and **Patient** entity types.

Analysing the Hospital scenario

We will continue to use the hospital enterprise to illustrate the approach that is used to analyse textual descriptions of an enterprise because it describes the data requirements of the hospital completely and hence it is easier to illustrate the steps that we need to undertake to develop an entity–relationship model that represents the data requirements of that enterprise using this approach.

The first step is to scan the text to identify all the nouns and noun phrases. In the following copy of the *Hospital scenario* all the nouns and noun phrases are underlined.

> <u>The hospital</u> is organised into <u>a number of wards</u>, each of which may be empty or may be occupied by <u>one or more patients</u>. <u>Each ward</u> is identified by <u>a ward number</u>; it has <u>a name</u> and contains <u>a fixed number of beds</u>. <u>Each ward</u> is staffed by <u>one or more nurses</u>. <u>Each nurse</u> is identified by <u>a staff number</u> and has <u>a name</u>. <u>A nurse</u> is assigned to <u>a single ward</u>. <u>Some nurses</u> are designated to supervise <u>one or more other nurses</u> on <u>the same ward</u>. <u>A nurse</u> has <u>at most one supervisor</u>.
>
> <u>Each patient</u> in <u>the hospital</u> has <u>a patient identification number</u> and <u>name</u> recorded; <u>their gender</u>, <u>height</u> and <u>weight</u> is kept on record. <u>Each patient</u> is assigned to <u>a single ward</u> and is under the care of (is the responsibility of) <u>a single doctor</u> who must have <u>a position of consultant</u>. <u>Each consultant</u> is responsible for <u>a number of patients</u>. Details of <u>the junior doctors</u> in <u>the hospital</u>, who have <u>a position</u> of either <u>registrar</u> or <u>house officer</u>, are also recorded. <u>Consultants</u> must have <u>a specialism</u>, but <u>registrars</u> and <u>house officers</u> are not <u>specialists</u> and do not have <u>a specialism</u>. <u>All specialists</u> are <u>consultants</u>. <u>Each doctor</u> (whether <u>consultant</u> or <u>junior doctor</u>) in <u>the hospital</u> has <u>a staff number</u> and <u>name</u> recorded. <u>Each consultant</u> must head <u>a single group</u>, known as <u>a team</u>, consisting of <u>one or more house officers</u> and <u>registrars</u>. <u>A team</u> must be headed by <u>a consultant</u>. <u>A house officer</u> or <u>registrar</u> cannot head <u>a team</u>, but must be a member of <u>one team</u>, and <u>consultants</u> cannot be members of <u>a team</u>. <u>Each team</u> has <u>a team code</u> and <u>a telephone number</u> that <u>people</u> can use to leave <u>messages</u> for <u>the team</u>.
>
> <u>Each doctor</u> may provide <u>treatment</u> for <u>several patients</u> and <u>each patient</u> may receive <u>treatment</u> from <u>a number of doctors</u>. <u>Any doctor</u> treating <u>a patient</u> must be a member of <u>the same team</u> as <u>the consultant</u> responsible for <u>that patient</u>. <u>A patient</u> may receive <u>more than one treatment</u> from <u>each doctor</u>, for which <u>the start date</u> and <u>the reason</u> (e.g. <u>a chest infection</u>) for <u>the treatment</u> are recorded. <u>Such a treatment</u> may require <u>several prescriptions</u>, each of which

has a prescription number and specifies a total quantity and daily dosage of some drug. A drug may appear on different prescriptions. Each drug has a unique code, a type and unit price as well as a name (e.g. Dolensol or Hallexanuran).

As you would expect, this step will usually result in a long list of candidate entity types and properties of entity types. So we need to establish appropriate criteria that will enable us to perform the second step, which is to prune the list and provide us with just those entity types and properties of entity types that are required to represent the data requirements of the enterprise.

As an entity represents a thing that has meaning in a given context and about which there is a need to record data, we can discard those candidate entity types that are not relevant because they are outside the scope of the database system being developed to represent data requirements of the enterprise. As an entity type is a collection of several entities with properties in common, we can discard those candidate entity types that will only ever have one occurrence. We can also discard those candidate entity types that have the same properties as another entity type because they are simply different names for the same thing: those that convey implementation details, and those that are values associated with attributes of entity types.

To summarise:

► we retain those candidates that represent entity types and properties of entity types that are required to represent the data requirements of the enterprise;

► we discard those that are outside the scope of the database being developed, those that represent entity types with only one occurrence, those that are synonymous with other entity types or properties of entity types, those that convey implementation details, and those that are values associated with attributes of entity types.

In Table 3.7, we list the *Hospital scenario* sentence by sentence. We consider each candidate entity type or property when it appears for the first time in the scenario, and say whether it should be retained as an entity type or a property of an entity type – an attribute – or whether it should be discarded, giving the justification.

Text	Noun or noun phrase	Outcome	Justification
The hospital is organised into a number of wards, each of which may be empty or may be occupied by one or more patients.	hospital	discard	has only one occurrence
	ward	**Ward** entity type	
	patient	**Patient** entity type	
Each ward is identified by a ward number; it has a name and contains a fixed number of beds.	ward number	identifying property of the **Ward** entity type – **WardNo** attribute	
	name	single-valued property of the **Ward** entity type – **WardName** attribute	
	number of beds	single-valued property of the **Ward** entity type – **NumberOfBeds** attribute	
Each ward is staffed by one or more nurses.	nurse	**Nurse** entity type	

Table 3.7   Analysis of the nouns and noun phrases from the *Hospital scenario*

Text	Noun or noun phrase	Outcome	Justification
Each nurse is identified by a staff number and has a name.	staff number	identifying property of the **Nurse** entity type – **StaffNo** attribute	
	name	single-valued property of the **Nurse** entity type – **NurseName** attribute	
A nurse is assigned to a single ward. Some nurses are designated to supervise one or more other nurses on the same ward. A nurse has at most one supervisor.	supervisor	**Supervisor** entity subtype	a specific type of nurse
Each patient in the hospital has a patient identification number and name recorded; their gender, height and weight is kept on record.	patient identification number	identifying property of the **Patient** entity type – **PatientId** attribute	
	name	single-valued property of the **Patient** entity type – **PatientName** attribute	
	gender	single-valued property of the **Patient** entity type – **Gender** attribute	
	height	single-valued property of the **Patient** entity type – **Height** attribute	
	weight	single-valued property of the **Patient** entity type – **Weight** attribute	
Each patient is assigned to a single ward and is under the care of (is the responsibility of) a single doctor who must have a position of consultant.	doctor	**Doctor** entity type	
	position	single-valued property of the **Doctor** entity type – **Position** attribute	
	consultant	discard	a value of the **Position** attribute
Each consultant is responsible for a number of patients.	consultant	**Consultant** entity subtype	a specific type of doctor
	patients	discard	**Patient** is an entity type
Details of the junior doctors in the hospital, who have a position of either registrar or house officer, are also recorded.	junior doctor	**JuniorDoctor** entity subtype	a specific type of doctor
	registrar	discard	a value of the **Position** attribute
	house officer	discard	a value of the **Position** attribute

Table 3.7   *continued*

Text	Noun or noun phrase	Outcome	Justification
Consultants must have a specialism, but registrars and house officers are not specialists and do not have a specialism.	specialism	single-valued property of the **Consultant** entity subtype – **Specialism** attribute	
	specialists	discard	synonymous with specialism
All specialists are consultants. Each doctor (whether consultant or junior doctor) in the hospital has a staff number and name recorded.	staff number	identifying property of the **Doctor** entity supertype – **StaffNo** attribute	
	name	single-valued property of the **Doctor** entity supertype – **DoctorName** attribute	
Each consultant must head a single group, known as a team, consisting of one or more house officers and registrars.	group	discard	synonymous with team
	team	**Team** entity type	
A team must be headed by a consultant.			
A house officer or registrar cannot head a team, but must be a member of one team, and consultants cannot be members of a team.			
Each team has a team code and a telephone number that people can use to leave messages for the team.	team code	single-valued property of the **Team** entity type – **TeamCode** attribute	
	telephone number	single-valued property of the **Team** entity type – **TelephoneNo** attribute	
	people	discard	outside the scope of the database being developed
	messages	discard	outside the scope of the database being developed
Each doctor may provide treatment for several patients and each patient may receive treatment from a number of doctors.	treatment	**Treatment** entity type	

Table 3.7   *continued*

Text	Noun or noun phrase	Outcome	Justification
Any doctor treating a patient must be a member of the same team as the consultant responsible for that patient.			
A patient may receive more than one treatment from each doctor, for which the start date and the reason (e.g. a chest infection) for the treatment are recorded.	start date	single-valued property of the **Treatment** entity type – **StartDate** attribute	
	reason	single-valued property of the **Treatment** entity type – **Reason** attribute	
	chest infection	discard	a value of the **Reason** attribute
Such a treatment may require several prescriptions, each of which has a prescription number and specifies a total quantity and daily dosage of some drug.	prescriptions	**Prescription** entity type	
	prescription number	single-valued property of the **Prescription** entity type – **PrescriptionNo** attribute	
	total quantity	single-valued property of the **Prescription** entity type – **TotalQuantity** attribute	
	daily dosage	single-valued property of the **Prescription** entity type – **DailyDosage** attribute	
	drug	**Drug** entity type	
A drug may appear on different prescriptions.			
Each drug has a unique code, a type and unit price as well as a name (e.g. Dolensol or Hallexanuran).	unique code	identifying property of the **Drug** entity type – **DrugCode** attribute	
	type	single-valued property of the **Drug** entity type – **DrugType** attribute	
	unit price	single-valued property of the **Drug** entity type – **UnitPrice** attribute	
	name	single-valued property of the **Drug** entity type – **DrugName** attribute	
	Dolensol	discard	a value of the **DrugName** attribute
	Hallexanuran	discard	a value of the **DrugName** attribute

Table 3.7 *continued*

In Table 3.7, we have identified specific forms of other entity types by defining them as entity subtypes. For example, **Supervisor** as a subtype of the **Nurse** entity type, and **Consultant** and **JuniorDoctor** as subtypes of the **Doctor** entity type. All the entity types that are deemed to be required to represent the data requirements of the hospital are those that have discernable properties relevant to that enterprise.

Note that the noun 'consultant' appears twice in Table 3.7 with different outcomes: first it was discarded as a value of the **Position** attribute; second it was accepted as a subtype of **Doctor** – a specific type of doctor.

At the end of the second step we are in a position to start writing down the entity type definitions of the entity–relationship model that will represent the data requirements of the enterprise whose textual descriptions we have analysed for nouns and noun phrases. Figure 3.13 gives the entity type definitions developed from Table 3.7 for an entity–relationship model that will eventually represent the data requirements of the hospital described in the *Hospital scenario*.

Entity types

Ward (<u>WardNo</u>, WardName, NumberOfBeds)

Patient (<u>PatientId</u>, PatientName, Gender, Height, Weight)

Nurse (<u>StaffNo</u>, NurseName)

      Supervisor ( )

Doctor (<u>StaffNo</u>, DoctorName, Position)

      Consultant (Specialism)

      JuniorDoctor ( )

Team (<u>TeamCode</u>, TelephoneNo)

Treatment (<u>?</u>, StartDate, Reason)

Prescription (<u>PrescriptionNo</u>, TotalQuantity, DailyDosage)

Drug (<u>DrugCode</u>, DrugType, UnitPrice, DrugName)

Additional constraint

      Doctors can be consultants, registrars or house officers. That is, the attribute Position (of entity supertype Doctor) may have a value of Consultant, Registrar or House Officer.

Working assumptions

      The identifier of the Team entity type is TeamCode.

      The identifier of the Prescription entity type is PrescriptionNo.

Figure 3.13   A partial entity–relationship model of the hospital described in the *Hospital scenario*

In Figure 3.13, we have had to assume the identifiers of the **Team** and **Prescription** entity types because they are not stated explicitly in the *Hospital scenario*. Noun phrases that describe the properties of entity types that combine the name of the entity with words like 'number' or 'code', are usually indicative of an identifying property.

We have been unable to deduce the identifier of the **Treatment** entity type at this stage in the analysis as neither has it been explicitly stated nor is it evident as with the identifiers of the **Team** and **Prescription** entity types. Once we have completed the third step of the analysis, determining the relationships between entity types and the properties of those relationships, then we should be able to determine the identifier of this entity type.

EXERCISE 3.29

The entity–relationship model shown in Figure 3.13 that was developed from Table 3.7 includes two inaccuracies in the representation of the data requirements of the hospital. Identify these two inaccuracies and suggest appropriate revisions to Figure 3.13 to correct these problems.

The third step of this approach to analysing textual descriptions of an enterprise is to rescan the text, and look for sentences in which two or more of the entity types that we identified in the second step are associated with each other by a verb or verb phrase. A copy of the *Hospital scenario* is given below, where the entity types that we have identified appear in **bold**, every associated noun phrase is underlined, and the associated verb and verbs phrases are *italicised*.

The hospital is organised into a number of **wards**, each of which *may be empty or may be occupied by* one or more **patients**. Each **ward** is identified by a ward number; it has a name and contains a fixed number of beds. Each **ward** *is staffed by* one or more **nurses**. Each **nurse** is identified by a staff number and has a name. A **nurse** *is assigned to* a single **ward**. Some **nurses** are designated to *supervise* one or more other **nurses** on the same **ward**. A **nurse** *has* at most one **supervisor**.

Each **patient** in the hospital has a patient identification number and name recorded; their gender, height and weight is kept on record. Each **patient** is *assigned to* a single **ward** and *is under the care of* (*is the responsibility of*) a single **doctor** who must have a position of consultant. Each **consultant** *is responsible for* a number of **patients**. Details of the **junior doctors** in the hospital, who have a position of either registrar or house officer, are also recorded. **Consultants** must have a specialism, but registrars and house officers are not specialists and do not have a specialism. All specialists are **consultants**. Each **doctor** (whether **consultant** or **junior doctor**) in the hospital has a staff number and name recorded. Each **consultant** *must head* a single group, known as a **team**, *consisting of* one or more house officers and registrars [**junior doctors**]. A **team** *must be headed by* a **consultant**. A house officer or registrar [**junior doctor**] cannot head a **team**, but *must be a member of* one **team**, and **consultants** cannot be members of a **team**. Each **team** has a team code and a telephone number that people can use to leave messages for the **team**.

Each **doctor** *may provide* **treatment** for several **patients** and each **patient** *may receive* **treatment** from a number of **doctors**. Any **doctor** treating a **patient** must be a member of the same **team** as the **consultant** responsible for that **patient**. A **patient** *may receive* more than one **treatment** from each **doctor**, for which the start date and the reason (e.g. a chest infection) for the **treatment** are recorded. Such a **treatment** *may require* several **prescriptions**, each of which has a prescription number and specifies a total quantity and daily dosage of some **drug**. A **drug** *may appear* on different **prescriptions**. Each **drug** has a unique code, a type and unit price as well as a name (e.g. Dolensol or Hallexanuran).

The fourth step is to identify from these sentences the properties of the relationships. A relationship between entity types may be described by a single sentence, or by two sentences if the relationship is described in both directions. For example, the *Hospital scenario* describes the relationship between the **Ward** and **Patient** entity types by two sentences, one for each direction:

> <u>The hospital</u> is organised into <u>a number of **wards**</u>, each of which *may be empty* or *may be occupied by* <u>one or more **patients**</u>.
>
> ...
>
> Each **patient** is *assigned to* <u>a single **ward**</u> ...

For each relationship, we will need to determine the properties of that relationship – its name, its degree and its participation conditions – by analysing the nouns and noun phrases, and verbs and verb phrases that comprise the one or more sentences that describe the relationship.

We will usually name a relationship after the verb or verb phrase that associates the two nouns or noun phrases representing the related entity types, or choose one of the verbs or verb phrases when two sentences are used to describe the relationship. This naming convention ensures that a reading of the relationship will correspond to its description in the textual account of the enterprise we are analysing. By convention, relationships on an entity–relationship diagram are read from left to right and from top to bottom. So it is useful at this stage to select two names for each relationship, so that the relationship can be read in either direction, and this convention can be easily followed when drawing an entity–relationship diagram for the entity–relationship model.

The degree of a relationship can be deduced by analysing the sentences for noun phrases that indicate the number of occurrences – the multiplicity – at a particular end of the relationship. A multiplicity of one (1) is often indicated explicitly by noun phrases including numerals or quantifiers like 'one', 'single', 'at most one', 'exactly one', and so on; a multiplicity of many (n) by 'many', 'several', 'more than one', 'different', and so on. Often, it may be necessary to make a reasonable assumption about the degree of a relationship because it is not conveyed explicitly by the text.

The participation conditions of associated entity types with respect to the relationship can be deduced by analysing the sentences for verb phrases that indicate optional or mandatory participation. Optional participation is often indicated explicitly by verb phrases including a word like 'may'; mandatory participation by the word 'must' or implicitly by the absence of a word like 'may'. Often, it may be necessary to make a reasonable assumption about the participation conditions of an entity type because it is not conveyed explicitly by the text.

In Table 3.8 we have grouped together sentences that describe the same relationship. For each relationship, we have drawn an entity–relationship diagram to represent that relationship, naming it in both directions, and deducing its degree by examining the noun phrases that describe the entity types at each end of the relationship, and its participation conditions by examining the verb phrases which describe that relationship. The arrows, →, ←, ↑ and ↓, have been included just to indicate the direction in which the relationship should be read and are not part of the notation for entity–relationship diagrams.

Text	Entity–relationship diagram
The hospital is organised into <u>a number of</u> **wards**, each of which may be empty or *may be occupied by* <u>one or more</u> **patients**. ... <u>Each</u> **patient** *is assigned to* <u>a single</u> **ward** ...	Ward —OccupiedBy→ / ←IsAssignedTo— Patient
<u>Each</u> **ward** *is staffed by* <u>one or more</u> **nurses**. ... A **nurse** *is assigned to* <u>a single</u> **ward**.	Ward —StaffedBy→ / ←IsAssignedTo— Nurse
Some **nurses** are designated to *supervise* <u>one or more other</u> **nurses** <u>on the same</u> **ward**. A **nurse** *has* <u>at most one</u> **supervisor**.	Nurse: Supervisor —Supervises→ / ←IsSupervisedBy— Supervisee We have chosen to name the relationship from Supervisee to Supervisor as IsSupervisedBy instead of Has (as given by the sentence) because Has is rather general.
<u>Each</u> **patient** ... *is under the care of (is the responsibility of)* <u>a single</u> **doctor** who must have a position of consultant. <u>Each</u> **consultant** *is responsible for* <u>a number of</u> **patients**.	Consultant —IsResponsibleFor→ / ←IsUnderTheCareOf— Patient We have assumed that a consultant may not (currently) be responsible for any patients (for whatever reason). Hence the participation of the Consultant entity type with respect to the IsResponsibleFor relationship is optional.
<u>Each</u> **consultant** *must head* <u>a single group</u>, known as a **team**, *consisting of* <u>one or more</u> house officers and registrars [**junior doctors**]. A **team** *must be headed by* a **consultant**. A house officer or registrar [**junior doctor**] cannot head a **team**, but *must be a member of* <u>one</u> **team**, and **consultants** cannot be members of a **team**.	Team / ↓ConsistsOf IsAMemberOf↑ / ↓HeadedBy Heads↑ / Doctor: JuniorDoctor, Consultant We have assumed that there must be at least one junior doctor in the team. Hence the participation of the Team entity type with respect to the ConsistsOf relationship is mandatory.

Table 3.8   Analysis of sentences from the *Hospital scenario* that describe relationships between entity types

continued

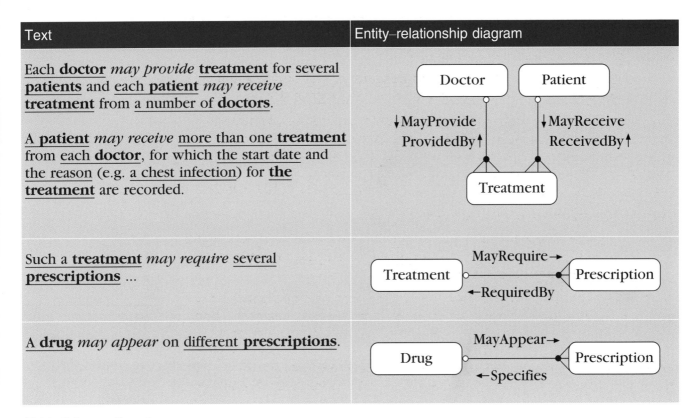

Text	Entity–relationship diagram
Each **doctor** *may provide* **treatment** for several **patients** and each **patient** *may receive* **treatment** from a number of **doctors**. A **patient** *may receive* more than one **treatment** from each **doctor**, for which the start date and the reason (e.g. a chest infection) for the **treatment** are recorded.	
Such a **treatment** *may require* several **prescriptions** ...	
A **drug** *may appear* on different **prescriptions**.	

Table 3.8   *continued*

At the end of the fourth step, we are in a position to add the entity–relationship diagram to the entity–relationship model that we are developing. Figure 3.14 gives the entity–relationship diagram for the entity–relationship model shown in Figure 3.13.

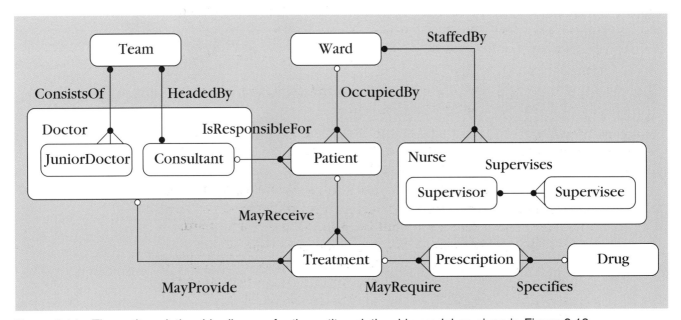

Figure 3.14   The entity–relationship diagram for the entity–relationship model as given in Figure 3.13

We are now in a position to determine the identifier of the **Treatment** entity type, which we were unable to do so at the end of the second step. The first sentence from the *Hospital scenario* that describes treatment says:

> Each **doctor** *may provide* **treatment** for several **patients** and each **patient** *may receive* **treatment** from a number of **doctors**.

This sentence describes a many-to-many (*m:n*) relationship between doctors and patients, where each occurrence of that relationship represents a treatment provided by a particular doctor to a particular patient. In Table 3.8, this relationship is decomposed into two 1:*n* relationships, **MayProvide** and **MayReceive**, and an intersection entity type, **Treatment**, which represents occurrences of this relationship.

The second sentence describing treatment says:

> A **patient** *may receive* more than one **treatment** from each **doctor**, for which the start date and the reason (e.g. a chest infection) for the **treatment** are recorded.

This sentence extends the notion of a relationship between doctors and patients so that each occurrence of that relationship now represents a treatment provided by a particular doctor to a particular patient, on a particular start date, for a particular reason. So occurrences of the **Treatment** entity type, which represent occurrences of this relationship, are distinguished by the identifiers of the **Patient** and **Doctor** entity types, and start date of the treatment, corresponding to the **PatientId**, **StaffNo** and **StartDate** attributes.

The fifth, and final, step of this approach to analysing textual descriptions of an enterprise is to rescan the text, looking for any other restrictions on the entity–relationship model we are developing that are not explicitly represented by the model, in particular, general constraints that involve dependencies between two or more entity types.

The following sentences from the *Hospital scenario* describe explicitly restrictions on the entity–relationship model as shown in Figure 3.13:

> Some nurses are designated to supervise one or more other nurses on the same ward.

> Any doctor treating a patient must be a member of the same team as the consultant responsible for that patient.

These restrictions on the entity–relationship model that we are developing can be represented by the addition of the conditions to the *Additional constraints* section of the entity–relationship model shown in Figure 3.13:

> A nurse can only supervise nurses in the same ward. That is, the two instances of the entity type Nurse that are involved in an occurrence of the Supervises relationship must be assigned to the same ward.

> A doctor who treats a patient must be in the same team as the consultant who is responsible for that patient. That is, an instance of the entity type Doctor that provides treatment for a patient must be from the same team as the consultant who is responsible for that patient.

The following sentences from the *Hospital scenario* imply that further restrictions are required on the entity–relationship model shown in Figure 3.13:

> The hospital is organised into a number of wards, each of which may be empty or may be occupied by one or more patients. Each ward is identified by a ward number; it has a name and contains a fixed number of beds.

> Each nurse is identified by a staff number and has a name. ... Each doctor (whether consultant or junior doctor) in the hospital has a staff number and name recorded.

The first pair of sentences concerns the relationship between the **Ward** and **Patient** entity types, **OccupiedBy**, which may be read from **Ward** to **Patient** as 'Each ward is occupied by zero, one or more patients' (see Table 3.8). However, the meaning of the word 'more' is unbounded; it could represent an infinite number of patients, which is clearly inappropriate as we have been told that there are a fixed number of beds in each ward. So the following condition needs to be included in the *Additional constraints* section of the entity–relationship model shown in Figure 3.13:

> The number of patients on a ward cannot exceed the number of beds on that ward. That is, the number of occurrences of the Patient entity type associated with a given occurrence of the Ward entity type cannot exceed the value specified by the NumberOfBeds attribute of the occurrence of that entity type.

The second pair of sentences states that both nurses and doctors are identified by their staff numbers. It is not unreasonable to assume that as medical staff, nurses and doctors will be assigned staff numbers drawn from the same value set. That is, a nurse cannot have the same staff number as a doctor, and vice versa. So the following condition needs to be included in the *Additional constraints* section of the entity–relationship model shown in Figure 3.13:

> A nurse cannot have the same staff number as a doctor. That is, the value of the StaffNo attribute for each occurrence of the Nurse entity type cannot be the same as the value of the StaffNo attribute for any occurrence of the Doctor entity type.

Before we complete the entity–relationship model for the hospital enterprise that we have developed using a grammatical analysis of the *Hospital scenario*, we need to include the conditions required for any weak entity types.

EXERCISE 3.30

How do you identify weak entity types in an entity–relationship model?

Figure 3.15 gives the complete entity–relationship model for the hospital enterprise that we have developed by using a grammatical analysis of the *Hospital scenario*.

Entity–relationship diagram

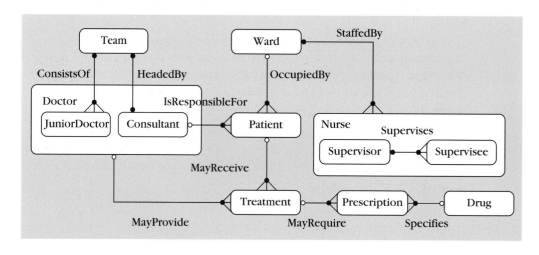

Entity types

Team (<u>TeamCode</u>, TelephoneNo)

Ward (<u>WardNo</u>, WardName, NumberOfBeds)

Doctor (<u>StaffNo</u>, DoctorName)

      Consultant (Specialism)

      JuniorDoctor (Position)

Patient (<u>PatientId</u>, PatientName, Gender, Height, Weight)

Nurse (<u>StaffNo</u>, NurseName)

      Supervisor ( )

      Supervisee ( )

Treatment (<u>StaffNo</u>, <u>PatientId</u>, <u>StartDate</u>, Reason)

Prescription (<u>PrescriptionNo</u>, TotalQuantity, DailyDosage)

Drug (<u>DrugCode</u>, DrugType, UnitPrice, DrugName)

Additional constraints

A doctor who treats a patient must be in the same team as the consultant who is responsible for that patient. That is, an instance of the entity type Doctor that provides treatment for a patient must be from the same team as the consultant who is responsible for that patient.

A nurse can only supervise nurses in the same ward. That is, the two instances of the entity type Nurse that are involved in an occurrence of the Supervises relationship must be assigned to the same ward.

Junior doctors can be registrars or house officers. That is, the attribute Position (of entity subtype JuniorDoctor) may have a value of Registrar or House Officer.

Treatment is a weak entity type dependent on the entity type Doctor. So, each value of the StaffNo attribute in entity type Treatment must be the same value as the StaffNo attribute of the Doctor instance to which the Treatment entity type is related by the relationship Provides (a consequence of weak–strong entity types).

Treatment is a weak entity type dependent on the entity type Patient. So, each value of the PatientId attribute in entity type Treatment must be the same value as the PatientId attribute of the Patient instance to which the Treatment entity type is related by the relationship Receives (a consequence of weak–strong entity types).

The number of patients on a ward cannot exceed the number of beds on that ward. That is, the number of occurrences of the Patient entity type associated with a given occurrence of the Ward entity type cannot exceed the value specified by the NumberOfBeds attribute of the occurrence of that entity type.

A nurse cannot have the same staff number as a doctor. That is, the value of the StaffNo attribute for each occurrence of the Nurse entity type cannot be the same as the value of the StaffNo attribute for any occurrence of the Doctor entity type.

Working assumptions

The identifier of the Team entity type is TeamCode.

The identifier of the Prescription entity type is PrescriptionNo.

Limitations

Only the details of a patient's current stay in hospital are recorded (i.e. only as an in-patient with no patient history of previous stays in the hospital).

Figure 3.15   The complete entity–relationship model for the hospital enterprise developed by using a grammatical analysis of the *Hospital scenario*

If we compare the entity–relationship model shown in Figure 3.15 with the *Hospital conceptual data model*, and take account of the use of entity supertypes/subtypes in Figure 3.15 and the naming of relationships (which are usually the choice of the analyst), the only significant difference between them is the representation of the supervision of nurses. This is described in the *Hospital scenario* as:

Some nurses are designated to supervise one or more other nurses on the same ward. A nurse has at most one supervisor.

Figure 3.16(a) shows the representation of the supervision of nurses as described in the *Hospital conceptual data model*, whereas Figure 3.16(b) shows the representation of the supervision of nurses as described in Figure 3.15.

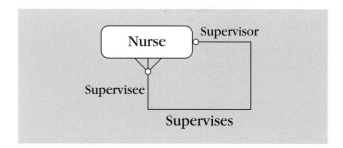

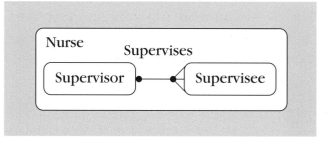

Entity types

Nurse (StaffNo, NurseName)

(a)

Entity types

Nurse (StaffNo, NurseName)
   Supervisor ( )
   Supervisee ( )

(b)

Figure 3.16   The different representations of the supervision of nurses as described (a) in the *Hospital conceptual data model*, and (b) in Figure 3.15

Let us compare these different representations in order to determine exactly what they define in terms of occurrences. In the *Hospital conceptual data model*, the recursive **Supervises** relationship on the **Nurse** entity type may be read as:

A nurse (supervisor) may supervise one or more nurses (supervisees). A nurse (supervisee) may be supervised by at most one nurse (supervisor).

The word 'may' is included in the above reading because the **Supervises** relationship has optional participation with the **Nurse** entity type at both ends. The representation does not preclude a nurse being neither a supervisor nor a supervisee. Neither does it preclude a nurse being both a supervisor and a supervisee. Figure 3.17 shows a diagram that describes the hierarchical data structure that the **Supervises** relationship represents in the *Hospital conceptual data model*.

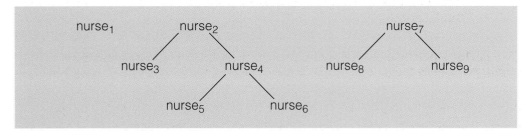

Figure 3.17   A diagrammatic representation of the Supervises relationship as described by the *Hospital conceptual data model*

In Figure 3.17, $nurse_1$ is neither a supervisor nor a supervisee; $nurse_2$ supervises $nurse_3$ and $nurse_4$; $nurse_4$ supervises $nurse_5$ and $nurse_6$; and $nurse_7$ supervises $nurse_8$ and $nurse_9$. That is, $nurse_1$ is neither a supervisor nor a supervisee; $nurse_2$ and $nurse_7$ are supervisors; $nurse_3$, $nurse_5$, $nurse_6$, $nurse_8$ and $nurse_9$ are supervisees; and $nurse_4$ is both a supervisor and a supervisee.

In Figure 3.15, the **Supervises** relationship between the **Nurse** entity subtypes may be read as:

> **A nurse is either a supervisor or a supervisee. A supervisor supervises one or more supervisees. A supervisee is supervised by one supervisor.**

Figure 3.18 shows a diagram that describes the data structure that the **Supervises** relationship represents in Figure 3.15.

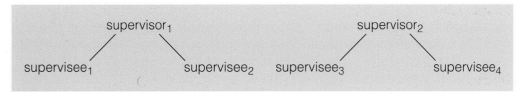

Figure 3.18   A diagrammatic representation of the Supervises relationship as described by Figure 3.15

Either representation satisfies the requirements specified in the *Hospital scenario*. However, if you look at the examples of occurrences of the **Supervises** relationship in the *Hospital domain* of *discourse summary,* you will find that all nurses participate in occurrences that are consistent with the representation of that relationship as given in the *Hospital conceptual data model* – Figure 3.16(a). All the nurses participate in the occurrences of the **Supervises** relationship, implying that a nurse is always a supervisor or supervisee, but there is one example of a nurse being both a supervisor and a supervisee (**StaffNo 834**).

This comparison of the different representations of the supervision of nurses raises two important points about analysing textual descriptions of an enterprise in order to determine the data requirements of that enterprise.

First, textual descriptions of an enterprise written in a natural language, such as English, are often ambiguous and incomplete. They are ambiguous as a consequence of the brevity of some descriptions, which we illustrated in the solution to Exercise 3.4. They are incomplete because descriptions of an enterprise are often written by the client who addresses them to colleagues who are familiar with the enterprise and who will understand terminology used and procedures employed, but often these will be unfamiliar to the contractor responsible for developing a database to support the enterprise.

Second, access to documents created and used by an enterprise to facilitate its day-to-day operations is important, in order to confirm the decisions made during the analysis of the textual descriptions of that enterprise. Such documents provide examples of occurrences of the entity types and relationships between those entity types that are consistent with their definitions in the entity–relationship model of the enterprise.

In Subsection 3.5, we will illustrate how the comparison of the examples of occurrences of entity types and relationships given in the *Hospital domain of discourse summary* with those found in the various documents created and used by an enterprise to facilitate its day-to-day operations, can be employed to validate an entity–relationship model.

ACTIVITY 3.1

Using the approach to analysing textual descriptions of an enterprise that we have described in this section, analyse the *University scenario* given on the laminated card entitled *M359: Scenarios* in order to develop an entity–relationship model of that enterprise. Compare your model with the one provided on the laminated card entitled *University conceptual data model*. You should see a good correspondence between your model and *University conceptual data model* provided.

Analysing the description of Walton Stores

The approach to analysing textual descriptions of an enterprise that we have described in this subsection has worked well when applied to both the *Hospital scenario* and *University scenario*. This is because these textual descriptions, as the sole descriptions of the hospital and university enterprises, have been written with the intention of providing complete and unambiguous descriptions of the data requirements of these enterprises.

We will now apply this approach to a textual description of Walton Stores that was presented in Subsection 2.1. As this description only provides an overview of the enterprise with little detail, the approach will only yield a limited representation of actual data requirements. However, this analysis represents a necessary step in the development of an entity–relationship model for Walton Stores because the textual description often provides an overview of the enterprise as a whole, whereas the documents we will analyse in Subsection 3.4 will only provide the detail of specific areas. That is, the analysis of a description of Walton Stores will result in an outline or skeleton of an entity–relationship model, which can be extended with the models developed as a result of the analysis of documents created or used by the enterprise.

The description of Walton Stores presented in Subsection 2.1 is more typical of what a data analyst might encounter in the field than that found in the *Hospital scenario*.

Using the approach to analysing textual descriptions of enterprise we described in this subsection, we will analyse the description of Walton Stores found in Subsection 2.1, but without analysing the figures that provide examples of the various documents created and used by the enterprise to facilitate its day-to-day operations. We will aim to develop an outline or skeleton of an entity–relationship model that represents the data requirements of the enterprise as a whole.

Step 1: Scan the description of Walton Stores in Subsection 2.1 to identify all the nouns and noun phrases.

In the following copy of the description of Walton Stores, all the nouns and noun phrases are underlined.

Walton Stores is a supermarket chain selling an extensive range of foodstuffs and household goods from stores located in many towns throughout England. The company plans to establish itself as a leading food retailer in a very competitive marketplace by meeting the demands of both its customers and its suppliers. For its customers, the company aims to make shopping a more pleasant experience by stocking the products they require, offering them a range of alternatives and discounts, and arranging the layout of products on the shelves in its stores to make shopping easier by locating those products that are commonly purchased on the same shopping trip close together. For its suppliers, who provide all the products that Walton Stores sells at its stores, the company aims to provide them with profiles of the kinds of customers who purchase their products. The suppliers can then select households to be targeted by their promotional and marketing strategies.

Walton Stores has divided its operation in England into four geographical regions covering the north-east (NE), south-east (SE), south-west (SW) and north-west (NW) quadrants of the country. Each region has a large distribution centre where packs of products from the suppliers are held until they are delivered to individual stores that the region is responsible for. Although a distribution centre can dispatch goods to a particular store within 24 hours, it may take several days for goods to be received from the suppliers. Therefore, a distribution centre has to ensure that it has adequate stock to meet all the demands from the stores within its region. In particular, it needs to monitor carefully stocks of perishable goods, such as fresh fruit and vegetables, which can be held for only a limited period before they need to be on the shelves of the stores.

A store can request deliveries of goods from its distribution centre in two different ways: by a standing order, where the goods requested are required at regular intervals throughout the year; and by a special order, where the goods requested are in demand only at certain times of the year. A store may need to revise standing orders to meet seasonal fluctuations in the demand for certain products.

Walton Stores operates a regional pricing policy where prices of goods at the stores may vary from region to region, but are the same at all the stores within a region. Prices are reviewed daily and are revised to take account of changes in the purchase cost, customer demand and product promotions. The stores receive current prices from their distribution centre on a daily basis.

Individual stores have a limited warehousing capacity for storing goods before they are put on the shelves, or in the compartments of refrigerators and freezers, as appropriate. Stores need to monitor carefully the stocks of each product and when necessary adjust the appropriate standing order to ensure that supply meets demand.

Foodstuffs with a short shelf-life – perishable goods – will have a 'display until' date and it is important that such items that are not sold on or before this date are removed from the shelves, or the compartments of refrigerators and freezers. Other foodstuffs will have a 'use by' date. With both types of foodstuffs a sensible shelf and compartment stocking policy will be to minimise the incidence of the shelves and compartments being stocked with the same product with different 'display until' dates or 'use by' dates, because customers have a tendency to choose items with a later date, which can result in wastage.

Each product line is classified by the type of product, such as fresh vegetables, and lines are typically grouped on the shelves by product type. Each product line sold by Walton Stores has a unique product code. With the exception of unpackaged goods, such as some fresh fruit and vegetables that customers select and package themselves, the product code is found on each item in the form of a barcode. The cost of each item is usually only found on prepacked goods that are sold by varying weights, such as meat, fish and cheese. The cost of an item, however, will be displayed on a label by the shelf or the compartment of a refrigerator or freezer where the item is found. The database will need to hold the current price of each item and be able to produce product and shelf/compartment labels.

The checkout tills at every store will be equipped with barcode scanners that are linked to the database system to enable the total cost of the customers' purchases to be calculated and recorded. For items without barcodes, which are packaged by the customers themselves, the checkout operator will need to weigh each product and enter the product code manually to calculate and record the cost.

A customer may apply for a loyalty (or reward) card – Walton Stores' Frequent Shopper Card – which gives points on all purchases. The customer's details are held only by the store where they applied for their Frequent Shopper Card. Holders of the Frequent Shopper Card, selected by their known purchasing habits and/or the data they supplied on their card application form, may be sent coupons to promote a product. Since a coupon will have a barcode, its redemption also becomes an entry on the customer's purchase history held by the database system, and so the supermarket chain can assess the success of a particular promotion.

Step 2: Prune the list of nouns and noun phrases so that it contains just those entity types and properties of entity types that are required to represent the data requirements of the enterprise.

The following table gives the description of Walton Stores sentence by sentence. We will consider each candidate entity type or property of an entity type when it appears for the first time in the description, and decide whether it should be retained as an entity type or a property of an entity type, or whether it should be discarded, giving the justification. Each entity type identified represents something that is relevant to Walton Stores and about which there is a need to record data. In this table we have neither named attributes nor attempted to identify any entity supertypes/subtypes.

Don't be surprised, or worried, if you disagree with the solution shown below. Because the description of Walton Stores given in Subsection 2.1 is incomplete, it is open to different interpretations, which themselves are dependent on your background knowledge of supermarkets and how they operate.

Text	Noun or noun phrase	Outcome	Justification
Walton Stores is a supermarket chain selling an extensive range of foodstuffs and household goods from stores located in many towns throughout England.	Walton Stores	discard	only one occurrence
	supermarket chain	discard	synonymous with Walton Stores
	foodstuffs	**Product** entity type	
	household goods	**Product** entity type	
	stores	**Store** entity type	
	towns	a single-valued property of the **Store** entity type	part of a store's address
The company plans to establish itself as a leading food retailer in a very competitive marketplace by meeting the demands of both its customers and its suppliers.	company	discard	synonymous with Walton Stores
	food retailer	discard	synonymous with Walton Stores
	marketplace	discard	outside the scope of the database being developed
	demands	unspecified properties of the **Customer** and **Supplier** entity types	
	customers	**Customer** entity type	
	suppliers	**Supplier** entity type	
For its customers, the company aims to make shopping a more pleasant experience by stocking the products they require, offering them a range of alternatives and discounts, and arranging the layout of products on the shelves in its stores to make shopping easier by locating those products that are commonly purchased on the same shopping trip close together.	alternatives	discard	synonymous with the **Product** entity type
	discounts	property of the **Product** entity type	
	shelves	discard	outside the scope of the database being developed
	shopping trip	the **CheckoutTillReceipt** entity type	checkout till receipts record the customers' purchases on a shopping trip
For its suppliers, who provide all the products that Walton Stores sells at its stores, the company aims to provide them with profiles of the kinds of customers who purchase their products.	profiles	unspecified properties of the **Customer** entity type	
The suppliers can then select households to be targeted by their promotional and marketing strategies.	households	discard	synonymous with the **Customer** entity type
	promotional and marketing strategies	properties of the **Supplier** entity type	

Text	Noun or noun phrase	Outcome	Justification
Walton Stores has divided its operation in England into four geographical regions covering the north-east (NE), south-east (SE), south-west (SW) and north-west (NW) quadrants of the country.	region	**Region** entity type	
	quadrant	identifying property of the **Region** entity type with values of north-east (NE), south-east (SE), south-west (SW) and north-west (NW)	
Each region has a large distribution centre where packs of products from the suppliers are held until they are delivered to individual stores that the region is responsible for. Although a distribution centre can dispatch goods to a particular store within 24 hours, it may take several days for goods to be received from the suppliers.	distribution centre	discard	synonymous with the **Region** entity type
	packs of products	property of the **Product** entity type	
	goods	discard	synonymous with the **Product** entity type
Therefore, a distribution centre has to ensure that it has adequate stock to meet all the demands from the stores within its region. In particular, it needs to monitor carefully stocks of perishable goods, such as fresh fruit and vegetables, which can be held for only a limited period before they need to be on the shelves of the stores.	stock	property of the **Region** entity type	
	demands	property of the **Store** entity type	'demands' are requests for products to distribution centres from the stores they supply, which become orders for those products
	perishable goods	**Product** entity type	
A store can request deliveries of goods from its distribution centre in two different ways: by a standing order, where the goods requested are required at regular intervals throughout the year; and by a special order, where the goods requested are in demand only at certain times of the year. A store may need to revise standing orders to meet seasonal fluctuations in the demand for certain products.	standing order	**StandingOrder** entity type	
	at regular intervals throughout the year	properties of the **StandingOrder** entity type	
	special order	**SpecialOrder** entity type	
	in demand only at certain times of the year	properties of the **SpecialOrder** entity type	
Walton Stores operates a regional pricing policy where prices of goods at the stores may vary from region to region, but are the same at all the stores within a region. Prices are reviewed daily and are revised to take account of changes in the purchase cost, customer demand and product promotions. The stores receive current prices from their distribution centre on a daily basis.	price	a property of the **Product** entity type that is dependent on the region	
	purchase cost	discard	synonymous with price

Text	Noun or noun phrase	Outcome	Justification
Individual stores have a limited warehousing capacity for storing goods before they are put on the shelves, or in the compartments of refrigerators and freezers, as appropriate. Stores need to monitor carefully the stocks of each product and when necessary adjust the appropriate standing order to ensure that supply meets demand.	compartments	discard	synonymous with shelves
	stock	property of the **Store** entity type	
Foodstuffs with a short shelf-life – perishable goods – will have a 'display until' date and it is important that such items that are not sold on or before this date are removed from the shelves, or the compartments of refrigerators and freezers. Other foodstuffs will have a 'use by' date. With both types of foodstuffs a sensible shelf and compartment stocking policy will be to minimise the incidence of the shelves and compartments being stocked with the same product with different 'display until' dates or 'use by' dates because customers have a tendency to choose items with a later date, which can result in wastage.	'display until' date	discard	outside the scope of the database being developed as we need only to record the particular products sold, and not the particular occurrences of those products
	'use by' date	discard	outside the scope of the database being developed as we need only to record the particular products sold, and not the particular occurrences of those products
	items	discard	synonymous with the **Product** entity type
Each product line is classified by the type of product, such as fresh vegetables, and lines are typically grouped on the shelves by product type. Each product line sold by Walton Stores has a unique product code. With the exception of unpackaged goods, such as some fresh fruit and vegetables that customers select and package themselves, the product code is found on each item in the form of a barcode. The cost of each item is usually only found on prepacked goods that are sold by varying weights, such as meat, fish and cheese. The cost of an item, however, will be displayed on a label by the shelf or the compartment of a refrigerator or freezer where the item is found. The database will need to hold the current price of each item and be able to produce product and shelf/compartment labels.	product line	discard	synonymous with the **Product** entity type
	type of product	a single-valued property of the **Product** entity type	
	unique product code	identifying property of the **Product** entity type	
	unpackaged goods	**Product** entity type	
	barcode	discard	implementation details – product code
	prepacked goods	**Product** entity type	
	database	discard	implementation details
	product and shelf/ compartment labels	discard	synonymous with the **Product** entity type

Text	Noun or noun phrase	Outcome	Justification
The checkout tills at every store will be equipped with barcode scanners that are linked to the database system to enable the total cost of the customers' purchases to be calculated and recorded. For items without barcodes, which are packaged by the customers themselves, the checkout operator will need to weigh each product and enter the product code manually to calculate and record the cost.	checkout tills	discard	implementation details
	barcode scanners	discard	implementation details
	database system	discard	implementation details
	total cost of customers' purchases	a single-valued property of the **CheckoutTillReceipt** entity type	
	checkout operator	a single-valued property of the **CheckoutTillReceipt** entity type	
A customer may apply for a loyalty (or reward) card – Walton Stores' Frequent Shopper Card – which gives points on all purchases. The customer's details are held only by the store where they applied for their Frequent Shopper Card. Holders of the Frequent Shopper Card, selected by their known purchasing habits and/or the data they supplied on their card application form, may be sent coupons to promote a product. Since a coupon will have a barcode, its redemption also becomes an entry on the customer's purchase history held by the database system, and so the supermarket chain can assess the success of a particular promotion.	loyalty (or reward) card, Walton Stores' Frequent Shopper Card	**Customer** entity type	the only customers that Walton Stores will be able to identify will be those who hold the chain's Frequent Shopper Card
	'home store' – the store where a customer applied for their Frequent Shopper Card	property of the **Customer** entity type	
	points on all purchases	a single-valued property of the **CheckoutTillReceipt** entity type	
	customer's details	properties of the **Customer** entity type	
	holders of the Frequent Shopper Card	discard	synonymous with the **Customer** entity type

Table 3.9 summarises the results of Step 2 by stating the entity types provisionally identified in the description of Walton Stores (Subsection 2.1), their synonyms, identifiers (where specified) and other properties.

Entity type	Synonyms	Identifier	Properties
Region	distribution centre	quadrant	stock (products)
Store			stock (products)
StandingOrder			'regular intervals throughout the year'
SpecialOrder			'certain times of the year'
Product	goods, product lines, foodstuffs, household goods, perishable goods, unpackaged goods, prepacked goods	product code	discounts packs price type stocks sales
Supplier			'demands' 'promotional and marketing strategies'
Customer	household, Frequent Shopper Card		'demands' 'profiles' 'details' 'home store'
CheckoutTillReceipt	customers' purchases		total cost points checkout operator

Table 3.9   A summary of the results of Step 2

Figure 3.19 gives an outline of the entity type definitions for an entity–relationship model that represents the data requirements of Walton Stores as described in Subsection 2.1.

Entity types

Region (<u>Quadrant</u>, ...)

Store (...)

Order (...)

      StandingOrder (...)

      SpecialOrder (...)

Product (<u>ProductCode</u>, ...)

Supplier (...)

Customer (...)

CheckoutTillReceipt (...)

Figure 3.19   Outline of the entity type definitions for an entity–relationship model that represents the data requirements of Walton Stores as described in Subsection 2.1

In Figure 3.19, as standing orders and special orders are two different (specific) ways that a store can request packs of products from its distribution centre (region), we have decided to make **StandingOrder** and **SpecialOrder** subtypes of the generic supertype **Order**. We have not introduced any subtypes of the **Product** entity type that represent the different types of products sold by Walton Stores because they do not appear to have any distinct properties. Only the identifiers of the **Region** and **Product** entity types are given by the description of Walton Stores.

Step 3: Rescan the description of Walton Stores in Subsection 2.1. Look for sentences in which two or more of the entity types are associated with each other by a verb or verb phrase.

In the following copy of the description of Walton Stores, the entity types appear in **bold**, all associated noun phrases are underlined, and all associated verbs and verb phrases are *italicised*.

Walton Stores is a supermarket chain *selling* an extensive range of foodstuffs [**product**] and household goods [**product**] *from* **stores** located in many towns throughout England. The company plans to establish itself as a leading food retailer in a very competitive marketplace by meeting the demands of both its **customers** and its **suppliers**. For its **customers**, the company aims to make shopping a more pleasant experience by stocking the **products** they *require*, offering them a range of alternatives and discounts, and arranging the layout of **products** on the shelves in its **stores** to make shopping easier by locating those **products** that are commonly purchased on the same shopping trip close together. For its **suppliers**, who *provide* all the **products** that Walton Stores sells at its **stores**, the company aims *to provide* them [**suppliers**] with profiles of the kinds of **customers** who purchase their **products**. The **suppliers** can then *select* households [**customers**] to be targeted by their promotional and marketing strategies.

Walton Stores has divided its operation in England into four geographical **regions** covering the north-east (NE), south-east (SE), south-west (SW) and north-west (NW) quadrants of the country. Each **region** has a large distribution centre where packs of **products** from the **suppliers** are *held* until they are delivered to individual **stores** that the **region** *is responsible for*. Although a distribution centre [**region**] can dispatch goods [**products**] to a particular **store** within 24 hours, it may take several days for goods to be *received* from the **suppliers**. Therefore, a distribution centre [**region**] has to *ensure* that it has adequate stock [**products**] to meet all the demands from the **stores** within its **region**. In particular, it needs to *monitor* carefully stocks of perishable goods, such as fresh fruit and vegetables, which can be held for only a limited period before they need to be on the shelves of the **stores**.

A **store** can *request* deliveries of goods from its distribution centre in two different ways: by a **standing order**, where the goods [**products**] *requested* are required at regular intervals throughout the year; and by a **special order**, where the goods *requested* are in demand only at certain times of the year. A **store** may need to revise **standing orders** to meet seasonal fluctuations in the demand for certain **products**.

Walton Stores operates a regional pricing policy where prices of goods at the **stores** may vary from **region** to **region**, but are the same at all the **stores** within a **region**. Prices are reviewed daily and are revised to take account of changes in the purchase cost, **customer** demand and **product** promotions. The **stores** *receive* current prices from their distribution centre [**region**] on a daily basis.

Individual **stores** have a limited warehousing capacity for storing goods before they are put on the shelves, or in the compartments of refrigerators and freezers, as appropriate. **Stores** need to *monitor* carefully the stocks of each **product** and when necessary adjust the appropriate **standing order** to *ensure* that supply meets demand. Foodstuffs with a short shelf-life – perishable goods – will have a 'display until' date and it is important that such items that are not sold on or before this date are removed from the shelves, or the compartments of refrigerators and freezers. Other foodstuffs will have a 'use by' date. With both types of foodstuffs a sensible shelf and compartment stocking policy will be to minimise the incidence of the shelves and compartments being stocked with the same **product** with different 'display until' dates or 'use by' dates because **customers** have a tendency to choose items with a later date, which can result in wastage.

Each **product** line is classified by the type of **product**, such as fresh vegetables, and lines are typically grouped on the shelves by **product type**. Each **product** line sold by Walton Stores has a unique **product** code. With the exception of unpackaged goods, such as some fresh fruit and vegetables that **customers** select and package themselves, the **product** code is found on each item in the form of a barcode. The cost of each item [**product**] is usually only found on prepacked goods that are sold by varying weights, such as meat, fish and cheese. The cost of an item, however, will be displayed on a label by the shelf or the compartment of a refrigerator or freezer where the item is found. The database will need to hold the current price of each item and be able to produce **product** and shelf and compartment labels.

The checkout tills at every **store** will be equipped with barcode scanners that are linked to the database system to enable the total cost of the **customers**' purchases [**checkout till receipt**] to be calculated and *recorded*. For items [**products**] without barcodes, which are packaged by the **customers** themselves, the checkout operator will need to weigh each **product** and enter the **product** code manually to calculate and *record* the cost.

A customer may apply for a loyalty (or reward) card – Walton Stores' Frequent Shopper Card – which gives points on all purchases. The **customer's** details are *held* only by the **store** where they applied for their Frequent Shopper Card. Holders of the Frequent Shopper Card [**customer**], selected by their known purchasing habits and/or the data they supplied on their card application form, may be sent coupons to promote a **product**. Since a coupon will have a barcode, its redemption also becomes an entry on the **customer**'s purchase history held by the database system, and so the supermarket chain can assess the success of a particular promotion.

Step 4: For each relationship identified in Step 3, determine the properties of that relationship – its name, degree and participation conditions – by analysing the noun and noun phrases, and the verb and verb phrases that comprise one or more sentences describing the relationship.

The table below contains sentences from the description of Walton Stores, which associate two or more of the entity types (as shown in Table 3.9) with each other by a verb or verb phrase. For each relationship, we have drawn an entity–relationship diagram to represent that relationship, naming it in both directions, and deducing its degree by examining the noun phrases that describe the entity types at each end of the relationship, and its participation conditions by examining the verb phrases which describe that relationship. The arrows, →, ←, ↑ and ↓, have been included just to indicate the direction in which the relationship should be read and are not part of the notation for entity–relationship diagrams.

Text	Entity–relationship diagram
Walton Stores is a supermarket chain *selling* an extensive range of foodstuffs [**products**] and household goods [**products**] *from* **stores** located in <u>many towns</u> throughout England.	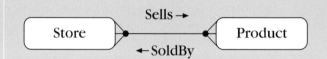 Each store sells several products; each product is sold by several stores.
For <u>its</u> **customers**, <u>the company</u> aims to make shopping <u>a more pleasant experience</u> by stocking the **products** they *require* ... [Assumption: A requirement by customers for the products is indicated by the customers purchasing those products.]	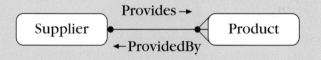 Each customer purchases several products; each product may be purchased by several customers (possibly none).
For <u>its</u> **suppliers**, who *provide* all <u>the</u> **products** that <u>Walton Stores</u> sells at <u>its</u> **stores** ... [Assumption: Each product is provided by a single supplier.]	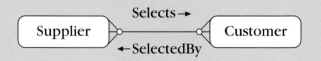 Each supplier provides several products; each product is provided by a single supplier.
The **suppliers** can then *select* households [**customers**] to be targeted by <u>their promotional and marketing strategies</u>.	Selects → Supplier ———— Customer ← SelectedBy A supplier may select several customers (possibly none); a customer may be selected by several suppliers (possibly none).

Text	Entity–relationship diagram
... individual **stores** that the **region** *is responsible for*.	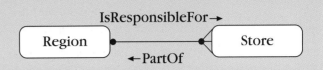 Each region is responsible for several stores; a store is part of one region.
Although a distribution centre [**region**] can dispatch goods [**products**] to a particular **store** within 24 hours, it may take several days for goods to be *received* from the **suppliers**. [Assumption: A region orders products from its suppliers.]	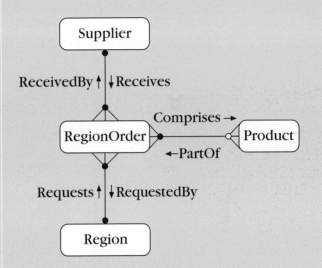 A region may request products from their suppliers by an order; a supplier may receive requests for products from regions by an order. An order comprises requests for several products; a product may form part of several orders.
Therefore, a distribution centre [**region**] has to *ensure* that it has adequate stock [**products**] to meet all the demands from the stores within its **region**.	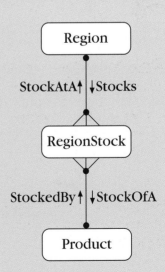 There is an *m:n* relationship between the Region and Product entity types: each region stocks several products; each product is stocked by several regions. This relationship is decomposed so that stock of each product at each region can be recorded by an occurrence of the RegionStock intersection entity type.

Text	Entity–relationship diagram
A **store** can *request* deliveries of goods from its distribution centre in two different ways: by a **standing order**, where the goods [**products**] *requested* are required at regular intervals throughout the year; and by a **special order**, where the goods *requested* are in demand only at certain times of the year. A **store** may need to revise **standing orders** to meet seasonal fluctuations in the demand for certain **products**.	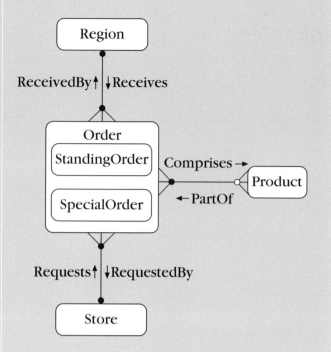 A store may request products from their region by a standing order or a special order; a region may receive requests for products from several regions by a standing order or a special order. An order comprises requests for several products; a product may form part of several orders.
Walton Stores operates a regional pricing policy where prices of goods at the **stores** may vary from **region** to **region**, but are the same at all the **stores** within a **region**. Prices are reviewed daily and are revised to take account of changes in the purchase cost, **customer** demand and **product** promotions. The **stores** *receive* current prices from their distribution centre [**region**] on a daily basis.	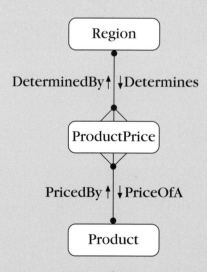 There is an *m:n* relationship between the Region and Product entity types: each product is priced by the regions in whose stores the product is sold; each region determines the price of each product sold in their stores. This relationship is decomposed so that the price of each product in each region can be recorded by an occurrence of the ProductPrice intersection entity type.

Text	Entity–relationship diagram
Stores need to *monitor* carefully the stocks of each **product** and ...	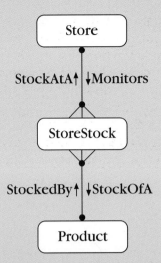 There is an *m:n* relationship between the Store and Product entity types: each store stocks several products; each product is stocked by several stores. This relationship is decomposed so that stock of each product at each store can be recorded by an occurrence of the StoreStock intersection entity type.
The checkout tills at every **store** will be equipped with barcode scanners linked to the database system to enable the total cost of the **customers'** purchases [**checkout till receipt**] to be calculated and *recorded*.	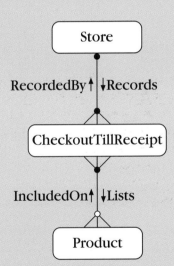 Each store records the purchases of products on checkout till receipts. Each checkout till receipt is recorded by a store and lists the products purchased. A product may be included on several checkout till receipts.

Text	Entity–relationship diagram
A customer may apply for a loyalty (or reward) card – Walton Stores' Frequent Shopper Card – which gives points on all purchases.	**Customer** PurchasedBy↑ ↓Purchases **CheckoutTillReceipt** A customer may use their Frequent Shopper Card to purchase products.
The customer's details are *held* only by the **store** where they applied for their Frequent Shopper Card.	**Store** HeldBy↑ ↓Holds **Customer** A store holds details of several customers who have a Frequent Shopper Card; a customer who has a Frequent Shopper Card has their details held by a single store (where they applied for their card).

Figure 3.20 below shows an outline entity–relationship model that represents the data requirements of Walton Stores as given in the description in Subsection 2.1.

Entity–relationship diagram

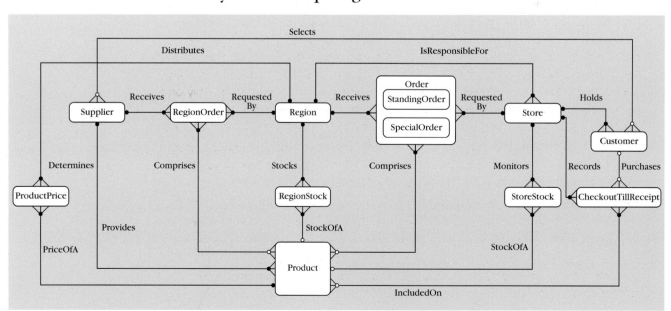

Entity types

Region (<u>Quadrant</u>, ...)

RegionOrder (...)

RegionStock (...)

Store (...)

Order (...)

> StandingOrder (...)
>
> SpecialOrder (...)

StoreStock (...)

Product (<u>ProductCode</u>, ...)

ProductPrice (...)

Supplier (...)

Customer (...)

CheckoutTillReceipt (...)

Working assumptions

> The only customers that Walton Stores will be able to identify will be those who hold the chain's Frequent Shopper Card.

Figure 3.20   An outline entity–relationship model that represents the data requirements of Walton Stores as given in the description in Subsection 2.1

We can develop the outline entity–relationship model shown in Figure 3.20 further in order to represent *all* the data requirements of Walton Stores by analysing the documents created and used by the supermarket chain to facilitate its day-to-day operations. We will do this in Subsection 3.4.

Summary of Subsection 3.3

In this subsection, we have described an approach to analysing textual descriptions of an enterprise in order to develop an entity–relationship model that represents the data requirements of that enterprise. With this approach, we undertake the following steps to develop this entity–relationship model.

1   Scan the text to identify all the nouns and noun phrases.

2   Prune the list of nouns and noun phrases so that it contains just those entity types and properties of entity types (attributes) that are required to represent the data requirements of the enterprise. That is, we retain those candidates that represent entity types and properties of entity types that are required to represent the data requirements of the enterprise; we discard those that are outside the scope of the database system being developed, those that represent entity types with only one occurrence, those that are synonymous with other entity types or properties of entity types, and those that are the values associated with attributes of entity types.

At the end of the second step we are in a position to start writing down the entity type definitions of the entity–relationship model that will represent the data requirements of the enterprise whose textual descriptions we are analysing.

3   Rescan the text and look for sentences in which two or more of the entity types that we identified in Step 2 are associated with each other by a verb or verb phrase.

4   For each relationship identified in the third step, we determine the properties of that relationship – its name, its degree and its participation conditions – by analysing the noun and noun phrases, and the verb and verb phrases in the relationship description, which may comprise one or more sentences.

At the end of the fourth step, we are in a position to add the entity–relationship diagram to the entity–relationship model that we are developing.

5   Rescan the text and look for any other restrictions on the entity–relationship model we are developing that are not explicitly represented by the model. These restrictions are represented by additional conditions in the *Additional constraints* section of the entity–relationship model. Finally, include the conditions required for any weak entity types.

We have used this approach to analyse the textual descriptions of the *Hospital scenario* and Walton Stores (Subsection 2.1). We were able to produce a complete entity–relationship model for the *Hospital scenario* because the description, as the sole description of the hospital enterprise, has been written with the intention of providing a complete and unambiguous description of the data requirements of this enterprise. When the approach was used to analyse the description of Walton Stores, we were only able to produce an outline entity–relationship model because the description only provided an overview of the enterprise, and detail is provided in the documents created and used by the enterprise. The description of Walton Stores and the accompanying documents presented in Section 2 are more typical of what a data analyst might encounter in the field than that found in the *Hospital scenario*.

3.4   Analysing documents

In this subsection, we describe an approach to analysing documents in order to develop an entity–relationship model that represents the data requirements of that enterprise, using the guidelines we developed in Subsection 3.2. Such documents are those created and used by an enterprise to facilitate its day-to-day operations, for example, those documents that are shown in Section 2.

With this approach, we start with the premise that a document will be represented by an entity type in the entity–relationship model, and the contents of the document describe the properties of, or facts about, that entity type. Analysing several documents of the same type, relating to different occurrences of the corresponding entity type, will enable us to gain a good understanding of the meaning and nature of the data associated with that entity type. The results of analysing several different documents can be pieced together, like a jigsaw, to develop an entity–relationship model that represents the data requirements of the enterprise.

Depending on the number and the nature of the documents associated with an enterprise made available for analysis, this approach may not necessarily yield an entity–relationship model that represents all the data requirements of the enterprise. So the approach is used typically in combination with the approach described in Subsection 3.3, which concerns the analysis of textual descriptions of the enterprise either provided by the client or produced as a result of the establishing requirements activity.

Using this approach, we analyse several documents of the same type to answer the following questions about the corresponding entity type.

1   What exactly does each occurrence of the entity type actually represent?

2   What are the properties of, or facts about, the entity type?

3   For each property, is it:

> ▶   single- or multi-valued?

> ▶   optional or mandatory?

> ▶   derivable from other properties?

> ▶   temporal? If so, do we need to record a history of changes to the values associated with the property?

4   How should each property be represented by the entity–relationship model that we are developing according to the guidelines we established in Subsection 3.2?

5   Which, if any, single-valued property or combination of single-valued properties, represented by an attribute or combination of attributes respectively, can act as an assertion of existence, a reference, and a uniqueness constraint, and so form the identifier of the entity type?

If more than one single-valued property or combination of single-valued properties can fulfil these three roles, then which property or combination of properties should be the identifier of the entity type?

If no one single-valued property or combination of single-valued properties can fulfil these three roles, then how can we distinguish between occurrences of the entity type?

6   For each single-valued property that is represented by an attribute:

▶   Are data values complex?

▶   Are they dependent on the data values of other attributes?

▶   What is the value set?

To help us answer these questions, we will probably also need to consult textual descriptions of the enterprise provided by the client or produced as a result of the establishing requirements task. An example is the overview of the Walton Stores enterprise presented in Subsection 2.1. As we answer these questions, we both develop the entity–relationship model and produce the accompanying domain of discourse summary.

We will illustrate this approach using the supermarket case study, which relates to Walton Stores. In the description of Walton Stores (Subsection 2.1), we noted that the supermarket chain will need to develop and install several different databases, each facilitating the day-to-day operations of a particular area of the business. As we describe this approach to analysing documents, we shall be focusing on just the data requirements of individual stores because, as we stated in Section 1, we will initially be concerned with the development and maintenance of a database that will be needed at an individual store. Such a database will need to record details of the products stocked at the store, their provision by the store's regional distribution centre, and their purchase by the store's customers.

Product labels

Let us start by first analysing the documents shown in Figure 2.4, which are examples of product labels that are displayed by the shelf or the compartment of the refrigerator or freezer where the product is found in a store.

The first question asks us to determine 'What exactly does each occurrence of the entity type actually represent?' In Figure 2.4, each label describes a product sold by Walton Stores, and the labels relate to particular foodstuffs. The supermarket chain also sells household goods but we will assume that the labels for such products will have the same content as those shown in Figure 2.4. We will name the corresponding entity type **Product**, where each occurrence represents a particular product sold by Walton Stores.

The second question asks us to determine what the properties of, or facts about, the entity type are. In Figure 2.4, labels 1 and 2 show examples of product lines that are sold by varying quantities (or measures), typically by weight: prepacked goods (label 1) and goods packaged and weighed by the customers themselves (label 2). Figure 2.5 shows corresponding examples of labels that would be affixed to products sold by varying weights packaged by store staff (label 1) or by customers (label 2). In Figure 2.4, labels 3 to 8 show examples of product lines that are sold by the same (fixed) quantities (or measures), by weight or by volume.

At the bottom of each label in Figure 2.4, there is a barcode where the number encoded by that barcode is unique for each product. As the description of Walton Stores (Subsection 2.1) states that

> **Each product line sold by Walton Stores has a unique product code.**

we can reasonably assume that the number encoded by the barcode is this product code. In Figure 2.4, a product like 'Pasteurised skimmed milk' is supplied in two quantities – 1 pint and 2 pints – distinct products having distinct product codes, 01015277 and 01015279 respectively.

Looking at the contents of each label above the barcode, from top to bottom, we can identify the following properties of the corresponding **Product** entity type:

> **Each product has a description (Gorgonzola, Pasteurised skimmed milk, ...), may have a quantity that may be expressed in more than one unit of measurement (568ml, 1 pint, ...), may include additional information for customers (Full-fat, soft blue-veined cheese, ...), has a price and this price may be expressed per unit of measurement (£10.99 per kg, 26p, ...), may have a cost per unit of measurement (45.8p per litre, ...), may be the subject of a special offer (Buy 2 and receive 2 extra points, ...), and has a unique product code (06002669, 01015277, ...).**

We can conveniently refer to these properties of the **Product** entity type as the product description, quantity, additional information, price, unit cost, special offer, and product code.

The third question asks us to characterise each property of the entity type, which is shown in Table 3.10.

Product entity type

Property	SVF/MVF	Mandatory/optional	Temporal/derivable
description	SVF	mandatory	
quantity	SVF	optional	
additional information	SVF	optional	
price	SVF	mandatory	temporal
unit cost	SVF	optional	derivable
special offer	SVF	optional	temporal
product code	SVF	mandatory	

Table 3.10   The characteristics of the properties of the Product entity type

The quantity of product is an optional property of the **Product** entity type because it is only relevant to those product lines sold by the same (fixed) quantities (or measures). Where the quantity of product is displayed both in metric and imperial units, we only need to record one value since the other is derivable from that value.

As unit cost is derivable from the price and quantity properties, we can remove it from the list of properties.

Since the description of Walton Stores (Subsection 2.1) states that

> **Prices are reviewed daily and are revised to take account of changes in the purchase cost, customer demand and product promotions.**

the price of a product is a temporal property of the **Product** entity type as it can vary over time. The promotion of a product by special offers is also a temporal property because a product is likely to be promoted at different times, for different periods and by various special offers.

As we have identified temporal properties of an entity type, we need to establish whether there is a requirement to record historical data values associated with these properties: a history of product prices and special offers. Since this requirement is not stated explicitly in the description of Walton Stores (Subsection 2.1), we will need to consult the client in order to determine whether or not this is a necessary requirement. However, it will be instructive to consider how we can develop separate entity–relationship models to satisfy each option: recording just current prices and special offers, and recording a history of product prices and special offers.

EXERCISE 3.31

How does the recording of the history of product prices and special offers affect the price and special offer properties of the **Product** entity type given in Table 3.10?

The fourth question asks us to consider 'How should each property be represented by the entity–relationship model that we are developing according to the guidelines we established in Subsection 3.2?' Table 3.11 describes how we can represent properties of the **Product** entity type by an entity–relationship model.

As we are considering both options for the temporal properties of price and special offer, representing either current or historical data values, Table 3.11 shows price and special offer as both single-valued and multi-valued properties.

Product entity type

Property	SVF/MVF	Mandatory/optional	Representation
description	SVF	mandatory	by an attribute that records descriptions of products
quantity	SVF	optional	via a :1 relationship with an entity type that records the quantities of those products sold by fixed quantities
additional information	SVF	optional	via a :1 relationship with an entity type that records additional information about products
price	SVF	mandatory	by an attribute that records the current prices of products
	MVF	mandatory	via a :n relationship with an entity type that records a history of prices of products
special offer	SVF	optional	via a :1 relationship with an entity type that records the details of current special offers
	MVF	optional	via a :n relationship with an entity type that records a history of the details of special offers
product code	SVF	mandatory	by an attribute that records product codes

Table 3.11   The representation of the properties of the **Product** entity type

We will now consider each property of the **Product** entity type, justify the representation that is presented in Table 3.11 and choose appropriate names for the attribute, or entity type and relationship required to represent that property.

According to our guidelines, product description, price and code, as mandatory single-valued properties of the **Product** entity type, are each represented by an attribute of that entity type. We will name these attributes **Description**, **Price** and **ProductCode**, respectively.

'Quantity', 'additional information' and 'special offer', as optional single-valued properties of the **Product** entity type, are each represented by a :1 relationship with an entity type that records quantities of those products sold by fixed quantities, additional information about products, and current special offers, respectively. We will name these entity types **ProductQuantity**, **ProductInformation** and **SpecialOffer**, and the appropriate names for the :1 relationships between **Product** and these entity types are **SoldByAFixed**, **MayIncludeAdditional** and **MayBeTheSubjectOf**. We will determine the degree at the **Product** end of these relationships when we consider the properties of the new entity types later. However, the participation condition of these relationships with respect to the **Product** entity type will be optional, as quantity, additional information and special offer are optional single-valued properties of that entity type.

'Price' and 'special offer', as multi-valued properties of the **Product** entity type, are each represented by a :*n* relationship with an entity type that records a history of product prices and special offers, respectively. We will name these entity types **PriceHistory** and **SpecialOfferHistory**, and the names of the :*n* relationships between **Product** and these entity types are **HasBeenSoldAt** and **HasBeenTheSubjectOf**, respectively. We will determine the degree at the **Product** end of these relationships when we consider the properties of these new entity types. The participation conditions of the **HasBeenSoldAt** and **HasBeenTheSubjectOf** relationships with respect to the **Product** entity type are mandatory and optional respectively, as price and special offer are mandatory and optional properties of that entity type.

Table 3.12 describes how we can represent the properties of the **Product** entity type by an entity–relationship model using the attributes, entity types and relationships that we have named above.

The fifth question asks us to determine 'Which, if any, single-valued property or combination of single-valued properties, represented by an attribute or combination of attributes respectively, can act as an assertion of existence, a reference, and a uniqueness constraint, and so form the identifier of the entity type?' As each product line sold by Walton Stores has a unique product code, each occurrence of the **Product** entity type is distinguished by the **ProductCode** attribute.

We complete the analysis of the product labels in Figure 2.4 by answering the sixth question, which requires us to determine the value set and other characteristics of the data values associated with each single-valued property of the entity type that is represented by an attribute of that entity type. Table 3.13 gives the value set and other characteristics of the data values for each attribute of the **Product** entity type.

Product entity type

Property	SVF/MVF	Mandatory/ optional	Representation
description	SVF	mandatory	by an attribute that records descriptions of products, **Description**
quantity	SVF	optional	via a :1 relationship, **SoldByAFixed**, with an entity type that records the quantities of those products sold by fixed quantities, **ProductQuantity**, where the **Product** end has optional participation
additional information	SVF	optional	via a :1 relationship, **MayIncludeAdditional**, with an entity type that records additional information about products, **ProductInformation**, where the **Product** end has optional participation
price	SVF	mandatory	by an attribute that records the current prices of products, **Price**
	MVF	mandatory	via a :*n* relationship, **HasBeenSoldAt**, with an entity type that records a history of prices of products, **PriceHistory**, where the **Product** end has mandatory participation
special offer	SVF	optional	via a :1 relationship, **MayBeTheSubjectOf**, with an entity type that records current special offers, **SpecialOffer**, where the **Product** end has optional participation
	MVF	optional	via a :*n* relationship, **HasBeenTheSubjectOf**, with an entity type that records a history of special offers, **SpecialOfferHistory**, where the **Product** end has optional participation
product code	SVF	mandatory	by an attribute that records product codes, **ProductCode**

Table 3.12   The representation of the properties of the **Product** entity type

Product entity type

Attribute	Value set	Characteristics
ProductCode	{00000000...99999999}	identifier
Description	{character strings}	
Price	{prices}	complex

Table 3.13   The value set and other characteristics of the data values for each attribute of the **Product** entity type

The labels displayed in Figure 2.4 show the product code encoded by each barcode as comprising eight digits. In Table 3.13, we have assumed initially that the data values held by the **ProductCode** can comprise all possible permutations of eight digits, 00000000...99999999, but we would need to confirm the range of values of the product codes with the client.

In Figure 2.4, as the prices are quoted either per item for products sold by fixed quantities (labels 3–8) or per unit of measurement for products sold by varying quantities (labels 1 and 2), they are considered to be complex data values, comprising either one data field, money, or two data fields, money and the unit of measurement, respectively.

EXERCISE 3.32

The description of Walton Stores (Subsection 2.1) states that:

> Walton Stores operates a regional pricing policy where prices of goods at the stores may vary from region to region, but are the same at all the stores within a region.

Why have we not indicated a dependency on the **Price** attribute in Table 3.13 with respect to the regional pricing policy of Walton Stores?

Before we can complete the entity–relationship model that represents all the data requirements described in Figure 2.4, we need to obtain answers to the above six questions for each of the new entity types we have introduced to represent the properties of the **Product** entity type – **ProductQuantity**, **ProductInformation**, **SpecialOffer**, **PriceHistory** and **SpecialOfferHistory**.

ProductQuantity entity type

Figure 2.4 shows that different products may be sold by the same quantities. For example, 'Goats' milk yoghurt' and 'Vegetable fat spread' are sold in quantities of 250g. Other examples such as different types of milk are sold in 1- and 2-pint quantities. Thus, each occurrence of the **ProductQuantity** entity type records the quantities of one or more products, and the **Product** end of the **SoldByAFixed** relationship will be :n. The properties of the **ProductQuantity** entity type, their characteristics, and how they can be represented by the entity–relationship model we are developing, are shown in Table 3.14.

ProductQuantity entity type

Property	SVF/MVF	Mandatory/ optional	Representation
quantity	SVF	mandatory	by an attribute that records the quantities of products, **Quantity**
product	MVF	mandatory	via a :n relationship, **SoldByAFixed**, with an entity type that records details of products, **Product**, where the **ProductQuantity** end has mandatory participation

Table 3.14   The representation of the properties of the ProductQuantity entity type

As **Quantity** is the only attribute of the **ProductQuantity** entity type, then this attribute will be the identifier for the entity type. Table 3.15 gives the value set and other characteristics of the data values for the sole attribute of the **ProductQuantity** entity type.

ProductQuantity entity type

Attribute	Value set	Characteristics
Quantity	{quantities}	identifier complex

Table 3.15   The value set and other characteristics of the data values for the Quantity attribute of the ProductQuantity entity type

As the quantities of products shown in Figure 2.4 are given in different units of measurement, imperial or metric, by weight or by volume of product, they are considered to be complex data values, comprising two data fields – the numeric quantity and the unit of measurement.

ProductInformation entity type

Each occurrence of the **ProductInformation** entity type provides additional information about a product for customers. In Figure 2.4, labels 3 and 4 show that the information can pertain to more than one product.

The **ProductInformation** entity type has the following property:

> **Each piece of additional information can be about one or more products.**

the characteristics of which and how they should be represented by the entity–relationship model that we are developing are shown in Table 3.16.

ProductInformation entity type

Property	SVF/MVF	Mandatory/optional	Representation
information	SVF	mandatory	by an attribute that records additional information about products, **Information**
product	MVF	mandatory	via a :n relationship, **MayIncludeAdditional**, with an entity type that records details of products, **Product**, where the **ProductInformation** end has mandatory participation

Table 3.16   The representation of the properties of the ProductInformation entity type

As **Information** is the only attribute of the **ProductInformation** entity type, then this attribute will be the identifier for the entity type.

Table 3.17 gives the value set and other characteristics of the data values for the sole attribute of the **ProductInformation** entity type.

ProductInformation entity type

Attribute	Value set	Characteristics
Information	{character strings}	identifier

Table 3.17   The value set and other characteristics of the data values for the Information attribute of the ProductInformation entity type

SpecialOffer entity type

Each occurrence of the **SpecialOffer** entity type records the details of a special offer to promote the products that Walton Stores sells. Figure 2.4 shows that a particular special offer may involve more than one product – see label 8 for *Prunes in syrup* and *Prunes in apple juice*. It is reasonable to assume that a particular promotion will only run for a finite period, having definite start and end dates.

The **SpecialOffer** entity type has the following properties:

> **Each special offer comprises details of a particular promotion of one or more products for a particular period of time.**

the characteristics of which, and how they can be represented by the entity–relationship model that we are developing, are shown in Table 3.18.

SpecialOffer entity type

Property	SVF/MVF	Mandatory/ optional	Representation
details	SVF	mandatory	by an attribute that records the details of current special offers, **Details**
product	MVF	mandatory	via a :*n* relationship, **MayBeTheSubjectOf**, with an entity type that records details of products, **Product**, where the **SpecialOffer** end has mandatory participation
start date	SVF	mandatory	by an attribute that records the start date of the current special offer, **StartDate**
end date	SVF	mandatory	by an attribute that records the end date of the current special offer, **EndDate**

Table 3.18   The representation of the properties of the SpecialOffer entity type

Labels 6 and 7 in Figure 2.4 show that products may have the same special offer even though these are distinct promotions of different products. If we assume that these offers have the same promotion period, then no single-valued property, or combination of single-valued properties, of the **SpecialOffer** entity type can form its identifier. That is, it is not possible to distinguish between occurrences of the **SpecialOffer** entity type by the values of its attributes.

Since in the entity–relationship model every entity type must have an identifier, we will have to invent a single-valued property for the **SpecialOffer** entity type that will allow us to distinguish between occurrences of this entity type. We will choose to convey this identifying property by an attribute named **SpecialOfferCode**; its proposed value set, together with those of the other attributes, is shown in Table 3.19.

SpecialOffer entity type

Attribute	Value set	Characteristics
SpecialOfferCode	{00000000...99999999}	identifier
Details	{special offers}	complex
StartDate	{dates}	dependency: the start date of a special offer must be earlier than the end date
EndDate	{dates}	

Table 3.19   The value set and other characteristics of the data values for each of the attributes of the SpecialOffer entity type

As the special offers shown in Figure 2.4 involve either a reduction in the cost of products, or rewards of points to customers who use their Frequent Shopper Cards to purchase products, special offers are considered to be complex data values, comprising two data fields – the condition (Buy 2, Buy any 2) and the nature of the discount or reward (save £1, receive 2 extra points, save 45p).

PriceHistory entity type

The **PriceHistory** entity type represents a temporal property of the **Product** entity type, recording a history of product prices. As the description of Walton Stores (Subsection 2.1) states that

> Prices are reviewed daily and are revised to take account of changes in the purchase cost, customer demand and product promotions.

each occurrence of the **PriceHistory** entity type records the price of a particular product on the date the price is changed. The current price of a particular product will be that relating to the latest change.

The properties of the **PriceHistory** entity type, their characteristics, and how they can be represented by the entity–relationship model we are developing, are shown in Table 3.20.

PriceHistory entity type

Property	SVF/MVF	Mandatory/ optional	Representation
price	SVF	mandatory	by an attribute that records the prices of products on a specified date, **Price**
product	SVF	mandatory	via a 1: relationship, **HasBeenSoldAt**, with an entity type that records details of products, **Product**, where the **PriceHistory** end has mandatory participation
date	SVF	mandatory	by an attribute that specifies the date that prices of products were recorded, **Date**

Table 3.20   The representation of the properties of the PriceHistory entity type

As each occurrence of the entity type records the price of a particular product on a particular date, the identifier of the **PriceHistory** entity type will be a combination of the product and date properties. So, **ProductCode** must become an attribute of the **PriceHistory** entity type so that the combination of **ProductCode** and **Date** attributes, (ProductCode, Date), can be the identifier of **PriceHistory**.

As the identifiers of the **Product** and **PriceHistory** entity types are **ProductCode** and (ProductCode, Date) respectively, **HasBeenSoldAt** will be a 1:*n* relationship, from **Product** to **PriceHistory**. As every product must have a purchase price, every occurrence of the **Product** entity type is associated with at least one occurrence of the **PriceHistory** entity type, and hence **Product** has mandatory participation with respect to the **HasBeenSoldAt** relationship.

Table 3.21 gives the value set and other characteristics of the data values for each attribute of the **ProductHistory** entity type.

PriceHistory entity type

Attribute	Value set	Characteristics
Price	{prices}	complex
ProductCode	{00000000...99999999}	identifier dependency: must be a known product code
Date	{dates}	identifier

Table 3.21   The value sets and other characteristics of the data values for each of the attributes of the PriceHistory entity type

As the prices of products shown in Figure 2.4 are quoted either per item (labels 3–8) or per unit of measurement (labels 1 and 2), they are considered to be complex data values, comprising one data field, money, or two data fields, money and the unit of measurement, respectively.

EXERCISE 3.33

Why is **PriceHistory** a weak entity type?

SpecialOfferHistory entity type

The **SpecialOfferHistory** entity type represents a temporal property of the **Product** entity type, recording a history of special offers to promote products. Each occurrence of the **SpecialOfferHistory** entity type records the details of a particular special offer to promote one or more products for a particular period. It records both current and historical special offers to promote products.

The properties of the **SpecialOfferHistory** entity type, their characteristics, and how they should be represented by the entity–relationship model we are developing, are shown in Table 3.22.

SpecialOfferHistory entity type

Property	SVF/MVF	Mandatory/ optional	Representation
details	SVF	mandatory	by an attribute that records the details of special offers, **Details**
product	MVF	mandatory	via a :*n* relationship, **HasBeenTheSubjectOf**, with an entity type that records details of products, **Product**, where the **SpecialOfferHistory** end has mandatory participation
start date	SVF	mandatory	by an attribute that records the start date of current special offers, **StartDate**
end date	SVF	mandatory	by an attribute that records the end date of current special offers, **EndDate**

Table 3.22   The representation of the properties of the SpecialOfferHistory entity type

If you compare the representation of the properties of the **SpecialOfferHistory** entity type in Table 3.22 with those of the **SpecialOffer** entity type in Table 3.18, you will see that they are identical, apart from the naming of the relationship with the **Product** entity type. To facilitate the recording of a history of special offers, the degree of the **HasBeenTheSubjectOf** relationship between the **Product** entity type and the **SpecialOfferHistory** entity type is *m:n*.

The value set and other characteristics of the data values for each attribute of the **SpecialOfferHistory** entity type will be identical to those of the **SpecialOffer** entity type (see Table 3.19).

Entity–relationship model

As we have now completed our analysis of the product labels shown in Figure 2.4, we can proceed to produce an entity–relationship model that represents the data requirements that we have described. Figure 3.21 shows the entity–relationship model that represents the current situation, recording only current prices and special offers. Figure 3.22 shows (part of) the accompanying domain of discourse summary.

Entity–relationship diagram

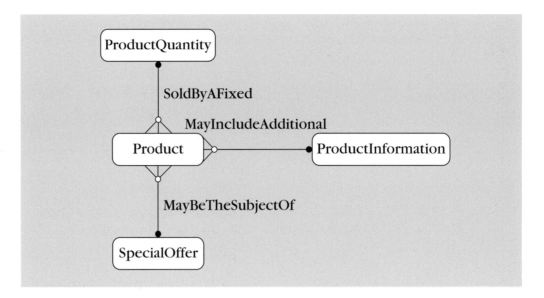

Entity types

Product (ProductCode, Description, Price)

ProductQuantity (Quantity)

ProductInformation (Information)

SpecialOffer (SpecialOfferCode, Details, StartDate, EndDate)

Additional constraint

c.1   For each instance of the SpecialOffer entity type, the value of StartDate should be less than or equal to the value of EndDate.

Working assumptions

The data values held by the ProductCode attribute can comprise all possible permutations of eight digits, 00000000...99999999.

A particular special offer will only run for a finite period, having definite start and end dates. Hence there is justification for including the StartDate and EndDate attributes in the SpecialOffer entity type.

Limitation

l.1   Only the details of a product's current price and special offers, if any, are recorded.

Figure 3.21   An entity–relationship model representing the data requirements described by product labels where only the current situation is represented

Entity type catalogue

Entity name:	**Product**
Description:	A representation of the properties of the products sold by Walton Stores. Each occurrence represents a particular product sold by the supermarket chain.
Attribute details:	Each product has an identifying product code, a description and a price. Product codes are in the range 00000000 to 99999999. Descriptions of products are character strings. Prices are complex data values, comprising either one data field – money, for products sold by a specific quantity – or two data fields – money and the unit of measurement, for products sold by variable weights.
Sample data (from Figure 2.4):	

ProductCode	Description	Price (£)
06002669	Gorgonzola	10.99 per kg
02524730	Carrots (Class 1)	0.31 per kg
01015277	Pasteurised skimmed milk	0.26
01015279	Pasteurised skimmed milk	0.50
04789217	Goats' milk yoghurt	0.89
08562411	Vegetable fat spread	2.49
07214781	Château Haut d'Allard 1996	5.45
02348126	Prunes in syrup	0.62
02348187	Prunes in apple juice	0.65

Entity name:	**ProductQuantity**
Description:	A representation of the quantities of those products that are sold by a specific (fixed) quantity, by weight or by volume. Each occurrence represents the quantity by which one or more products are sold.
Attribute details:	Product quantities are complex data as values are given in different units of measurement, imperial or metric, by weight or by volume of product, comprising two data fields – the numeric quantity and the unit of measurement.
Sample data (from Figure 2.4):	

Quantity
568ml
1.136 litres
250g
75cl
420g
410g

Figure 3.22   Part of the domain of discourse summary accompanying Figure 3.21 *continued*

Entity name:	**ProductInformation**
Description:	A representation of the additional information about products found on some shelf (product) labels. Each occurrence provides additional information about one or more products.
Attribute details:	Product descriptions are character strings.
Sample data (from Figure 2.4):	**Information**

Information

Full-fat, soft blue-veined cheese.

A healthy choice. Virtually fat-free and high in calcium.

Similar in style to a lighter St Emilion, this elegant claret shows much Merlot character.

Entity name:	**SpecialOffer**
Description:	A representation of the properties of special offers that give either a reduction in the cost of products or rewards of points to customers who present their Frequent Shopper Cards (FSCs) to the checkout operator when purchasing products. Each occurrence represents a special offer that relates to the purchase of one or more particular products.
Attribute details:	Each special offer has an identifying special offer code, details of the offer, start and end dates of the offer. Special offer codes are in the range 00000000 to 99999999. Special offer details are complex data values comprising two fields – the condition of the offer, and the discount (money) or reward (FSC points).

Sample data (from client):

SpecialOffer Code	Details	StartDate	EndDate
00005462	Buy 2 and receive 2 extra points	01-May-2006	29-May-2006
00005463	Buy 2 and save £1	15-May-2006	11-June-2006
00005464	Buy 2 and save £1	15-May-2006	11-June-2006
00005465	Buy any 2 and save 45p	15-May-2006	29-May-2006

Notes: The sample data presented above is not included in Section 2.

The special offers identified by the codes 00005463 and 00005464, though offering the same discount, are distinct promotions of different products.

Figure 3.22 *continued*

Relationship catalogue

Relationship name:	**SoldByAFixed** (conversely, associated with)
Description:	Certain products are sold by a specific (fixed) quantity, by weight or by volume.
Reading:	A product may be sold by a specific quantity.
	A specific quantity is associated with one or more products.
Additional information:	None
Sample relationship occurrences (from Figure 2.4):	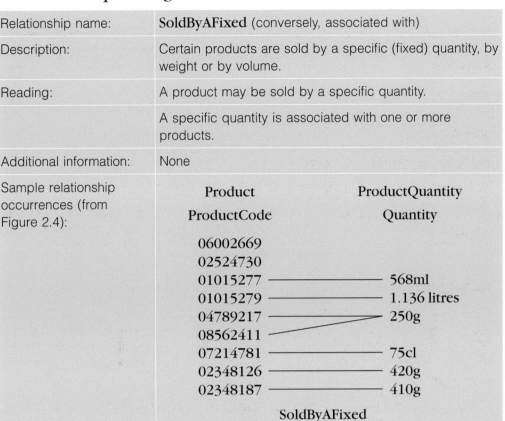

Relationship name:	**MayIncludeAdditional** (conversely, provided for)
Description:	A shelf (product) label may provide additional information about a product for customers.
Reading:	A product may include additional product information.
	Additional product information is provided for one or more products.
Additional information:	None
Sample relationship occurrences (from Figure 2.4):	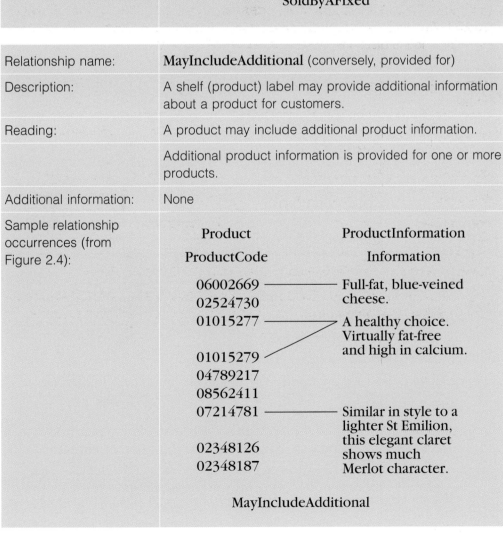

Figure 3.22   (*continued overleaf*)

Relationship name:	**MayBeTheSubjectOf** (conversely, promotes)
Description:	A special offer promotes one or more products by offering either a reduction in the cost of products, or rewards of points to customers who use their Frequent Shopper Cards to purchase products.
Reading:	A product may be the subject of a special offer.
	A special offer promotes one or more products.
Additional information:	None
Sample relationship occurrences (from client):	

Product
ProductCode

SpecialOffer
SpecialOfferCode

06002669
02524730
01015277
01015279
04789217 ——————— 00005462
08562411 ——————— 00005463
07214781 ——————— 00005464
02348126 ——————— 00005465
02348187

MayBeTheSubjectOf

Figure 3.22   *continued*

Figure 3.23 below shows the entity–relationship model that represents the historical situation, recording a history of prices and special offers.

Entity–relationship diagram

Entity types

Product (ProductCode, Description)

ProductQuantity (Quantity)

ProductInformation (Information)

PriceHistory (ProductCode, Date, Price)

SpecialOfferHistory (SpecialOfferCode, Details, StartDate, EndDate)

Additional constraints

c.1   For each instance of the SpecialOfferHistory entity type, the value of StartDate should be less than or equal to the value of EndDate.

c.2   PriceHistory is a weak entity type dependent on Product. So, each value of ProductCode in the entity type PriceHistory must be the same value as the ProductCode of the Product instance to which the

PriceHistory is related by the relationship HasBeenSoldAt
(a consequence of weak–strong entity types).

Working assumptions

The data values held by the ProductCode and SpecialOfferCode
attributes can comprise all possible permutations of eight digits,
00000000...99999999.

A particular special offer will only run for a finite period, having
definite start and end dates. Hence there is justification for including
the StartDate and EndDate attributes in the SpecialOfferHistory entity
type.

Limitation

None

Figure 3.23   An entity–relationship model representing the data requirements described
by product labels where the historical situation is represented

When we answered the third question associated with our approach to analysing
documents, which asks us to characterise each property of the entity type, we decided
that both the price of a product and the promotion of a product by special offers were
temporal properties. If you compare the entity–relationship model representing the
data requirements described by product labels where only the current situation is
represented (Figure 3.21) with the model where the historical situation is represented
(Figure 3.23), then you should note the following differences.

1   In the model representing only the current situation, the price of a product is
    recorded by the **Price** attribute of the **Product** entity type, whereas in the model
    representing the historical situation, the price is recorded by a :*n* relationship
    HasBeenSoldAt, with the **PriceHistory** entity type.

2   In the model representing only the current situation, the promotion of a product by
    a special offer is recorded by a :1 relationship **MayBeTheSubjectOf**, with the
    SpecialOffer entity type, whereas in the model representing the historical
    situation, it becomes a :*n* relationship **HasBeenTheSubjectOf**.

In both cases, these differences are consistent with the recording of a history of
product prices and special offers. This means that price and special offer become
multi-valued properties of the **Product** entity type, where each value is dependent on
time (see Exercise 3.31).

We have spent some considerable time working methodically through the steps of our
approach to analysing documents, outlined at the start of this section, in order to
develop an entity–relationship model that records the data described by the product
labels shown in Figure 2.4. As we use this approach to analyse other documents
created and used by Walton Stores, we will include a little less detail because we hope
that you will have become a little more experienced at analysing the data and
relationships between the data that are conveyed by the documents, and representing
them by an entity–relationship model. We should emphasise that this is just *one*
approach to developing an entity–relationship model; it is a methodical approach and
should not be performed mechanically, as you need to develop a good understanding
of an enterprise and its data in order to model it accurately.

EXERCISE 3.34

The analysis of the examples of shelf (product) labels shown in Figure 2.4 revealed two
types of product: those sold by fixed quantities, and those sold by varying quantities,

typically by weight. Identify the properties that these two types have in common and those properties that are specific to each type. Revise the entity–relationship model representing the data requirements described by the product labels shown in Figures 3.21 and 3.22 where only the current situation is represented, by using entity supertypes/subtypes to represent the generic and specific properties of the two types of product explicitly.

Standing and special orders

In Section 2, which describes the case study of Walton Stores, we stated that:

> A store can request deliveries of goods from its distribution centre in two different ways: by a standing order, where the goods requested are required at regular intervals throughout the year (see Figure 2.1); and by a special order, where the goods requested are in demand only at certain times of the year (see Figure 2.2).

In this section, we will analyse examples of standing and special orders by employing the same approach that we used to analyse product labels in the previous section.

Standing orders

We will start by analysing the examples of standing orders shown in Figure 2.1.

The first question asks us to determine 'What exactly does each occurrence of the entity type actually represent?' Each standing order shown in Figure 2.1 lists the packs of products that a particular store requests its distribution centre to deliver to the store at regular intervals. We will name the corresponding entity type **StandingOrder**, where each occurrence represents a particular order for the periodic delivery of one or more packs of products requested by the store from its distribution centre.

EXERCISE 3.35

What information is provided by the standing orders shown in Figure 2.1?

The second question asks us to determine the properties of, or facts about, the entity type. From the solution to Exercise 3.35, we can identify the following properties of the corresponding **StandingOrder** entity type:

> Each standing order has an order number and a date, and lists the requests for the delivery of the packs of products. Each request on the standing order has a unique item number within that standing order, a product code and a description of the product, and includes details relating to pack size, number of packs required, delivery days, and frequency of delivery.

EXERCISE 3.36

Why have we excluded the name of the store and its distribution centre from our list of properties of the **StandingOrder** entity type?

We can conveniently refer to these properties of the **StandingOrder** entity type as the order number, order date, item numbers, product codes, product descriptions, pack sizes, numbers of packs, delivery days, and delivery frequencies.

The third question asks us to characterise each property of the entity type, as shown in Table 3.23.

StandingOrder entity type

Property	SVF/MVF	Mandatory/ optional	Temporal/ derivable
order number	SVF	mandatory	
order date	SVF	mandatory	
item numbers	MVF	mandatory	
product codes	MVF	mandatory	
product descriptions	MVF	mandatory	
pack sizes	MVF	mandatory	
numbers of packs	MVF	mandatory	temporal
delivery days	MVF	mandatory	temporal
delivery frequencies	MVF	mandatory	temporal

Table 3.23 The characteristics of the properties of the StandingOrder entity type

Since the description of Walton Stores (Subsection 2.1) states that

> **A store may need to revise standing orders to meet seasonal fluctuations in the demand for certain products.**

the numbers of packs, delivery days and delivery frequencies are temporal properties of the **StandingOrder** entity type as they could vary over time.

Evidence from Figures 2.1 and 2.2 suggests that each product is supplied solely in packs of the same size. We will assume that pack sizes do not vary over time for a given product, thus pack sizes are not a temporal property of standing orders, but we will need to confirm this with the client.

As we have identified temporal properties of an entity type, we need to establish whether there is a requirement to record historical data values associated with these properties: a history of revisions to standing orders. This requirement is not stated explicitly in the description of Walton Stores (Subsection 2.1), therefore we will need to consult the client in order to determine whether or not this is a necessary requirement. For the moment, we will develop an entity–relationship model that records just the current standing orders.

The fourth question asks us to consider how each property should be represented by the entity–relationship model we are developing, according to the guidelines we have established in Subsection 3.2. Table 3.24 describes how we can represent properties of the **StandingOrder** entity type by an entity–relationship model.

StandingOrder entity type

Property	SVF/MVF	Mandatory/ optional	Representation
order number	SVF	mandatory	by an attribute that records order numbers
order date	SVF	mandatory	by an attribute that records the dates of the orders
	MVF	mandatory	

product codes, product descriptions, pack sizes			via a :*n* relationship with an entity type that records details about products
item numbers, numbers of packs, delivery days, delivery frequencies	MVF	mandatory	via a :*n* relationship with an entity type that records details about requests for products

Table 3.24   The representation of the properties of the **StandingOrder** entity type

We will now consider each property of the **StandingOrder** entity type, justify the representation presented in Table 3.24 and choose appropriate names for the attribute, or entity type and relationship required to represent that property.

Order number and order date, as mandatory single-valued properties of the **StandingOrder** entity type, are each represented by an attribute of that entity type. We will name these attributes **OrderNumber** and **OrderDate**, respectively.

In Table 3.24, you should note the distinction made between properties of products, which are product codes, product descriptions and pack sizes, and properties of the requests for the delivery of packs of products such as item numbers, numbers of packs, delivery days and delivery frequencies.

Product codes, product descriptions and pack sizes, as mandatory multi-valued properties of the **StandingOrder** entity type, are represented by a :*n* relationship with an entity type that records details about products, the **Product** entity type, which we established in the previous section when we analysed the product labels shown in Figure 2.4. We will name the :*n* relationship between the **StandingOrder** and **Product** entity types, **RequestsRegularDeliveryOf**. The entity type **StandingOrder** has mandatory participation with respect to the **RequestsRegularDeliveryOf** relationship because a standing order must comprise at least one request for the delivery of packs of a product.

Item numbers, numbers of packs, delivery days and delivery frequencies, as mandatory multi-valued properties of the **StandingOrder** entity type, are represented by a :*n* relationship with an entity type that records details about requests for the delivery of products. However, as each occurrence of the **RequestsRegularDeliveryOf** relationship records a particular request for the delivery of a particular product, these properties will be properties of the **RequestsRegularDeliveryOf** relationship itself or, as we will describe below, of an intersection entity type representing the **RequestsRegularDeliveryOf** relationship.

Table 3.25 describes how we can represent the properties of the **StandingOrder** entity type by an entity–relationship model, the attributes, the entity type and the relationship we named above.

StandingOrder entity type

Property	SVF/MVF	Mandatory/ optional	Representation
order number	SVF	mandatory	by an attribute that records order numbers, **OrderNumber**
order date	SVF	mandatory	by an attribute that records the dates of the orders, **OrderDate**
	MVF	mandatory	via a :*n* relationship, **RequestsRegularDeliveryOf**,

product codes, product descriptions, pack sizes			with an entity type that records details about products, **Product**, where the **StandingOrder** end has mandatory participation
item numbers, numbers of packs, delivery days, delivery frequencies	MVF	mandatory	via an intersection entity type representing the **RequestsRegularDeliveryOf** relationship

Table 3.25   The representation of the properties of the StandingOrder entity type

Table 3.26 shows the additional properties of the **Product** entity type as a result of the analysis of standing orders – pack sizes and standing orders. These properties should be added to those listed in Table 3.12.

Product entity type

Property	SVF/MVF	Mandatory/ optional	Representation
pack size	SVF	mandatory	by an attribute that records pack sizes, **PackSize**
standing orders	MVF	optional	via a :*n* relationship, **RequestsRegularDeliveryOf**, with an entity type that records details about standing orders, **StandingOrder**, where the **Product** end has optional participation

Table 3.26   The representation of the new properties of the Product entity type

In Table 3.26, we have decided to make pack size a mandatory single-valued property of the **Product** entity type because it is reasonable to assume that every product sold by Walton Stores will be provided by their supplier in a convenient pack comprising several items.

We have decided to make the participation condition of the **Product** entity type, with respect to the **RequestsRegularDeliveryOf** relationship, optional because the residual stocks of discontinued product lines should be available to customers to purchase even though they are no longer being ordered from the suppliers. Products may only be seasonal and may not have a standing order but only special orders. We have chosen to make the **StandingOrder** end of the **RequestsRegularDeliveryOf** relationship :*n* because we have assumed that a particular product could be supplied by more than one standing order (though this is not shown in Figure 2.1).

Tables 3.25 and 3.26 show **RequestsRegularDeliveryOf** as an *m:n* (many-to-many) relationship between the **StandingOrder** and **Product** entity types: each standing order may request one or more packs of different products; a product may be requested by one or more standing orders. As we noted above, item numbers, numbers of packs, delivery days and delivery frequencies are properties of the **RequestsRegularDeliveryOf** relationship. According to the guidelines for representing properties of relationships between entity types by an entity–relationship model that we have developed in Subsection 3.2, such properties become properties of an intersection entity type that represents that relationship.

We will represent the **RequestsRegularDeliveryOf** relationship by an intersection entity type named **StandingOrderItem**, as shown in Figure 3.24.

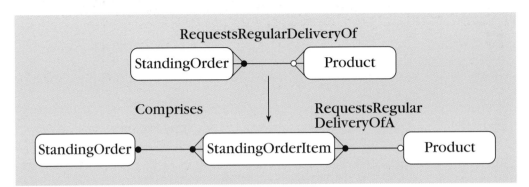

Figure 3.24   The representation of the RequestsRegularDeliveryOf relationship by an intersection entity type named StandingOrderItem

Each occurrence of the **StandingOrderItem** intersection entity type records a specific request for the regular delivery of packs of a product found on a particular standing order. The properties of the **StandingOrderItem** intersection entity type are shown in Table 3.28, together with how they may be represented by an entity–relationship model. Tables 3.27 and 3.29 show revised Tables 3.25 and 3.26, respectively, to reflect the introduction of the **StandingOrderItem** entity type.

StandingOrder entity type

Property	SVF/MVF	Mandatory/ optional	Representation
order number	SVF	mandatory	by an attribute that records order numbers, **OrderNumber**
order date	SVF	mandatory	by an attribute that records the dates of the orders, **OrderDate**
requests for the regular delivery of packs of products	MVF	mandatory	via a :n relationship, **Comprises**, with an entity type that records details about requests for the regular delivery of packs of products, **StandingOrderItem**, where the **StandingOrder** end has mandatory participation

Table 3.27   The representation of the properties of the StandingOrder entity type

StandingOrderItem entity type

Property	SVF/MVF	Mandatory/ optional	Representation
order number	SVF	mandatory	by an attribute that records order numbers, **OrderNumber**
item number	SVF	mandatory	by an attribute that records item numbers, **ItemNumber**
number of packs	SVF	mandatory	by an attribute that records the number of packs, **NumberOfPacks**
delivery days	MVF	mandatory	via a :*n* relationship, **DeliveredOn**, with an entity type that records delivery days, **DeliveryDay**, where the **StandingOrderItem** end has mandatory participation
delivery frequency	SVF	mandatory	by an attribute that records the frequency of delivery, **DeliveryFrequency**
standing order	SVF	mandatory	via a :1 relationship, **Comprises**, with an entity type that records details about standing orders, **StandingOrder**, where the **StandingOrderItem** end has mandatory participation
product	SVF	mandatory	via a :1 relationship, **RequestsRegularDeliveryOfA**, with an entity type that records details about products, **Product**, where the **StandingOrderItem** end has mandatory participation

Table 3.28   The representation of the properties of the StandingOrderItem entity type

Product entity type

Property	SVF/MVF	Mandatory/ optional	Representation
pack size	SVF	mandatory	by an attribute that records pack sizes, **PackSize**
requests for the regular delivery of packs of the product	MVF	optional	via a :*n* relationship, **RequestsRegularDeliveryOfA**, with an entity type that records details about requests for products, **StandingOrderItem**, where the **Product** end has optional participation

Table 3.29   The representation of the new properties of the Product entity type

In Table 3.28, as delivery days is a multi-valued property of the **StandingOrderItem** entity type, according to our guidelines, we have introduced a new entity type, **DeliveryDay**, to record the days of the week that deliveries of packs of products are made. Its properties are shown in Table 3.30, together with how they may be represented by an entity–relationship model.

DeliveryDay entity type

Property	SVF/MVF	Mandatory/optional	Representation
delivery day	SVF	mandatory	by an attribute that records the days that deliveries are made, **DeliveryDay**
requests for the regular delivery of packs of products	MVF	optional	via a :*n* relationship, **DeliveredOn**, with an entity type that records details about requests for packs of products, **StandingOrderItem**, where the **DeliveryDay** end has optional participation

Table 3.30   The representation of the properties of the DeliveryDay entity type

The fifth question asks us to determine 'Which, if any, single-valued property or combination of single-valued properties, represented by an attribute or combination of attributes respectively, can act as an assertion of existence, a reference, and a uniqueness constraint, and so form the identifier of the entity type?'

EXERCISE 3.37

Which attribute or combination of attributes should form the identifiers of the **StandingOrder**, **StandingOrderItem** and **DeliveryDay** entity types?

We complete the analysis of the standing orders shown in Figure 2.1 by answering the sixth question, which requires us to determine the value set and other characteristics of the data values associated with each single-valued property of the entity type that is represented by an attribute of that entity type.

EXERCISE 3.38

What are the value sets and other characteristics of the attributes of the **StandingOrder**, **StandingOrderItem** and **DeliveryDay** entity types?

We need also to determine the value set and other characteristics of the data values for the **PackSize** attribute of the **Product** entity type. The **PackSize** attribute has complex data values comprising two data fields – the number of items of the product in a pack, and the weight or volume of each item. However, if you compare the examples of standing orders in Figure 2.1 with the examples of product labels in Figure 2.4, you will see that each of the pack sizes displayed on standing orders for the products sold by fixed amounts (labels 3 to 8) includes the quantity of the product which is also shown on product labels.

EXERCISE 3.39

Although we do not want to duplicate the quantities of products sold by fixed amounts in the **PackSize** attribute of the **Product** entity type, we do have to record the weight or volume of individual items comprising packs of products sold by variable amounts. How can we achieve this?

Hint: see the solution to Exercise 3.34.

Entity–relationship model

As we have now completed our analysis of the standing orders shown in Figure 2.1, we can proceed to produce an entity–relationship model that represents the data requirements described by this document. Figure 3.25 shows an extended Figure 3.21, where products are represented using entity subtypes according to the solution to Exercise 3.34 and standing orders as a result of the above analysis. Figure 3.26 shows (part of) the accompanying domain of discourse summary.

Entity–relationship diagram

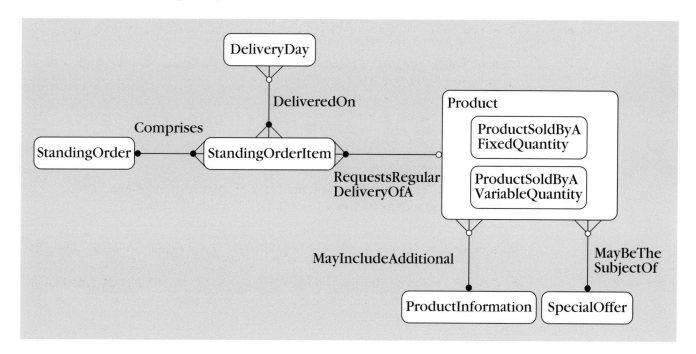

Entity types

StandingOrder (<u>OrderNumber</u>, OrderDate)

StandingOrderItem (<u>OrderNumber</u>, <u>ItemNumber</u>, NumberOfPacks,
                   DeliveryFrequency)

DeliveryDay (<u>DeliveryDay</u>)

Product (<u>ProductCode</u>, Description, Price)

   ProductSoldByAFixedQuantity (Quantity, NumberInPack)

   ProductSoldByAVariableQuantity (PackSize)

ProductInformation (<u>Information</u>)

SpecialOffer (<u>SpecialOfferCode</u>, Details, StartDate, EndDate)

Additional constraints

c.1   For each instance of the SpecialOffer entity type, the value of StartDate should be less than or equal to the value of EndDate.

c.3   StandingOrderItem is a weak entity type dependent on StandingOrder. So, each value of OrderNumber in the entity type StandingOrderItem must be the same value as the OrderNumber of the StandingOrder instance to which the StandingOrderItem entity type is related by the relationship Comprises (a consequence of weak–strong entity types).

Working assumptions

The data values held by the ProductCode and SpecialOfferCode attributes can comprise all possible permutations of eight digits, 00000000...99999999.

A particular special offer will only run for a finite period, having definite start and end dates. Hence there is justification for including the StartDate and EndDate attributes in the SpecialOffer entity type.

A product may be requested by more than one standing order. Hence there is justification for the degree of the RequestARegularDeliveryOfA relationship being n:1 from StandingOrderItem to Product.

Every product is supplied as a pack comprising several items that is the same size for a given product.

Deliveries of packs of products are not made on Sundays.

Limitations

l.1   Only the details of a product's current price and special offers, if any, are recorded.

l.2   There is no requirement to record a history of changes to standing orders.

Figure 3.25   An entity–relationship model representing the data requirements described by product labels and standing orders where only the current situation is represented

Entity type catalogue

Entity name:	StandingOrder
Description:	A representation of standing orders whereby a store can request the delivery of product lines at regular intervals throughout the year from its distribution centre. Each occurrence represents a particular order that requests the regular delivery of packs of products.
Attribute details:	Each standing order has an identifying order number and an order date. Order numbers are in the range 0000000 to 9999999.
Sample data (from Figure 2.1):	OrderNumber OrderDate 0014588 13-May-2006 0014589 13-May-2006

Figure 3.26   Part of the domain of discourse summary accompanying Figure 3.25

Entity name:	**StandingOrderItem**
Description:	A representation of requests for the regular delivery of product lines found on standing orders. Each occurrence represents a specific request for the regular delivery of packs of a product found on a particular standing order.
Attribute details:	Each standing order item is identified by the combination of the order number and item number, and records the number of packs of the product to be delivered and the frequency of the delivery. Order numbers are in the range 0000000 to 9999999. Item numbers for each standing order follow the sequence 1, 2, 3, ..., n. The frequency of delivery is recorded as either *Weekly* or *Monthly*.

Sample data (from Figure 2.1):

Order Number	Item Number	Number OfPacks	Delivery Frequency
0014588	1	5000	Weekly
0014588	2	8000	Weekly
0014588	3	5000	Weekly
0014588	4	8000	Weekly
0014588	5	1000	Weekly
0014588	6	1000	Weekly
0014588	7	50	Monthly
0014589	1	1000	Monthly
0014589	2	2000	Monthly
0014589	3	10	Weekly
0014589	4	20	Weekly

Entity name:	**DeliveryDay**
Description:	A representation of the days of the week when regular deliveries of packs of products are required by a request on a standing order. Each occurrence represents a particular day of the week when deliveries of packs of products are made by a store's distribution centre.
Attribute details:	A sole attribute identifies the day of the week.

Sample data (from Figure 2.1):

DeliveryDay

Monday
Tuesday
Wednesday
Thursday
Friday
Saturday

Figure 3.26 *continued*

Entity name:	**Product** (supertype)
Description:	A representation of the properties of the products sold by Walton Stores.
Attribute details:	Each product has an identifying product code and a description. Product codes are in the range 00000000 to 99999999. Descriptions of products are character strings.

Entity name:	**ProductSoldByAVariableQuantity** (subtype)
Description:	A representation of the properties of those products sold by varying quantities: prepacked goods, and goods packaged and weighed by the customers themselves. Each occurrence represents a particular product sold by varying quantities.
Attribute details:	Prices and pack sizes both have complex data values comprising two data fields: prices – money and the unit of measurement; pack sizes – number of items in a pack and the quantity of each item.

Sample data (from Figures 2.1 and 2.4):

ProductCode	Description	Price (£)	PackSize
06002669	Gorgonzola	10.99 per kg	10 x 10kg
02524730	Carrots (Class 1)	0.31 per kg	1 x 50kg

Entity name:	**ProductSoldByAFixedQuantity** (subtype)
Description:	A representation of the properties of those products sold by fixed amounts. Each occurrence represents a particular product sold by fixed amounts.
Attribute details:	Quantities are complex data values comprising two data fields – the numeric quantity and the unit of measurement. Prices are money, pounds. NumberInPack the number of product items in a pack.

Sample data (from Figures 2.1, 2.2 and 2.4):

The catalogue entries for the **ProductInformation** and **SpecialOffer** entity types are unchanged from Figure 3.22.

ProductCode	Description	Quantity	Price (£)	Number InPack
01015277	Pasteurised skimmed milk	568ml	0.26	72
01015279	Pasteurised skimmed milk	1.136 litres	0.50	72
04789217	Goats' milk yoghurt	250g	0.89	36
08562411	Vegetable fat spread	250g	2.49	144
07214781	Château Haut d'Allard 1996	75cl	5.45	6
02348126	Prunes in syrup	420g	0.62	48
02348187	Prunes in apple juice	410g	0.65	48

Figure 3.26 *continued*

Relationship catalogue

Relationship name:	**Comprises**
Description:	Standing orders comprise requests for the regular delivery of products.
Reading:	A standing order comprises one or more requests for the regular delivery of products.
	Each request for the regular delivery of products is part of a particular standing order.
Additional information:	None
Sample relationship occurrences (from Figure 2.1):	

StandingOrder
OrderNumber

StandingOrderItem
(OrderNumber, ItemNumber)

```
0014588          (0014588, 1)
                 (0014588, 2)
                 (0014588, 3)
                 (0014588, 4)
                 (0014588, 5)
                 (0014588, 6)
                 (0014588, 7)
0014589          (0014589, 1)
                 (0014589, 2)
                 (0014589, 3)
                 (0014589, 4)
```

Comprises

Relationship name:	**RequestsADeliveryOfA**
Description:	Standing order items request the regular delivery of specified products.
Reading:	Each standing order item requests a regular delivery of a single product.
	Each product may be requested in several standing order items.
Additional information:	None
Sample relationship occurrences (from Figure 2.1):	

StandingOrderItem
(OrderNumber, ItemNumber)

Product
ProductCode

```
(0014588, 1)          01015277
(0014588, 2)
(0014588, 3)          01015279
(0014588, 4)
(0014588, 5)          04789217
(0014588, 6)          08562411
(0014588, 7)          06002669
(0014589, 1)          02348126
(0014589, 2)          02348187
(0014589, 3)          02524730
(0014589, 4)
```

RequestsDeliveryOfA

Figure 3.26 *continued*

Relationship name:	**DeliveredOn**
Description:	Standing order items request the regular delivery of products on specified days of the week.
Reading:	Each standing order item requests a regular delivery of a single product on one or more days of the week.
	For each day of the week, one or more standing order items request the delivery of a single product on that day.
Additional information:	None
Sample relationship occurrences (from Figure 2.1):	**StandingOrderItem** **DeliveryDay** (OrderNumber, DeliveryDay ItemNumber) (0014588, 1) Monday (0014588, 2) Tuesday (0014588, 3) Wednesday (0014588, 4) Thursday ... Friday Saturday DeliveredOn

The catalogue entries for the **MayIncludeAdditional** and **MayBeTheSubjectOf** relationships are unchanged from Figure 3.22.

Figure 3.26   *continued*

Special orders

We will now analyse the examples of the special orders in Figure 2.2.

EXERCISE 3.40

Analyse the examples of special orders in Figure 2.2 in order to produce an entity–relationship model. Before you start, first compare the contents of the special orders with those of the standing orders (Figure 2.1).

Exercise 3.40 illustrates an important aspect of data analysis and how experienced analysts develop entity–relationship models that represent the data requirements of some enterprise. It was not necessary to work through all the steps of our approach to analysing documents to produce an entity–relationship model; we could simply recognise the similarities and differences between standing orders and special orders, and then adapt the results of the previous analysis of examples of standing orders. As you become more experienced in data analysis, you will begin to recognise similar (or even the same) situations to those you have encountered before and for which you have developed entity–relationship models that represent their requirements. Standing orders and special orders are simply a variation of a common business document, an order form or invoice document.

As standing orders and special orders are different means by which a store may request the delivery of packs of products from its distribution centre, and since they have properties in common and also distinct properties, we can sensibly employ entity

supertypes/subtypes in our entity–relationship model. Further evidence for the connection between standing orders and special orders can be found by looking at Figures 2.1 and 2.2, where all the orders were created on the same date (13-May-2006) and have consecutive order numbers (0014588, 0014589, 0014590 and 0014591).

Figure 3.27 shows an entity–relationship model that represents the data requirements of both standing and special orders. It combines the models shown in Figure 3.25 and the solution to Exercise 3.40, and uses the entity supertypes/subtypes to represent the common and distinct properties of those orders.

Entity–relationship diagram

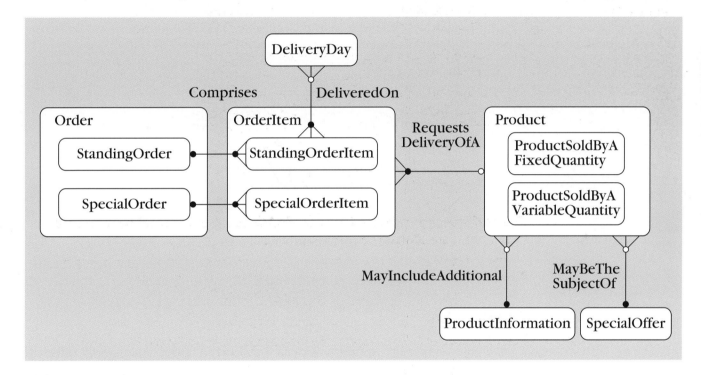

Entity types

Order (<u>OrderNumber</u>, OrderDate)

    StandingOrder ()

    SpecialOrder ()

OrderItem (<u>OrderNumber</u>, <u>ItemNumber</u>, NumberOfPacks)

    StandingOrderItem (DeliveryFrequency)

    SpecialOrderItem (DeliveryDate)

DeliveryDay (<u>DeliveryDay</u>)

Product (<u>ProductCode</u>, Description, Price)

    ProductSoldByAFixedQuantity (Quantity, NumberInPack)

    ProductSoldByAVariableQuantity (PackSize)

ProductInformation (<u>Information</u>)

SpecialOffer (<u>SpecialOfferCode</u>, Details, StartDate, EndDate)

Additional constraints

c.1   For each instance of the SpecialOffer entity type, the value of StartDate should be less than or equal to the value of EndDate.

c.3   StandingOrderItem is a weak entity type dependent on StandingOrder. So, each value of OrderNumber in the entity type StandingOrderItem must be the same value as the OrderNumber of the StandingOrder instance to which the StandingOrderItem entity type is related by the relationship Comprises (a consequence of weak–strong entity types).

c.4   SpecialOrderItem is a weak entity type dependent on SpecialOrder. So, each value of the OrderNumber in the entity type SpecialOrderItem must be the same value as the OrderNumber of the SpecialOrder instance to which the SpecialOrderItem entity type is related by the relationship Comprises (a consequence of weak–strong entity types).

Working assumptions

The data values held by the ProductCode and SpecialOfferCode attributes can comprise all possible permutations of eight digits, 00000000...99999999.

A particular special offer will only run for a finite period, having definite start and end dates. Hence there is justification for including the StartDate and EndDate attributes in the SpecialOffer entity type.

A product may be requested by more than one order. Hence there is justification for the degree of the RequestsDeliveryOfA relationship being n:1 from OrderItem to Product.

Every product is supplied as a pack comprising several items that is the same size for a given product.

Deliveries of packs of products are not made on Sundays.

Limitations

l.1   Only the details of a product's current price and special offers, if any, are recorded.

l.2   There is no requirement to record a history of changes to standing orders.

Figure 3.27   An entity–relationship model representing the data requirements described by product labels, standing orders and special orders where only the current situation is represented

Frequent Shopper Card (FSC) application form

We will now analyse the application form for a Frequent Shopper Card that is shown in Figure 2.7. An example of an FSC is shown in Figure 2.8. We will name the corresponding entity type **Customer** because when a customer presents their FSC to the checkout operator when purchasing goods at a store to benefit from the rewards and credit facility that the card provides, they identify themselves as the purchaser of those goods – a customer of Walton Stores.

EXERCISE 3.41

Analyse the application form for a Frequent Shopper Card shown in Figure 2.7, using the approach we have employed previously for analysing documents.

Checkout till receipts

Finally, we will analyse the examples of checkout till receipts shown in Figure 2.6. Each receipt shown in Figure 2.6 lists the products purchased by a customer on a visit to a particular store in the Walton Stores supermarket chain. We will name the corresponding entity type **CheckoutTillReceipt**, where each occurrence represents a record of a particular transaction between a customer and a store whereby the customer purchases particular products at a particular time.

EXERCISE 3.42

What do the checkout till receipts shown in Figure 2.6 record about a transaction between a customer and a store?

From the solution to Exercise 3.35, we can identify the following properties of the **CheckoutTillReceipt** entity type:

> Each checkout till receipt names the checkout operator and lists the products purchased, giving a description of each product, the quantity, the unit cost for those products sold by variable quantity, the purchase price and any discount or reward (points) resulting from special offers. It also gives the total purchase price, the method of payment, the amount tendered, and the change returned if cash was tendered. It may give the Frequent Shopper Card (FSC) number together with the points earned for the transaction and total points accrued, if appropriate. It has a transaction date and time.

We have excluded the name of the store where the products were purchased from our list of properties of the **CheckoutTillReceipt** entity type because we are focusing just on the data requirements of individual stores.

We can conveniently refer to these properties of the **CheckoutTillReceipt** entity type as the checkout operator, the products purchased – descriptions, quantities, unit costs, purchase prices and discounts/rewards – the total purchase price, method of payment, amount tendered, change given, FSC number, points earned, total points accrued, transaction time.

EXERCISE 3.43

Characterise each property of the **CheckoutTillReceipt** entity type.

In the solution to Exercise 3.43 we noted that some properties of the **CheckoutTillReceipt** entity type were dependent on whether the product purchased was sold by fixed or variable quantities. Before we consider how we might represent properties of the **CheckoutTillReceipt** entity type by the entity–relationship model we are developing to represent the data requirements of individual stores in the supermarket chain, we need to consider carefully how the purchase of the two different types of product – those sold by fixed quantities and those sold by variable quantities – relate to the properties and their characteristics that are identified in the solution to Exercise 3.43.

For a particular product sold by fixed quantities, the quantity and the purchase price will be fixed for all purchases of that product, as recorded by the corresponding occurrence of the **ProductSoldByAFixedQuantity** entity subtype. The unit cost is not applicable to such products.

For a particular product sold by variable quantities, the quantity and the purchase price could be different for each purchase of that product, the purchase price being derived from the quantity recorded by the barcode on the label affixed to the prepacked product (see Figure 2.5), and the unit cost as recorded by the corresponding occurrence of the **ProductSoldByAVariableQuantity** entity subtype.

Table 3.31 shows a revised version of the table presented in the solution to Exercise 3.43, which distinguishes between the generic properties of products purchased and the specific properties associated with products sold by fixed or variable quantities. Derivable properties are excluded from Table 3.31.

CheckoutTillReceipt entity type

Property	SVF/MVF	Mandatory/optional
checkout operator	SVF	mandatory
products purchased:		
- descriptions	MVF	mandatory
- discounts/rewards	MVF	optional
- sold by fixed quantities		
- quantities	MVF	mandatory
- purchase prices	MVF	mandatory
- sold by variable quantities		
- quantities	MVF	mandatory
- unit costs	MVF	mandatory
method of payment	SVF	mandatory
amount tendered	SVF	mandatory
FSC number	SVF	optional
transaction time	SVF	mandatory

Table 3.31   The characteristics of the properties of the CheckoutTillReceipt entity type

EXERCISE 3.44

How do we represent properties of the **CheckoutTillReceipt** entity type by the entity–relationship model we are developing to represent the data requirements of individual stores in the supermarket chain? Choose suitable names for any new attributes, entity types and relationships required to represent the properties of the **CheckoutTillReceipt** entity type. Update the properties of any existing entity type that has a relationship with the **CheckoutTillReceipt** entity type.

EXERCISE 3.45

Which, if any, single-valued property or combination of single-valued properties, represented by an attribute or combination of attributes, respectively, shown in the solution to Exercise 3.44, can act in the roles of an assertion of existence, a referenceand a uniqueness constraint, and so form the identifier of the **CheckoutTillReceipt** entity type?

The solution to Exercise 3.44 has established two inclusive/exclusive $m:n$ (many-to-many relationships between the **CheckoutTillReceipt** entity type and the **ProductSoldByAFixedQuantity** and **ProductSoldByAVariableQuantity** entity subtypes as described by the entity–relationship diagram in Figure 3.28.

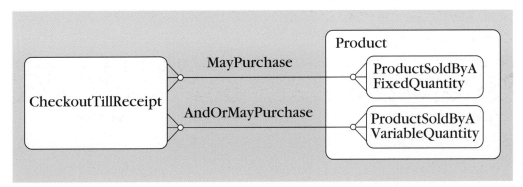

Figure 3.28

A transaction, as shown on a checkout till receipt (Figure 2.6), may involve the purchase of one or more products sold by fixed quantities and/or the purchase of one or more products sold by variable quantities. A particular product sold either by fixed or variable quantities may have been purchased as a result of one or more transactions.

EXERCISE 3.46

Why is it necessary to decompose both the **MayPurchase** and **AndOrMayPurchase** relationships?

A question that data analysts often have to ask when analysing various documents created and used by an enterprise to facilitate its day-to-day operations, is 'What exactly needs to be recorded?' The checkout till receipts in Figure 2.6 provide us with an example of the importance of considering this question when analysing documents. In Figure 2.6, each till receipt shows the order in which each item selected by the customer was passed over the barcode scanner by the checkout operator. Although no examples are shown in Figure 2.6, according to the transcript (Figure 2.9) of the interview with the checkout operator Gerda, a till receipt could display items that were cancelled either because of operator error or because the customer had insufficient funds to pay for the goods that they had brought to the checkout till.

Considering the question 'What exactly needs to be recorded?', we need to decide whether there is a requirement to record the order in which items are scanned by the checkout operator, and/or any errors and their correction, or just a requirement to record those products that are actually purchased by the customer. The former would allow us to reproduce the exact contents of the till receipt as given to the customer who purchased the goods; the latter would not. As with many decisions that a data analyst has to make when analysing the requirements of an enterprise, it will be necessary to consult the client for the basis of a decision, as the requirement has not been stated explicitly.

For the moment, however, we will assume that there is a requirement to record the order in which items are scanned by the checkout operator, but we will not concern ourselves about recording errors and their correction because we need to look at examples of till receipts first. Since the decision about what to record affects how we decompose the **MayPurchase** and **AndOrMayPurchase** relationships, we will consider the other option, which is the requirement to record just those products that are actually purchased by the customer but not the order in which they are purchased, later.

Figure 3.29 gives an entity–relationship model that represents the checkout till receipts as shown in Figure 2.6. Figure 3.30 shows the relevant part of the accompanying domain of discourse summary for Figure 3.29.

Entity–relationship diagram

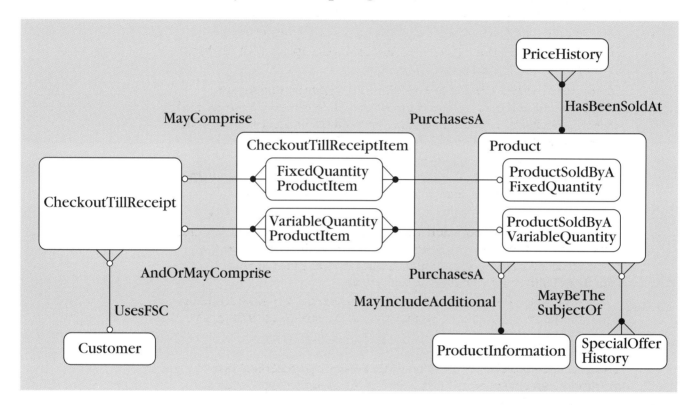

Entity types

Customer (<u>FSCNumber</u>, Title, Forenames, FamilyName, Address,
DateOfBirth, Gender, Occupation, AnnualIncome, Residence,
FurtherInformation?, ApplicationDate, CreditLimit)

CheckoutTillReceipt (<u>CheckoutTillNumber</u>, <u>Time</u>, CheckoutOperator,
MethodOfPayment, AmountTendered)

CheckoutTillReceiptItem (<u>CheckoutTillNumber</u>, <u>Time</u>, <u>ItemNumber</u>)

    FixedQuantityProductItem ( )

    VariableQuantityProductItem (Quantity)

Product (<u>ProductCode</u>, Description)

    ProductSoldByAFixedQuantity (Quantity, NumberInPack)

    ProductSoldByAVariableQuantity (PackSize)

PriceHistory (<u>ProductCode</u>, <u>Date</u>, Price)

ProductInformation (<u>Information</u>)

SpecialOfferHistory (<u>SpecialOfferCode</u>, Details, StartDate, EndDate)

Additional constraints

c.1 For each instance of the SpecialOffer entity type, the value of StartDate should be less than or equal to the value of EndDate.

c.2 PriceHistory is a weak entity type dependent on Product. So, each value of ProductCode in the entity type PriceHistory must be the same value as the ProductCode of the Product instance to which the PriceHistory is related by the relationship HasBeenSoldAt (a consequence of weak–strong entity types).

c.5 The customer should be at least 18 years old when they apply for a Frequent Shopper Card. That is, for each instance of the Customer entity type, the value of the ApplicationDate attribute should be at least 18 years greater than that of the DateofBirth attribute.

c.6 Each instance of CheckoutTillReceipt must participate in the MayComprise relationship, or the AndOrMayComprise relationship, or both.

c.7 FixedQuantityProductItem is a weak entity type dependent on CheckoutTillReceipt. So, each value pair of CheckoutTillNumber and Time in the entity type FixedQuantityProductItem must be the same value pair as the CheckoutTillNumber and Time of the CheckoutTillReceipt instance to which the FixedQuantityProductItem entity type is related by the relationship MayComprise (a consequence of weak–strong entity types).

c.8 VariableQuantityProductItem is a weak entity type dependent on CheckoutTillReceipt. So, each value pair of CheckoutTillNumber and Time in the entity type VariableQuantityProductItem must be the same value pair as the CheckoutTillNumber and Time of the CheckoutTillReceipt instance to which the VariableQuantityProductItem entity type is related by the relationship AndOrMayComprise (a consequence of weak–strong entity types).

Working assumptions

The data values held by the ProductCode and SpecialOfferCode attributes can comprise all possible permutations of eight digits, 00000000...99999999.

A particular special offer will only run for a finite period, having definite start and end dates. Hence there is justification for including the StartDate and EndDate attributes in the SpecialOffer entity type.

Limitations

None

Figure 3.29   An entity–relationship model representing the data requirements described by product labels and checkout till receipts

Entity type catalogue

Entity name:	**Customer**
Description:	A representation of the details provided by an applicant for a Frequent Shopper Card (FSC). Each occurrence represents a particular customer who may purchase products using their FSC.
Attribute details:	Each customer has an identifying FSC number, a title, forename(s), a family name, an address, a date of birth, a gender, an occupation, an annual income, a type of residence, an indicator to show whether they want further information, the date of application for an FSC, and a credit limit. FSC numbers are in the range 0000-0000-0000 to 9999-9999-9999. Titles, forenames, family names and addresses are character strings, addresses being complex data. Dates of birth and application dates are dates. Customers' genders are recorded as either Male or Female. Their occupations are Professional, Managerial, Clerical, Skilled, Unskilled or Unemployed. Their annual incomes are £10k, £10k – £20k, £20k – £30k, £30k – £40k, £40k – £50k or > £50k. Their types of residence are Owner, Tenant or Other. Whether they want to receive further information is indicated by Yes or No.
Sample data (from Figure 2.8):	<table><tr><th>FSCNumber</th><th>Title</th><th>Forenames</th><th>FamilyName</th><th>...</th></tr><tr><td>1567-2711-5223</td><td>Miss</td><td>Christie</td><td>Malakite</td><td>...</td></tr></table>

Entity name:	**CheckoutTillReceipt**
Description:	A representation of a checkout till receipt. Each occurrence represents a particular transaction between a customer and a store whereby the customer purchases particular products at a particular time.
Attribute details:	Each checkout till receipt has an identifying checkout till number and transaction time, and records the name of the checkout operator, the method of payment and the amount tendered. As the checkout till number is not included on the checkout till receipt, sample data has been provided by the client. Checkout till receipt numbers are in the range 1 to 99. Each transaction time is the date and time (hh:mm) of the transaction completed by the checkout operator. Checkout operators are characters strings. Methods of payment are Cash, Cheque, FSC (Frequent Shopper Card), Debit Card and Credit Card. Amounts tendered are sums of money.
Sample data (checkout till numbers from client and other transaction data from Figure 2.6):	<table><tr><th>Checkout TillNumber</th><th>Time</th><th>Checkout Operator</th><th>MethodOf Payment</th><th>Amount Tendered</th></tr><tr><td>1</td><td>25-May-2006 15:43</td><td>Jason</td><td>Debit Card</td><td>£ 4.14</td></tr><tr><td>2</td><td>25-May-2006 16:04</td><td>Selena</td><td>Cheque</td><td>£ 10.16</td></tr><tr><td>7</td><td>25-May-2006 16:04</td><td>Gerda</td><td>FSC</td><td>£ 10.72</td></tr><tr><td>4</td><td>27-May-2006 11:24</td><td>Anne</td><td>Cash</td><td>£ 10.00</td></tr></table>

Figure 3.30   Part of the accompanying domain of discourse summary for Figure 3.29

Entity name:	**CheckoutTillReceiptItem** (supertype)
Description:	A representation of the items listed on a checkout till receipt.
Attribute details:	Each checkout till receipt item has an identifying checkout till number, transaction time and item number. Checkout till receipt numbers are in the range 1 to 99. Each transaction time is the date and time (hh:mm) of the transaction completed by the checkout operator. Item numbers are in the range 1 to 999.

Entity name:	**FixedQuantityProductItem** (subtype)
Description:	Each occurrence represents a particular item on a particular checkout till receipt, which is a product sold by a fixed quantity (or measure).
Attribute details:	Checkout till receipt number, transaction time and item number are inherited from the supertype, **CheckoutTillReceiptItem**.

Sample data (from Figure 2.6):

CheckoutTillNumber	Time	ItemNumber
1	25-May-2006 15:43	1
1	25-May-2006 15:43	2
1	25-May-2006 15:43	3
1	25-May-2006 15:43	4
2	25-May-2006 16:04	1
2	25-May-2006 16:04	2
2	25-May-2006 16:04	3
7	25-May-2006 16:04	1
7	25-May-2006 16:04	2
7	25-May-2006 16:04	3
7	25-May-2006 16:04	4
7	25-May-2006 16:04	5
7	25-May-2006 16:04	6
4	27-May-2006 11:24	3
4	27-May-2006 11:24	4

Entity name:	**VariableQuantityProductItem** (subtype)
Description:	Each occurrence represents a particular item on a particular checkout till receipt, which is a product sold by a variable quantity (or measure).
Attribute details:	Checkout till receipt number, transaction time and item number are inherited from the supertype, **CheckoutTillReceiptItem**. The quantity of product is recorded.

Sample data (from Figure 2.6):

CheckoutTillNumber	Time	ItemNumber	Quantity
4	27-May-2006 11:24	1	0.95kg
4	27-May-2006 11:24	2	0.242kg

Figure 3.30   *continued*

Entity name:	**Product** (supertype)
Description:	A representation of the properties of products sold by Walton Stores.
Attribute details:	Each product has an identifying product code and a description. Product codes are in the range 00000000 to 99999999. Descriptions of products are character strings.

Figure 3.30   *continued*

In the entity–relationship model shown in Figure 3.29, each occurrence of the subtypes of the **CheckoutTillReceiptItem** entity type represents an item on a till receipt either as a product sold by a fixed quantity or as a product sold by a variable quantity. The quantity of a product sold by varying quantities is recorded by the **Quantity** attribute of the **VariableQuantityProductItem** entity subtype.

Since checkout till receipts record a history of purchases of products by customers, then the temporal properties of products, prices and special offers, are recorded by the entity–relationship model as shown in Figure 3.29.

The following entity–relationship model (Figure 3.31) represents the checkout till receipts shown in Figure 2.6 and satisfies the requirement to record those products that were purchased by the customer but not in the order they were scanned. Figure 3.32 gives the relevant part of the accompanying domain of discourse summary for Figure 3.31.

Entity–relationship diagram

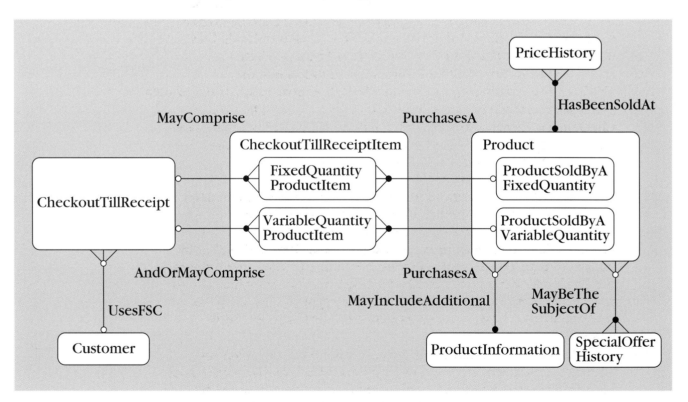

Entity types

Customer (<u>FSCNumber</u>, Title, Forenames, FamilyName, Address,
         DateOfBirth, Gender, Occupation, AnnualIncome, Residence,
         FurtherInformation?, ApplicationDate, CreditLimit)

CheckoutTillReceipt (<u>CheckoutTillNumber</u>, <u>Time</u>, CheckoutOperator,
         MethodOfPayment, AmountTendered)

CheckoutTillReceiptItem (<u>CheckoutTillNumber</u>, <u>Time</u>, <u>ProductCode</u>)
    FixedQuantityProductItem (NumberOfItems)
    VariableQuantityProductItem (TotalQuantity)

Product (<u>ProductCode</u>, Description)
    ProductSoldByAFixedQuantity (Quantity, NumberInPack)
    ProductSoldByAVariableQuantity (PackSize)

PriceHistory (<u>ProductCode</u>, <u>Date</u>, Price)

ProductInformation (<u>Information</u>)

SpecialOfferHistory (<u>SpecialOfferCode</u>, Details, StartDate, EndDate)

Additional constraints

c.1   For each instance of the SpecialOffer entity type, the value of
       StartDate should be less than or equal to the value of EndDate.

c.2   PriceHistory is a weak entity type dependent on Product. So, each
       value of ProductCode in the entity type PriceHistory must be the
       same value as the ProductCode of the Product instance to which the
       PriceHistory is related by the relationship HasBeenSoldAt (a
       consequence of weak–strong entity types).

c.5   The customer should be at least 18 years old when they apply for a
       Frequent Shopper Card. That is, for each instance of the Customer
       entity type, the value of the ApplicationDate attribute should be at
       least 18 years greater than that of the DateofBirth attribute.

c.6   Each instance of CheckoutTillReceipt must participate in the
       MayComprise relationship, or the AndOrMayComprise relationship, or both.

c.7   FixedQuantityProductItem is a weak entity type dependent on
       CheckoutTillReceipt. So, each value pair of CheckoutTillNumber and
       Time in the entity type FixedQuantityProductItem must be the same
       value pair as the CheckoutTillNumber and Time of the
       CheckoutTillReceipt instance to which the
       FixedQuantityProductItem entity type is related by the relationship
       MayComprise (a consequence of weak–strong entity types).

c.7a   FixedQuantityProductItem is a weak entity type dependent on
       ProductSoldByAFixedQuantity. So, each value of ProductNumber in
       the entity type FixedQuantityProductItem must be the same value as
       the ProductNumber of the ProductSoldByAFixedQuantity instance to
       which the FixedQuantityProductItem entity type is related by the
       relationship PurchasesA (a consequence of weak–strong entity
       types).

c.8   VariableQuantityProductItem is a weak entity type dependent on
       CheckoutTillReceipt. So, each value pair of CheckoutTillNumber and
       Time in the entity type VariableQuantityProductItem must be the
       same value pair as the CheckoutTillNumber and Time of the
       CheckoutTillReceipt instance to which the
       VariableQuantityProductItem entity type is related by the relationship
       AndOrMayComprise (a consequence of weak–strong entity types).

c.8a VariableQuantityProductItem is a weak entity type dependent on ProductSoldByAVariableQuantity. So, each value of ProductNumber in the entity type VariableQuantityProductItem must be the same value as the ProductNumber of the ProductSoldByAVariable instance to which the VariableQuantityProductItem entity type is related by the relationship PurchasesA (a consequence of weak–strong entity types).

Working assumptions

The data values held by the ProductCode attribute can comprise all possible permutations of eight digits, 00000000...99999999.

A particular special offer will only run for a finite period, having definite start and end dates. Hence there is justification for including the StartDate and EndDate attributes in the SpecialOffer entity type.

Limitation

None

Figure 3.31   An entity–relationship model representing the data requirements described by product labels and checkout till receipts where the products on the till receipt are recorded not according to the order of the scanning

---

Entity type catalogue

Entity name:	**CheckoutTillReceiptItem** (supertype)
Description:	A representation of the products on a checkout till receipt.
Attribute details:	Each checkout till receipt item has an identifying checkout till number, transaction time and product code. Checkout till receipt numbers are in the range 1 to 99. Each transaction time is the date and time (hh:mm) of the transaction completed by the checkout operator. Product codes are in the range 00000000 to 99999999.

Entity name:	**FixedQuantityProductItem** (subtype)
Description:	Each occurrence represents a particular product sold by a fixed quantity (or measure) on a particular checkout till receipt.
Attribute details:	The number of items of the particular product purchased. The number of items is in the range 1 to 99.

Sample data (from Figure 2.6):

Checkout TillNumber	Time	ProductCode	NumbersOfItems
1	25-May-2006 15:43	01015279	2
1	25-May-2006 15:43	02348187	1
1	25-May-2006 15:43	08562411	1
2	25-May-2006 16:04	01015277	1
2	25-May-2006 16:04	07214781	2
7	25-May-2006 16:04	01015279	1
7	25-May-2006 16:04	02348126	2
7	25-May-2006 16:04	07214781	1
7	25-May-2006 16:04	08562411	2
4	27-May-2006 11:24	04789217	2

Entity name:	**VariableQuantityProductItem** (subtype)			
Description:	Each occurrence represents a particular product sold by a varying quantity (or measure) on a particular checkout till receipt.			
Attribute details:	The total quantity of the particular product purchased.			
Sample data (from Figure 2.6):	Checkout TillNumber	Time	ProductCode	TotalQuantity
	4	27-May-2006 11:24	02524730	0.95kg
	4	27-May-2006 11:24	06002669	0.242kg

Figure 3.32   Part of the accompanying domain of discourse summary for Figure 3.31

In the entity–relationship model shown in Figure 3.31, each occurrence of the subtypes of the **CheckoutTillReceiptItem** entity type represents a product purchased in the transaction, which records either the numbers of the product sold by a fixed quantity, or the total quantity of a product sold by a variable quantity.

Both the entity–relationship models presented in Figures 3.29 and 3.31 represent the data and the relationships between the data described by the examples of checkout till receipts (Figure 2.6). The entity–relationship model in Figure 3.29 has the advantage that it records the order in which the items were scanned by the checkout operator and could be further developed to record the operator's errors.

Entity–relationship model for Walton Stores

We have analysed a few of the documents created and used by Walton Stores to facilitate its day-to-day operations at individual stores. An important point to note is that we have developed not just a single entity–relationship model, but several that represent the data requirements for individual stores. This is not only because we require decisions to be made by the client with respect to whether there is a requirement to record certain historical data, but also because we have seen that for a given set of data requirements more than one entity–relationship model can represent those requirements. These entity–relationship models differ with respect to how explicitly they represent the requirements and whether they offer any flexibility to extend the model in the light of new requirements.

In Figure 3.33 we present an entity–relationship model for Walton Stores based on the analysis of the documents presented in this section. It is a combination of the entity–relationship models in Figures 3.27 and 3.29.

Entity–relationship diagram

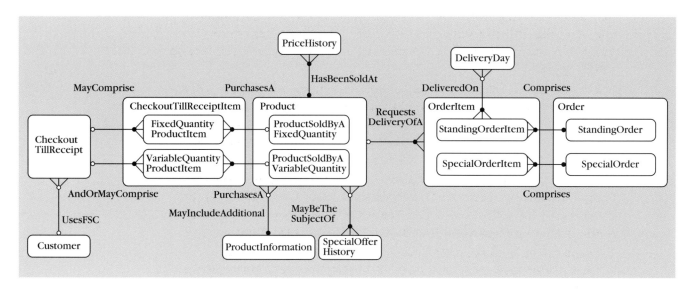

Entity types

Customer (<u>FSCNumber</u>, Title, Forenames, FamilyName, Address,
  DateOfBirth, Gender, Occupation, AnnualIncome, Residence,
  FurtherInformation?, ApplicationDate, CreditLimit)

CheckoutTillReceipt (<u>CheckoutTillNumber</u>, <u>Time</u>, CheckoutOperator,
  MethodOfPayment, AmountTendered)

CheckoutTillReceiptItem (<u>CheckoutTillNumber</u>, <u>Time</u>, <u>ItemNumber</u>)

    FixedQuantityProductItem ( )

    VariableQuantityProductItem (Quantity)

Product (<u>ProductCode</u>, Description)

    ProductSoldByAFixedQuantity (Quantity, NumberInPack)

    ProductSoldByAVariableQuantity (PackSize)

PriceHistory (<u>ProductCode</u>, <u>Date</u>, Price)

ProductInformation (<u>Information</u>)

SpecialOfferHistory (<u>SpecialOfferCode</u>, Details, StartDate, EndDate)

Order (<u>OrderNumber</u>, OrderDate)

    StandingOrder ( )

    SpecialOrder ( )

OrderItem (<u>OrderNumber</u>, <u>ItemNumber</u>, NumberOfPacks)

    StandingOrderItem (DeliveryFrequency)

    SpecialOrderItem (DeliveryDate)

DeliveryDay (<u>DeliveryDay</u>)

Additional constraints

c.1   For each instance of the SpecialOffer entity type, the value of
StartDate should be less than or equal to the value of EndDate.

c.2   PriceHistory is a weak entity type dependent on Product. So, each
value of ProductCode in the entity type PriceHistory must be the
same value as the ProductCode of the Product instance to which the
PriceHistory is related by the relationship HasBeenSoldAt (a
consequence of weak–strong entity types).

c.3 StandingOrderItem is a weak entity type dependent on StandingOrder. So, each value of OrderNumber in the entity type StandingOrderItem must be the same value as the OrderNumber of the StandingOrder instance to which the StandingOrderItem is related by the relationship Comprises (a consequence of weak–strong entity types).

c.4 SpecialOrderItem is a weak entity type dependent on SpecialOrder. So, each value of OrderNumber in the entity type SpecialOrderItem must be the same value as the OrderNumber of the SpecialOrder instance to which the SpecialOrderItem is related by the relationship Comprises (a consequence of weak–strong entity types).

c.5 The customer should be at least 18 years old when they apply for a Frequent Shopper Card. That is, for each instance of the Customer entity type, the value of the ApplicationDate attribute should be at least 18 years greater than that of the DateofBirth attribute.

c.6 Each instance of CheckoutTillReceipt must participate in the MayComprise relationship, or the AndOrMayComprise relationship, or both.

c.7 FixedQuantityProductItem is a weak entity type dependent on CheckoutTillReceipt. So, each value pair of CheckoutTillNumber and Time in the entity type FixedQuantityProductItem must be the same value pair as the CheckoutTillNumber and Time of the CheckoutTillReceipt instance to which the FixedQuantityProductItem entity type is related by the relationship MayComprise (a consequence of weak–strong entity types).

c.8 VariableQuantityProductItem is a weak entity type dependent on CheckoutTillReceipt. So, each value pair of CheckoutTillNumber and Time in the entity type VariableQuantityProductItem must be the same value pair as the CheckoutTillNumber and Time of the CheckoutTillReceipt instance to which the VariableQuantityProductItem entity type is related by the relationship AndOrMayComprise (a consequence of weak–strong entity types).

Working assumptions

The data values held by the ProductCode attribute can comprise all possible permutations of eight digits, 00000000...99999999.

A particular special offer will only run for a finite period, having definite start and end dates. Hence there is justification for including the StartDate and EndDate attributes in the SpecialOffer entity type.

Limitation

l.1 There is no requirement to record a history of changes to standing orders.

Figure 3.33 An entity–relationship model representing the data requirements described by product labels and checkout till receipts

Summary of Subsection 3.4

In this subsection, we have described an approach to analysing the various documents created and used by an enterprise to facilitate its day-to-day operations, in order to develop an entity–relationship model that represents the data requirements of that enterprise, using the guidelines we developed in Subsection 3.2. With this approach, we start with the premise that a document will be represented by an entity type in the entity–relationship model, and the contents of the document describe the properties of, or facts about, that entity type. Analysing several documents of the same type, different occurrences of the corresponding entity type, will enable us to gain a good understanding of the meaning and nature of the data associated with that entity type. The results of analysing several different documents can be pieced together, like a jigsaw, to develop an entity–relationship model that represents the data requirements of the enterprise.

Using this approach, we analyse several documents of the same type to answer the following questions about the corresponding entity type.

1   What exactly does each occurrence of the entity type actually represent?

2   What are the properties of, or facts about, the entity type?

3   For each property, is it:

> ► single or multi-valued?
>
> ► optional or mandatory?
>
> ► derivable from other properties?
>
> ► temporal? If so, do we need to record a history of changes to the values associated with the property?

4   How should each property be represented by the entity–relationship model that we are developing according to the guidelines we established in Subsection 3.2?

5   Which, if any, single-valued property or combination of single-valued properties, represented by an attribute or combination of attributes respectively, can act as an assertion of existence, a reference, and a uniqueness constraint, and so form the identifier of the entity type?

      If more than one single-valued property or combination of single-valued properties can fulfil these three roles, then which property or combination of properties should be the identifier of the entity type?

      If no one single-valued property or combination of single-valued properties can fulfil these three roles, then how can we distinguish between occurrences of the entity type?

6   For each single-valued property that is represented by an attribute:

> ► Are data values complex?
>
> ► Are they dependent on the data values of other attributes?
>
> ► What is the value set?

To help us answer these questions, we will probably also need to consult the textual descriptions of the enterprise provided by the client or produced as a result of establishing the requirements. As we answer these questions, we both develop the entity–relationship model and produce the accompanying domain of discourse summary.

3.5 Validating an entity–relationship model

An entity–relationship model represents the data requirements of an enterprise. To validate an entity–relationship model we need to demonstrate that it does in fact represent those data requirements. That is, if the entity–relationship model were to be subsequently implemented as a relational database (or by any other software artefact), would it record the data and the relationships between the data that are required by the enterprise?

There are two complementary activities that we can perform to help us demonstrate that an entity–relationship model does represent the data requirements of an enterprise.

The first activity that we can perform involves reconstituting the description of the data requirements from the entity–relationship model and the accompanying domain of discourse summary. As an entity–relationship model is a formal representation of the data requirements of an enterprise, we can translate it back into an unambiguous description of the data requirements of that enterprise by 'reading' the model with the help of the domain of discourse summary.

We 'read' the model by describing with a few concise sentences each entity type definition, each relationship on the entity–relationship diagram, and the additional constraints, assumptions and limitations sections of the entity–relationship model. We then compare this reconstituted description of the data requirements with those found in the textual descriptions of the enterprise.

The second activity that we can perform involves checking whether the data and relationships between the data are recorded by an entity–relationship model. We determine this by comparing the example occurrences of entity types and relationships given in the accompanying domain of discourse summary with those found in the various documents created and used by an enterprise to facilitate its day-to-day operations.

Activities that are designed to validate an entity–relationship model, such as those described above, are best performed independently by individuals who are unfamiliar with the enterprise because those individuals are more likely to identify any discrepancies between the entity–relationship model and the documents from which it was developed. This is because such individuals will be able to look at the enterprise untainted by any prior knowledge about it, whether or not this knowledge is correct.

In Figure 3.34, we illustrate how the first activity can be used to validate an entity–relationship model by considering a fragment of the model for the hospital as given in Figure 3.15.

Entity–relationship diagram

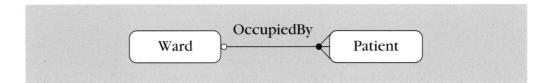

Entity types
Ward (<u>WardNo</u>, WardName, NumberOfBeds)
Patient (<u>PatientId</u>, PatientName, Gender, Height, Weight)

Additional constraints

The number of patients on a ward cannot exceed the number of beds on that ward. That is, the number of occurrences of the Patient entity type associated with a given occurrence of the Ward entity type cannot exceed the value specified by the NumberOfBeds attribute of the occurrence of that entity type.

Working assumptions

None

Limitations

Only the details of a patient's current stay in hospital are recorded (i.e. only as an in-patient with no patient history of previous admissions to the hospital).

Figure 3.34   A fragment of the entity–relationship model for the hospital as given in Figure 3.15

A reading of the definition of the **Ward** entity type could be as follows:

Each occurrence of the Ward entity type represents a particular ward that is identified by its ward number, and records the ward's name and the number of beds on that ward.

The **Patient** entity type:

Each occurrence of the Patient entity type represents a particular patient who is currently resident in the hospital and is identified by their patient identifier; their name, gender, height and weight are recorded.

The OccupiedBy relationship:

Each occurrence of the OccupiedBy relationship represents the current occupancy of a particular patient on a particular ward. A ward may be empty or occupied by one or more patients. A patient currently occupies a single ward.

The *Additional constraints* section:

The number of patients on a ward cannot exceed the number of beds on that ward.

If we compare these 'readings' with the following extract from the *Hospital scenario,*
you will see that there is a good agreement between them – all the information about
wards and patients has been recorded by the entity–relationship model shown in
Figure 3.34.

> The hospital is organised into a number of wards, each of which may
> be empty or may be occupied by one or more patients. Each ward is
> identified by a ward number; it has a name and contains a fixed
> number of beds. ...
>
> Each patient in the hospital has a patient identification number and
> name recorded; their gender, height and weight is kept on record.
> Each patient is assigned to a single ward ...

We can illustrate how the second activity can be used to validate an entity–relationship
model by comparing Figure 3.21 and the occurrences shown in Figure 3.22 with
Figure 2.4.

If you compare this entity–relationship model and the associated domain of discourse
summary with the examples of the product labels, you will see that there is a good
agreement between them – all the data and relationships between the data are all
recorded.

Although neither of these activities 'proves' that an entity–relationship model does
represent the data requirements of an enterprise, their outcomes do provide the
evidence, or otherwise, to the data analyst that their model is an adequate
representation.

3.6 Summary

This section has focused on the data analysis task, which entails all of the activities that
need to be completed before a database development can move from the information
requirements stage to the next stage of its life cycle, which is the conceptual data
model stage. Data analysis is the key task in database development as it results in a
detailed understanding of the meaning of the data and the relationships between the
data, which is expressed in the form of a conceptual data model.

In this section on the data analysis task, we have:

▶ Provided a review of the entity–relationship model and extended the notation for
the model.

▶ Developed guidelines on how we might analyse the data requirements of an
enterprise in order to develop an entity–relationship model.

▶ Described an approach to analysing textual descriptions of an enterprise, either
provided by the client or produced as a result of the requirements gathering and
analysis activity, in order to develop an entity–relationship model that represents
the data requirements of that enterprise.

▶ Described an approach to analysing the various documents created and used by
an enterprise to facilitate its day-to-day operations, in order to develop an
entity–relationship model that represents the data requirements of that enterprise.

▶ Considered briefly how we can demonstrate that an entity–relationship model is an
accurate representation of the data requirements of an enterprise.

LEARNING OUTCOMES

Having completed your study of this section of the course, you will be able to:

▶ Develop an entity–relationship model from the various documents created and used by an enterprise to facilitate its day-to-day operations, which represents the data requirements of that enterprise.

▶ Develop an entity–relationship model from textual descriptions of an enterprise, either provided by the client or produced as a result of requirements gathering and analysis, which represents the data requirements of that enterprise.

▶ Demonstrate that an entity–relationship model is an accurate representation of the data requirements of an enterprise.

4 Database design

This section focuses on the database design task, which entails all of the activities that need to be completed before a database development can move from the conceptual data model stage to the next stage of its life cycle, that is, the specification of the logical schema. The logical schema describes the table structure of a database and is commonly referred to as a **database schema**.

The aim of the database design task is to develop a **first-cut design** for a database that is a relational representation of an entity–relationship model that represents the data requirements of an enterprise, where the database tables are normalised, that is, they do not include any redundant duplication that may result in insertion, amendment and deletion anomalies. The database design task concerns primarily the direct transformation of an entity–relationship model into a database schema. The basic transformation from an entity–relationship model to a database schema is as follows:

▶ each entity type becomes a table;

▶ each attribute of that entity type becomes a column of the corresponding table;

▶ each identifying attribute of the entity type becomes a primary key column of that table;

▶ each value set of each attribute becomes the domain over which the corresponding column is defined.

In our model of database development (see *Block 1*, Figure 4.5) we postpone consideration of the operational requirements of an enterprise until the implementation task when the user processes (application software) and associated external schemas are developed. Thus, an entity–relationship model represents just the data requirements of that enterprise as the model was developed without concern about how the data and the relationships between the data will satisfy the operational requirements of the enterprise. The direct transformation of an entity–relationship model, therefore, will result in a database that will similarly represent just the data requirements.

As a consequence, a database resulting from the implementation of a first-cut design will have integrity, which is a desirable property (see Exercise 1.2), but it may subsequently prove inflexible or inefficient, or offer poor usability. As the desirable properties of a database – flexibility, efficiency and usability – cannot be assessed until after a database design has been implemented, the database populated with data, application software developed and the system tested, a first-cut design often needs to be **flexed** during the activities associated with the implementation and maintenance tasks in order to improve the quality of the database design with respect to these particular desirable properties. Figure 4.6 of *Block 1* summarised the iterative steps involved in ensuring that a database design meets the information requirements of an enterprise and can be adapted to satisfy new requirements during the implementation and maintenance tasks respectively through a series of **second-cut designs**.

Before we proceed with a description of the activities associated with the database design task, there are two important points that we need to consider. They both concern the transformation of an entity–relationship model into a logical schema and will emphasise that this transformation is not simply a mechanical process but one that will require a certain number of decisions to be made.

The first point is, as we noted in Section 1, that the complete separation of the development of a database from the user processes is an ideal scenario. In reality, there are often situations where at the database design stage how we represent certain data is dependent on how it is to be processed. A particular situation is with regard to how complex data values are recorded in a database. In Section 3, we stated that complex data values are typically represented by single attributes in an entity–relationship model. However, it is useful during the database design task to be able to establish how this data will be processed, in order to determine whether complex data needs to be recorded as a single column or several columns, or even using a separate table. In Subsection 4.3, we will consider the options for recording complex data in an SQL database to satisfy different operational requirements.

Another situation is with regard to how temporal data are recorded in a database. In Section 3, we stated that when representing historical data and historical relationships between data, we need to establish whether there is a requirement to distinguish between current and historical values, but this decision was dependent on knowing how the data is to be processed. Early decisions on how complex and historical data need to be recorded in order to satisfy the operational requirements of an enterprise will facilitate the development of user processes (application software) and associated external schemas during the implementation task.

The second point is that we have significant choices in how we transform an entity–relationship model into a logical schema. These choices arise because an entity–relationship model describes *what* the data requirements are and not *how* these requirements are to be implemented by any particular database approach. Design choices occur in the following areas.

▶ Optional single-valued properties

According to our guidelines for representing the properties of entity types by an entity–relationship model, which we developed in Section 3, an optional single-valued property that is not related to any occurrences of another entity type is represented by a :1 relationship with a *new* entity type, where the participation condition of the entity type, whose properties we are representing, with respect to this relationship is optional.

For example, in Table 3.12, the optional single-valued properties – quantity, additional information and special offer – are represented by :1 relationships with new entity types where the **Product** ends have optional participation (see Figure 3.21).

We have to represent optional single-valued properties by a new entity type because with the entity–relationship model, for each occurrence of a particular entity type, every attribute has a value, that is, an occurrence is a complete set of data values. However, in *Block 3*, Subsection 4.1, we discussed the use of the marker **NULL** in SQL to indicate the absence of a value. So, in our database design we may be able to choose either to use a table corresponding to the new entity type, or to use a column that allows **NULL** in the table corresponding to the entity type whose single-valued properties we are representing. We will elaborate on these alternatives in Subsection 4.2.

▶ Relationships

In *Block 2*, Section 2, we described two methods for representing relationally a relationship between entity types: by using a *foreign key alone approach* (which might be posted and pre-posted) or by the *relation for relationship approach*. The former method is employed to represent 1:1 and 1:*n* relationships where the entity type at the :1 or:*n* (foreign key) end has *mandatory* participation with the relationship. The latter method is employed for 1:1 and 1:*n* relationships where the entity type at the :1 or :*n* end has *optional* participation; this method is also used for *m:n* relationships. The solution to Exercise 2.34 of *Block 2* summarises the use of the methods for representing relationships of varying degree and participation conditions between two entity types.

As a consequence of SQL supporting the marker **NULL** to indicate the absence of a value, the *foreign key alone approach* can also be used in a database design to represent 1:1 and 1:*n* relationships where the entity type at the :1 or :*n* end has *optional* participation with the relationship because posted foreign key columns can be allowed to take **NULL** (see *Block 3*, Subsection 4.4). So, in our database design we may choose to represent 1:1 and 1:*n* relationships by using either the *foreign key alone approach* or the *relation for relationship approach*, but *m:n* relationships are represented only by the latter approach. We will elaborate on these alternatives in Subsection 4.2.

▶ Constraints

In *Block 3*, we described two kinds of constraint in SQL where the constraint is specified as a search condition, **check constraints** (see *Block 3*, Subsection 5.4) and **triggers** (see *Block 3*, Subsection 7.4). These constraints are comparable to a general constraint as described in *Block 2*, Subsection 4.3, but may be used also to enforce referential and domain constraints, as we will describe later. So, in our database design we may choose to represent a general constraint with either a check constraint or a trigger. We will elaborate on these alternatives in Subsection 4.4.

▶ Entity subtypes

The entity subtype concept has no direct counterpart in relational theory. Although the SQL:1999 Standard introduced the equivalent concepts of supertables and subtables, at the time of writing, many SQL implementations, including SQL Anywhere, do not support supertables and subtables. So, we will consider just how entity subtypes can be represented by conventional SQL tables.

In our database design we may choose either to represent all subtypes by a single table, or to represent each subtype by a separate table. We will consider these alternatives in Subsection 4.5.

This section has two aims: First, to provide you with a review of the transformation of an entity–relationship model into a relational representation, as initially described in *Block 2*, from the viewpoint of relational theory, then in *Block 3*, from the viewpoint of the practical realisation of relational theory by SQL. The second aim is to provide you with a detailed overview of the choices available, when transforming an entity–relationship model into a logical (database) schema for a first-cut design.

Where SQL provides alternatives for representing a particular aspect of an entity–relationship model, we will indicate the relative support for these alternatives by SQL Anywhere specifically and by other SQL implementations generally. Later, in Section 5, when we consider the implementation of the database designs that we develop in this section, we will focus on SQL Anywhere.

Table 4.1 provides a summary of the mapping between the elements of an entity–relationship model and the corresponding elements of an SQL database definition, indicating the areas where we have some choice in the representation to consider during the database design task.

Entity–relationship model	SQL database definition
entity type - entity subtype	table - table[*]
attribute - identifier - value set - complex data	column - primary key[*] - domain or check constraint[*] - column(s) or another table[*]
relationship - 1:1 and 1:n - m:n	 - foreign key alone or relation for relationship[*] - relation for relationship
constraint	check constraint or trigger[*]

Table 4.1   A summary of the mapping between the elements of an entity–relationship model and the corresponding elements of an SQL database definition. Note that an asterisk (*) indicates an area where we have some choice in the representation, which we will consider during the database design task.

4.1   Representing entity types

In the solution to Exercise 3.41 we gave the definition of the **Customer** entity type, each occurrence of which represents a customer of Walton Stores who has been issued with a Frequent Shopper Card. The entity type records the information that the customer has supplied on their application form for a Frequent Shopper Card, together with their card number and credit limit as determined by Walton Stores. Each attribute represents a mandatory single-valued property of, or fact about, the **Customer** entity type. We will use this entity type to illustrate the representation of entity types by SQL tables.

The entity–relationship model for the **Customer** entity type is given in Figure 4.1, and the value set and other characteristics of the data values associated with each attribute of this entity type are shown in Table 4.2.

Entity–relationship diagram

Entity types

Customer (FSCNumber, Title, Forename, FamilyName, Address,
          DateOfBirth, Gender, Occupation, AnnualIncome, Residence,
          FurtherInformation, ApplicationDate, CreditLimit)

Additional constraints

c.5   The customer should be at least 18 years old when they apply for a Frequent Shopper Card. That is, for each instance of the Customer entity type, the value of the ApplicationDate attribute should be at least 18 years greater than that of the DateOfBirth attribute.

Working assumptions

None

Limitations

1.1   Only a customer's current details are recorded.

Figure 4.1   The entity–relationship model for the Customer entity type (from the solution to Exercise 3.41)

Customer entity type

Attribute	Value set	Characteristics
Title	{character strings}	
Forename	{character strings}	
FamilyName	{character strings}	
Address	{character strings}	complex
DateOfBirth	{dates}	dependency: the application date should be at least 18 years greater than the date of birth (c.1).
Gender	{Male, Female}	
Occupation	{Professional, Managerial, Clerical, Skilled, Unskilled, Unemployed}	
AnnualIncome	{< £10k, £10k – £20k, £20k – £30k, £30k – £40k, £40k – £50k, > £50k}	
Residence	{Owner, Tenant, Other}	
FurtherInformation?	{Yes, No}	
ApplicationDate	{dates}	dependency: the application date should be at least 18 years greater than the date of birth (c.1).
CreditLimit	{money}	
FSCNumber	{nnnn-nnnn-nnnn}	identifier

Table 4.2   The value set and other characteristics of the data values associated with each attribute of the Customer entity type

As given in Table 4.1, the basic transformation from an entity–relationship model to an SQL database definition is as follows:

▶ each entity type becomes a table;

▶ each attribute of that entity type becomes a column of the corresponding table;

▶ each identifying attribute of the entity type becomes a primary key column of that table;

▶ each value set of an attribute becomes the domain over which the corresponding column is defined.

Figure 4.2 shows a database schema diagram for a database design that represents the properties of the **Customer** entity type as given in Figure 4.1. A **database schema diagram** describes the table structure of a database design by using a table–relationship diagram and a list of table definitions where the foreign keys (both posted and pre-posted) are shown in italics. The table–relationship diagram uses the same notation as an entity–relationship diagram except that a table is denoted by a rectangle. We will use a database schema diagram primarily to describe how relationships are to be represented in a database design.

```
                              ┌─────────────┐
                              │  Customer   │
                              └─────────────┘

   customer (fsc_number, title, forename, family_name,
             address, date_of_birth, gender, occupation,
             annual_income, residence, further_information,
             application_date, credit_limit)
```

Figure 4.2 A database schema diagram for a database design that represents the properties of the **Customer** entity type

Figures 4.1 and 4.2 follow the naming conventions used throughout this course for entity–relationship models and SQL database definitions, respectively. So, for example, during the transformation from the **Customer** entity type to the `customer` table, the **FamilyName** attribute becomes the `family_name` column.

Figure 4.3 gives an outline SQL definition of the `customer` table, which represents the **Customer** entity type and illustrates the basic transformation from an entity–relationship model to an SQL data definition. It is an incomplete definition (the missing elements are indicated by ...) because the value sets shown in Table 4.2 have not been represented by appropriate column data types. We have not considered how the complex data values associated with the **Address** attribute should be recorded to facilitate the operational requirements of Walton Stores, nor have we considered how the condition c.1 specified in the *Additional constraint* section should be represented. Note, however, that each column is defined as being **NOT NULL** because it represents a *mandatory* single-valued property of the **Customer** entity type (see the solution to Exercise 3.41).

```
    CREATE TABLE customer
        (fsc_number ... NOT NULL,
         title ... NOT NULL,
         forename ... NOT NULL,
         family_name ... NOT NULL,
         address ... NOT NULL,
         date_of_birth ... NOT NULL,
         gender ... NOT NULL,
         occupation ... NOT NULL,
         annual_income ... NOT NULL,
         residence ... NOT NULL,
         further_information ... NOT NULL,
         application_date ... NOT NULL,
         credit_limit ... NOT NULL,
        PRIMARY KEY (fsc_number),
         ...
        )
```

Figure 4.3 An outline SQL definition of the `customer` table

In this course, we specify a database schema for a database design by using a database schema diagram (Figure 4.2) and the SQL data definition language (DDL) statements that are required to implement the database design (Figure 4.3).

Column names

We have noted the naming conventions used throughout this course for entity–relationship models and SQL database definitions. Although we have not stipulated how we should name attributes of an entity–relationship model, other than that each word (noun or noun-phrase) comprising the name of an attribute should start with a capital letter, some care is needed when naming columns of a table, for two main reasons.

The first reason is that SQL has a number of reserved words, notably **DATE** and **TIME**, which may conflict with intended column names. A list of SQL Anywhere reserved words can be found in the Sybase online book: *ASA SQL Reference, Part I SQL, Chapter 1, SQL Language Elements.*

The second reason is related to the way the SQL **natural join** works, which was described in *Block 3*, Subsection 2.4. When a **NATURAL JOIN** keyword is specified in a **FROM** clause of a **SELECT** statement, it performs a natural join on the two tables specified by this keyword by matching the values of any column or columns that have the same name in both tables (and that are defined over the same SQL data type). So, in our database design, if we have two (or more) tables with columns that have the same name, we should always check carefully to determine whether it makes sense for these commonly named columns to be joined (possibly inadvertently) by an SQL natural join. If not, we should rename the columns to ensure that they have unique names across the database schema. We can effect this simply by prefixing the column name with the name of the table in which the column is defined.

Domains

In the transformation from an entity–relationship model to an SQL database definition, the value set of each attribute becomes the domain that the corresponding column is defined over. In *Block 3*, Subsection 5.5, we described a domain as having two components: the underlying SQL data type and, if necessary, a constraint that restricts the range of values that are possible for that chosen SQL data type.

Some of the SQL predefined data types are given in Figure 2.3 of *Block 3*, and some of the implementation details for the other data types in SQL Anywhere are given in Figure 2.4. A more detailed account of the data types supported by SQL Anywhere, including conformance with particular SQL standards and vendor extensions, can be found in the Sybase online book: *ASA SQL Reference, Part I SQL, Chapter 2, SQL Data Types.*

EXERCISE 4.1

Using the information provided in Table 4.2 and Figure 2.7, suggest suitable SQL data types for the columns of the outline definition of the **customer** table shown in Figure 4.3, which you might use to implement the table with SQL Anywhere. Assume for the moment that the customers' addresses will be represented by a single column in the **customer** table (as shown in Figure 4.3).

In the solution to Exercise 4.1 we have simply chosen the underlying SQL data type that allows us to record the data in the format that it was presented on the Frequent Shopper Card application form. During the database design task, we may choose to transform the data values of a particular column of a table to another value set in order to minimise the storage requirements. For example, the **occupation** column in the solution to Exercise 4.1 takes the values *Professional*, *Managerial*, *Clerical*, *Skilled*, *Unskilled* and *Unemployed*, which requires 12 bytes of storage as the underlying SQL data type is **VARCHAR(12)**. By storing customers' occupations as a series of categorical values where, for example, the value 1 represents *Professional*, 2 represents *Managerial*, and so on, the underlying SQL data type would be **SMALLINT**, which would require only 2 bytes of storage (see *Block 3*, Figure 2.4).

The above transformation of data values results in a significant saving in the storage requirements for recording customers' occupations if the **customer** table has many rows. However, the semantics of the data will be lost unless the database also records the meaning of the devised occupation codes (1, 2, ...). Figure 4.4 gives a database schema diagram for a database design that would record the mapping between the devised occupation codes and customers' occupations.

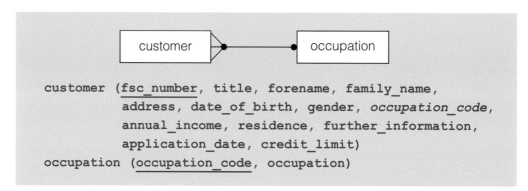

```
customer (fsc_number, title, forename, family_name,
          address, date_of_birth, gender, occupation_code,
          annual_income, residence, further_information,
          application_date, credit_limit)
occupation (occupation_code, occupation)
```

Figure 4.4   A database schema diagram for the relational representation of the Customer entity type

In Figure 4.4, the **customer** table records the devised occupation codes instead of the customers' occupations. The **occupation_code** column of the **customer** table is a foreign key (shown in italics) referencing the primary key of the **occupation** table, which records the mapping between the devised occupation codes and the customers' occupations.

Throughout Section 4, in our database designs we will continue to record the data values as presented by the various documents created and used by Walton Stores to facilitate its day-to-day operations. That is, we will not be looking for opportunities to make savings in the storage requirements of the database tables.

Having determined the appropriate underlying SQL data type for a particular column, if necessary, we can restrict the range of values possible for that chosen SQL data type by using an appropriate check constraint.

EXERCISE 4.2

For each column of the **customer** table shown in Figure 4.3, state whether the range of values possible for the underlying SQL data type chosen in the solution to Exercise 4.1 will need to be restricted and, if so, state whether the restriction is to a particular data format or to specified data values. For example, the **fsc_number** column with the underlying SQL data type of **CHAR(14)** should be restricted to a particular data format, {nnnn-nnnn-nnnn} (see Figure 2.8), and the **further_information** column with the underlying SQL data type of **VARCHAR(3)** should be restricted to the specified data values of *Yes* and *No*.

Having determined the underlying SQL data type for each column of the **customer** table and whether the range of values possible for that data type needs to be restricted to a particular data format or to specified data values, we can now define the appropriate SQL domain for each column. As described in *Block 3*, Subsection 5.5, an SQL domain is defined using a **CREATE DOMAIN** statement.

Figure 4.5 illustrates how SQL domains may be defined using standard SQL for the **title**, **occupation** and **fsc_number** columns of the **customer** table, and how these domains are used in the definition of this table.

```
CREATE DOMAIN titles AS VARCHAR(4)
CREATE DOMAIN occupations AS VARCHAR(12)
   CHECK (VALUE IN ('Professional', 'Managerial', 'Clerical',
                    'Skilled', 'Unskilled', 'Unemployed'))
CREATE DOMAIN fsc_numbers AS VARCHAR(14)
   CHECK ((CHAR_LENGTH(VALUE) = 14) AND
          ((CAST(SUBSTRING(VALUE FROM 1 FOR 4))
            AS INTEGER) BETWEEN 0 AND 9999) AND
           (SUBSTRING(VALUE FROM 5 FOR 1) = '-') AND
          ((CAST(SUBSTRING(VALUE FROM 6 FOR 4))
            AS INTEGER) BETWEEN 0 AND 9999) AND
           (SUBSTRING(VALUE FROM 10 FOR 1) = '-') AND
          ((CAST(SUBSTRING(VALUE FROM 11 FOR 4))
            AS INTEGER) BETWEEN 0 AND 9999)
          )
CREATE TABLE customer
   (fsc_number fsc_numbers NOT NULL,
    title titles NOT NULL,
    ...
    occupation occupations NOT NULL,
    ...
   )
```

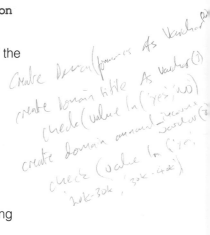

Figure 4.5   Illustrating how SQL domains may be defined for the **title**, **occupation** and **fsc_number** columns of the **customer** table, and used in the table definition

In Figure 4.5, we have adopted the convention of naming a domain as the plural of the column name.

In the definition of the **fsc_numbers** domain given in Figure 4.5, we have used a search condition of the following form:

```
((CAST( ... VALUE ... ) AS INTEGER) BETWEEN 0 AND 9999)
```

rather than

```
(( ... VALUE ... ) BETWEEN '0000' AND '9999')
```

because the latter will also evaluate to TRUE for any 4-character alphanumeric string starting with a digit, example the string '0ABC'.

EXERCISE 4.3

Figure 4.5 illustrates how SQL domains may be defined using standard SQL for certain columns of the **customer** table. Define domains for all the columns of the **customer** table so that the table could be implemented with SQL Anywhere. Assume that customers' credit limits are in the range £1,000 to £10,000.

Although an SQL domain provides a convenient means of establishing a global definition of a value set through a user-defined data type, as we noted in *Block 3*, Subsection 5.5, unlike SQL Anywhere, many SQL implementations do not support domains. So, before completing this section on SQL domains we need to consider how we might represent a value set with an SQL implementation that does not support domains.

Figures 4.6 and 4.7 show respectively the representation of the value set for the customers' genders using an SQL domain and the alternative of a table constraint.

```
CREATE DOMAIN genders AS VARCHAR(6)
   CHECK (VALUE IN ('Male', 'Female'))
CREATE TABLE customer
   ( ...
      gender genders NOT NULL,
      ...
   )
```

Figure 4.6   The representation of the value set for customers' genders using an SQL domain defined for the `gender` column of the `customer` table

```
CREATE TABLE customer
   ( ...
      gender VARCHAR(6) NOT NULL,
      ...
      CONSTRAINT genders
         CHECK (gender IN ('Male', 'Female'))
   )
```

Figure 4.7   The representation of the value set for customers' genders using a table constraint defined for the `gender` column of the `customer` table

The disadvantage of using a table constraint to define a value set, as in Figure 4.7, is that the combination of an SQL data type and check constraint has to be duplicated for every column that should be defined over the same value set. As with every form of duplication, there is always the risk that when a definition needs revising not every copy will be amended.

The definition of the `customer` table given in the solution to Exercise 4.3 is nearly a complete one. We will consider the options for recording the customers' addresses in Subsection 4.3, and the representation of the condition c.1 in Subsection 4.4.

Normalised tables

We stated in the introduction to this section on the database design task that an aim of the task was to ensure that the database tables are normalised; that is, they do not include any redundant duplication that may result in insertion, amendment and deletion anomalies. Following the approach to developing an entity–relationship model to represent the data requirements of an enterprise that we described in Section 3 should result in a model that does not include any duplicated data. Thus the database tables of a first-cut design that results from the direct transformation of that entity–relationship model should already be normalised. However, we should check that the database tables of a first-cut design are normalised.

In *Block 2*, Subsection 5.5, we described the highest normal form considered in this course, Boyce–Codd Normal Form (BCNF). As we noted, BCNF neither eliminates all redundancies nor precludes insertion or deletion anomalies. However, these situations are very rare and are unlikely to arise when following our approach to developing an entity–relationship model to represent the data requirements of an enterprise (as described in Section 3). So, for practical purposes, we can define a normalised table as one being in BCNF.

In Subsection 5.5 of *Block 2*, we defined this normal form as follows:

> A relation is in BCNF if, and only if, each irreducible determinant of a non-trivial functional dependency (FD) is a candidate key.

As a database table is the practical realisation of a relation in relational theory, BCNF (and other normal forms) is also applicable to database tables. A less rigorous definition of BCNF in the context of database tables is as follows:

> The value of each non-candidate key column of a row of a table is solely dependent on the value(s) of the candidate key column(s) of that row, where the candidate key is the primary key of that table or any other column that is the subject of a uniqueness constraint (alternate key).

To verify that a database table is in BCNF, we need to check that the values of each non-candidate key column are not determined by any other non-candidate key column and, in the case of a composite candidate key, by any individual column that comprises that candidate key. We can accomplish this by reviewing the semantics of the entity type that the table represents and/or inspecting the values included in the domain of discourse summary.

If a database table is not in BCNF then it may be necessary to normalise that table as described in *Block 2*, Section 5, for relations. However, if insertion, amendment and deletion anomalies are unlikely to arise either because the table has not been updated since it was initially populated or because the rows have not been updated since they were inserted, the table does not need to be normalised.

The **customer** table, described in Figure 4.2, would not be in BCNF if a customer's initial credit limit (**credit_limit** column) was determined solely by the information supplied on the Frequent Shopper Card application form (other non-primary key columns). However, as a customer's credit limit is likely to vary according to their use of the credit facilities provided by the card, the **customer** table will be in BCNF because the values of each non-primary key column are not determined by any other non-candidate key column.

4.2　Representing relationships

In a relational database, a relationship between two tables is represented by both tables having one or more columns in common. That is, the columns have the same meaning in both tables and are defined over the same domains. These columns may correspond to the attributes of the entity types that the tables represent, or have been added (posted) to a table to enable the relationship to be established. In this section, we will review the mechanism that you first encountered in *Block 2* for representing relationships and their properties – name, degree and participation conditions – and compare the different options we have for representing relationships and their properties, which we can choose during the database design task.

Figure 4.8 shows a fragment of the entity–relationship model representing the data requirements as described by the checkout till receipts that are used by Walton Stores. The entity–relationship model is a simplified version of the model shown in Figure 3.29 that does not use entity subtypes. As a consequence, the conditions c.7 and c.8 are combined as c.7&8. In Figure 4.8, for reasons of brevity, we have only shown the identifying attributes in the definitions of the entity types.

Entity–relationship diagram

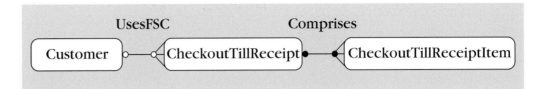

Entity types

Customer (<u>FSCNumber</u>, ...)

CheckoutTillReceipt (<u>CheckoutTillNumber</u>, <u>Time</u>, ...)

CheckoutTillReceiptItem (<u>CheckoutTillNumber</u>, <u>Time</u>, <u>ItemNumber</u>)

Additional constraints

c.5   The customer should be at least 18 years old when they apply for a Frequent Shopper Card. That is, for each instance of the Customer entity type, the value of the ApplicationDate attribute should be at least 18 years greater than that of the DateOfBirth attribute.

c.7&8   CheckoutTillReceiptItem is a weak entity type dependent on CheckoutTillReceipt. So, each pair of (CheckoutTillNumber, Time) values in the entity type CheckoutTillReceiptItem must be the same pair of values as the (CheckoutTillNumber, Time) of the CheckoutTillReceipt instance to which the CheckoutTillReceiptItem is related by the relationship Comprises (a consequence of weak–strong entity types).

Working assumption

None

Limitation

None

Figure 4.8   A fragment of an entity–relationship model representing the data requirements described by the checkout till receipts used by Walton Stores

Figure 4.9 shows some valid occurrences of the entity types and relationships between those entity types defined in Figure 4.8. These occurrences were included in the domain of discourse summary (Figure 3.30) that accompanied the entity–relationship model representing the data requirements described by the checkout till receipts and product labels (Figure 3.29).

In *Block 2*, Section 2, we described two methods for representing relationally a relationship between entity types, either by using a *foreign key alone approach* (which might be posted and pre-posted) or by the *relation for relationship approach*. The *foreign key alone approach* was employed to represent 1:1 and 1:*n* relationships where the entity type at the :1 or :*n* (foreign key) end has *mandatory* participation with the relationship; the *relation for relationship approach* for 1:1 and 1:*n* relationships where the entity type at the :1 or :*n* end has *optional* participation, and for *m*:*n* relationships.

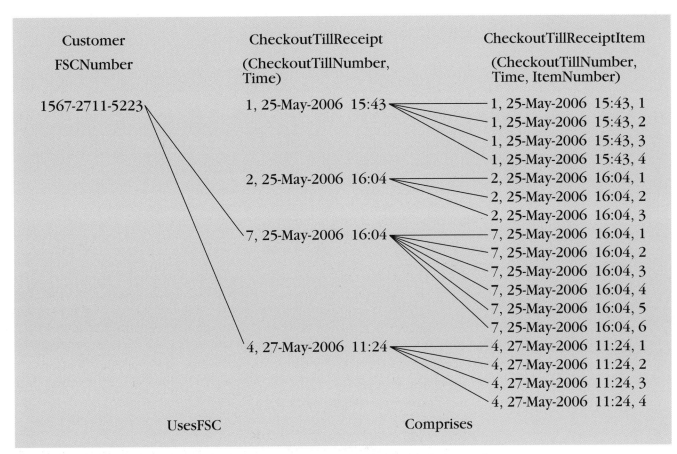

Figure 4.9   Some valid occurrences of the entity types and relationship between those entity types defined in Figure 4.8

As a consequence of SQL supporting the marker **NULL** to indicate the absence of a value, the *foreign key alone approach* can also be used in a database design to represent 1:1 and 1:*n* relationships where the entity type at the :1 or :*n* end has *optional* participation with the relationship because posted foreign key columns can be allowed to take **NULL** (see *Block 3*, Subsection 4.4). So, in our database design we may choose to represent 1:1 and 1:*n* relationships either by using a *foreign key alone approach* or by the *relation for relationship approach*; for *m*:*n* relationships, only the latter approach is used.

In this subsection, we will compare and contrast the two approaches, the *foreign key alone* and the *relation for relationship*, for representing a relationship by considering different database designs for the entity–relationship model shown in Figure 4.8.

Foreign key alone approach

Figure 4.10 shows a database schema diagram for a database design that represents the entity–relationship model as shown in Figure 4.8, using the *foreign key alone approach*.

```
customer (fsc_number, … )
checkout_till_receipt (checkout_till_number, checkout_time, … ,
                       fsc_number)
checkout_till_receipt_item (checkout_till_number,
                            checkout_time, item_number, … )
```

Figure 4.10   A database schema diagram of a database design for the
entity–relationship model shown in Figure 4.8, using the *foreign key alone approach*

In Figure 4.10, the foreign keys are indicated by the column names being italicised.
Since **TIME** is a reserved word in SQL, we have named the **time** attributes of the
CheckoutTillReceipt and **CheckoutTillRecipeItem** entity types, **checkout_time** in
the corresponding tables.

Figure 4.11 shows an outline SQL definition of the database schema diagram given in
Figure 4.10. Although each column in Figure 4.11 is defined using an SQL domain, for
reasons of brevity, the definitions of these domains have not been included.

```
CREATE TABLE customer
   (fsc_number fsc_numbers NOT NULL,
    ... ,
   PRIMARY KEY (fsc_number),
    ...
   )
CREATE TABLE checkout_till_receipt
   (checkout_till_number checkout_till_numbers NOT NULL,
    checkout_time checkout_times NOT NULL,
    fsc_number fsc_numbers,
    ... ,
   PRIMARY KEY (checkout_till_number, checkout_time),
   CONSTRAINT relationship_uses_fsc
     FOREIGN KEY (fsc_number) REFERENCES customer
   )
CREATE TABLE checkout_till_receipt_item
   (checkout_till_number checkout_till_numbers NOT NULL,
    checkout_time checkout_times NOT NULL,
    item_number item_numbers NOT NULL,
    ... ,
   PRIMARY KEY (checkout_till_number, checkout_time, item_number),
   CONSTRAINT relationship_comprises
     FOREIGN KEY (checkout_till_number, checkout_time)
     REFERENCES checkout_till_receipt
   )
```

Figure 4.11   An outline SQL definition of the database schema diagram given
in Figure 4.10

Figure 4.12 shows some valid rows of the tables of the database design given in
Figure 4.10 and defined in Figure 4.11. These rows correspond to some of the
occurrences of the entity types and the relationships between those entity types as
shown in Figure 4.9.

`customer`

fsc_number	...
1567-2711-5223	...

`checkout_till_receipt`

checkout_till _number	checkout_time	fsc_number	...
1	25-May-2006 15:43	NULL	...
2	25-May-2006 16:04	NULL	...
7	25-May-2006 16:04	1567-2711-5223	...
4	27-May-2006 11:24	1567-2711-5223	...

`checkout_till_receipt_item`

checkout_till _number	checkout_time	item_number	...
1	25-May-2006 15:43	1	...
1	25-May-2006 15:43	2	...
1	25-May-2006 15:43	3	...
1	25-May-2006 15:43	4	...
2	25-May-2006 16:04	1	...
2	25-May-2006 16:04	2	...
2	25-May-2006 16:04	3	...
7	25-May-2006 16:04	1	...
7	25-May-2006 16:04	2	...
7	25-May-2006 16:04	3	...
7	25-May-2006 16:04	4	...
4	27-May-2006 11:24	1	...
4	27-May-2006 11:24	2	...
4	27-May-2006 11:24	3	...
4	27-May-2006 11:24	4	...

Figure 4.12   Some valid rows of the tables of the database design given in Figure 4.10 and defined in Figure 4.11

Comprises relationship

The 1:n relationship between the **CheckoutTillReceipt** and **CheckoutTillReceiptItem** entity types, **Comprises**, is represented relationally in Figures 4.10 and 4.11 by the corresponding tables, `checkout_till_receipt` and `checkout_till_receipt_item`, having two columns, `checkout_till_number` and `checkout_time`, in common. The pair of `checkout_till_number` and `checkout_time` columns of the `checkout_till_receipt_item` table at the :n end of the relationship is declared as a foreign key referencing the primary key columns, `checkout_till_number` and `checkout_time`, of the `checkout_till_receipt` table at the :1 end of the relationship. Each of the `checkout_till_number` and `checkout_time` columns is defined over the same domains in both tables (see Figure 4.11).

Note that it is the fact that the two tables, `checkout_till_receipt` and `checkout_till_receipt_item`, have columns, `checkout_till_number` and `checkout_time`, with the same meaning in both tables that are defined over the same domains, which represents the **Comprises** relationship; and not that the columns simply have the same names. We have adopted the naming convention whereby related primary and foreign key columns are given the same names (where possible), which will facilitate the use of the SQL natural join to realise the relationship.

In *Block 3*, Subsection 4.4, we gave the definition of a foreign key as:

> A foreign key is a column (or collection of columns) in a table, T2, whose values match those of a candidate key of some other table, T1 (where T1 and T2 are not necessarily distinct).

If we rewrite this definition specifically for the representation of the **Comprises** relationship given in Figures 4.10 and 4.11, we will get the following definition:

> The foreign key columns `checkout_till_number` and `checkout_time` in the table `checkout_till_receipt_item` match the values of the primary key columns `checkout_till_number` and `checkout_time` of the table `checkout_till_receipt`.

Compare this definition with the definition of the condition c.7&8 in the *Additional constraints* section of the corresponding entity–relationship model that is given in Figure 4.8:

> c.7&8   CheckoutTillReceiptItem is a weak entity type dependent on CheckoutTillReceipt. So, each pair of (CheckoutTillNumber, Time) values in the entity type CheckoutTillReceiptItem must be the same pair of values as the (CheckoutTillNumber, Time) of the CheckoutTillReceipt instance to which the CheckoutTillReceiptItem is related by the relationship Comprises (a consequence of weak–strong entity types).

These two definitions are comparable. So, a foreign key declaration in the table at the :*n* end of a 1:*n* relationship not only represents this relationship but also represents any condition that defines the corresponding entity type as a weak entity type with respect to that relationship.

In Figure 4.8, the **CheckoutTillReceiptItem** entity type has mandatory participation with respect to the **Comprises** relationship. Mandatory participation of a table at the :*n* end of a 1:*n* relationship is represented by not allowing the foreign key column, or columns, representing that relationship to be **NULL**. In Figures 4.10 and 4.11, the foreign key columns of the `checkout_till_receipt_item` table representing the **Comprises** relationship, `checkout_till_number` and `checkout_time`, cannot be **NULL** because they also form part of the primary key of that table, and the entity integrity rule states that no column that forms part of the primary key may be **NULL**.

We will consider how to represent the participation conditions of the table at the :1 end of a 1:*n* relationship with that table later in this section.

UsesFSC relationship

The 1:*n* relationship between the **Customer** and **CheckoutTillReceipt** entity types, **UsesFSC**, is represented relationally in Figures 4.10 and 4.11 by the corresponding tables, `customer` and `checkout_till_receipt`, having one column, `fsc_number`, in common. The `fsc_number` column has been added (posted) to the `checkout_till_receipt` table, which is the :*n* end of the relationship, and is declared as a foreign key referencing the primary key column, `fsc_number`, of the `customer` table at the :1 end of the relationship. The `fsc_number` column is defined over the same domain in both tables (see Figure 4.11).

In Figure 4.8, the **CheckoutTillReceipt** entity type has optional participation with respect to the **UsesFSC** relationship. Optional participation of a table at the :*n* end of a 1:*n* relationship is represented by allowing the foreign key column, or columns, representing that relationship to be **NULL**. In Figures 4.10 and 4.11, the foreign key column of the `checkout_till_receipt` table representing the **UsesFSC** relationship, `fsc_number`, can be **NULL** because in Figure 4.11 the **NOT NULL** keyword has not been included in the definition of the `fsc_number` column.

In Figure 4.12, you will see that in the first two rows of the `checkout_till_receipt` table the `fsc_number` column is **NULL** because the customers did not use a Frequent Shopper Card, so no card number is recorded.

Relation for relationship approach

Figure 4.13 gives a database schema diagram for a database design that represents the entity–relationship model shown in Figure 4.8 using the relation for relationship approach.

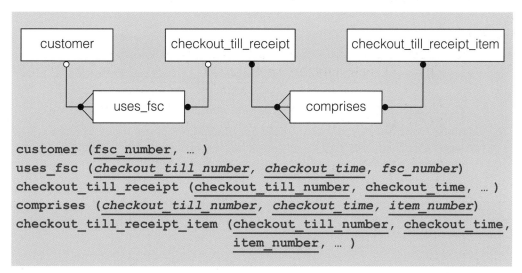

Figure 4.13   A database schema diagram for a database design that represents the entity–relationship model shown in Figure 4.8 using the *relation for relationship approach*

In Figure 4.13, each relationship that is shown in Figure 4.8 is represented by a table that is named after that relationship. By convention, we do not name the new relationships that arise when employing the *relation for relationship approach*.

Figure 4.14 shows an outline SQL definition of the database schema diagram given in Figure 4.13. Although each column in Figure 4.14 is defined using an SQL domain, for reasons of brevity, the definitions of these domains have not been included.

```
CREATE TABLE customer
  (fsc_number fsc_numbers NOT NULL,
   ... ,
  PRIMARY KEY (fsc_number),
   ...
  )
CREATE TABLE uses_fsc
  (checkout_till_number checkout_till_numbers NOT NULL,
   checkout_time checkout_times NOT NULL,
   fsc_number fsc_numbers NOT NULL,
  PRIMARY KEY (checkout_till_number, checkout_time),
  CONSTRAINT customer_in_uses_fsc
    FOREIGN KEY (fsc_number) REFERENCES customer,
  CONSTRAINT checkout_till_receipt_in_uses_fsc
    FOREIGN KEY (checkout_till_number, checkout_time)
    REFERENCES checkout_till_receipt
  )
CREATE TABLE checkout_till_receipt
  (checkout_till_number checkout_till_numbers NOT NULL,
   checkout_time checkout_times NOT NULL,
   ... ,
  PRIMARY KEY (checkout_till_number, checkout_time),
   ...
  )
CREATE TABLE comprises
  (checkout_till_number checkout_till_numbers NOT NULL,
   checkout_time checkout_times NOT NULL,
   item_number item_numbers NOT NULL,
  PRIMARY KEY (checkout_till_number, checkout_time, item_number),
  CONSTRAINT checkout_till_receipt_in_comprises
    FOREIGN KEY (checkout_till_number, checkout_time)
    REFERENCES checkout_till_receipt,
  CONSTRAINT checkout_till_receipt_item_in_comprises
    FOREIGN KEY (checkout_till_number, checkout_time, item_number)
    REFERENCES checkout_till_receipt_item
  )
CREATE TABLE checkout_till_receipt_item
  (checkout_till_number checkout_till_numbers NOT NULL,
   checkout_time checkout_times NOT NULL,
   item_number item_numbers NOT NULL,
   ... ,
  PRIMARY KEY (checkout_till_number, checkout_time, item_number),
   ...
  )
```

Figure 4.14   An outline SQL definition of the database schema diagram given in Figure 4.13

Figure 4.15 shows some valid rows of the tables of the database design that is given in Figure 4.13 and defined in Figure 4.14. These rows correspond to some of the occurrences of the entity types and relationships between those entity types as shown in Figure 4.9.

checkout_till_receipt_item

checkout_till _number	checkout_time	item_ number	...
1	25-May-2006 15:43	1	...
1	25-May-2006 15:43	2	...
1	25-May-2006 15:43	3	...
1	25-May-2006 15:43	4	...
2	25-May-2006 16:04	1	...
2	25-May-2006 16:04	2	...
2	25-May-2006 16:04	3	...
7	25-May-2006 16:04	1	...
7	25-May-2006 16:04	2	...
7	25-May-2006 16:04	3	...
7	25-May-2006 16:04	4	...
4	27-May-2006 11:24	1	...
4	27-May-2006 11:24	2	...
4	27-May-2006 11:24	3	...
4	27-May-2006 11:24	4	...

customer

fsc_number	...
1567-2711-5223	...

checkout_till_receipt

checkout_till _number	checkout_time	...
1	25-May-2006 15:43	...
2	25-May-2006 16:04	...
7	25-May-2006 16:04	...
4	27-May-2006 11:24	...

comprises

checkout_till _number	checkout_time	item_ number
1	25-May-2006 15:43	1
1	25-May-2006 15:43	2
1	25-May-2006 15:43	3
1	25-May-2006 15:43	4
2	25-May-2006 16:04	1
2	25-May-2006 16:04	2
2	25-May-2006 16:04	3
7	25-May-2006 16:04	1
7	25-May-2006 16:04	2
7	25-May-2006 16:04	3
7	25-May-2006 16:04	4
4	27-May-2006 11:24	1
4	27-May-2006 11:24	2
4	27-May-2006 11:24	3
4	27-May-2006 11:24	4

uses_fsc

checkout_till _number	checkout_time	fsc_number
7	25-May-2006 16:04	1567-2711-5223
4	27-May-2006 11:24	1567-2711-5223

Figure 4.15   Some valid rows of the tables of the database design given in Figure 4.13 and defined in Figure 4.14

Comprises relationship

The 1:*n* relationship between the **CheckoutTillReceipt** and **CheckoutTillReceiptItem** entity types, **Comprises**, is represented relationally in Figures 4.13 and 4.14 by the `comprises` table. Each occurrence of the **Comprises** relationship is recorded by a row of the `comprises` table (see Figure 4.15). Thus its primary key, `(checkout_till_number, checkout_time, item_number)`, will be the same as the primary key of the table at the :*n* end of the original **Comprises** relationship, `checkout_till_receipt_item`, and there will be a 1:1 relationship between the `comprises` and `checkout_till_receipt_item` tables (because they have the same primary key).

In the definition of the `comprises` table given in Figures 4.13 and 4.14, the columns `(checkout_till_number, checkout_time)` form a foreign key referencing the `checkout_till_receipt` table, and the columns `(checkout_till_number, checkout_time, item_number)` form a foreign key referencing the `checkout_till_receipt_item` table. Since these columns are part of the primary key of the `comprises` table, and hence cannot be **NULL**, the `comprises` table has mandatory participation with the relationships with the `checkout_till_receipt` and `checkout_till_receipt_item` tables.

We will consider how to represent the participation conditions of the table at the :1 end of a 1:1 or 1:*n* relationship with that table later in this section.

UsesFSC relationship

The 1:*n* relationship between the **Customer** and **CheckoutTillReceipt** entity types, **UsesFSC**, is represented relationally in Figures 4.13 and 4.14 by the `uses_fsc` table. Each occurrence of the **UsesFSC** relationship is recorded by a row of the `uses_fsc` table (see Figure 4.15). Thus, its primary key, `(checkout_till_number, checkout_time)`, will be the same as the primary key of the table at the :*n* end of the original **UsesFSC** relationship, `checkout_till_receipt`, and there will be a 1:1 relationship between the `uses_fsc` and `checkout_till_receipt` tables (because they have the same primary key).

In the definition of the `uses_fsc` table given in Figures 4.13 and 4.14, the column `fsc_number` forms a foreign key referencing the `customer` table, and the columns `(checkout_till_number, checkout_time)` form a foreign key referencing the `checkout_till_receipt` table. Since these columns are part of the primary key of the `uses_fsc` table, and hence cannot be **NULL**, the `uses_fsc` table has mandatory participation with the relationships with the `customer` and `checkout_till_receipt` tables.

Representing relationships

During the database design task, we will need to choose how we are going to represent 1:1 and 1:*n* relationships. We have no choice with *m*:*n* relationships: they have to be represented using the *relation for relationship approach* by decomposing the *m*:*n* relationship into two 1:*n* relationships and an intersection table that records occurrences of the relationship. But with 1:1 and 1:*n* relationships, as we illustrated above, we can use either the *foreign key alone approach* or the *relation for relationship approach*.

Using the *relation for relationship approach*, that is, employing a table to represent relationships in a database design, has the following benefits:

 ▶ It provides a uniform treatment for the representation of 1:1, 1:*n* and *m*:*n* relationships.

▶ It enables the name of a relationship to be recorded by naming the table that represents that relationship after the relationship.

▶ It avoids foreign keys being **NULL** to represent optional participation in the relationship.

▶ It enables data about a relationship to be recorded by having non-primary key columns added to the table that represents that relationship.

Despite these benefits, the usual practice adopted by database designers when representing relationships in a database design is to use the *foreign key alone approach* for representing 1:1 and 1:*n* relationships, and because this approach does not support *m:n* relationships, the *relation for relationship approach* is used to represent *m:n* relationships.

The main reason for representing 1:1 and 1:*n* relationships using the *foreign key alone approach* is that it employs fewer tables to represent relationships. Hence, it requires fewer relational joins, a relatively resource-intensive operation, that may be required to realise the information that it is recorded by a relationship between two entity types.

We can demonstrate this by comparing the SQL queries that would be required to join the **customer** and **checkout_till_receipt** tables together in the different database designs using the *foreign key alone approach* (Figure 4.10) and the *relation for relationship approach* (Figure 4.13) in order, for example, to obtain information about the purchases made by customers who have a Frequent Shopper Card.

The following SQL query would be required to join the **customer** and **checkout_till_receipt** tables in the database design using the *foreign key alone approach* as shown in Figure 4.10:

```
SELECT *
FROM customer
    NATURAL JOIN checkout_till_receipt
```

Whereas the following SQL query would be required to join the **customer** and **checkout_till_receipt** tables in the database design using the *relation for relationship approach* shown in Figure 4.13:

```
SELECT *
FROM (customer NATURAL JOIN uses_fsc)
    NATURAL JOIN checkout_till_receipt
```

Throughout the remainder of this section, when considering database designs for the entity–relationship models that we developed in Section 3, we will use the *foreign key alone approach* for representing 1:1 and 1:*n* relationships, and the *relation for relationship approach* for representing *m:n* relationships.

Representing optional single-valued properties

According to our guidelines for representing the properties of entity types by an entity–relationship model, which we developed in Section 3, an optional single-valued property that is not related to any occurrences of another entity type is represented by a :1 relationship with a *new* entity type, where the participation condition of the entity type, whose properties we are representing, with respect to this relationship is optional.

For example, in Table 3.12, the optional single-valued properties – *quantity, additional information* and *special offer* – are represented by :1 relationships with new entity types where the **Product** ends have optional participation (see Figure 3.21). Compare this representation with that used for the mandatory single-valued properties of the **Product** entity type – *description*, *price* and *product code* – which are represented by the **Description**, **Price** and **ProductCode** attributes of the **Product** entity type.

We have to represent such optional single-valued properties by a new entity type because with the entity–relationship model, for each occurrence of a particular entity type, every attribute has a value; that is, an occurrence is a complete set of data values. However, in *Block 3*, Subsection 4.1, we discussed the use of the marker **NULL** in SQL to indicate the absence of a value. So, in our database design we may be able to choose either to use a table corresponding to the new entity type or to use a column that allows **NULL** in the table corresponding to the entity type whose single-valued properties we are representing.

We will compare these approaches by considering database designs for the **Product** entity type. Figure 4.16 reproduces Figure 3.21, but for reasons of brevity, we have only shown the identifying attributes in the definitions of the entity types, and have omitted additional constraints, assumptions and limitations.

Entity–relationship diagram

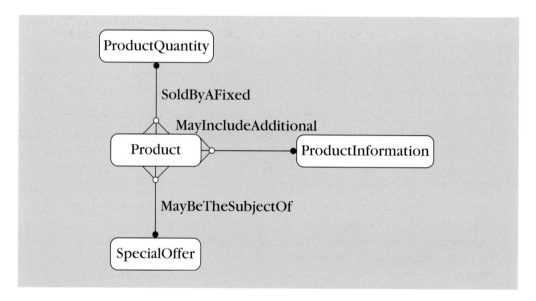

Entity types
Product (<u>ProductCode</u>, ...)
ProductQuantity (<u>Quantity</u>)
ProductInformation (<u>Information</u>)
SpecialOffer (<u>SpecialOfferCode</u>, ...)

Figure 4.16   An entity–relationship model representing the data requirements described by product labels where only the current situation is represented

Figure 4.17 gives a database schema diagram for a database design that results from the direct transformation of the entity–relationship model shown in Figure 4.16 and as described in Table 4.1.

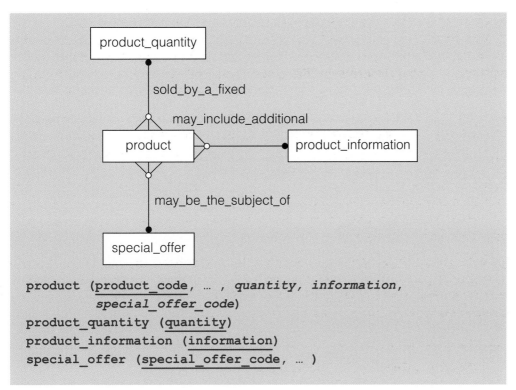

product (**product_code**, ... , *quantity, information,*
        special_offer_code)
product_quantity (**quantity**)
product_information (**information**)
special_offer (**special_offer_code**, ...)

Figure 4.17   A database schema diagram for a database design that results from the direct transformation of the entity–relationship model shown in Figure 4.16 and as described by Table 4.1

In Figure 4.17, relationships shown in the entity–relationship model (see Figure 4.16) are represented as follows:

The 1:*n* **SoldByAFixed** relationship is represented by adding (posting) the primary key of the table at the :1 end of the relationship, **product_quantity.quantity**, as a foreign key in the table at the :*n* end of the relationship, **product.quantity**, which will be allowed to take **NULL** as **Product** has optional participation with respect to the **SoldByAFixed** relationship.

The 1:*n* **MayIncludeAdditional** relationship is represented by adding (posting) the primary key of the table at the :1 end of the relationship, **product_information.information**, as a foreign key in the table at the :*n* end of the relationship, **product.information**, which will be allowed to take **NULL** as **Product** has optional participation with respect to the **MayIncludeAdditional** relationship.

The 1:*n* **MayBeTheSubjectOf** relationship is represented by adding (posting) the primary key of the table at the :1 end of the relationship, **special_offer.special_offer_code**, as a foreign key in the table at the :*n* end of the relationship, **product.special_offer_code**, which will be allowed to take **NULL** as **Product** has optional participation with respect to the **MayBeTheSubjectOf** relationship.

In Figure 4.17, the **product_quantity** and **product_information** tables are redundant because the information they record is already recorded by the **quantity** and **information** columns of the **product** table, which are the columns posted to that table to represent the **SoldByAFixed** and **MayIncludeAdditional** relationships, respectively. This redundancy arises because of the nature of the relational representation of relationships whereby an occurrence of a relationship exists between two tables because the primary key and the foreign key columns have the same values. Since each of the **product_quantity** and **product_information** tables has a single column for their primary key, and as they have mandatory participation with respect to the **SoldByAFixed** and **MayIncludeAdditional** relationships, respectively, the quantity and information foreign key columns in the product table will record the same information as that recorded in the primary key columns of those tables.

Figure 4.18 gives a database schema diagram for another database design that represents the entity–relationship model shown in Figure 4.16. This design makes use of the SQL NULL marker to represent the optional single-valued properties of the Product entity type, product quantity and further information about a product by the quantity and information columns of the product table instead of the product_quantity and product_information tables. These columns are allowed to be NULL as these properties are optional for occurrences of the Product entity type.

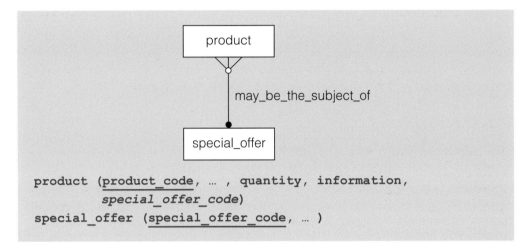

Figure 4.18   A database schema diagram for another database design that represents the entity–relationship model shown in Figure 4.16

EXERCISE 4.4

In Section 3, we gave an entity–relationship model representing the data requirements described by product labels, where the historical situation is represented in Figure 3.23. The figure is reproduced below, but for reasons of brevity, we have only shown the identifying attributes in the definitions of the entity types, and have omitted additional constraints, assumptions and limitations.

Give a database schema diagram to show how this entity–relationship model could be represented by using the *foreign key alone approach* for 1:*n* relationships and the *relation for relationship approach* for *m:n* relationships.

Entity–relationship diagram

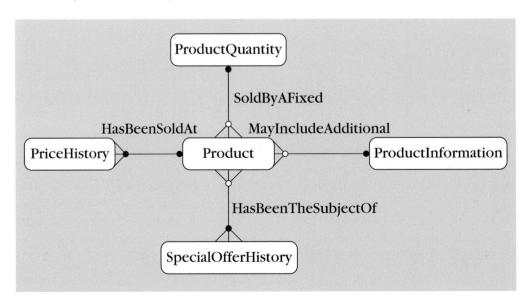

Entity types
Product (ProductCode, ...)
ProductQuantity (Quantity)
ProductInformation (Information)
PriceHistory (ProductCode, Date, ...)
SpecialOfferHistory (SpecialOfferCode, ...)

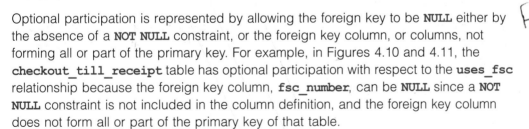

In most situations, we will choose to represent optional single-valued properties by a column that allows **NULL** in the table corresponding to the entity type whose single-valued properties we are representing. The advantage of using a table is that it builds flexibility into the database design, which would allow us to record more details about a property by using non-primary columns. This is what effectively happened with the representation of special offers during the analysis task when we decided that we would need to record the start and end dates for each promotion.

Participation conditions

The :*n* (foreign key) end of a relationship

We considered how the participation condition of the table at the :*n* end of a 1:*n* relationship should be represented in the section on the foreign key alone approach. We said that the participation condition was determined by whether the foreign key representing the relationship in that table could be **NULL** or not.

Mandatory participation of a table at the :*n* end of a 1:*n* relationship is represented by not allowing the foreign key column(s), representing that relationship to be **NULL**. This can be effected either explicitly by including a **NOT NULL** constraint in the definition of the foreign key column(s), or implicitly by the foreign key column(s) forming all or part of the primary key of that table because the entity integrity rule states that no column that forms part of the primary key may be **NULL**. For example, in Figures 4.10 and 4.11, the **checkout_till_receipt_item** table has mandatory participation with respect to the **comprises** relationship because the foreign key columns, **checkout_till_number** and **checkout_time**, cannot be **NULL** because they also form part of the primary key of that table.

Optional participation is represented by allowing the foreign key to be **NULL** either by the absence of a **NOT NULL** constraint, or the foreign key column, or columns, not forming all or part of the primary key. For example, in Figures 4.10 and 4.11, the **checkout_till_receipt** table has optional participation with respect to the **uses_fsc** relationship because the foreign key column, **fsc_number**, can be **NULL** since a **NOT NULL** constraint is not included in the column definition, and the foreign key column does not form all or part of the primary key of that table.

The 1: end of a relationship

By default, the participation condition of the table at the 1: end of a 1:*n* relationship is optional because the optional participation condition does not correspond to any constraint on the valid states of a database. So, we only need to define a constraint if the participation condition is mandatory.

In *Block 2*, Subsection 4.3, we considered the relational representation of mandatory participation of a relation at the 1: end of a 1:*n* relationship. In an SQL database definition, mandatory participation of a table at the 1: end of a 1:*n* relationship means that each row of this table is associated with at least one row of the table at the :*n* end by an occurrence of the 1:*n* relationship. As each row of a table is distinguished by the value of its primary key, mandatory participation of a table at the 1: end of a 1:*n* relationship means that each primary key value of that table is matched by the foreign key value present in at least one row of the table at the :*n* end by an occurrence of the 1:*n* relationship.

In an SQL database definition, we can represent this constraint using an SQL check constraint where the search condition specifies that the primary key values match the foreign key values. Figure 4.19 gives an outline definition of an SQL check constraint that represents mandatory participation of a table at the 1: end of a 1:*n* relationship.

```
CREATE TABLE <table at the 1: end>
  ( . . .
    . . .
  CONSTRAINT mandatory_participation_at_the_1:_end
    CHECK (EXISTS
      (SELECT *
       FROM <table at the :n end>
       WHERE <table at the 1: end>.<primary key> =
             <table at the :n end>.<foreign key>))
  )
```

Figure 4.19   An outline definition of an SQL check constraint that represents mandatory participation of a table at the 1: end of a 1:*n* relationship

The SQL check constraint given in Figure 4.19 ensures that when we insert a row into the table at the 1: end of a 1:*n* relationship, its primary key value is matched by a foreign key value present in at least one row in the table at the :*n* end by an occurrence of the 1:*n* relationship. This constraint also ensures that we cannot delete a row from the table at the :*n* end of the relationship, so that a primary key value at the 1: end is no longer matched by a foreign key value present in any row in the table at the :*n* end by an occurrence of the 1:*n* relationship.

Figure 4.20 shows the SQL check constraint that is required to be included in the definition of the **checkout_till_receipt** table shown in Figure 4.11 to represent mandatory participation of the **checkout_till_receipt** table in the **comprises** relationship.

```
CREATE TABLE checkout_till_receipt
  ( . . .
    . . .
  CONSTRAINT mandatory_participation_in_comprises
    CHECK (EXISTS
      (SELECT *
       FROM checkout_till_receipt_item
       WHERE checkout_till_receipt.checkout_till_number =
             checkout_till_receipt_item.checkout_till_number
         AND checkout_till_receipt.checkout_time =
             checkout_till_receipt_item.checkout_time))
  )
```

Figure 4.20   The SQL check constraint that is required to be included in the definition of the **checkout_till_receipt** table shown in Figure 4.11 to represent mandatory participation of the **checkout_till_receipt** table in the **comprises** relationship

EXERCISE 4.5

Give an outline SQL database definition (only primary and foreign keys) for the database schema diagram given in the solution to Exercise 4.4.

The **price_history** table has mandatory participation with respect to the 1:*n*
has_been_sold_at relationship because the foreign key representing the
relationship, **product_code**, is part of the primary key of that table and therefore
cannot be **NULL**. The **product** table has mandatory participation with respect to
the 1:*n* **has_been_sold_at** relationship because the constraint
mandatory_participation_in_has_been_sold_at has been included in the
definition of that table. Since the primary key of the **product** table comprises just a
single column, the constraint can also be written as follows:

```
    ...
    CONSTRAINT mandatory_participation_in_has_been_sold_at
      CHECK (product_code IN
        (SELECT product_code
         FROM price_history)),
    ...
```

The **has_been_the_subject_of** table has mandatory participation with respect to
the relationships with the **product** and **special_offer_history** tables
because the foreign keys representing these relationships, **product_code** and
special_offer_code, form the primary key of that table and therefore cannot be
NULL. The **special_offer_history** table has mandatory participation with
respect to the 1:*n* relationship because the constraint
mandatory_participation_in_has_been_the_subject_of has been included in
the definition of that table. Since the primary key of the **special_offer_history**
table comprises just a single column, the constraint could also have been written as
follows:

```
    ...
    CONSTRAINT mandatory_participation_in_has_been_the_subject_of
      CHECK (special_offer_code IN
        (SELECT special_offer_code
         FROM has_been_the_subject_of))
    ...
```

Primary keys

In Table 4.1 where we summarised the transformation of an entity–relationship model
into an SQL database definition, we stated that the identifiers of entity types became
the primary keys of the corresponding tables. However, in the case of composite
identifiers that comprise several attributes, this direct transformation may result in an
inefficient database design. This is because of the overheads associated with indexing
primary key values to facilitate, for example, the joining of tables to realise the
relationships between those tables.

During the database design task, we may decide to replace a composite primary key
with a single-column primary key to improve the overall efficiency of the design. Such
primary keys are known as **surrogate keys** because they are invented solely for the
purpose of distinguishing rows of a table and have no meaning within the enterprise for
which the database is being built. Their values are often generated by the DBMS. SQL
Anywhere enables you to define a numeric column as **DEFAULT AUTOINCREMENT**. This
has the effect that when a new row is inserted, it does not need a value for this column
because a new unique value is generated automatically by adding one to the current
maximum for the column. A surrogate key is usually immutable, that is, the value does
not change while the row exists.

In Figure 4.10, we defined the `checkout_till_receipt` and `checkout_till_receipt_item` tables as follows:

> `checkout_till_receipt` (`checkout_till_number`, `checkout_time`, ...,
> `fsc_number`)
>
> `checkout_till_receipt_item` (`checkout_till_number`, `checkout_time`,
> `item_number`, ...)

We could replace the composite primary key of the `checkout_till_receipt` table with a single primary key as follows:

> `checkout_till_receipt` (`transaction_number`, `checkout_till_number`,
> `checkout_time`, ..., `fsc_number`)

The new primary key would have a numeric SQL data type to save in the storage space required for indexing and the values generated by the DBMS. Note that the original primary key columns are retained as the data has meaning within the enterprise. The `checkout_till_receipt_item` table would be revised as follows:

> `checkout_till_receipt_item` (`transaction_number`, `item_number`, ...)

The main advantage of surrogate keys is improved indexing, which facilitates DBMS operations such as searching and joining tables. The main disadvantage is that surrogate keys are usually unrelated to the other data stored in a row of a table because they have no meaning within the enterprise for which the database is being built.

4.3 | Representing complex data

We stated in the introduction to Section 4 that early decisions on how complex data needs to be recorded in a database in order to satisfy the operational requirements of an enterprise would facilitate the development of the application software during the implementation stage. We will explore the options we have for recording complex data to satisfy different operational requirements by considering designs for the **Address** attribute of the **Customer** entity type (see Figure 4.1), which is designated as having complex data values in Table 4.2.

An address of a property in the UK comprises a number of data fields (or address lines). It could comprise the number or name of the property, the name of the street, the neighbourhood, suburb, district or estate, the village, town or city, and county where the property is located, and the postcode. There are many possible variations: for example, the property may be subdivided into individual apartments, each of which may be identified by a number or name. Each property in the UK can be identified uniquely by the combination of its property number or name, and its postcode.

Let us consider the different ways that customers' addresses may be utilised by Walton Stores, and the database designs that would facilitate them. One way that Walton Stores might use customers' addresses is simply to produce address labels to enable the supermarket chain to send promotional materials and coupons to all those customers who have a Frequent Shopper Card (FSC) and have indicated on their FSC application forms that they are willing to receive such materials. For this particular application, we are concerned not with the detail that each field of an address records, but just with the ability to retrieve each address line by line to facilitate the printing of the labels.

The database schema diagrams in Figures 4.21, 4.22 and 4.23 show the three basic approaches for representing complex data: using a single column, several columns and a separate table, respectively.

Figure 4.21   A database schema diagram for the representation of the Address attribute of the Customer entity type using a single column

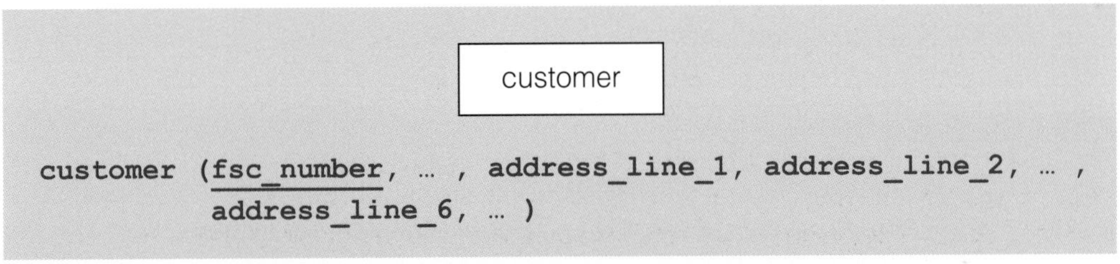

Figure 4.22   A database schema diagram for the representation of the Address attribute of the Customer entity type using several columns

Figure 4.23   A database schema diagram for the representation of the Address attribute of the Customer entity type using a separate table

With the database design specified in Figure 4.21, a customer's address is stored as a single data value where each address line and the postcode recorded on the Frequent Shopper Card (FSC) application form (see Figure 2.7) would be delimited by some special code, for example, by using the end-of-line marker ($\backslash$n). The application software, which is written to print the address labels for promotional mailings, could execute the following SQL query, process the resultant table using cursors (see *Block 3*, Subsection 7.3) and unpack the address data recorded by the **address** column of each row of the resultant table into address lines and postcode, ready for printing.

Block 5, Application development, describes how SQL statements can be executed by application processes and the resultant tables handled using cursors.

> **SELECT address**
> **FROM customer**
> **WHERE further_information = 'Yes'**

With the database design specified in Figure 4.22, a customer's address is stored in the **address_line_1** to **address_line_6** columns. These six columns store the five address lines and postcode recorded on the FSC application form. The application software, which is written to print the address labels, could execute the following SQL query, process the resultant table using cursors and print the **address_line_1** to **address_line_6** columns of each row of the resultant table on separate lines.

> **SELECT address_line_1, address_line_2, ...**
> **FROM customer**
> **WHERE further_information = 'Yes'**

With the database design specified in Figure 4.23, a customer's address is stored in a separate table, **address_line**, where each row records a particular line of the address of a particular customer. The **fsc_number** of the **address_line** table is a foreign key referencing the **customer** table. The application software that is written to print address labels could execute the following SQL query, process the resultant table using cursors and print the **address_line** column of each row of the resultant table.

```
SELECT address_line
FROM customer NATURAL JOIN address_line
WHERE further_information = 'Yes'
ORDER BY fsc_number, address_line_number
```

It be Sure about the order

EXERCISE 4.6

Why is it necessary to include the **ORDER BY** clause in the SQL query that is used to retrieve the customers' addresses from the database design presented in Figure 4.23, even though these addresses are likely be added to the database in the order that the address lines and postcode are presented on the FSC application form?

All three database designs presented in Figures 4.21, 4.22 and 4.23 are capable of satisfying the operational requirement to produce address labels to enable Walton Stores to send promotional materials and coupons to all those customers who have a Frequent Shopper Card (FSC) and have indicated on their FSC application form that they are willing to receive such materials.

Processing Speed reduction of null values flexibility

EXERCISE 4.7

What other criteria could be used to select, for example, one of the database designs presented in Figures 4.21, 4.22 and 4.23?

There is another way that Walton Stores might use the customers' addresses. When analysing the customers' purchases they might find the customers addresses useful if they wish to relate the customers' purchasing behaviour to where they live. This depends on the analysis undertaken, which could be any one of the address fields – the neighbourhood, suburb, district, estate, village, town, city, county or postcode where the property is located. For example, Walton Stores may wish to analyse the use of a small store located within a particular housing estate by customers who live on that estate, and compare its use with that of a larger 'out of town' store located several miles away. There are numerous ways that such analyses could be performed, but they all require that the various address fields are distinguishable; this would enable Walton Stores to search the particular locations where the customers are resident.

Figure 4.24 presents a database schema diagram for the database design given in Figure 4.22, which could facilitate the operational requirements described above.

```
              ┌──────────────────┐
              │     customer     │
              └──────────────────┘

customer (fsc_number, ... , property, street, locality,
          town, county, postcode, ... )
```

Figure 4.24   A database schema diagram for the representation of the **Address** attribute of the **Customer** entity type by several columns

Details of the various columns in Figure 4.24 are as follows:

▶ the **property** column records the number or name of the property;

▶ the **street** column records the name of the street;

▶ the **locality** column records the neighbourhood, suburb, district or estate where the property is located;

▶ the **town** column records the village, town or city;

▶ the **county** column records the county, unitary authority or metropolitan area;

▶ the **postcode** column records the postcode of the property.

This design would also facilitate the printing of address labels.

Finally, Walton Stores might use the customers' addresses in their comparison of customers' addresses for administrative purposes. The database design given in Figure 4.24 will facilitate this operational requirement. However, we cannot simply compare the various address columns of the different rows of the **customer** table because the elements of an address may be abbreviated. For example, the **county** column may have the value 'Buckinghamshire' in one row and 'Bucks' in another, but both of them refer to the same county. As each property in the UK can be identified uniquely by the combination of its property number or name, and its postcode, address comparisons can be performed on the **property** and **postcode** columns of the **customer** table.

EXERCISE 4.8

Suppose that Walton Stores restricts its Frequent Shopper Card to one per household (property). How would you enforce this condition on an SQL database definition of the database design given in Figure 4.24?

EXERCISE 4.9

In this subsection we have considered both the requirements of Walton Stores and our database designs for recording the customers' addresses, which involve recording address lines as multiple columns of the **customer** table. Under what circumstances would it be expedient to employ a separate **address** table?

4.4 Representing constraints

In *Block 3*, we described two kinds of constraint in SQL where the constraint is specified as a search condition: **check constraints** (see *Block 3*, Subsection 5.4) and **triggers** (see *Block 3*, Subsection 7.4). These constraints are comparable to a general constraint as described in *Block 2*, Subsection 4.3, but may be used also to enforce referential and domain constraints. So, in our database design we may choose to represent a general constraint with either a check constraint or a trigger. In this subsection, we will elaborate on these alternatives, in particular, their support by the different SQL implementations.

Check constraints

An SQL check constraint that is specified as a table constraint has the following form:

```
CREATE TABLE <table name>
  ( ...
  [CONSTRAINT <constraint name>]
    CHECK (<search condition>),
  ...
  )
```

The search condition must not evaluate to FALSE for any row of a table where the check constraint is defined, otherwise the constraint will be violated. This means that the search condition must evaluate to either TRUE or UNKNOWN for every row of the table.

An SQL check constraint has two basic forms. The first form is where the search condition simply references one or more columns of the table where the check constraint is defined. This form enables the value(s) of a column or columns of the row or rows being inserted into the table or updated in the table, where the check constraint is defined, to be compared in some way. The search condition will be evaluated whenever rows are inserted into the table or updated in the table by an SQL **INSERT** or **UPDATE** statement, respectively. If the search condition evaluates to FALSE then the SQL statement fails and the table remains unchanged.

Figure 4.25 shows the representation of the value set for the customers' residences using a check constraint defined for the **residence** column of the **customer** table. This is an alternative to using an SQL domain, as we described in Subsection 4.1. The check constraint in Figure 4.25 is used to restrict the range of values possible for the SQL data type specified for the **residence** column, **VARCHAR(6)**, to just **'Owner'**, **'Tenant'** and **'Other'**.

```
CREATE TABLE customer
  ( ...
    residence VARCHAR(6) NOT NULL,
    ...
  CONSTRAINT residences
    CHECK (residence IN ('Owner', 'Tenant', 'Other'))
  )
```

Figure 4.25   The representation of the value set for the customers' residences using a check constraint defined for the **residence** column of the **customer** table

In the entity–relationship model for the **Customer** entity type shown in Figure 4.1, the *Additional constraint* section includes the following condition:

c.1   The customer should be at least 18 years old when they apply for a Frequent Shopper Card. That is, for each instance of the Customer entity type, the value of the ApplicationDate attribute should be at least 18 years greater than that of the DateOfBirth attribute.

Figure 4.26 shows the representation of the condition c.1 using a check constraint defined on the **customer** table.

```
CREATE TABLE customer
  ( ...
    date_of_birth dates NOT NULL,
    ...
    application_date dates NOT NULL,
    ...
  CONSTRAINT condition_c1
    CHECK (DATEDIFF(year, date_of_birth, application_date) >= 18)
  )
```

Figure 4.26   The representation of the condition c.1 using a check constraint defined on the **customer** table

The check constraint in Figure 4.26 uses the SQL Anywhere function **DATEDIFF** to determine the number of years between a customer's date of birth and the date of their application for a Frequent Shopper Card. It returns the specified interval, **year**, between the two dates specified by the **application_date** and **date_of_birth** columns. See the following Sybase online book *ASA SQL Reference, Part I SQL, Chapter 3, SQL Functions* for a description of the **DATEDIFF** function.

If the definition of the **customer** table includes the two check constraints shown in Figures 4.25 and 4.26, then both conditions must be satisfied. If any change to the **customer** table causes either search condition to evaluate to FALSE, the change will fail and the **customer** table will remain unchanged.

The first form of an SQL check constraint is supported by most SQL implementations, including SQL Anywhere.

The second form of an SQL check constraint is where the search condition includes a subquery. This form enables the value(s) of a column or columns of the row or rows being inserted into the table, updated in the table, or deleted from the table where the check constraint is defined, to be compared with the columns of the rows of another, or the same, table. The search condition will be evaluated whenever there are rows to be inserted into the table, updated in the table, or deleted from the table by an SQL **INSERT**, **UPDATE** or **DELETE** statement, respectively, *and* any of the tables listed in the **FROM** clause(s) of the subquery. If a **FROM** clause of the subquery includes the table where the check constraint is defined, then the table will include the changes made by the SQL statement that invoked the evaluation of that check constraint.

Figure 4.27 shows the representation of mandatory participation of the **product** table with respect to the **has_been_sold_at** relationship as given in the solution to Exercise 4.5, which uses this second form of an SQL check constraint.

```
CREATE TABLE product
  (product_code product_codes NOT NULL,
   ... ,
  PRIMARY KEY (product_code),
  CONSTRAINT mandatory_participation_in_has_been_sold_at
    CHECK (product_code IN
      (SELECT product_code
       FROM price_history)),
  ...
  )
```

Figure 4.27   The representation of mandatory participation of the **product** table with respect to the **has_been_sold_at** relationship as given in the solution to Exercise 4.5

Mandatory participation of the **product** table with respect to the **has_been_sold_at** relationship means that each row of the **product** table is related to at least one row of the **price_history** table. That is, the primary key values of the **product** table must be matched by the foreign key values of the **price_history** table. The check constraint in Figure 4.27 ensures that the above condition is not violated when rows are either inserted into the **product** table or deleted from the **price_history** table.

In the *Hospital conceptual data model*, the *Additional constraints* section includes the following condition:

> **c.11 The number of patients in a ward cannot exceed the number of beds in that ward.**

Figure 4.28 shows the representation of the condition c.11 using a check constraint defined on the **ward** table.

```
CREATE TABLE ward
  ( ...
    number_of_beds ... ,
    ...
  CONSTRAINT condition_c11
    CHECK (
      (SELECT COUNT(*)
       FROM patient
       WHERE ward.ward_no = patient.ward_no) <= number_of_beds)
  ...
  )
```

Figure 4.28   The representation of the condition c.11 as specified in the *Additional constraints* section of the *Hospital conceptual data model* using a check constraint defined on the **ward** table

The check constraint given in Figure 4.28 has two main purposes. First, it ensures that when we update the **number_of_beds** column of a particular row (ward) of the **ward** table, its value is greater than or equal to the number of patients currently on that ward. Second, it ensures that when we insert a row into the **patient** table, the total number of patients on the same ward as that patient is less than or equal to the number of beds available on that ward.

If the definition of the **ward** table includes the check constraint shown in Figure 4.28, then each time an SQL **INSERT**, **UPDATE** or **DELETE** statement respectively inserts, updates or deletes one or more rows of either the **ward** table or the **patient** table, this constraint is evaluated once for each of those rows. If the search condition evaluates to FALSE for any one of those rows, then the SQL statement fails and the **ward** or **patient** table is unchanged.

The second form of an SQL check constraint, where the search condition includes a subquery, is NOT supported by most SQL implementations. Although SQL Anywhere supports this second form of an SQL check constraint, as we noted in *Block 3*, Subsection 5.7, it does not evaluate the constraint according to the SQL standard. First, it does NOT evaluate a check constraint when changes are made by the SQL **DELETE** statement. Second, it does NOT evaluate a check constraint whenever rows are inserted into the table, updated in the table, or deleted from any of the tables listed in the **FROM** clause(s) of the subquery. Third, if a **FROM** clause of the subquery includes the table where the check constraint is defined, then the table does NOT include any of the changes made by the SQL **INSERT**, **UPDATE** or **DELETE** statement that invoked the evaluation of that check constraint.

We will consider how SQL Anywhere evaluates the check constraints shown in Figures 4.27 and 4.28, and if possible, how we might be able to overcome the above limitations of how SQL Anywhere implements the second form of the check constraint.

Using SQL Anywhere to define the check constraint on the **product** table shown in Figure 4.27, will ensure that whenever we insert a row into the **product** table, the value of its primary key, **product_code**, is matched by a foreign key value present in at least one row of the **price_history** table. As the check constraint will not be evaluated for any change made to the **price_history** table, it will not prevent the deletion of a row from the **price_history** table that will result in a primary key value of the **product** table that no longer matches a foreign key value present in any row of the **price_history** table. However, we are unable to prevent such a deletion because SQL Anywhere does not evaluate a check constraint when changes are made by the SQL **DELETE** statement. Later in this subsection, we will show how this aspect of mandatory participation of the table at the 1: end of a 1:*n* relationship can be represented using SQL triggers.

Where SQL Anywhere is used to define the check constraint on the **ward** table shown in Figure 4.28, then each time an SQL **INSERT** or **UPDATE** statement respectively inserts or updates one or more rows of the **ward** table, this constraint is evaluated. The check constraint will not be evaluated for any change made to the **patient** table, but we can define the check constraint shown in Figure 4.29 to prevent rows being inserted into the **patient** table from violating the constraint.

```
CREATE TABLE patient
  ( ...

    ...
  CONSTRAINT condition_c11
    CHECK (
      (SELECT COUNT(*) + 1
       FROM patient p
       WHERE p.ward_no = patient.ward_no) <=
      (SELECT number_of_beds
       FROM ward w
       WHERE w.ward_no = patient.ward_no))
    ...
  )
```

Figure 4.29   The representation of the condition c.11 specified in the *Additional constraints* section of the *Hospital conceptual data model* using a check constraint defined on the **patient** table

If the definition of the **patient** table includes the check constraint shown in Figure 4.29, then each time an SQL **INSERT** statement inserts one or more rows into the **patient** table, this constraint will be evaluated once for each of those rows. For the ward specified by the **ward_no** column of the patient row being inserted, the first subquery returns the number of patients in that ward *after* the row has been inserted. Since SQL Anywhere does NOT include the changes made to the table where the check constraint is defined when evaluating the check constraint, **COUNT(*)** does not include the patient being inserted, so we have appended **+ 1** to the expression. The second subquery returns the number of beds on the ward as specified by the **ward_no** column of the patient row being inserted. If this value is less than the number of patients, then the search condition will evaluate to FALSE and the SQL statement fails. The **patient** table

Unfortunately, the suggested 'work around' for SQLAnywhere shown in Figure 4.29 has the unintentional side-effect of not allowing updates to patients occupying full wards.

EXERCISE 4.10

Consider the following fragment of the *Hospital conceptual data model*. Give an SQL database definition of the outline database definition for an SQL implementation that supports standard SQL that represents this entity–relationship model.

Entity–relationship diagram

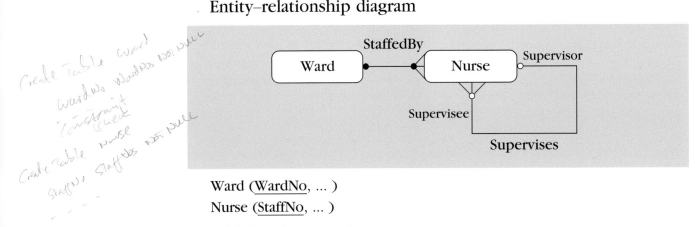

Ward (WardNo, ...)

Nurse (StaffNo, ...)

Additional constraints

c.5   A nurse can only supervise nurses in the same ward. That is, the two instances of the entity type Nurse that are involved in an occurrence of the Supervises relationship must be assigned to the same ward.

Working assumptions

None

Limitations

None

Triggers

Triggers were introduced in *Block 3*, Subsection 7.4. They provide a comprehensive means of enforcing constraints on data and the relationships between data in an SQL database, as well as contributing to meeting the operational requirements of an enterprise by monitoring database changes and taking appropriate actions.

Here, however, we will focus only on triggers as an alternative to using check constraints to enforce database integrity because triggers are well-supported by SQL implementations, unlike SQL check constraints. More information about SQL triggers and their implementation by SQL Anywhere can be found in the Sybase online book: *ASA SQL User's Guide, Part VI Stored Procedures and Triggers, Introduction to Triggers*.

The general form of an SQL trigger definition is:

```
CREATE TRIGGER <trigger-name>
  {BEFORE|AFTER} {INSERT|DELETE|UPDATE|
    UPDATE OF <column-name>[<,column-name>,...]}
  ON <table-name>
    [REFERENCING [OLD AS <old-name>] [NEW AS <new-name>]]
  FOR EACH {ROW|STATEMENT}
    [WHEN <search condition>]
  BEGIN ATOMIC
    <triggered SQL statement(s)>
  END
```

Each trigger is associated with a table (as specified by the **ON** clause) and is invoked whenever this table is modified by a particular SQL statement (as specified by the **INSERT, DELETE, UPDATE** or **UPDATE OF** keyword) either before or after the modification is made to the table (as specified by the **BEFORE** or **AFTER** keyword). The **REFERENCING** keyword allows us to reference the columns of the new rows being inserted into the table, or the old rows being deleted from the table, or existing and replacement rows during an update to the table.

The **FOR EACH** clause specifies whether the trigger action is fired either as each row is updated or when all processing of the triggering statement is completed (as specified by the **ROW** or **STATEMENT** keyword, respectively). The optional **WHEN** clause specifies a search condition that, if it evaluates to TRUE, causes the trigger to 'fire', executing the triggered SQL statement(s).

Figure 4.30 gives the triggers that are required to represent the value set for the customers' residences by the **residence** column of the **customer** table. This was represented previously using the first form of an SQL check constraint that we described earlier (see Figure 4.25).

```
CREATE TRIGGER insert_residences
   BEFORE INSERT ON customer
   REFERENCING NEW AS new_customer
   FOR EACH ROW
      WHEN (new_customer.residence NOT IN ('Owner', 'Tenant',
                                           'Other'))
      BEGIN ATOMIC
         DECLARE invalid_residences_value
            EXCEPTION FOR SQLSTATE '99999';
         SIGNAL invalid_residences_value;
      END


CREATE TRIGGER update_residences
   BEFORE UPDATE OF residence ON customer
   REFERENCING NEW AS new_customer
   FOR EACH ROW
      WHEN (new_customer.residence NOT IN ('Owner', 'Tenant',
                                           'Other'))
      BEGIN ATOMIC
         DECLARE invalid_residences_value
            EXCEPTION FOR SQLSTATE '99999';
         SIGNAL invalid_residences_value;
      END
```

Figure 4.30   The triggers required to represent the value set for the customers' residences by the **residence** column of the **customer** table

Figure 4.30 shows that when using triggers, the disadvantage is that it is necessary to define a separate trigger for each trigger event, **INSERT**, **DELETE** and **UPDATE**, which is relevant to the constraint being represented. However, some SQL implementations do allow you to specify more than one trigger event in the definition of a trigger.

You may have queried whether we need to include a trigger for an **UPDATE** event to the **residence** column of the **customer** table because once the value has been copied from the Frequent Shopper Card application form and entered into the database (as a row of the **customer** table) it is unlikely that the value will be revised. However, without this trigger it would be possible change the value to one outside the range specified by the value set.

Note the complementary logic of the specifications of the search conditions of the **CHECK** clause of a check constraint compared with that of the **WHEN** clause of a trigger. In the **CHECK** clause shown in Figure 4.25, the search condition is:

```
residence IN ('Owner', 'Tenant', 'Other')
```

In the **WHEN** clause of the trigger shown in Figure 4.30, the search condition is:

```
residence NOT IN ('Owner', 'Tenant', 'Other')
```

This is because with a check constraint, the search condition must not evaluate to FALSE for any row of a table, otherwise the constraint is violated and the change will fail. But with a trigger, the search condition must not evaluate to TRUE for any row of a table, otherwise the constraint is violated and will cause the trigger to 'fire'. However, the change will only fail if the triggered SQL statements include the following sequence (as in Figure 4.30):

```
BEGIN ATOMIC
   ... ;
   DECLARE <variable name>_value
       EXCEPTION FOR SQLSTATE '99999';
      SIGNAL <variable name>_value;
   END
```

EXERCISE 4.11

Give the triggers required to represent condition c.5 specified in the *Additional constraint* section of the entity–relationship model for the **Customer** entity type shown in Figure 4.1.

Since the first form of a check constraint that we described above is supported by most SQL implementations, it is easier to represent constraints that need to compare the value(s) of a column or columns of the row or rows being inserted into a table or updated in a table using a check constraint rather than writing two triggers, one to handle an **INSERT** statement and another the **UPDATE** statement.

Figure 4.31 gives the triggers required to represent mandatory participation of the **product** table with respect to the **has_been_sold_at** relationship. This was represented previously using the second form of an SQL check constraint that we have described (see Figure 4.27).

```
CREATE TRIGGER insert_product
   BEFORE INSERT ON product
   REFERENCING NEW AS new_product
   FOR EACH ROW
      WHEN (new_product.product_code NOT IN
        (SELECT  product_code
         FROM price_history))
      BEGIN ATOMIC
        DECLARE invalid_product_row
           EXCEPTION FOR SQLSTATE '99999';
        SIGNAL invalid_product_row;
      END


CREATE TRIGGER delete_price_history
   AFTER DELETE ON price_history
   REFERENCING OLD AS old_price_history
   FOR EACH ROW
      WHEN (old_price_history.product_code NOT IN
        (SELECT product_code
         FROM price_history))
      BEGIN ATOMIC
        DECLARE invalid_price_history_row
           EXCEPTION FOR SQLSTATE '99999';
        SIGNAL invalid_price_history_row;
      END
```

Figure 4.31   The triggers required to represent mandatory participation of the **product** table with respect to the **has_been_sold_at** relationship

The first trigger shown in Figure 4.31 ensures that whenever we insert a row into the **product** table, the value of its primary key, **product_code**, is matched by a foreign key value present in at least one row of the **price_history** table. The second trigger ensures that we cannot delete a row from the **price_history** table so that a primary key value of the **product** table is no longer matched by a foreign key value present in any row of the **price_history** table.

EXERCISE 4.12

Give the triggers required to represent the condition c.11 specified in the *Additional constraints* section of the *Hospital conceptual data model*, which was previously represented using a check constraint (see Figures 4.28 and 4.29).

Since the second form of a check constraint, where the search conditions includes a subquery, is NOT supported by most SQL implementations, and in the case of SQL Anywhere, not supported according to the SQL standards, then a trigger will need to be written in those situations where you need to compare the value(s) of a column or columns of the row or rows being inserted into the table, updated in the table, or deleted from the table with the columns of the rows of another, or the same, table.

4.5 Representing entity subtypes

In Section 3, we extended the notation for an entity–relationship diagram and the entity type definitions to introduce the concept of entity subtypes. In this section, we will describe how entity subtypes may be represented in a database (logical) schema.

EXERCISE 4.13

What do entity subtypes facilitate in an entity–relationship model? What is the advantage of employing subtypes in an entity–relationship model?

Figure 4.32 shows a fragment of the *Hospital conceptual data model* employing entity subtypes to distinguish between the properties associated with doctors in general, and those specific to either consultants or junior doctors. In Figure 4.32, **Doctor** is an entity supertype, and **JuniorDoctor** and **Consultant** are entity subtypes. As an entity supertype, **Doctor** has no occurrences and serves solely to define the properties common to all of its subtypes, **JuniorDoctor** and **Consultant**. We will use this example to illustrate how entity subtypes may be represented in a database design.

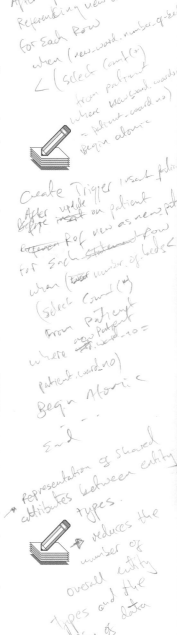

Entity–relationship diagram

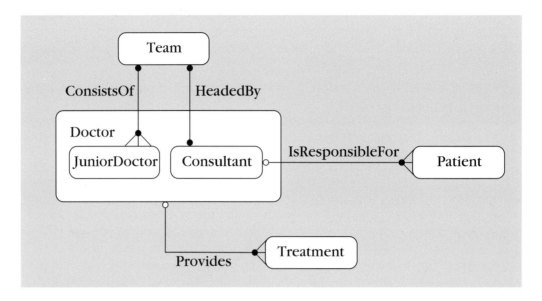

Entity types

Team (<u>TeamCode</u>, TelephoneNo)

Doctor (<u>StaffNo</u>, DoctorName)

    JuniorDoctor (Position)

    Consultant (Specialism)

Patient (<u>PatientId</u>, PatientName, Gender, Height, Weight)

Treatment (<u>StaffNo</u>, <u>PatientId</u>, <u>StartDate</u>)

Additional constraints

c.6   Junior doctors can be registrars or house officers. That is, the attribute Position (of entity type JuniorDoctor) may have a value of Registrar or House Officer.

c.8   Treatment is a weak entity type dependent on the entity type Doctor. So, each value of the StaffNo attribute in the entity type Treatment must be the same value as the StaffNo attribute of the Doctor instance to which the Treatment entity type is related by the relationship Provides (a consequence of weak–strong entity types).

Figure 4.32   A fragment of the *Hospital conceptual data model* employing entity subtypes to distinguish between the properties associated with doctors in general, and those specific to either consultants or junior doctors

The entity subtype concept has no direct counterpart in relational theory, and although the SQL:1999 Standard introduced the equivalent concepts of supertables and subtables, at the time of writing, relational DBMS vendors have not implemented supertables and subtables. So, in this section we will consider how entity subtypes can be represented by conventional SQL tables.

For a relational representation of entity subtypes, we usually choose to represent:

▶ either all subtypes by a single table   *involves null + exclusive constraints*

▶ or each subtype by a separate table.   *involves overlapping primary key constraint + exclusive relationship*

With the first approach, we construct the table simply by combining all the attributes of the entity supertype and its subtypes as columns of that table. We may include an additional column to indicate which subtype each row of the table is an occurrence of.

With the second approach, the attributes of the entity supertype are included as columns of each of the tables representing the subtypes. We also need an additional constraint to ensure that the primary key values of the tables representing the entity subtypes do not overlap. This is necessary because as the identifier is defined in the entity supertype, occurrences of all of the subtypes are mutually exclusive. That is, there cannot be an occurrence of one subtype with the same identifier as occurrences of any of the other subtypes.

Figure 4.33 gives the database schema diagram for the relational representation of the entity–relationship model shown in Figure 4.32, using the first approach – representing all subtypes by a single table. In Figure 4.33, the **doctor** table is constructed by combining all the attributes of the entity supertype, **Doctor**, and its subtypes, **JuniorDoctor** and **Consultant**.

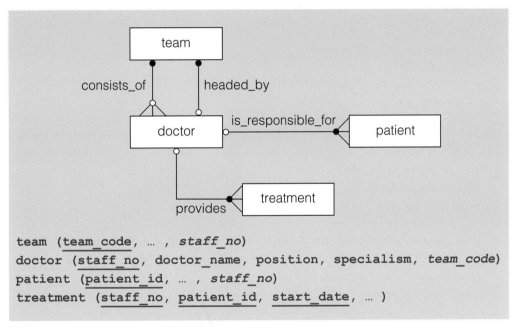

```
team (team_code, ... , staff_no)
doctor (staff_no, doctor_name, position, specialism, team_code)
patient (patient_id, ... , staff_no)
treatment (staff_no, patient_id, start_date, ... )
```

Figure 4.33   The database schema diagram for the relational representation of the entity–relationship model shown in Figure 4.32, using the first approach

In Figure 4.33, the **headed_by** relationship is represented by adding the **staff_no** column to the **team** table as a foreign key referencing the **doctor** table, and as the degree for the relationship is 1:1, the column is also an alternate key. The **consists_of** relationship is represented by adding the **team_code** column to the **doctor** table as a foreign key referencing the **team** table. The **is_responsible_for** relationship is represented by adding the **staff_no** column to the **patient** table as a foreign key referencing the **doctor** table. The **provides** relationship is represented by making the primary key column of the **treatment** table, **staff_no**, a foreign key referencing the **doctor** table.

Figure 4.34 gives an SQL database definition of the database schema for the relational representation of the entity–relationship model shown in Figure 4.32, using the first approach.

```
CREATE DOMAIN positions AS VARCHAR(20)
  // constraint C6 "Doctors can be consultants, registrars
  // or house officers"
  CHECK (value IN ('Consultant', 'Registrar', 'House Officer')
  )


CREATE TABLE team
  (team_code team_codes,
   ... ,
   staff_no staff_nos UNIQUE NOT NULL,
  PRIMARY KEY (team_code),
  CONSTRAINT relationship_headed_by
    FOREIGN KEY (staff_no) REFERENCES doctor,
  // mandatory participation in relationship consists_of
  CONSTRAINT team_in_consists_of
    CHECK (team_code IN
      (SELECT team_code
       FROM doctor)
  // constraint C2 "A doctor that is the head of a team
  // must be a consultant"
  CONSTRAINT C2
    CHECK (staff_no IN
      (SELECT staff_no
       FROM doctor
       WHERE position = 'Consultant'))
  )


CREATE TABLE doctor
  (staff_no staff_nos,
   ... ,
   position positions NOT NULL,
   ... ,
   team_code team_codes,
  PRIMARY KEY (staff_no),
  CONSTRAINT relationship_consists_of
    FOREIGN KEY (team_code) REFERENCES team,
  // constraint C3 "A consultant must head a team. Doctors
  // who are not consultants must be members of a team"
  CONSTRAINT C3
    CHECK ((position = 'Consultant' AND team_code IS NULL) OR
            (position <> 'Consultant' AND team_code IS NOT NULL))
  )


CREATE TABLE patient
  (patient_id patient_ids,
   ... ,
   staff_no staff_nos NOT NULL,
  PRIMARY KEY (patient_id),
  CONSTRAINT relationship_is_responsible_for
    FOREIGN KEY (staff_no) REFERENCES doctor
  )
```

```
CREATE TABLE treatment
  (staff_no staff_nos NOT NULL,
   patient_id patient_ids NOT NULL,
   start_date dates NOT NULL,
   ... ,
  PRIMARY KEY (staff_no, patient_id, start_date),
  CONSTRAINT relationship_provides
    FOREIGN KEY (staff_no) REFERENCES doctor,
  )
```

Figure 4.34   An SQL database definition of the database schema for the relational representation of the entity–relationship model shown in Figure 4.32, using the first approach

Figure 4.35 gives the database schema diagram for the relational representation of the entity–relationship model shown in Figure 4.32, using the second approach – representing each subtype by a separate table. In Figure 4.35, the **consultant** and **junior_doctor** tables include all the attributes of the entity supertype, **Doctor**, the **consultant** table all the attributes of the **Consultant** entity subtype, and the **junior_doctor** table all the attributes of the **JuniorDoctor** entity subtype.

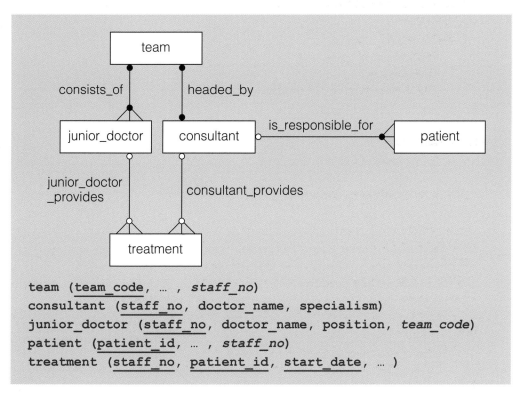

```
team (team_code, … , staff_no)
consultant (staff_no, doctor_name, specialism)
junior_doctor (staff_no, doctor_name, position, team_code)
patient (patient_id, … , staff_no)
treatment (staff_no, patient_id, start_date, … )
```

Figure 4.35   The database schema diagram for the relational representation of the entity–relationship model shown in Figure 4.32, using the second approach

In Figure 4.35, the **headed_by** relationship is represented by adding the **staff_no** column to the **team** table as a foreign key referencing the **consultant** table, and as the degree for the relationship is 1:1, the column is also an alternate key. The **consists_of** relationship is represented by adding the **team_code** column to the **junior_doctor** table as a foreign key referencing the **team** table. The **is_responsible_for** relationship is represented by adding the **staff_no** column to the **patient** table as a foreign key referencing the **consultant** table. The **junior_doctor_provides** and **consultant_provides** relationships are exclusive relationships on the **treatment** table and are represented by making the primary key column of the **treatment** table, **staff_no**, a foreign key referencing both the **junior_doctor** and **consultant** tables.

Figure 4.36 gives an SQL database definition of the database schema for the relational representation of the entity–relationship model shown in Figure 4.32, using the second approach.

```
CREATE DOMAIN positions AS VARCHAR(20)
  // constraint C6 "Junior doctors can be
  // registrars or house officers"
  CHECK (value IN ('Registrar', 'House Officer')
  )

CREATE TABLE team
  (team_code team_codes,
   ... ,
   staff_no staff_nos UNIQUE NOT NULL,
  PRIMARY KEY (team_code),
  CONSTRAINT relationship_headed_by
    FOREIGN KEY (staff_no) REFERENCES consultant,
  // mandatory participation in relationship consists_of
  CONSTRAINT team_in_consists_of
    CHECK (team_code IN
      (SELECT team_code
       FROM junior_doctor))

CREATE TABLE junior_doctor
  (staff_no staff_nos,
   ... ,
   position positions NOT NULL,
   ... ,
   team_code team_codes NOT NULL,
  PRIMARY KEY (staff_no),
  CONSTRAINT relationship_consists_of
    FOREIGN KEY (team_code) REFERENCES team,
  // primary keys of the junior_doctor and consultant
  // tables must not overlap
  CONSTRAINT no_overlapping_primary_keys
    CHECK (staff_no NOT IN
      (SELECT staff_no
       FROM consultant))
  )

CREATE TABLE consultant
  (staff_no staff_nos,
   ... ,
   specialism specialisms NOT NULL,
   ... ,
  PRIMARY KEY (staff_no),
  // constraint C3 "A consultant must head a team. Doctors
  // who are not consultants must be members of a team"
  CONSTRAINT c3
    CHECK (staff_no IN
      (SELECT staff_no
       FROM team))
  )
```

```
CREATE TABLE patient
  (patient_id patient_ids,
   ... ,
   staff_no staff_nos NOT NULL,
  PRIMARY KEY (patient_id),
  CONSTRAINT relationship_is_responsible_for
    FOREIGN KEY (staff_no) REFERENCES consultant
  )

CREATE TABLE treatment
  (staff_no staff_nos NOT NULL,
   patient_id patient_ids NOT NULL,
   start_date dates NOT NULL,
   ... ,
  PRIMARY KEY (staff_no, patient_id, start_date),
  // exclusive relationships junior_doctor_provides
  // and consultant_provides
  CONSTRAINT exclusive_relationships
    CHECK ((staff_no IN
             (SELECT staff_no FROM junior_doctor)) OR
           (staff_no IN
             (SELECT staff_no FROM consultant))
          )
  ...
  )
```

Figure 4.36   An SQL database definition of the database schema for the relational representation of the entity–relationship model shown in Figure 4.32, using the second approach

There are two important points to note in the SQL database definition given in Figure 4.36. The first point is the need for an additional constraint to ensure that the primary key values of the tables representing the **JuniorDoctor** and **Consultant** entity subtypes do not overlap. This is necessary because as the identifier is defined in the entity supertype, occurrences of all of the subtypes are mutually exclusive. That is, there cannot be an occurrence of one subtype with the same identifier as the occurrences of any of the other subtypes. This restriction is represented by the following constraint in Figure 4.36:

```
CREATE TABLE junior_doctor
  (staff_no staff_nos,
   ... ,
  PRIMARY KEY (staff_no)
   ... ,
  // primary keys of the junior_doctor and consultant
  // tables must not overlap
  CONSTRAINT no_overlapping_primary_keys
    CHECK (staff_no NOT IN
      (SELECT staff_no
        FROM consultant))
  )
```

According to the SQL standard, it is not necessary to include the corresponding constraint (see below) in the **consultant** table because any constraint that references data in more than one table is checked after a change to any one or more of those tables (**junior_doctor** and **consultant**, in this case) (see page 174). This constraint,

therefore, will also cause a faulture if an attempt is made to insert a row into the
consultant table with a **staff_no** that is the same as some **staff_no** in the
junior_doctor table.

It is necessary, however, to include the corresponding constraints (see below) in the
consultant table when implementing the database definition (Fig. 4.36) using
SQLAnywhere for reasons outlined on page 174.

```
CREATE TABLE consultant
  (staff_no staff_nos,
  ( ... ,
  PRIMARY KEY (staff_no)
  ...,
  // primary keys of the junior_doctor and consultant tables
  // must not overlap
  CONSTRAINT no_overlapping_primary_keys
    CHECK (staff_no NOT IN
      (SELECT staff_no ,
      FROM junior_doctor))
  )
```

The second point that we need to note in the SQL database definition given in
Figure 4.36 is the representation of the exclusive **junior_doctor_provides** and
consultant_provides relationships on the **treatment** table, which is represented by
making the primary column of the treatment table, **staff_no**, a foreign key referencing
both the **junior_doctor** and **consultant** tables. Since SQL does not allow the
REFERENCE clause of a **FOREIGN KEY** statement to specify more than one table, we
have use the following check constraint to represent the exclusive
junior_doctor_provides and **consultant_provides** relationships in Figure 4.36:

```
CREATE TABLE treatment
  ( ... ,
  // exclusive relationships junior_doctor_provides and
  // consultant_provides
  CONSTRAINT exclusive_relationships
    CHECK ((staff_no IN
          (SELECT staff_no FROM junior_doctor)) OR
          (staff_no IN
            (SELECT staff_no FROM consultant))
          )
  ...
  )
```

EXERCISE 4.14

Consider the following fragment of an entity–relationship model that represents the
data requirements of the checkout till receipts used by Walton Stores (see Figure 3.29).
For reasons of brevity, we have only shown the identifying attributes in the definitions of
the entity types, and omitted assumptions and limitations.

Give both a database schema diagram and outline SQL database definition for each of
the approaches to representing entity subtypes described above.

Entity–relationship diagram

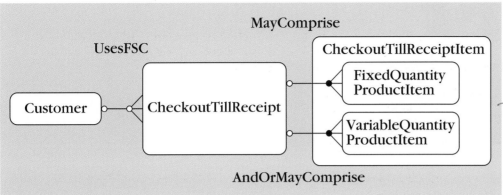

MayComprise

UsesFSC

Customer

CheckoutTillReceipt

CheckoutTillReceiptItem

FixedQuantity
ProductItem

VariableQuantity
ProductItem

AndOrMayComprise

Entity types

Customer (<u>FSCNumber</u>, ...)

CheckoutTillReceipt (<u>CheckoutTillNumber</u>, <u>Time</u>, ...)

CheckoutTillReceiptItem (<u>CheckoutTillNumber</u>, <u>Time</u>, <u>ItemNumber</u>)

    FixedQuantityProductItem ( )

    VariableQuantityProductItem ( )

Additional constraint

c.2 Each instance of CheckoutTillReceipt must participate in the
MayComprise relationship, or the AndOrMayComprise relationship,
or both.

4.6 | Summary

This section has focused on the database design task, which entails all of the activities that need to be completed before a database development can move from the conceptual data model stage to the next stage of its life cycle, that is, the specification of the logical (database) schema.

In this section on the database design task, we have:

▶ Provided a review of the transformation of an entity–relationship model into a relational representation as an SQL database.

▶ Provided a detailed overview of the choices available when transforming an entity–relationship model into a logical (database) schema for a first-cut design.

LEARNING OUTCOMES

Having completed your study of this section of the course, you will be able to:

▶ Develop a database design from an entity–relationship model and accompanying domain of discourse summary.

▶ Describe the choices that are available when transforming an entity–relationship model into a logical (database) schema for a first-cut design.

5 Implementation

This section focuses on the implementation task, which entails all of the activities that need to be completed before a database development can move from the logical (database) schema stage to the next stage of its life cycle, that is, a database system that satisfies all of the information requirements of an enterprise.

Implementation will typically involve the following activities:

► Implementation of the first-cut database design for the database using the relational DBMS that is chosen to manage that database.

► Population of the database with sufficient data to facilitate the development of application software.

► Development of user schemas (views) and application software (user processes) to satisfy the different information requirements of the users of the database. This will usually include the design and development of appropriate user interfaces, and often interfaces to specialist hardware and other computer systems.

► Acceptance testing – demonstrating that the database system will satisfy the information requirements of the enterprise, and is acceptable to both the client who commissioned the database development and users of the database system.

► Integrating the database system into the client's existing hardware and software systems. If the database system replaces an existing system, then ensuring a smooth transition between the old and new system.

► Documenting the database development and the database system implemented – providing the appropriate documentation and user guides for the client, database administrators and users of the database system.

► Training the client, database administrators and users of the database system to use, maintain and adapt the database system, as appropriate.

As the development of application software (user processes) proceeds, a first-cut database design often needs to be flexed in order to improve the quality of the database design with respect to the desirable properties of a database – integrity, flexibility, efficiency and usability. This necessitates revisiting the activities associated with the database design task described in Section 4 to develop second-cut designs.

The database schema is a working document that evolves as the database design and implementation tasks proceed, going through a series of second-cut designs, until not only the information requirements of the enterprise have been satisfied, but also these desirable database properties are met. That is, the implementation task and the development of the final database schema proceed incrementally. They also proceed iteratively because, in reality, the implementation task cannot be done in isolation; it requires feedback from both the client and, most importantly, users of the database system (possibly even the client's customers) throughout the task.

As the above list of activities implies, implementation is about not just developing and testing a database system, but also integrating the database system into a client's existing hardware and software systems, and providing the client with adequate documentation and training for their staff and users.

EXERCISE 5.1

Consider a database designed to satisfy the information requirements of a store in the Walton Stores supermarket chain. What specialist hardware and other computer systems do you think the database system needs to interface with?

[handwritten margin note: checkout tills, Bar code reader for accepting stock]

The aim of this section is to provide you with some basic guidelines for implementing database designs, expressed as SQL database definitions, using SQL Anywhere. It will provide overviews on:

▶ implementing an SQL database definition;

▶ populating a database with data;

▶ developing and testing application software.

A detailed description of the design and implementation of application software is beyond the scope of the course; but in *Block 5* we will describe how software that is written using programming languages such as Java can interface with a relational DBMS such as SQL Anywhere. However, as application software can only access and modify a relational database using SQL statements, in this section we will provide a framework for developing application software in terms of the SQL statements needed to satisfy the operational requirements of the software. This framework can also be the basis for testing a database system to ensure that it satisfies the information requirements of an enterprise.

5.1 | Implementing a database schema

In Section 4, for the sake of brevity, we gave SQL Anywhere database definitions in the course text and as solutions to exercises without any concern to whether they would be interpreted by SQL Anywhere without errors because of the order in which definitions of tables, columns and domains are declared. The aim of this section is to provide you with some guidelines for writing SQL database definitions that are acceptable to SQL Anywhere, and to ensure that you are aware of limited checking of constraint, function, procedure and trigger definitions performed by SQL Anywhere.

Figure 5.1 shows a fragment of a database schema diagram for a simplified database design that represents the checkout till receipts used by Walton Stores.

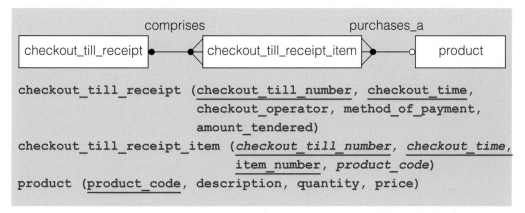

Figure 5.1   A fragment of a database schema diagram for a simplified database design that represents the checkout till receipts used by Walton Stores

Figure 5.2 gives an SQL database definition for the database schema diagram given in Figure 5.1.

```
CREATE DOMAIN checkout_till_numbers AS SMALLINT
   CHECK (@VALUE BETWEEN 1 AND 99)
CREATE DOMAIN checkout_times AS TIMESTAMP
CREATE DOMAIN checkout_operators AS VARCHAR(20)
CREATE DOMAIN methods_of_payment AS VARCHAR(11)
   CHECK (@VALUE IN ('Cash', 'Cheque','Debit card', 'credit card', 'FSC'))
CREATE DOMAIN amounts_tendered AS DECIMAL(6, 2)
   CHECK (@VALUE > 0.00)
CREATE DOMAIN item_numbers AS SMALLINT
   CHECK (@VALUE BETWEEN 1 AND 999)
CREATE DOMAIN product_codes AS VARCHAR(8)
   CHECK ((CHAR_LENGTH(TRIM(@VALUE)) = 8) AND
          (CAST(@VALUE AS INTEGER) BETWEEN 0 AND 99999999))
CREATE DOMAIN descriptions_of_products AS VARCHAR(200)
CREATE DOMAIN quantities_of_products AS VARCHAR(20)
CREATE DOMAIN prices_of_products AS DECIMAL(6, 2)
   CHECK (@VALUE > 0.00)

CREATE TABLE checkout_till_receipt
   (checkout_till_number checkout_till_numbers NOT NULL,
    checkout_time checkout_times NOT NULL,
    checkout_operator checkout_operators NOT NULL,
    method_of_payment methods_of_payment NOT NULL,
    amount_tendered amounts_tendered NOT NULL,
   PRIMARY KEY (checkout_till_number, checkout_time),
   CONSTRAINT mandatory_participation_in_comprises
     CHECK (EXISTS
       (SELECT *
        FROM checkout_till_receipt_item
        WHERE checkout_till_receipt.checkout_till_number =
              checkout_till_receipt_item.checkout_till_number
          AND checkout_till_receipt.checkout_time =
              checkout_till_receipt_item.checkout_time)
     )
   )

CREATE TABLE checkout_till_receipt_item
   (checkout_till_number checkout_till_numbers NOT NULL,
    checkout_time checkout_times NOT NULL,
    item_number item_numbers NOT NULL,
    product_code product_codes NOT NULL,
   PRIMARY KEY (checkout_till_number, checkout_time, item_number),
   CONSTRAINT relationship_comprises
     FOREIGN KEY (checkout_till_number, checkout_time)
     REFERENCES checkout_till_receipt,
   CONSTRAINT relationship_purchases_a
     FOREIGN KEY (product_code)
     REFERENCES product
   )

CREATE TABLE product
   (product_code product_codes NOT NULL,
    description descriptions_of_products NOT NULL,
    quantity quantities_of_products NOT NULL,
    price prices_of_products NOT NULL,
   PRIMARY KEY (product_code)
   )
```

Figure 5.2   An SQL database definition for the database schema diagram given in Figure 5.1

The SQL database definition given in Figure 5.2 will fail with an error when interpreted by SQL Anywhere because the foreign declaration in the definition of the `checkout_till_receipt_item` table representing the **purchases_a** relationship references the **product** table which at that point is not defined. An SQL database definition will be acceptable to SQL Anywhere only if:

▶ the definition employs the correct SQL syntax for the **CREATE DOMAIN** and **CREATE TABLE** statements;

▶ column definitions reference domains that have been previously defined;

▶ the **FOREIGN KEY** declarations reference tables that have been previously defined.

The SQL database definition would produce errors when interpreted by SQL Anywhere if any SQL keyword had been misspelt or misplaced in the definition, or if any of the domains or tables referenced in the **CREATE TABLE** statements had not been previously defined by **CREATE DOMAIN** or **CREATE TABLE** statements, respectively.

To enable the SQL database definition given in Figure 5.2 to be interpreted by SQL Anywhere without errors, we could simply define the **product** table before the `checkout_till_receipt_item` table. Alternatively, we could defer the foreign key declaration in the definition of the `checkout_till_receipt_item` table representing the **purchases_a** relationship until after the **product** table has been defined. This is shown in Figure 5.3 where an **ALTER TABLE** statement is used to add the **FOREIGN KEY** declaration to the `checkout_till_receipt_item` table after the **product** table has been defined. In Figure 5.3 the definitions of the domains and the `checkout_till_receipt` and **product** tables are the same as those in Figure 5.2.

```
CREATE TABLE checkout_till_receipt
   . . .


CREATE TABLE checkout_till_receipt_item
   (checkout_till_number checkout_till_numbers NOT NULL,
    checkout_time checkout_times NOT NULL,
    item_number item_numbers NOT NULL,
   PRIMARY KEY (checkout_till_number, checkout_time, item_number),
   CONSTRAINT relationship_comprises
      FOREIGN KEY (checkout_till_number, checkout_time)
      REFERENCES checkout_till_receipt)


CREATE TABLE product
   . . .


ALTER TABLE checkout_till_receipt_item
   ADD CONSTRAINT relationship_purchases_a
      FOREIGN KEY (product_code)
      REFERENCES product
```

Figure 5.3   Another SQL database definition for the database schema diagram in Figure 5.1, which is acceptable to SQL Anywhere and will be interpreted by SQL Anywhere without error

The SQL database definition given in Figure 5.3 would NOT produce any errors when interpreted by SQL Anywhere if we replaced the **CONSTRAINT** declared in the `checkout_till_receipt` table with the following definition, where we have misspelt the table specified on the **FROM** clause (`chuckout_till_receipt_item`) and a column referenced by the **WHERE** clause (`checkout_toll_number`):

```
CONSTRAINT mandatory_participation_in_comprises
  CHECK (EXISTS
    (SELECT *
     FROM chuckout_till_receipt_item
     WHERE checkout_till_receipt.checkout_toll_number =
           checkout_till_receipt_item.checkout_till_number
       AND checkout_till_receipt.checkout_time =
           checkout_till_receipt_item.checkout_time)
    )
    ...
```

Such errors will only be identified when an attempt is made to insert a row into the **checkout_till_receipt** table when the check constraint will be evaluated.

SQL Anywhere does not check table and column references in the search conditions specified by check constraints and triggers, or in the bodies of procedures and functions. Any errors in the table and column references will be identified only when the check constraint, trigger, procedure or function is evaluated.

An appropriate approach to developing an SQL database definition for a particular database design using SQL Anywhere is as follows:

1   Define all of the domains using **CREATE DOMAIN** statements.

2   Define all the columns of all the tables using **CREATE TABLE** statements and include all the column, primary key and uniqueness constraints.

3   Define all of the foreign keys using **ALTER TABLE** statements.

4   Define table constraints by using either check constraints or triggers; check constraints are added to a table using **ALTER TABLE** statements, and triggers using **CREATE TRIGGER** statements.

The table and column references in the search conditions, specified by check constraints and triggers, can be checked during step 4 by evaluating them as queries against the tables defined by earlier steps. For example, the search condition specified by the check constraint given in Figure 5.2 could be checked simply by evaluating the following query:

```
SELECT *
    FROM checkout_till_receipt, checkout_till_receipt_item
    WHERE checkout_till_receipt.checkout_till_number =
          checkout_till_receipt_item.checkout_till_number
      AND checkout_till_receipt.checkout_time =
          checkout_till_receipt_item.checkout_time
```

EXERCISE 5.2

A fragment of the entity–relationship model of the *Hospital conceptual data model*, describing the formation of consultants and junior doctors into teams, is shown below.

Entity–relationship diagram

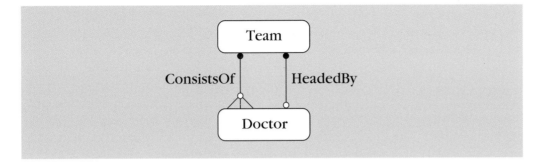

Entity types

Team (<u>TeamCode</u>, TelephoneNo)
Doctor (<u>StaffNo</u>, DoctorName, Position)

Additional constraints

c.2   A doctor who is the head of a team must be a consultant. That is, an instance of the entity type Doctor that is involved in the relationship HeadedBy must have a position of consultant.

c.3   A consultant must head a team. Doctors who are not consultants must be members of a team. That is, an instance of the entity type Doctor whose position is that of a consultant belongs to a team via the HeadedBy relationship, whereas other doctors belong to a team via the ConsistsOf relationship.

Show how you would implement the following database schema diagram that represents the above fragment of the *Hospital conceptual data model* with SQL Anywhere using the approach that we have described. You will need to consult the *Hospital domain of discourse summary* to determine the domains over which the columns should be defined.

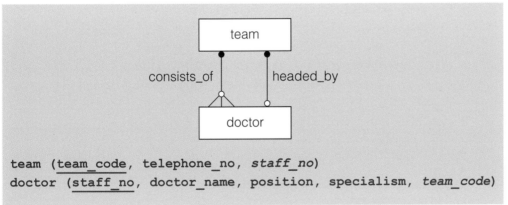

```
team (team_code, telephone_no, staff_no)
doctor (staff_no, doctor_name, position, specialism, team_code)
```

5.2 Populating a database with data

Once we have implemented some or all of a database schema we are in a position to start populating the database with some data, not only to check that the database design satisfies the data requirements, but also to facilitate the development of application software to satisfy the operational requirements.

Before we outline the approaches to populating a database with data using SQL Anywhere, we first need to consider the issue of when constraints that enforce the integrity of the data are checked. By default, constraints are checked at the end of the execution of every SQL statement even though those SQL statements may form part of an SQL transaction. There will be many situations where this default will be inappropriate and so we need to describe how standard SQL and SQL Anywhere allow us to defer constraint checking until a more appropriate time.

EXERCISE 5.3

Suppose we have just implemented one of the SQL database definitions given in Figures 5.2 and 5.3 for the database schema diagram shown in Figure 5.1. Explain why attempting to populate the `checkout_till_receipt` and `checkout_till_receipt_item` tables using SQL `INSERT` statements will fail without adding any rows to either table.

The solution to Exercise 5.3 illustrates the limitation of the default of checking some constraints immediately after an SQL statement has been executed.

Standard SQL allows you to declare each individual constraint as being **INITIALLY IMMEDIATE** (the default) or **INITIALLY DEFERRED** at the start of each transaction. Immediate constraints are checked at the end of every SQL statement; deferred constraints are checked at the end of an SQL transaction.

Figure 5.4 shows how the two constraints, identified in the solution to Exercise 5.3 as preventing the population of the `checkout_till_receipt` and `checkout_till_receipt_item` tables, could be defined as initially deferred to allow those tables to be populated with data using an SQL transaction.

```
CREATE TABLE checkout_till_receipt
  ( ... ,
  CONSTRAINT mandatory_participation_in_comprises
    INITIALLY DEFERRED
    CHECK (EXISTS
      (SELECT *
       FROM checkout_till_receipt_item
       WHERE checkout_till_receipt.checkout_till_number =
             checkout_till_receipt_item.checkout_till_number
         AND checkout_till_receipt.checkout_time =
             checkout_till_receipt_item.checkout_time)
    )
  )


CREATE TABLE checkout_till_receipt_item
  ( ... ,
  CONSTRAINT relationship_comprises
    INITIALLY DEFERRED
    FOREIGN KEY (checkout_till_number, checkout_time)
    REFERENCES checkout_till_receipt
  )
```

Figure 5.4   A partial SQL database definition for the database schema diagram given in Figure 5.1 that allows the population of the `checkout_till_receipt` and `checkout_till_receipt_item` tables

The standard SQL **SET CONSTRAINTS** statement can be used to change the initial modes for individual constraints, if permitted by the definition, and also force the checking of a deferred constraint upon demand (before the transaction completes).

SQL Anywhere does NOT fully support deferred constraint checking but does allow deferred checking of foreign key (referential) integrity. This facility is provided by the

SQL Anywhere **WAIT_FOR_COMMIT** database option. We will illustrate the use of this SQL Anywhere database option by considering how we could populate the **checkout_till_receipt** and **checkout_till_receipt_item** tables defined in Figure 5.3 with the data supplied on the checkout till receipt number 1 shown in Figure 2.6, which we have reproduced as Figure 5.5 below.

WALTON STORES

Ramsgard
Your checkout operator today was
JASON

	£
Pasteurised skimmed milk 1.136 litres	0.50
Pasteurised skimmed milk 1.136 litres	0.50
Prunes in apple juice 410g	0.65
Vegetable fat spread 250g	2.49
Total	**4.14**
Debit card	4.14

25-May-2006 15:43

Figure 5.5   An example of a checkout till receipt (from Figure 2.6)

Figure 5.6 gives an SQL transaction that incorporates the **WAIT_FOR_COMMIT** database option provided by SQL Anywhere.

```
BEGIN
SET OPTION WAIT_FOR_COMMIT = ON;
INSERT INTO checkout_till_receipt_item
   VALUES(1, '2006-05-25 15:43', 1, '01015279');
INSERT INTO checkout_till_receipt_item
   VALUES(1, '2006-05-25 15:43', 2,'01015279');
INSERT INTO checkout_till_receipt_item
   VALUES(1, '2006-05-25 15:43', 3, '02348187');
INSERT INTO checkout_till_receipt_item
   VALUES(1, '2006-05-25 15:43', 4, '08562411');
INSERT INTO checkout_till_receipt
   VALUES(1, '2006-05-25 15:43', 'Jason', 'debit card', 4.14);
END
```

Figure 5.6   Populating the **checkout_till_receipt** and **checkout_till_receipt_item** tables using the **WAIT_FOR_COMMIT** database option provided by SQL Anywhere

In Figure 5.6, setting the SQL Anywhere database option **WAIT_FOR_COMMIT** to ON causes referential integrity to remain unchecked until a commit executes when a transaction completes. If the database is in an inconsistent state at the end of a transaction, then the transaction does not commit and SQL Anywhere reports an error.

The approach that is used to populate the **checkout_till_receipt** and **checkout_till_receipt_item** tables, as shown in Figure 5.6, is as follows:

Rows are initially added to the table at the :*n* (foreign key) end of the **comprises** relationship, **checkout_till_receipt_item**, without checking the values assigned to the foreign key columns **checkout_till_number** and **checkout_time** referencing the **checkout_till_receipt** table, and the foreign key column **product_code** referencing the **product** table.

Rows are then added to the table at the :1 end of the **comprises** relationship, **checkout_till_receipt**, evaluating the constraint defined in that table to represent mandatory participation of that table in the **comprises** relationship for each row inserted.

When the transaction commits, the values assigned to the foreign key columns **checkout_till_number** and **checkout_time** of the **checkout_till_receipt_item** table will be checked against the primary key values of the **checkout_till_receipt** table, and the values assigned to the foreign key column **product_code** against the primary key values of the **product** table.

If we follow the approach of populating database tables using the SQL Anywhere database option **WAIT_FOR_COMMIT**, we will not be able to populate all database tables because the option only defers the checking of foreign key (referential) integrity, unlike the deferred constraint checking provided by standard SQL that can defer the checking of all constraints.

EXERCISE 5.4

Explain why it is not possible to populate the **team** and **doctor** tables in the database implementation given in the solution to Exercise 5.2 using the SQL Anywhere database option **WAIT_FOR_COMMIT** as we have described.

In those situations when we cannot populate database tables with data using the SQL Anywhere database option **WAIT_FOR_COMMIT**, we have to employ one of the following approaches:

1   Drop the minimum number of constraints to allow data to be inserted into the tables, check the integrity of the data, then reinstate those constraints that were dropped.

2   Drop some (as in 1) or all of the constraints, then use SQL procedures as the sole means of updating the database and to validate the constraints on the data. Each procedure needs an execute privilege, which enables users to update the database tables without requiring the privilege on the tables to use an SQL statement to update the tables directly.

5.3   Developing and testing application software

In this section we will outline a framework for developing application software (user processes), which can also be used as the basis for verifying that the database satisfies the information requirements of an enterprise.

An approach to satisfying the information requirements of an enterprise is to view all the functions of the database (operational requirements) as transactions. That is, a 'real world' event, such as a customer purchasing a selection of products at a store in the Walton Stores supermarket chain, is represented by a database transaction. A transaction as an operation may be viewed as sequence of steps initiated by a single process or individual that must succeed entirely, or fail completely.

A customer purchasing a selection of products is a transaction because it comprises a sequence of steps – the checkout operator scans each product selected by the customer, and handles the customer's payment for the purchases. It is initiated by an individual – the customer bringing the selected product(s) to the checkout till. It must succeed entirely – the customer has sufficient money to pay for purchases – or fail completely – the checkout operator fails to get authorisation for the customer's credit card and the customer leaves the store 'empty-handed'.

This approach of viewing all the functions of the database (operational requirements) as transactions is analogous to the **use case** which is used in object-oriented software development methods to describe the functionality of a system from a user's perspective.

The approach to developing application software described here is as follows:

1   Produce a detailed outline of steps that comprise some significant operation (event) – a scenario.

2   Describe how the scenario could be enacted using an SQL transaction, giving the SQL statements required to query and/or modify the database in order to effect the steps of the scenario.

3   Develop the application software by incorporating these SQL statements using, for example, the approaches described in *Block 5*.

The SQL statements produced for step 2 can be used to demonstrate that the database *could* satisfy the information requirements of an enterprise without writing the application software and user interfaces.

We will illustrate this approach by considering in more detail a customer purchasing a selection of products at a store in the Walton Stores supermarket chain.

In Section 2, we gave the transcript of the interview with the checkout operator Gerda in Figure 2.9, which outlined the steps involved in the purchase of products by a customer from the perspective of the checkout operator. The following description is a possible scenario for the purchase of products by a customer at a checkout till:

1   The checkout operator presses the **NEXT CUSTOMER** button on the operator's screen to start the operation (transaction).

2   The checkout operator scans each item to obtain its price and record the details on the checkout till receipt.

3   The checkout operator presses the **TOTAL** button on the operator's screen and the total cost of the purchases is displayed to the customer.

4   The checkout operator handles the customer's payment for the purchases.

5   The checkout operator presses the **NEXT CUSTOMER** button on the operator's screen to complete the operation (transaction), which also initiates the next transaction (see step 1).

This scenario only considers the situation where no problems are encountered during the purchase of products by a customer at a checkout till. We would need to extend this scenario to handle all possible problems and their solutions. For example, the checkout operator is unable to obtain authorisation for payment by credit card.

To facilitate the development and testing of application software, it is essential that we have some sample data. We will use the data supplied on the checkout till receipt that we reproduced in Figure 5.5.

In Figure 5.7 we show how the above scenario could be enacted using an SQL transaction, by giving the SQL statements that are required to query and/or modify the database in order to effect each step of this scenario.

```
// 1  The checkout operator presses the NEXT CUSTOMER button
// on the operator's screen to start the operation (transaction).
BEGIN
SET OPTION WAIT_FOR_COMMIT = ON;
// 2  The checkout operator scans each item to obtain its
// price and record the details on the checkout till receipt.
INSERT INTO checkout_till_receipt_item
   VALUES(1, '2006-05-25 15:43', 1, '01015279');
INSERT INTO checkout_till_receipt_item
   VALUES(1, '2006-05-25 15:43', 2, '01015279');
INSERT INTO checkout_till_receipt_item
   VALUES(1, '2006-05-25 15:43', 3,'02348187');
INSERT INTO checkout_till_receipt_item
   VALUES(1, '2006-05-25 15:43', 4, '08562411');
// 3  The checkout operator presses the TOTAL button on
// the operator's screen and the total cost of the
// purchases is displayed to the customer.
DECLARE total_cost DECIMAL(6, 2);
SELECT SUM(product.price) INTO total_cost
   FROM checkout_till_receipt_item JOIN product
   ON checkout_till_receipt_item.product_code =
      product.product_code
   WHERE checkout_till_number = 1
   AND checkout_time = '2006-05-25 15:43';
// 4  The checkout operator handles the customer's
// payment for the purchases.
INSERT INTO checkout_till_receipt
   VALUES(1, '2006-05-25 15:43', 'Jason', 'Debit card', 4.14);
// 5  The checkout operator presses the NEXT CUSTOMER button
// on the operator's screen to complete the
// operation (transaction).
IF 4.14 = total_cost THEN COMMIT WORK ELSE ROLLBACK WORK;
END
```

Figure 5.7   SQL statements that are required to query and/or modify the database in order to effect each step of the scenario at a supermarket checkout till

Figure 5.7 is only intended to outline the sequence of SQL statements required to effect the above scenario. Any application software written to process checkout till receipts would need to replace literal data embedded in the SQL statements with variables. This will be discussed in *Block 5*.

ACTIVITY 5.1

You will find the instructions for this activity on the course website. The aim of this activity is to enable you to engage with the practical activities associated with the database implementation task as described in this section, by implementing a database design using SQL Anywhere, populating it with data and demonstrating that the database could satisfy the specified information requirements.

5.4 Summary

This section has focused on the implementation task, which entails all of the activities that need to be completed before a database development can move from the database (logical) schema stage to the next stage of its life cycle, a database system that satisfies all of the information requirements of an enterprise.

In this section on the implementation task, we have provided overviews on:

▶ Implementing an SQL database definition using SQL Anywhere.

▶ Populating an SQL Anywhere database with data.

▶ Developing and testing application software.

LEARNING OUTCOMES

Having completed your study of this section of the course, you will be able to:

▶ Describe the purpose of each activity associated with the database implementation task.

▶ Implement a database design expressed as an SQL database definition using SQL Anywhere.

▶ Populate an SQL Anywhere database with data not only to check that the database design satisfies the data requirements, but also to facilitate the development of application software to satisfy the operational requirements.

▶ Outline a framework that could be used to facilitate the development application software and demonstrate that the database could satisfy the information requirements of an enterprise.

6 Database maintenance

In Section 1, we said that the database life cycle has two phases – database development and database maintenance. The database maintenance phase starts when the database development phase completes, when the database is accepted by the client and it becomes operational. The database maintenance phase continues until the database system is withdrawn from use, and this phase is usually much longer than the database development phase.

EXERCISE 6.1

Explain why the database development and database maintenance phases are equally important and critical to organisations that employ databases to facilitate their day-to-day operations.

Many organisations are wholly dependent on their databases once they are installed to facilitate their day-to-day operations. Walton Stores, and other businesses in the retail sector, for example, could not trade without a functioning database, that is, a database that continues to satisfy the information requirements of the enterprise.

Businesses wishing to maintain their position in the marketplace will often have to adapt their databases to meet new and changing requirements. Such changes in requirements arise not only from organisations wishing to exploit new business opportunities, for example selling a new range of products or services, but also from changes to government legislation that affect the way those organisations function.

There are two main forms of maintenance – operational and adaptive. **Operational maintenance** ensures that the database continues to satisfy the information requirements of an enterprise after it has been installed, by monitoring its performance and undertaking a database restructuring or database reorganisation when necessary. **Adaptive maintenance** concerns the restructuring of a database to meet new and changing requirements.

Once a database has been installed and is fully operational, close monitoring needs to take place to ensure that performance remains within acceptable levels. The acceptable levels of performance will have been defined in the specification of requirements. A DBMS normally provides proprietary **database tools** to enable the database administrator (DBA) to monitor the performance of the database. These tools give information on, for example, database usage, query execution strategy, use of database locks to support concurrent transactions and other performance indicators. The DBA can use this information to tune the database system in order to give better performance by restructuring and/or reorganising the database.

Database reorganisation involves changes to the storage schema, which specifies how the logical (database) schema is stored and accessed. Database reorganisation is usually performed using proprietary database tools as standard SQL does not provide any facility to define or modify the storage schema. Indexes may be defined on columns of tables to facilitate access to rows as described in *Block 3*, Subsection 5.8.

Database restructuring involves changes to the logical (database) schema, which defines the table structure of a database. Database restructuring is performed primarily using the SQL data definition statements **CREATE TABLE**, **ALTER TABLE** and **DROP TABLE** to define new tables, modify and delete existing tables, respectively.

This section focuses on database restructuring and has two aims: First, to illustrate how we can restructure an SQL Anywhere database to optimise the performance of data retrieval by relaxing the requirement that database tables should be in BCNF. Second, to describe how we can restructure an SQL Anywhere database to ensure that it continues to satisfy the information requirements after it has been installed, and/or to meet new and changing requirements.

6.1 Denormalisation

When we compared the *foreign key alone approach* to representing relationships with the *relation for relationship approach* in Subsection 4.2, we stated our preference for the former approach for representing 1:1 and 1:*n* relationships. The reasoning behind this preference was that because the *foreign key alone approach* employs fewer tables to represent relationships, fewer relational joins – relatively resource intensive operations – would be required to realise the information that is recorded by those relationships. In the database designs we presented in Section 4, we minimised the number of tables employed to represent an entity–relationship model by using columns rather than tables to record optional single-valued properties (see Subsection 4.1), and the *foreign key alone approach* to representing relationships whenever possible.

In this subsection, we will consider the advantages and disadvantages of merging two or more tables together, and the relationships between them, after the database has been installed. The goal of merging tables is to improve the efficiency of queries required to satisfy the operational requirements of an enterprise by reducing the number of joins that are needed to obtain the necessary information.

Figure 6.1 shows a database schema diagram for a database design that represents the data requirements as described by the checkout till receipts used by Walton Stores.

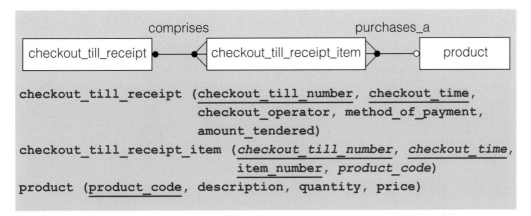

Figure 6.1   A database schema diagram for a database design that represents the data requirements described by the checkout till receipts used by Walton Stores

Figure 6.2 shows examples of the rows of the tables defined in Figure 6.1 that record the data shown on the checkout till receipt in Figure 5.5.

checkout_till_receipt

checkout_till _number	checkout_time	checkout_ operator	method_of _payment	amount_ tendered
1	25-May-2006 15:43	Jason	Debit card	4.14
...	...	...	...	...

checkout_till_receipt_item

checkout_till_number	checkout_time	item_number	product_code
1	25-May-2006 15:43	1	01015279
1	25-May-2006 15:43	2	01015279
1	25-May-2006 15:43	3	02348187
1	25-May-2006 15:43	4	08562411
...	...	...	...

product

product_code	description	quantity	price
01015279	Pasteurised skimmed milk	1.136 litres	0.50
02348187	Prunes in apple juice	410g	0.65
08562411	Vegetable fat spread	250g	2.49
...	...	...	...

Figure 6.2 Examples of the rows of the tables defined in Figure 6.1 that record the data shown on the checkout till receipt in Figure 5.5

Suppose an operational requirement of Walton Stores is to analyse customer purchases by running frequent queries similar to that shown in Figure 6.3. This query performs joins between the **checkout_till_receipt**, **checkout_till_receipt_item** and **product** tables.

```
SELECT *
FROM checkout_till_receipt A,
     checkout_till_receipt_item B,
     product C
WHERE  A.checkout_till_number = B.checkout_till_number
  AND  A.checkout_time = B.checkout_time
  AND  B.product_code = C.product_code
```

Figure 6.3 An SQL query to analyse customers' purchases

There are a number of ways that we could restructure the database design shown in Figure 6.1 that would reduce the number of joins required to satisfy the above operational requirement. One option would be to merge (join) the **checkout_till_receipt** and **checkout_till_receipt_item** tables as shown in Figures 6.4 and 6.5.

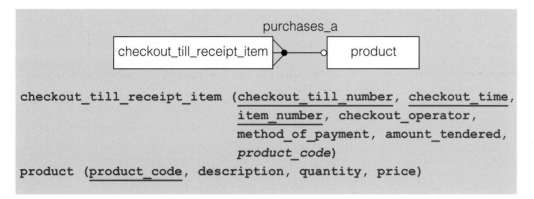

checkout_till_receipt_item (checkout_till_number, checkout_time,
                            item_number, checkout_operator,
                            method_of_payment, amount_tendered,
                            product_code)
product (product_code, description, quantity, price)

Figure 6.4   A database schema diagram for a database design that represents the data
requirements described by the checkout till receipts used by Walton Stores

checkout_till_receipt_item

checkout _till _number	checkout _time	item_ number	checkout _operator	method_of _payment	amount_ tendered	product _code
1	25-May-2006 15:43	1	Jason	Debit card	4.14	01015279
1	25-May-2006 15:43	2	Jason	Debit card	4.14	01015279
1	25-May-2006 15:43	3	Jason	Debit card	4.14	02348187
1	25-May-2006 15:43	4	Jason	Debit card	4.14	08562411
...	...	...	...	...	...	...

Figure 6.5   Example rows from a restructured checkout_till_receipt_item table

In the database design shown in Figures 6.4 and 6.5, we have merged the
checkout_till_receipt and checkout_till_receipt_item tables by copying the
data recorded by the checkout_till_receipt table into the
checkout_till_receipt_item table.

EXERCISE 6.2

What is the consequence of merging the checkout_till_receipt and
checkout_till_receipt_item tables?

Merging tables that are associated by 1:*n* relationships will result in tables that will
typically include duplicated information, and these tables are referred to as
unnormalised tables as they are not in BCNF. The process of merging tables to
speed up the retrieval process by deliberately introducing redundancy into the data is
known as **denormalisation**.

EXERCISE 6.3

Explain why denormalisation is usually not performed unless a performance need
arises.

As denormalisation results in duplicated information it often requires more disk space to store a merged table than the original tables. If you compare the example rows from the **checkout_till_receipt** and **checkout_till_receipt_item** tables shown in Figure 6.2 with those of the restructured **checkout_till_receipt_item** table shown in Figure 6.5, you will see that the restructured table requires more space to record the same information on the checkout till receipts than the **checkout_till_receipt** and **checkout_till_receipt_item** tables.

The possibility of insertion, amendment and deletion anomalies noted in the solution to Exercise 6.3 will be of no concern, however, if the rows of a denormalised table do not require to be updated after they have been inserted into the merged table. This will be true for the restructured **checkout_till_receipt_item** table shown in Figures 6.4 and 6.5 because the merged table records the products purchased by customers and that information will not need updating. So, we could amend our database design that represents the data requirements described by the checkout till receipts and product labels to that shown in Figure 6.4, to reduce the number of joins required to satisfy the operational requirement to analyse customers' purchases as shown by the SQL query in Figure 6.3.

EXERCISE 6.4

Explain why it would not be appropriate to merge (join) the **checkout_till_receipt**, **checkout_till_receipt_item** and **product** tables into a single table.

As explained in the solution to Exercise 6.4, merging the **checkout_till_receipt**, **checkout_till_receipt_item** and **product** tables into a single table to optimise the analysis of customer purchases would not be appropriate because it would complicate satisfying other requirements. However, we could merge the **checkout_till_receipt** and **checkout_till_receipt_item** tables into a single table as in the database design shown in Figure 6.4 but also include relevant data from the **product** table – the **description**, **quantity** and **price** columns – as shown in Figure 6.6.

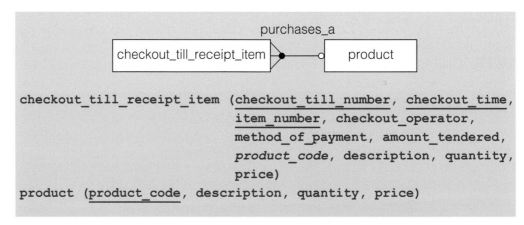

Figure 6.6   A database schema diagram for a database design that represents the data requirements described by the checkout till receipts used by Walton Stores

The database design shown in Figure 6.6 not only facilitates analyses of customers' purchases but also supports the other requirements that were considered in Section 3. The information presented on checkout till receipts shown in Figure 2.6 are represented by a single table, **checkout_till_receipt_item**, which is unnormalised but does not compromise the integrity of the information because the rows that are added to this table will not require updating. Using this table, analyses of customers' purchases are not required to perform any relational joins in order to obtain the basic information as this is all included in this single table.

Summary of Subsection 6.1

Denormalisation is the process of merging (joining) two or more related tables together as a single table to improve the performance of retrievals by reducing the number of joins needed to obtain the required information. As the name of the process implies, denormalisation typically results in unnormalised tables, that is, tables that are not in BCNF. Such tables include duplicated information that may result in insertion, amendment and deletion anomalies if the duplicated information needs to be updated.

6.2 | Database restructuring

There are many reasons why it may be necessary to restructure a database after it has been installed and accepted by the client. These reasons include:

1   Correcting errors or omissions in the database design and/or implementation that were not detected during acceptance testing.

2   Optimising retrieval performance.

3   Satisfying new and changing requirements.

EXERCISE 6.5

As we discussed in Subsection 6.1, optimising retrieval performance can be achieved by merging two or more tables together. What other ways are there to optimise retrieval performance?

Database restructuring involves adding, modifying and deleting tables, columns, relationships, domains, constraints and triggers. While adding new tables, columns, relationships, domains, constraints and triggers is usually straightforward, modifying and deleting them once the database has been populated with data can often be difficult and/or needs to be done with due consideration. Table 6.1 outlines the basic SQL Anywhere statements required to add, modify and delete tables, columns, relationships, domains, constraints and triggers.

- indexing
- creating views for static data
- improving hardware
- splitting the work of retrieval queries
- storing derived data

Add	SQL statement(s)	Comments
table	`CREATE TABLE <table-name> <table-definition>`	
column	`ALTER TABLE <table-name>` `    ADD <column-definition>`	

relationship	`ALTER TABLE <table-name>`
	`    ADD <column-name> <data-type> [NOT NULL]`
	`    CONSTRAINT <constraint-name> REFERENCES`
	`            <table-name> [<actions>]`
		For any relationship being represented using the *relation for relationship approach*, the table representing that relationship would have to be created first.

domain	`CREATE DOMAIN <domain-name> <domain-definition>`	
constraint	`ALTER TABLE <table-name>` `    ADD CONSTRAINT <constraint-name>` ` {UNIQUE (<column-name>, ...)	PRIMARY KEY` ` (<column-name>, ...)` `	<foreign-key-constraint>	CHECK (<search-condition>) }`	
trigger	`CREATE TRIGGER <trigger-name> <trigger-definition>`	

Modify	SQL statement(s)	Comments
table	`ALTER TABLE <table-name> <table-definition>`	
column	`ALTER TABLE <table-name>` `    MODIFY <column-definition>`	

relationship	`ALTER TABLE <table-name>`
	`    DELETE FOREIGN KEY <constraint-name>`
	`ALTER TABLE <table-name>`
	`    ADD <column-name> <data-type> [NOT NULL]`
	`    CONSTRAINT <constraint-name> REFERENCES`
	`            <table-name> [<actions>]`
		To modify the definition of a relationship, it is usually necessary to delete and then recreate it.

domain	`DROP DOMAIN <domain-name>` `CREATE DOMAIN <domain-name> <domain-definition>`	The SQL Anywhere **ALTER DOMAIN** statement only allows you to rename a domain name. To modify the definition of a domain, it is necessary to delete and then recreate it.
constraint	`ALTER TABLE <table-name>` `    DELETE CONSTRAINT <constraint-name>` `ALTER TABLE <table-name>` `    ADD CONSTRAINT <constraint-name>` ` {UNIQUE (<column-name>, ...)	PRIMARY KEY` ` (<column-name>, ...)` `	<foreign-key-constraint>	CHECK (<search-condition>) }`	To modify the definition of a constraint, it is usually necessary to delete and then recreate it.
trigger	`ALTER TRIGGER <trigger-name> <trigger-definition>`	

Table 6.1   An outline of the basic SQL Anywhere statements required to add, modify and delete tables, columns, relationships, domains, constraints and triggers

Delete	SQL statement(s)	Comments
table	DROP TABLE <table-name>	A populated table cannot be dropped if any column is referenced by another table.
column	ALTER TABLE <table-name> DELETE <column-name>	
relationship	ALTER TABLE <table-name> DELETE FOREIGN KEY <constraint-name>	
domain	DROP DOMAIN <domain-name>	A domain cannot be dropped if any column is defined over it.
constraint	ALTER TABLE <table-name> DELETE CONSTRAINT <constraint-name>	
trigger	DROP TRIGGER <trigger-name>	

Table 6.1   *continued*

Table 6.1 shows that the database restructure is accomplished primarily by using the SQL **ALTER TABLE** statement. This statement was introduced in *Block 3*, Subsection 5.6. A detailed description of the SQL Anywhere **ALTER TABLE** statement can be found in the Sybase online book: *ASA SQL Reference, Part I SQL, Chapter 4, SQL Statements.*

The SQL **ALTER TABLE** statement provides a comprehensive means of restructuring a database. However, we need to use the SQL **ALTER TABLE** statement with caution when attempting to change a table, column or constraint when it is associated with data because it may be necessary to transform the data or re-evaluate the data against a new or modified constraint. For example, if we decide to change the data type of a particular column from **VARCHAR(100)** to **VARCHAR(80)**, any existing data recorded by that column will be truncated to 80 characters as a result of the execution of the **ALTER TABLE** statement that effected the change to the data type, which may result in loss of data.

As Table 6.1 shows, not every aspect of database restructuring can be performed directly by the SQL **ALTER TABLE** statement. Database restructuring that requires the data to be transformed in some way may require the rows of a table to be moved to a temporary table first, the empty table restructured, the data transformed and then the table repopulated with transformed data.

ACTIVITY 6.1

You will find the instructions for this activity on the course website. The aim of this activity is to enable you to engage with the practical activities associated with database restructuring and explore some of the issues outlined above, by restructuring the database you implemented in Activity 5.1.

6.3 Summary

This section has focused on the maintenance phase of the database life cycle, which starts when the database development phase completes, when the database is accepted by the client and it becomes operational. There are two main forms of maintenance – operational and adaptive. Operational maintenance ensures that the database continues to satisfy the information requirements of an enterprise after it has been installed, by monitoring its performance and undertaking a database restructuring or database reorganisation when necessary. Adaptive maintenance concerns the restructuring of a database to meet new and changing requirements.

In this section on the maintenance phase, we have provided overviews on:

▶ Denormalisation – merging (joining) two or more related tables together as a single table to improve the performance of retrievals by reducing the number of joins needed to obtain the required information.

▶ Database restructuring – revising a database schema in order to meet new and changing information requirements.

LEARNING OUTCOMES

Having completed your study of this section of the course, you will be able to:

▶ Describe how we can denormalise database tables to optimise the performance of data retrieval by relaxing the requirement that database tables should be in BCNF.

▶ Describe how we can restructure a database to ensure that it continues to satisfy the information requirements after it has been installed, and meet new and changing requirements.

7 Distributed data management

In the preceding sections of *Block 4*, our focus has been on the development of a database to facilitate the day-to-day running of an enterprise where the data is located on a single computer system shared by its many users. In this section, we will consider the requirement to distribute and manage data over several computer systems – distributed data management.

The need to manage distributed data commonly arises in organisations such as supermarket chains that collect and process data in a number of geographical locations. The advantage of distributing data is that it is often possible to put the data close to the most frequent users of that data, while at the same time making it accessible to other users who may be more remote.

In *Block 1*, Subsection 3.5, where we described various information system architectures, we introduced the following three distinct approaches applicable to managing distributed data:

▶ The first approach, which we call **client–multiserver systems**, requires explicit navigation by the user process between multiple database servers that are independent of each other.

▶ The second approach, which we call a **distributed database**, aims to hide the location of the underlying data and how it is distributed so that it appears as a single database from the user's point of view.

▶ The third approach, which we call **replication systems**, makes use of data replication, distributing the copies to allow local processing of data within each local database system.

In the first approach, the client's user process must know where the remote data is located and how to reach it in order to construct a query. This places the burden of dealing with remote data upon each user process (the client). In contrast, the distributed database approach shifts that burden to the server side; clients do not see the work going on 'behind the scenes' when their queries are being processed. The third and final approach is somewhat different. Clients continue to operate with their local database, but a separate service is attached to the DBMS to enable remote data to be replicated locally. Processing is done locally for each user, and each local database retains its independence. The additional service becomes responsible for the coordination of updates to any remote data.

The aim of this section is to examine each of these three approaches in more detail.

7.1 Client–multiserver systems

This section describes the **client–multiserver** approach to distributed databases. It is an extension of the client–server approach which allows for several clients and several servers in a number of computer systems.

This first approach is to distribute the processing components in the architecture, as given in *Block 1*, so that there may be many user processes in a number of different computer systems and many databases, each having an associated DBMS. A DBMS in a computer system, which is separated from its users, is referred to as a **server** or, more specifically, a **database server**. The many user processes are known as its

clients. The kinds of requests for service from a client to a database server are no different from those requests to a DBMS described in *Block 1*, except that now they have to be communicated between computer systems.

When a client has established a link to a database server, the client may use SQL statements, which are expressed exactly as before, in order to access the data that is controlled by that server. Then the appropriate communication software transforms the statements into the required representation. Figure 7.1 illustrates a user process connected to two independent database servers. It represents a distributed user, who wants access to two databases (A and B in Figure 7.1).

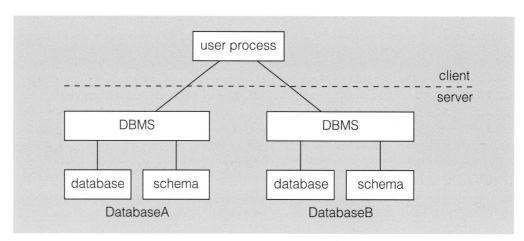

Figure 7.1   A single client connected to two independent DBMSs

In the **client–multiserver** approach, the distributed user needs to be connected to multiple database servers in order to satisfy a particular requirement. In *Block 1*, Subsection 3.5, we assumed that the University's logical database is physically split according to the geographic regions in which it has offices and there is a database server in each regional office, as shown in Figure 3.5 of *Block 1*. Each region physically stores data for only their students, staff and courses in that region's server. However, a user might want to write a query that involves all the students in the University, such as a request to count all the students on specific courses, or to change staff salaries globally. Such a query is possible but requires the client to access multiple physical servers, each with its own database.

In effect, the distributed user needs a mechanism to connect to each regional database server to perform queries that can take a view of the University database that is not confined to a single region. In addition, there must be a way of coordinating any changes to the data in the various databases so that data integrity may be maintained across the whole system.

Connection management

To satisfy the needs of both local and distributed users, we need a mechanism to make and break a client–server connection that also allows a client to communicate with different servers. This mechanism should be available to a user process that requires access to two or more servers in order to construct a query. SQL supports this way of working by providing statements for **connection management**. We can use the configuration shown in Figure 3.5 of *Block 1* as an example. Suppose the University data has been distributed to each of the regions using separate database servers, named *region1*, *region2*, and so on. A user, identified as `admin`, could establish a connection to the database server in Region 4 with the following SQL statement:

```
CONNECT region4 USER admin
```

The execution of this statement establishes a connection with the specified database server. Each subsequent SQL statement is processed by this database server, identified here as **region4**, and may gain access to data available to the user **admin** in this database. If the user had previously established a connection with another database server, then that connection would have become dormant since only one connection can be active; this is known as the **current connection**. However, a dormant connection, which had been established earlier, can be made the current connection by a **SET** statement as follows:

```
SET CONNECTION region1
```

Note that the connection with **region4** becomes dormant after the execution of this statement, since only one connection can be current.

Connection management also includes a **DISCONNECT** statement which, while not necessary from the database's point of view, enables the communication link for a connection to be closed down. Using the example of separate regions for our University database as in Figure 3.5 of *Block 1*, we can see what needs to be done using SQL. Figure 7.2 gives a sample of SQL code to transfer the data relating to a particular student between two regional database servers. (For simplicity, we have not shown how the user process deals with a change in tutor nor any of the other consequences of a change in region, such as the transfer of any study details.)

```
DECLARE local_student_id CHAR(3),
    local_name CHAR(20),
    local_address VARCHAR(120)
    local_email_address VARCHAR(40)
    local_registration_date DATE
CONNECT region1 USER admin
CONNECT region4 USER admin
SET CONNECTION region1
SELECT student_id, name, address, email_address, registration_date
INTO local_student_id, local_name, local_address,
        local_email_address, local_registration_date
FROM student WHERE student_id = 's38'
SET CONNECTION region4
INSERT INTO student (student_id, name, address, email_address,
    registration_date, region_number)
    VALUES (local_student_id, local_name, local_address,
            local_email_address, local_registration_date, '4')
SET CONNECTION region1
DELETE FROM student
    WHERE student_id = 's38'
DISCONNECT ALL
```

Figure 7.2   An example of SQL code within a user process that moves a student's data from one region to another

EXERCISE 7.1

What single SQL statement would you use to transfer a student from Region 1 to Region 4 in the (non-distributed) University database, which you studied in *Block 3*?

Comparing Figure 7.2 with the solution to Exercise 7.1 we can see that the client–multiserver approach requires quite a lot of extra work as a result of distributing the database.

How the data is distributed between servers is a design decision, similar to the choice of tables within a database. Decisions will be based on criteria such as ensuring that data to be processed together is kept together. However, each database server is autonomous, managing the data under its control and operating independently of any other database server, so that there is no sense in which the totality of the data in the different servers is being managed as a whole.

For example, if student data is stored using a database server in the region to which the students belong, instead of just one student table in a centralised database there will now be many tables. All the tables may have the same name, **student**, and the same columns (**student_id**, **name**, **address**, **email_address**, **registration_date**, and **region_number**), but they have to be accessed independently. So a program to retrieve all student data requires a separate connection to each server. Note that the only way of ensuring consistency of table names, columns and their formats, is for a database administrator (DBA) to monitor each database server regularly.

This requirement to look at all of the databases involved creates a number of difficulties when we consider the checking of constraints. For example, let us assume that the student data is distributed to a number of regional database servers. When a user process executes an **INSERT** statement, what would be necessary to enforce the requirement that a value for **student_id** is to be unique for all students? While each database server may enforce a unique constraint for the data it controls, it is necessary for the user process to establish connections to all servers and check the constraint for each one separately to ensure that the constraint for all students is checked. This is not a practical proposition and the problem may not be easy to resolve.

Transaction management

Any transaction that changes data in more than one database server (or location) will require a more complex mechanism than that used in a single, local database. It is no longer possible for a user process to request each DBMS to do a simple **COMMIT**, because some may succeed and some may fail, violating the 'all or nothing' principle. One way of supporting transactions for multiple servers is to implement a **COMMIT** in two phases – called a **two-phase commit**. In the first phase all locations involved in a transaction, whether they are separated logically or physically, are each sent a request asking them to prepare to commit. Only when all locations have responded that they are ready to commit can the second phase start, in which they are each sent a request to complete the commit. If any one location does not respond to the first request, or responds that it is unable to commit, then the commit fails.

The two-phase commit protocol – that is, the sequence of messages for a two-phase commit – is a mechanism that contributes to the integrity of distributed data, which we can illustrate here.

One location must take control of the overall transaction. The originator of a transaction will normally perform such a coordinating role. Every participant in the transaction must confirm their ability to perform their part of the transaction. The participants must, in the end, all confirm that their part of the transaction is valid in order to achieve a successful transaction.

The mechanism of a two-phase commit also plays a key role in the reliability of a system that includes distributed data. While it is transparent to the user of an application process, a knowledge of the underlying mechanism is necessary in planning access to distributed data. This is also important in terms of overall efficiency, as the two-phase commit can lead to longer processing times for distributed transactions.

Let us see how the mechanism works, using a simple example. Suppose we have a user process on System A and data distributed between System B and System C. What messages need to be exchanged for a transaction to allow System A to perform an **INSERT** on System B and a **DELETE** on System C? In the University example in Figure 3.5 of *Block 1*, where the **student** table is distributed by region, we might be moving a student from one region to another.

Since the user process on System A originated the transaction, System A acts as the coordinator so as to orchestrate the activities of Systems B and C. The **INSERT** and **DELETE** statements in Figure 7.2 are viewed as one transaction, which has been initiated by a distributed user of a user process in System A in the example that follows. System B and System C may be viewed as Regions 4 and 1, respectively.

Figure 7.3 illustrates the steps that System A must coordinate.

1 System A sends the **insert** to System B and the **delete** to System C.

2 System A begins the first phase of a **commit** for the transaction logging the start.

3 System A then sends a **get ready** message to Systems B and C.

4 When Systems B and C receive their **get ready** messages, each must prepare either to **commit** or to **rollback** their designated transaction.

5 If Systems B and C can **commit** their local transaction, each will reply with a simple **yes** message and record an entry in its log. A **no** message means that the system cannot complete the transaction.

6 System A waits for these replies from Systems B and C:

 ▶ if both replies are **yes**, System A will send the final **commit** to Systems B and C;

 ▶ if any reply is **no**, System A will send a **rollback** instead.

 Where a timeout period is exceeded, this is equivalent to a **no**. In either response, System A will make an entry into its log.

7 When Systems B and C receive their final **commit** or **rollback**, they must do as they are told. The **yes** message in step 5 has meant that Systems B and C have given up their ability to decide their local transaction's fate. Each local DBMS must now fulfil its part of the requested transaction, which results in a **commit** or **rollback** entry in its local log followed by an **OK** message returned to System A.

8 When System A receives an **OK** message from both Systems B and C, it can then return the appropriate value for **sqlstate** upon completion.

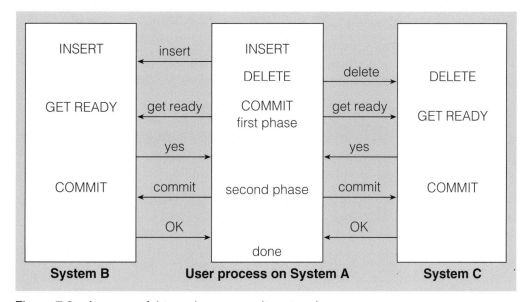

Figure 7.3   A successful two-phase commit protocol

The two-phase commit mechanism allows for the possibility of failures in any of the systems. Let us consider the possible failures in System C, noting that similar arguments will apply to System B.

If there is a failure on System C *before* it responds 'yes' to the 'get ready' request, then System A will record a timeout. Thus System A will send a 'rollback' to System B. As part of its recovery program, System C will find neither a 'yes' nor a 'commit' message in its transaction log, so it will perform a 'rollback' on the original request, which is a 'delete' in the above example.

If System C has a local failure *after* sending a 'yes' message, as in step 5, there will be no 'commit' or 'rollback' entry in its log to mark the end of the transaction. Now, System A will decide whether or not to 'commit', depending only on the reply from System B. So, the recovery program on System C must query the coordinator on System A about the final disposition of the transaction before taking the appropriate action. You can envisage a number of combinations of places and times where failure could occur, thus making the whole process quite complicated to manage.

EXERCISE 7.2

How long does System A, the coordinator in the above example, need to keep records of a distributed transaction in its log file?

The two-phase commit protocol generates additional network traffic in order to guarantee the integrity of a distributed transaction. Without including the statements that the user process sends, each system will contribute four messages to handle a transaction. So, if there are n systems involved, there will be a minimum of $4n$ messages, both sent and received, to allow successful completion of a transaction.

These additional messages increase the load on a communication network and can have a detrimental effect on response times for a transaction over two or more computer systems. Each communication bottleneck between any two systems involved could be visited more than eight times for a successful conclusion to the transaction. Thus we should aim to minimise the number of times that two or more remote systems are involved in a transaction. Consequently, an implementation that included distributed data would locate that data as close as possible to the processes which might change it.

Summary of Subsection 7.1

The client–multiserver approach requires that application programmers know how data is distributed between the database servers required by each distributed user. They have to ensure that processing hides the multiple connections, so that the end-user, whether distributed or local, is unaware of the number and nature of database servers involved.

We should note that incompatibilities between different implementations do cause problems for the client–multiserver approach. In particular, it is a significant task to include the two-phase commit protocol in a DBMS.

In general, the client–multiserver approach enables data, which was originally held in separate local databases, to be shared with the least change to those existing databases. The main additional feature is connection management.

7.2 | Distributed databases

In this second approach, the key requirement is that user processes do *not* have to know how data is distributed. Thus user processes use the same SQL as they would for a local database system.

In this approach there is no need for connection management within a user process. Users, through the processes that they interact with, do not have to know anything about where data is stored nor how it is processed to meet their requirements. This is referred to as **location independence**.

If the location of data is viewed as a storage characteristic, this requirement for location independence may be considered as just another aspect of data independence that we want to be provided by database management systems. However, the software to provide location independence involves a lot more than a local DBMS provides. We shall refer to a management system that meets this requirement as a **distributed database management system** (DDBMS). The notion of location independence may be viewed as a further level of abstraction that is required of a DDBMS.

The requirements for a DDBMS are very similar to the general requirements for data management that we introduced earlier in the course. You will recall from *Block 1* that a database has a logical schema to describe all the data in it. For a distributed database we use the term **global schema** or **global logical schema** which describes all the data for a distributed user. Similarly, a local database has a storage schema and the counterpart to this for the distributed database is the **distribution schema**, which defines where data is located, i.e. in which local database. The DBA for the distributed database is responsible for defining both the global schema and the distribution schema.

EXERCISE 7.3

What are the general characteristics we would expect to find in a DDBMS?

Figure 3.7 of *Block 1*, which we have reproduced here as Figure 7.4, shows an example of a distributed database where the user processes (such as user processes 1 and 2 in the figure) communicate with a DDBMS that manages the underlying, localised databases. Note that although Figure 7.4 shows a DDBMS component for each local system, we should regard the distributed database as having a single, unified, management system. The DDBMS components of Figure 7.4 should therefore be viewed as cooperating parts of a single DDBMS. Such a DDBMS will need to meet the above requirements. Suppose we split the University database into separate regions, as shown in Figure 3.5 of *Block 1*, so that each region has its own local database system. The only way for a distributed user to access all of the University's data transparently is to establish a connection to the DDBMS.

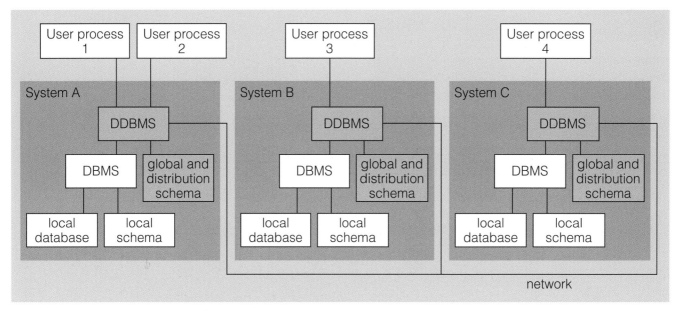

Figure 7.4   A simplified model for a distributed database

Location of the global schema and the distribution schema

The global schema and distribution schema are key components in providing location independence that allow a DBA to specify where data is to be distributed. Location independence does not determine the location of the contents of these schemas, but we can envisage a range of alternatives such as:

▶ to have complete replicated copies of the schemas in every location;

 ▶ to have just one copy of the schemas in one location;

▶ to have different parts of the schemas distributed in different locations.

Figure 7.4 shows replicated copies of the global and distribution schemas in every location. Is there anything to be gained in having just one copy of the schemas in one location?

Advantages:	One copy prevents the inconsistency that is possible with duplication and simplifies any modifications that may be necessary.
Disadvantages:	The user processes at every location have to access that one copy, as do the local databases below it. They all have to communicate with it, hence a processing bottleneck arises. If the distribution schema is unavailable to any other locations (whether it is due to software, computer or communication failure), they cannot access any part of the database, even at their own location.

For both the other options, the DDBMS will have an extra task to look after the consistency of the global and distribution schemas. A change to either or both schemas can have a number of implications, depending on the extent of the change. The final choice is very much dependent on the individual requirements for each distributed database, which is beyond the scope of this course.

EXERCISE 7.4

A single global schema may become an unwelcome bottleneck. What benefits and drawbacks might we find in the other two options: the complete replication and the distribution of parts of the schemas?

Local autonomy

In each of the local systems shown in Figure 7.4 there is a local DBMS. The purpose of this DBMS is to provide self-standing database management for all the data at that location. The aim is to preserve **local autonomy**. This is sometimes called **site autonomy**.

With local autonomy it should be possible to manage the local database for local users without having to depend in any way on the rest of the distributed system.

For simplicity we have omitted local users from Figure 7.4, but we may now see how local users can be accommodated in any one of the local systems in Figure 7.5. This figure shows the possibility of both local users and distributed users. Because of local autonomy a local user may interface directly with the local DBMS just as for a non-distributed system. However, a distributed user must use the DDBMS.

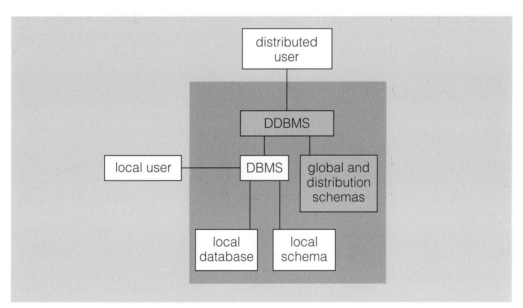

Figure 7.5   Local users and distributed users access one site

Distribution of the data into fragments

To consider what is involved in distributed database management, we first examine how the data in a database can be distributed in different locations. The simplest option when distributing data is to put some tables in one location and others in another. However, it will often be the case that what we really need to do is to partition the tables themselves, so that parts of each table are in a number of locations. Breaking a table into parts is known as **fragmentation**, and it can take different forms as follows:

▶ **horizontal fragmentation**, where a subset of complete rows of a table is stored in one location, such as keeping data for all students and staff in regional databases;

▶ **vertical fragmentation**, where some columns of a table are stored in one location and other columns in another (for example, keeping the names and registration data for all students in one place, and keeping their addresses and other personal details in another);

▶ a combination of horizontal and vertical fragmentation.

Distribution of data can also include making copies and storing them in more than one location, with the aim of ensuring that all data required for certain processes is available at the same location. This is known as replication, to which we shall return later.

Moving data between systems will usually be the slowest step in a query. This leads to the oft-quoted strategy:

Place data so that most processing is performed locally.

Let us now consider a simple SQL query involving just one table, such as listing all the students registered before 1996. When a DDBMS processes a query, it prepares a plan of how the query is to be executed (as described for a local database system in *Block 3*). This requires details of how the table is stored, which for a distributed database includes how the table is fragmented and replicated. The DDBMS obtains these details from the distribution schema and uses them to prepare a plan that involves many operations which, essentially, consist of two kinds.

▶ Retrieve some part of the required data from a given location. This kind of operation may be specified as a subsidiary query, which may be expressed in terms of just the data at that location and so can be processed as if it were a normal SQL statement for a local database.

▶ Combine the intermediate tables resulting from operations of the first kind at the separate locations into further intermediate tables, until the final table required by the original query is obtained. This second kind of operation involves moving data between locations and then performing relational operations such as:

   ▶ **union**, where the queried table has been horizontally fragmented;

   ▶ **join**, where the queried table has been vertically fragmented.

EXERCISE 7.5

Suppose the **student** table is horizontally fragmented such that each row is stored in the region given by the **region_number** column in that row, as we saw in Figure 3.5 of *Block 1*. We have the following query to find those students who were registered before 1996:

```
SELECT student_id, name, address, email_address, registration_date,
       region_number
FROM student
WHERE registration_date < 1996
```

(a) What subsidiary query should be executed at each regional location?

(b) What operations are needed to combine the results of part (a) to give the final result for the query?

The plan for query processing

As for a local database system, a query plan should be optimal in terms of some measure of efficiency. For a DDBMS there are three aspects to take into account for optimisation.

1   For any relevant data that is replicated, choose which copy to use and thus where operations of the first kind (local retrieval) are performed.

2   Choose how to execute each (local retrieval) operation most efficiently; this is essentially the same as the optimisation described in *Block 3*, since it is for a local system.

3   Choose where and how operations of the second kind (moving and combining) are to be performed (and thus which data has to be moved and to where).

The first and third of these aspects of optimisation are characteristic of a DDBMS, and we refer to this as **distribution optimisation**. It involves many factors, particularly those related to communication facilities and the specific capabilities of the computer systems in each location, which we cannot consider in any depth here. Needless to say it is a complex process for a DDBMS to take such details into account, so much so that there are no commercial products (at the time of writing) which provide the full capabilities of a DDBMS in a sufficiently efficient implementation. This should not deter us from looking at what would be involved in such distributed queries.

Since communication is the slowest step, we might apply one simple criterion when trying to optimise a distributed query:

> minimise the transfer of data over the network.

Based on this criterion, the process of query optimisation may select the most appropriate execution plan for each query. In effect, the process of query optimisation has to be distributed as well as the execution of each query. This results in a two-stage process:

▶ first, a consideration of the query at a global level;

▶ second, a number of local optimisation steps at each location.

Using Figure 7.4, for example, user process 4 might submit a query to the DDBMS in System C that involves two tables: one of 100 records in System A and another of 1 000 000 records in System B. The optimiser in the DDBMS, in System C, will choose the global strategy for the query. Assuming that the record size in both tables is similar, the global strategy will be to move the smaller table from System A to System B. The local optimiser in System B will determine the execution plan for the query. Following the optimising criteria above, a global strategy would rule out the transfer of both tables to System C and also the transfer of the larger table to System A.

We can illustrate the importance of an initial, global optimisation as follows. There are many organisations with large numbers of employees who might each be allocated to a department. Figure 7.6 shows the details for two tables that might be included in a distributed database: **staff** and **department**. This example assumes that there are 5000 members of staff or employees organised into 100 departments.

These definitions exclude the actual data types involved, since the focus is on data volume in this example.

staff

column	size (bytes)
staff_no	4
first_name	20
last_name	20
region	4
address	50
phone_no	10
department_no	4
total for record	112

department

column	size (bytes)
department_no	4
department_name	10
manager_no	4
total for record	18

Figure 7.6 Sizes of fields in two tables

Consider the following query to produce a list of the names of the departments and their managers, assuming that there is only one manager for each department:

```
SELECT department_name, first_name, last_name
FROM department, staff
WHERE manager_no = staff_no
```

If we assume that neither the **staff** table nor the **department** table is fragmented, but each is located on a separate site, and that the query originates from yet another site, we can envisage the following three possible plans for global optimisation.

1   Transfer both the **staff** and **department** tables to the originating site of the query and then perform the join.

2   Transfer the **staff** table to where the **department** table is, perform the join, and then send the result to the originating site.

3   Transfer the **department** table to where the **staff** table is, perform the join, and then send the result to the originating site.

EXERCISE 7.6

Perform the calculations for the total amount of data to be transferred for each of these three possible plans.

We can see from the solution to Exercise 7.6 that plan 3 offers the minimum amount of data transfer for query optimisation, by quite a large margin. For multi-site queries we should avoid moving large tables around and look for ways to take advantage of involving fewer rows.

The plans that we have considered so far involve transferring only whole tables, but this is not the only possibility. If we could find other ways of reducing the amount of data to be transferred between sites, it could make query processing more efficient. In other words, if a DDBMS could produce a subset of one or more of the tables involved in a distributed query, there could be a reduction in the time taken to process a query. This can be achieved by ignoring any columns not required to answer the query.

For example, a distributed query involving the **staff** table in Figure 7.6 would be checked during optimisation to see if the number of attributes could be reduced for any data transfer. If the optimum plan required the **staff** table to be moved, it might be possible first to eliminate the address and phone number.

However, we should also take into account any potential benefits of local processing. This is illustrated using another simple query to list the department names and the number of staff working in each department:

```
SELECT d.department_no, d.department_name, COUNT(s.staff_no)
FROM staff s, department d
WHERE s.department_no = d.department_no
GROUP BY d.department_no
```

Assuming that the query is submitted by a user process at a third separate site, it may be possible to exploit the benefits of local processing before transferring any data. Possible plans are as follows.

1   Process the aggregate function on the **staff** table to count the number of staff in each department and transfer the result (department number and count) to the originating site. Transfer the **department** table to the originating site and then perform the join.

2   Process the aggregate function on the **staff** table and transfer the **department** table to where the **staff** table is. Perform the join and then send the result to the originating site.

3   Process the aggregate function on the **staff** table and transfer the result to where the **department** table is. Perform the join and then send the result to the originating site.

EXERCISE 7.7

Perform the calculations for the total amount of data to be transferred for each of the three plans, assuming that a count needs 4 bytes.

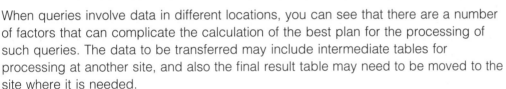

Without knowing any details about the processing and transfer times, the first plan minimises the amount of data transferred and the number of transfers, and also exploits local processing since the **staff** table can be processed in parallel to the transfer of the **department** table.

When queries involve data in different locations, you can see that there are a number of factors that can complicate the calculation of the best plan for the processing of such queries. The data to be transferred may include intermediate tables for processing at another site, and also the final result table may need to be moved to the site where it is needed.

It is not relevant to this course to discuss the problems of moving data around a communication network, but we have considered examples that show the factors involved in choosing the best plan. Query optimisation for a DDBMS will involve ways of reducing the amount of data transfers and making use of local processing, whenever it is possible.

Updating data

Updating a distributed database introduces further requirements. An update statement may result in changes to the data stored in many locations. A DDBMS can use a distribution schema to determine the effect of an update statement in each location, which can then be executed by a number of subsidiary update statements, each specifically related to a given location. If any data is replicated, there is a need to ensure that all copies are updated consistently. Furthermore, every transaction must have an acceptable completion time. However, there is a lot of work needed to guarantee data integrity, as we saw earlier, where we considered transaction management for the client–multiserver approach.

We have seen how the two-phase commit protocol contributes to data integrity for a transaction and how it protects in cases of failure of individual sites and/or network links. In the DDBMS approach this is all the responsibility of the DDBMS and not that of the user process. A DDBMS should be able to continue when a local database site fails, yet should provide a recovery method to help it get back up to date before rejoining the live DDBMS. We can see how recovery becomes arduous for a DDBMS, even when trying to find out if a system is operational. For example, in Figure 7.3 there were a number of messages to be exchanged between the coordinator on System A and the other two systems involved, Systems B and C. In the distributed database approach the DDBMS has to perform the coordinating role that was previously done by the user process in System A. There are three possibilities if System A sends a **COMMIT** message to System B and gets no response.

▶   System B is down and so cannot reply.

▶   A communication failure has prevented the message from reaching System B.

▶ System B is operational and has sent a response, but it has not been delivered back to System A.

It will be difficult to determine where the failure occurred without sending additional messages to gain more information, which can easily take up substantial processing time.

Constraints also introduce further problems relating to the consistency of data among the various locations, such as the need for uniqueness of student identifiers. Some constraints may be resolved by appropriate partitioning of data in each location, such as different sets of student identifiers for each region, which can be specified in a global schema and enforced by a DDBMS. Other mechanisms include keeping a global index that enables a constraint to be checked before updating is carried out in a location.

Replication under a DDBMS

Later, in Subsection 7.3, we shall be considering replication systems as an alternative approach to using a DDBMS. Here we consider the possibility that even under a DDBMS, parts of the distributed database may be replicated.

We saw earlier that making copies of the global and distribution schemas can create some problems while solving others. The same is true of data replication in a distributed database.

The amount of replication is a design choice. Some database fragments may be copied while others are not. Furthermore, the number of copies can range from one up to the total number of sites within the distributed database. It is easy to see that a database solution that includes replication of data can produce a very complex optimisation problem for the designer of a distributed database.

Each database system will have a number of performance and availability goals, and they will influence the actual choice of sites for data and the degree of replication. At each site, there is likely to be a different mix of both type and frequency of transaction, which adds to the complexity of the problem. The chosen level of replication will often depend on the relative use for queries compared with updates. For example, a high proportion of data retrieval with queries from many locations suggests that a high degree of replication will contribute to availability. But if the number of updates required is high, then there must be limits to the amount of replication to keep an acceptable level of performance. Performance degradation arises out of the need to maintain consistency via the use of the two-phase commit protocol, which is applied to update each replicate.

In a DDBMS that has incorporated some replication, there is an additional burden of maintaining consistency between the copies. When any one location or system fails, the recovery mechanisms have extra work to do to make copies on the restored system consistent with those found elsewhere in the DDBMS.

When there are replicated data items, there needs to be a way of managing the required locks for concurrency control during transactions. Imagine the problem that arises when more than one user wants to update replicated copies of the same data at the same time. One method involves the identification of one particular copy as unique within the distribution global schema, which is called a **primary copy**. Thus, all locking requests are sent to the location that contains the primary copy where these requests must be coordinated.

There are two ways of approaching the location of the primary copy:

▶ the allocation of a primary location which holds *all* the primary copies;

▶ the distribution of primary copies over different locations.

The primary location model uses the locking methods described in *Block 3*, but this location becomes a potential bottleneck because it must handle all locking requests for the DDBMS. This, in turn, might lead to overloading which is a potential source of failure of the primary location, and could paralyse the whole DDBMS. This problem is addressed in the distributed primary copies technique by spreading the load for lock coordination over a number of locations. Thus, failure at one location will affect locking data only for the primary copies it maintains. This is similar to the problems mentioned earlier when we introduced the notion of replicating all or part of the global schema.

Both methods can be modified to include one or more backup sites to aid recovery in the event of failure. The backup site can then take over lock coordination, but this does introduce the overhead of processing lock requests at the backup location.

Towards the goal of a distributed database

Having introduced some of the issues and complexities relating to distributed databases, we can again note that there are, at the time of writing, no DDBMSs that provide the full capabilities which we have described. However, there are developments of local DBMSs that provide various capabilities which allow data to be distributed, but involve various restrictions of the requirements described above. These restrictions may include any of the following:

▶ no horizontal fragmentation;

▶ no vertical fragmentation;

▶ no fragmentation;

▶ no replication or limited replication;

▶ queries limited to accessing data in one location;

▶ queries limited in form when accessing data in multiple locations;

▶ transactions limited to a single statement;

▶ transactions limited to a single location.

A combination of the above restrictions might seem to imply no more capabilities than a client–multiserver system, but there are still differences in the approach. For example, suppose a DDBMS does not allow fragmentation of tables. If each location is represented by a differently named schema within a global system, such as **region1**, **region2**, and so on, then references to tables could be expressed by qualifying their name, say, **region1.student**. Such a DDBMS may still provide a measure of location independence by interpreting this reference as being a table in a particular physical location, and hence provide access to it without the need for **CONNECT** statements by the user process. Thus a single statement may refer to tables in different locations.

We can illustrate the use of named schemas with reference to the student transfer example in Figure 7.2. Using the names **region1** and **region4** for the local databases, we can reduce the SQL shown to just two statements:

```
INSERT INTO region4.student (student_id, name, address, email_address,
                            registration_date, region_number)
    SELECT r1.student_id, r1.name, r1.address, r1.email_address,
        r1.registration_date, '4'
    FROM region1.student r1
    WHERE r1.student_id = 's38'
DELETE FROM region1.student
    WHERE region1.student_id = 's38'
```

If you compare the above statements with those in Figure 7.2 for the client–multiserver system, you will notice that all the navigation has disappeared.

Although there may be restrictions on the level of fragmentation and replication allowed within any DDBMS, it must be able to support location independence through a global schema. This location independence means that it is the database management software, and not the user processes, that determines the way that processing is distributed.

One way to provide a form of location independence requires those tables for distributed access from each local database to be registered with the global schema. Generally, the DBA of the distributed database may register a link between a table entry in the distribution schema and the actual table from a given local database. In this way, the global distribution schemas can be constructed from a number of separate and distinct databases. User processes, which use the global schema, may then access the registered tables. Thus we might say there is a high degree of schema integration, if a user sees just one schema that hides any information about data location.

There are different paths for providing more of the capabilities of a DDBMS, which means that there are varying levels of schema integration available for database designers. In the above example using named schemas, it is up to the user to provide an unambiguous specification of the relations or fragments for inclusion in a query.

This is an example of the **naming problem** in distributed systems. You can imagine how this will affect any DDBMS that is expected to expand such that it includes all the local databases in an organisation. Each local database is likely to have been developed independently of the others. Consequently, the same names may be used in two of the local databases, which creates problems when they are combined. If the DDBMS can provide an integrated schema, then naming becomes an internal system problem because each user sees an unambiguous global schema.

EXERCISE 7.8

If vertical fragmentation is not supported, how can the columns **student_id**, **name**, **address**, **email_address** and **registration_date** in the **student** table be distributed in a different location from the other column in the table?

Summary of Subsection 7.2

The key requirement of a distributed database is that user processes do *not* have to know how data is distributed. The interface between the user processes and the database is the distributed database management system (DDBMS). For the distributed database this takes over the roles that a DBMS plays in a localised system. The DDBMS employs a global (logical) schema which contains all the logical information about the tables available within the distributed database. It uses a distribution schema to show where the data is stored.

Each local database system has its own local DBMS. This provides local autonomy. Local users may use the local DBMS. Tables may be distributed among the various local databases and may be fragmented horizontally or vertically. Tables may also be replicated in whole or in part.

The optimum plan for query processing will minimise the amount of data that has to be copied from one local database to another. Local processing can often be done on a table to reduce the amount of data sent over the network. Updating a distributed database poses significant extra difficulties, especially when replication may also be used.

7.3 Replication systems

In this third approach to distributed data, the aim is to allow all application processing to be done locally. Data is copied and then distributed to other databases, where the replicated data is then included into each local database. There is no need to access remote data to process queries.

The replication systems that we consider in this section are different from the replication under a DDBMS as discussed in Subsection 7.2. The difference is that in this section we assume there is no DDBMS and no global schema. In effect we have only local users, not distributed users, but the local users are provided with replicas of the data that they need to access if the primary copy resides elsewhere.

The purposes of replication

In the model of a distributed database that we outlined in Subsection 7.2, we saw a number of ways of attempting to provide distributed processing for clients via location independence. But in using a DDBMS, when queries require access to multiple locations, response times begin to suffer as the number of locations increases.

When we need to update data over multiple locations, mechanisms such as the two-phase commit are needed to guarantee data integrity, which requires all locations to be operational in order to complete any distributed transaction. If a distributed database includes replication to provide better access, for example, then the two-phase commit protocol will be needed to keep the replicates in step with the primary copy. (The primary copy that we described in Subsection 7.2 applies equally to this subsection.)

Replication is a way of meeting the problems of a distributed database by providing copies of data to other database servers so that each user process can perform all processing locally. It makes data more available through local access by:

▶ minimising the use of remote connections;

▶ reducing the dangers of remote site failure or connection failure.

Replication may seem to be undesirable because it involves storing data more than once, which uses more space and introduces the possibility of disagreement between copies. However, there are advantages: shorter response time and higher availability.

For example, we make use of a simplified hospital database throughout this course, yet a working hospital is open all hours of the day, every day of the week. For an operational database system in a hospital, this represents an availability requirement for the data it stores.

There is another potential use for a replication system, since it can be used as an automated mechanism for taking 'snapshots' of data over a period of time. These snapshots may be combined to produce a separate table or tables such that certain auditing requirements can be met. For example, a series of snapshots may be taken to follow who changed what and when in a financial system.

In general, replication provides a mechanism for storing data that may change over time, which is a valuable benefit for users who want to look for patterns or trends in data. Thus replication allows the collection of historical data, which can be kept separate from operational data. In practice, this might amount to taking periodic copies of data from an operational database and storing the copies in a separate database to meet any auditing and statistical requirements. For example, we can look at a working hospital where operational data, concerning patients who receive treatment after they have been admitted to the wards, is typified by substantial routine updates as patients receive treatment. If replication is used as a mechanism to build historical data, hospital staff can access it to look for evidence relating to the effectiveness of different treatments, without hindering the operational data. For example, they might use a number of queries to find out how patients responded to their treatment over a period of time.

Providing a replication service

As with the DDBMS approach to distributed data, a specialised service is needed to provide the additional coordination of exchanges between participating databases. Figure 3.8 in *Block 1*, which we have reproduced here as Figure 7.7, shows a simplified connection between databases using a replication server at each site to act as the channel between them. A replication server is appended to each local database, which communicates with the DBMS and is consequently hidden from the user processes.

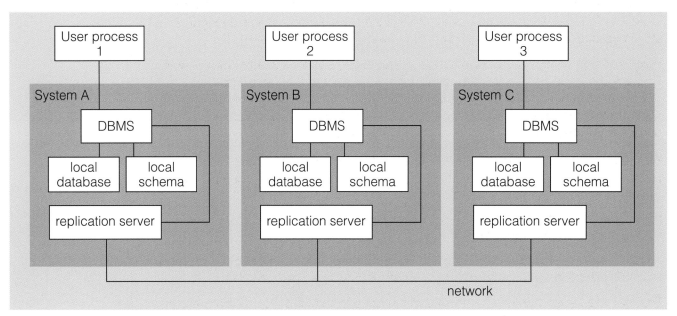

Figure 7.7   A simplified model of replication involving three database systems

A **replication server** both sends and receives data, and so has the following two main roles:

1   To receive or collect updates from its local database and pass copies on to other sites that require them.

2   To receive or collect updates from remote sites, via their replications servers, and apply them to the local database.

Once it has been agreed between the systems that replicates will be passed from one system to another, there are two ways in which such a transfer may be initiated: either from the sender or from the receiver. Referring to Figure 7.7, the DBA for System A may declare that System B should receive all changes to certain tables. So, whenever those items are updated on System A, replicates are *pushed* over to System B. In contrast, the DBA for System B may from time to time request copies of any changes to those same items located in System A. Now, replicates must be *pulled* across from System A on demand from System B.

The replication server will store descriptions of any replicated data and descriptions of how to reach other database servers. Users may continue to work with local copies of the data, even though there may be a system failure at the remote location that holds the primary copy of the data. For example, in Figure 7.7, user process 1 will be able to continue working if System B fails for some reason.

There are a number of ways that replication can be used within any particular design, but we shall give examples of just two ways, illustrated using the Hospital and University databases. The two ways that we shall describe are called **consolidation** and **dissemination**. Consolidation involves the collection of data fragments, from a number of locations, into one location to construct a global view. Dissemination begins with one database and copies of data fragments, which might contain data items that overlap, for distribution to different locations.

Consolidation of replicas

We shall illustrate the consolidation method of replication using the Hospital example. Since the treatment of patients involves their location in individual wards, we might choose to locate a dedicated database server within each ward. Here, we could keep the treatment details of the specific group of patients who are in that ward. We would expect a high frequency of updates that reflect the treatment to patients during their stay in hospital (i.e. the tables **patient**, **treatment** and **prescription**).

However, in addition to the ward databases, there is a need to take a broader view of the data accumulated within the hospital. For example, there is a requirement to monitor drug usage throughout the hospital. This means that we would expect a number of regular queries involving several wards at regular intervals. For such purposes we shall assume there is a central administration system.

We can now see two different ways of using the Hospital database:

▶ the use on the wards involves a high transaction rate on a few rows of data, over a small number of tables;

▶ the use for administration involves queries that can include a number of joins as well as intensive computations.

If there were only a single centralised database, there might be some conflict because of the difference in query types which might affect individual response times.

The replicated approach can be applied in this case to separate the different ways of using data within the hospital. We can say that each ward owns the primary copy of the tables within its database, such as **patient**, **treatment** and **prescription**. A single copy of each table may then pass, via the replication servers, to the administration database. The wards can thus operate without hindrance from administrative users making large-scale time-consuming queries. This is an example of *data consolidation*, where a single replica copy is made by drawing together a number of primary sources, as shown in Figure 7.8.

In terms of the outline given in Figure 7.7, user process 1 may represent a nurse recording the details of the daily drug doses given to patients, while user process 2 may represent an administrator trying to estimate how much of each drug to purchase.

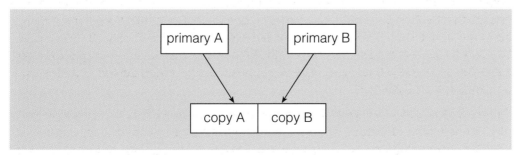

Figure 7.8   Data consolidation: making a single replica copy from multiple, primary sources

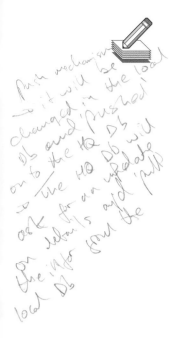

EXERCISE 7.9

Refer to Figure 3.5 of *Block 1*, which shows a regional fragmentation of student and staff data for the University database. If there is now a consolidated **student** table in a headquarters database, describe how this table may be kept up to date with changes to students' email addresses using (a) a push mechanism, and (b) a pull mechanism.

What is the disadvantage of the pull mechanism?

Dissemination of replicas

We shall illustrate the dissemination method of replication using the University example. Consider the tutors who want a connection to the University database to record the assignment grades for their groups of students. In terms of the University example, the tutor is responsible for marking assignments and recording the results.

Suppose the tutors wish to work with their own independent databases. How can replication help in this case where there are a large number of tutors who may be involved in more than one course? We want the primary copy to be the central copy. We now have to consider the copying of table fragments and distributing those fragments among the various tutors. This is an example of *data dissemination*, where one source provides many copies which are often subsets of a primary copy, as shown in Figure 7.9.

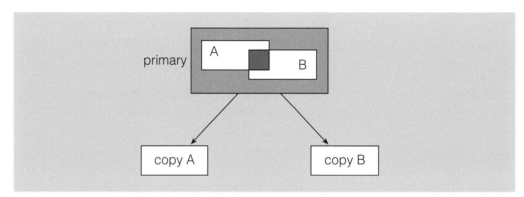

Figure 7.9   Data dissemination: making multiple copies from a single primary source

Tutors will want to know which students are taking the courses that they teach. They will also want to record the grade for each assignment from their students. Using the University database schema, we expect each tutor to have access to a subset of the **student**, **course**, **enrolment** and **assignment** tables. In this case, there would be an overlap where a student is taking two courses with two different tutors, which we can see as the shaded area in Figure 7.9 for the different tutor fragments A and B. Each tutor would have copies of different fragments of the **course**, **enrolment** and **assignment** tables. But each copy of their fragment of the **student** table would include the details of those students taking two courses.

The way in which a distributed system like this could work might be as follows. At the start of each course presentation, the University distributes the replicated fragments to each tutor via the replication servers. In terms of Figure 7.7, System A may represent the University database and user process 1 may be responsible for entering the details of each new enrolment, while user process 2 represents a tutor connected to a separate local database, that is, System B.

Now we need to consider what happens when each tutor records the grades for each assignment, that is, updates the data on their copies of the tables. We have already said that the replicated approach encourages local processing of data, but there is a problem because the primary versions of the data used by a tutor are stored in the University database where the permissions to update the original data reside.

In the example of data consolidation in a hospital, there was no such problem. In the hospital the replicated copies would be read-only, since user processes were performing queries that did not modify the data. However, in the University example we expect the replication servers to support changes to the primary data while allowing the tutors to maintain their independence. One way to satisfy the need to update primary data from a replication site involves the use of stored procedures, which we introduced in *Block 3*, taking advantage of their contribution to data independence and security.

For example, when a tutor records the marks for each student assignment, a procedure associated with that particular copy of the **assignment** table can be used to update the primary data. So, in their own database, tutors can change the values of the replicated items, but their replication server must coordinate the changes to the primary data (student grades, in this case). At the primary data location, tutors may be given permission to call the procedure which updates those data items. But remember that this additional work is undertaken by each replication server, as follows.

In Figure 7.7, the University database is on System A and the tutor, who teaches a particular course, is connected to System B which records the grades for a given assignment. Within System B, the updates to the **assignment** table might be used to initiate a database trigger which passes the new student grades over to its replication server. The replication server at System B will then communicate with the replication server at System A, which contains the University database, to update the primary **assignment** table. On System A, this can be achieved using a database procedure, representing an overall *push* mechanism from each tutor to the University. Other remote users may send a request via their local replication server to the University database for a different procedure to test for changes to the **assignment** table and return copies of the new values, if any. This represents a *pull* mechanism for remote users with permission to access the University database.

Since we do not generally have two tutors trying to mark the same assignment, we would expect no conflict because a student who is enrolled on a course is assigned to a particular tutor. However, we should expect to apply some constraint in the design to prevent such an error.

EXERCISE 7.10

In practice, students may do more than one course at a time, with a different tutor assigned to each course. Now, a realistic student record would include contact details, such as address and telephone number. In the data dissemination example, what problem would arise if a student, taking two courses at the same time, had moved to a new address and asked both tutors to record the new details?

Transactions involving replicated data

The notion of local processing of data for the replicated data approach relies upon each of the local database servers for transaction processing. In order to provide any guarantees of integrity for replicated data, the 'all or nothing' nature of a transaction must be maintained on each local database server that has data distributed in this way. Furthermore, the results of any transaction are considered to be permanent and the effects of each locally committed transaction must be recoverable after any local system failure.

Consequently, the replicated data approach relies upon local control and processing of data. The coordination of updates between replication servers is done separately and may involve protocols such as the two-phase commit to maintain consistency of the data. In general, the importance of maintaining local autonomy means that transaction management is implementation dependent, requiring agreement on which mechanisms to use and how to deal with failures at or between replication servers.

Summary of Subsection 7.3

The aim of a replication system is to provide all the data that is required at any local site by including replicas of any data that is held elsewhere. Thus the aim is to be able to answer all queries locally. Although replication introduces normally undesirable duplication, it turns this duplication to advantage by being able to reduce response times and giving higher availability.

The coordination that has to be maintained between the sites that contain replicas is provided by a replication server at each site. The replication servers may push data to another site or pull data from it.

7.4 Summary

We have shown how the need to manage distributed data commonly arises in organisations such as hospitals and universities. It is easy to think of many others: banks, supermarkets, factories; the list is endless.

One of the advantages of distributing data is that it is often possible to put the data close to the most frequent users of that data, while at the same time making it accessible to other users who may be more remote. Often a degree of local autonomy is desirable.

We have studied three distinct approaches to managing distributed data: *client–multiserver*, *distributed database* and *replication systems*.

▶ The client–multiserver approach enables data, which was originally held in separate local databases, to be shared, with the least changes made to those existing databases. However, it requires a user process to provide explicit navigational instructions on where to find the data.

▶ The distributed database management system (DDBMS) of the distributed database overcomes the need for user processes to have any knowledge of navigation. All the services that would have been provided by the DBMS in a local system are provided by the DDBMS. This simplifies the task of the user process but puts heavy demands upon a DDBMS. The problem of maintaining database integrity is much greater for the distributed database than for a local database, thus making a practical DDBMS difficult to implement.

▶ The replication system aims to provide responses to all queries through local processing using replicas, where necessary. The replicas of data are coordinated by having a replication server at each local site.

LEARNING OUTCOMES

Having completed your study of this section of the course, you will be able to:

▶ Describe how the need to handle distributed data arises.

▶ Compare the three approaches described in this section: client–multiserver, distributed database and replicated systems.

8 Data warehousing

In *Block 1*, Subsection 1.7, we described data warehousing as being concerned with the integration of large quantities of historical data from many different sources intended to support decision-making activities within an organisation. This repository of data, a data warehouse, is typically analysed using data mining techniques.

Data warehousing and data mining technologies have developed as a result of the need to store and analyse the increasing volume of operational data that is now collected. The last decade of the twentieth century saw a significant growth in our capabilities both to generate and to collect data. With the development of electronic data-gathering devices and the steady reduction in the cost of data-storage devices, data is now easy to capture and fairly inexpensive to store. The widespread introduction of barcodes for almost all retail products and the routine use of debit and credit cards for customer purchases have generated large volumes of data. Data warehousing technology has provided the means to store and effectively manage this increased volume of data for decision support purposes.

The increased collection and storage of data has outpaced our abilities to analyse this data using traditional manual methods of analysis such as spreadsheets and database queries. It is not realistic to expect that all this data can be carefully analysed by human analysts. This has created a significant need for a new generation of techniques and tools with the ability to assist organisations in analysing intelligently and automatically the increased volume of decision support data they are generating. These techniques and tools are the subject of data mining.

In this section we will consider:

▶ decision support systems (DSSs);

▶ the multidimensional data model;

▶ data warehouses and data warehousing.

Decision support systems (DSSs) are computer-based systems that incorporate data warehouses and employ data mining techniques to facilitate and improve strategic decision making by providing decision makers with relevant information.

The **multidimensional data model** is a conceptual data model that enables decision makers to view data from different, and multiple, perspectives. A multidimensional view of data allows decision makers to consolidate or aggregate the data collected from operational databases at different levels of detail.

A **data warehouse** is a repository of an organisation's operational data where the data is organised around the subjects of interest to the organisation, such as customers, products, locations and sales. It focuses on the modelling and analysis of data for decision makers. **Data warehousing** is the process of building, managing and using data warehouses.

Data mining is the process of finding significant, previously unknown, and potentially valuable knowledge hidden in data. Data mining provides the ability to automate the identification and extraction of information from an organisation's data warehouses, which can be used to make informed business decisions.

This section has two aims: First, to provide you with an introduction to decision support systems, the multidimensional data model, data warehouses and data warehousing.

Second, to enable you to acquire the practical skills that you will need to develop a simple design for a data warehouse using a relational database, which facilitates strategic decision making.

8.1 Decision support systems

Decision making is a process of choosing among alternative courses of action for the purpose of attaining a goal or goals. Managerial decision making embodies the whole process of management: planning, organising and controlling. Planning, for example, involves a series of decisions: What should be done? When? How? Where? By whom?

The purpose of decision support systems (DSSs) is to facilitate and improve decision making by providing decision makers with relevant information. The information advances the decision makers' knowledge in some way so as to assist them in making and planning policy decisions.

DSSs are primarily used for strategic decisions faced by senior management, and are implemented separately from operational systems. We need to consider the differences between the terms *strategic* and *operational* to understand why it is usual for organisations to have a database system solely for decision support that is separate from the operational databases that facilitate the day-to-day running of the organisation.

Strategic matters relate to the planning and policy making decisions made by senior management, which involves decision making with a long time horizon of a month to several years. Developing corporate goals, planning for mergers and acquisitions, capital budgeting, allocation and control of resources, and sale promotion planning are examples of strategic planning.

Operational matters relate to the day-to-day running of the organisation, involving decision making with a daily to monthly time horizon, and operational procedures that implement the organisation's strategy. Production scheduling, inventory control, maintenance planning and scheduling, and quality control are examples of operational decisions. The day-to-day ordering of supplies, satisfying customers' orders and hiring new employees according to an agreed strategy are examples of operational procedures.

The nature and source of the data required to facilitate strategic decision making and operational procedures of an organisation are different.

Strategic decision making requires summarised *historical* data in order to identify trends. The data is sourced by integrating operational data from the many systems on different computers that the organisation may use. Such data is required to provide answers to *strategic* questions such as:

> Which product lines are seasonal?
>
> Which product lines are increasing in popularity?
>
> Are some products more popular in different parts of the country?

Operational procedures require *current* data, which may be available from a single system the organisation may use. Such data is required to provide answers to *operational* questions such as:

> How many unfulfilled orders are there?
>
> Which items are out of stock?
>
> What is the status of a particular order?

The natures of the database systems required to facilitate strategic decision making and operational procedures of an organisation are also different.

Strategic decision making requires a system that facilitates the decision support tasks of an organisation. These tasks are unstructured and consist of mostly ad hoc, complex queries involving historical, summarised and consolidated data, and can access possibly millions of records (rows) of data. Query throughput and response times are the key performance metrics. These systems are known as **online analytical processing** (**OLAP**) systems. Such systems enable decision makers to gain insight into an organisation's data from different, and multiple, perspectives. OLAP is an element of decision support systems.

Operational procedures require a system that automates clerical data processing tasks that are the day-to-day operations of an organisation. These tasks are structured and repetitive, and consist of short, isolated transactions, and involve detailed, up-to-date raw data, and read or update tens of records. Consistency and recoverability of the database are critical, and maximising transaction throughput is the key performance metric. These systems are known as **online transaction processing** (**OLTP**) systems. Such systems support most of the day-to-day operations of an organisation, such as purchasing, inventory, manufacturing, banking, payroll and accounting.

The reason for the separation of operational database systems from decision support database systems is that the content, functional and performance requirements of the two systems are different. Operational database systems are finely tuned to support known transaction processing workloads. Trying to execute complex decision support queries against the operational databases would result in performance degradation. Decision support requires summarised historical data, whereas operational databases usually store only raw current data. Decision support usually requires consolidating data from many heterogeneous sources. These different sources might contain data of varying quality, or use inconsistent representations, codes and formats, which have to be reconciled.

DSSs have existed, in different forms, for many years. The concept of a DSS is extremely broad and its definition varies depending on the context. In this course, we define a DSS as an interactive computer-based system to facilitate and improve decision making by providing decision makers with relevant information.

DSSs have been successfully deployed in many areas: the retail sector (for customer profiling and product promotion), financial services (for claims analysis, risk analysis, credit card analysis, and fraud detection), health care (for outcomes analysis), and any area in which management will encounter complex decision situations. DSSs are primarily used for strategic decisions faced by senior management: decisions with a reasonably low frequency and high potential consequences, in which the time taken for thinking through and modelling the problem pays off generously in the long term.

Systematic decision making involves three main phases: *intelligence*, *design* and *choice*.

▶ The *intelligence* phase involves identifying problems to solve, or opportunities to explore, so that the organisation can continue to meet its goals. The existence of a problem or opportunity is often determined by collecting and analysing the organisation's data.

▶ The *design* phase involves identifying or developing alternative courses of action, and constructing models to evaluate each of these alternatives based on the information available.

▶ The *choice* phase involves selecting the best course to follow, and planning its implementation.

DSSs allow decision makers to make better, more consistent decisions in a timely manner, by supporting all the phases of the decision-making process, and providing factual answers to questions posed by the decision maker.

For instance, a manager of a supermarket store would probably be concerned if her actual product sales were falling short of the target set by the supermarket chain. The question she would like to be able to ask might be:

Why are my total sales not meeting the company's targets?

There are, as yet, no such computer systems available to answer such a question. Her questioning has to be more specific so that the DSS can give factual responses. So the first question might be:

For each product, what are the cumulative sales and targets for the year?

A DSS would respond with a list of products and the sales figures. It is likely that some of the products are above the target and some are below it. A well-constructed report might highlight the offending products to make them easier to see. The manager could have asked:

What are the cumulative sales and targets for the year for those products where the actual sales are lower than the target?

Having discovered which products are not achieving the target, she might ask what the company's market share is for those products, and whether the market share is decreasing. She might then develop alternative promotion campaigns for those products that have a declining market share. Using the DSS she can evaluate each of these promotion campaigns, select the best campaign and plan the campaign.

The purpose of the DSS is to respond to ad hoc questions like these, so that the decision maker can ultimately come to a conclusion and make a decision based upon an analysis of the available data.

8.2 Multidimensional data model

Getting answers to business questions often requires viewing business data from various perspectives. For example, Walton Stores' management, who want to improve sales activity, might want to examine sales data collected throughout the organisation. The examination would entail viewing historical sales figures from multiple perspectives such as:

▶ sales by product;

▶ sales by location of the store;

▶ sales over time.

Analysing the sales data from each of the above perspectives can yield answers to questions such as: 'What is the trend in sales over a period of time for a particular product across the stores in a particular region?' Having the ability to respond to these types of enquiries in a timely fashion allows decision makers to formulate effective business strategies, identify trends and improve their overall ability to make important business decisions.

In this subsection, we describe a conceptual data model, the multidimensional data model, which enables decision makers to view data from different, and multiple, perspectives.

The multidimensional data model has its origins in multidimensional matrix algebra, which has been used since the late nineteenth century for multidimensional data analysis. Statistical databases and online analytical processing (OLAP) systems deal with multidimensional data, and both are concerned with statistical summarisation over the dimensions of the data. Statistical databases were developed during the 1970s to analyse socio-economic data, such as census data. OLAP systems were developed during the 1990s for the analysis of operational data, such as retail sales data. Despite supporting the same data model, literature on statistical databases and OLAP systems uses different terminology to describe the structural and manipulative parts of the model. We shall use the terminology associated with OLAP systems throughout this course.

In this subsection, we will describe the structural and manipulative parts of the multidimensional data model, and approaches to implementing the model in OLAP systems. The structural part of the model defines the underlying data structure on which the model is based, and the manipulative part defines the operators which can act on the data structure.

The structural part of the model is based on *facts* and *dimensions*, each fact depending on a set of dimensions, which provides the context for the fact. The *n*-dimensional view of data can be visualised in two dimensions as a spreadsheet (cross tabulation) as we shall illustrate later.

The manipulative part of the model is concerned with the operators that present different perspectives of the data and perform statistical summarisation over the dimensions.

There are two different approaches to implementing the model, depending on the nature of the underlying database technology used to store the data: **relational OLAP** (**ROLAP**), and **multidimensional OLAP** (**MOLAP**). ROLAP systems employ a relational database system to store the data as *fact tables* and *dimension tables*. MOLAP systems implement the multidimensional data model directly using a multidimensional database system, a database system where data is conceptually stored in cells of a multidimensional array. In this course, we shall focus primarily on ROLAP systems. In particular, we will describe the mapping of multidimensional data onto a relational database schema, and the provisions in SQL, known SQL/OLAP, to support the manipulative part of the model.

The structure of the multidimensional data model

At the core of the multidimensional data model are **facts**, numerical **measures** of the subject area of interest, typically sales. The perspectives by which an organisation wishes to view these facts are called the **dimensions**. Each fact depends on a set of dimensions, which provides a context for the measure. Using Walton Stores' sales data as an example, the subject area of interest could be product sales. If the dimensions are *product*, *location* and *time*, a fact could be the total sales for a particular product, in a particular region where stores are located, over a specified time period.

We can visualise a fact as a cell, or point, in an *n*-dimensional (*n*-D) space, where *n* is the number of dimensions. For example, Figure 8.1 shows a 1-D view of Walton Stores' sales data as a spreadsheet. Each numeric cell in Figure 8.1 records a fact about, or measure of, the total revenue from product sales by the four quarters of 2000 (Q1, Q2, Q3 and Q4).

Sales (£ billions)		
Time	Q1	7.52
	Q2	8.93
	Q3	8.74
	Q4	9.26

Figure 8.1   A 1-D view of Walton Stores' sales data showing total revenue from product sales for 2000 according to the dimension of *time*

Figure 8.2 shows another 1-D view of Walton Stores' sales data as a spreadsheet giving a different perspective of the data. Each numeric cell in Figure 8.2 records a fact about, or measure of, the total revenue from product sales for 2000 by the region in which the stores are located (NE, SE, SW and NW).

Sales (£ billions)		
Location	NE	8.33
	SE	10.53
	SW	7.31
	NW	8.28

Figure 8.2   A 1-D view of Walton Stores' sales data showing total revenue from product sales for 2000 according to the dimension of *location*

Dimensions are used for two purposes: *selection* of data and *grouping* of data at the desired level of detail. Figure 8.3 shows the data presented in Figure 8.1 in more detail by adding another dimension, *location*, which denotes the region in which the stores are located. Each cell in Figure 8.3 records a fact about, or measure of, the total revenue from product sales by the quarters of 2000, by region. Note that the row totals match the data described by Figure 8.1, and column totals match the data described by Figure 8.2.

Sales (£ billions)		Location			
		NE	SE	SW	NW
Time	Q1	2.02	2.35	1.08	2.07
	Q2	2.14	2.64	2.05	2.10
	Q3	2.13	2.51	2.03	2.07
	Q4	2.04	3.03	2.15	2.04

Figure 8.3   A 2-D view of Walton Stores' sales data showing total revenue from product sales for 2000 according to the dimensions of *time* and *location*

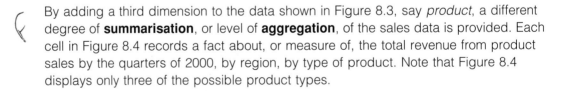

By adding a third dimension to the data shown in Figure 8.3, say *product*, a different degree of **summarisation**, or level of **aggregation**, of the sales data is provided. Each cell in Figure 8.4 records a fact about, or measure of, the total revenue from product sales by the quarters of 2000, by region, by type of product. Note that Figure 8.4 displays only three of the possible product types.

Sales (£ billions)				Product			
				Fish	Meat	Fruit	...
Time	Q1	Location	NE	0.21	0.68	0.41	
			SE	0.32	0.61	0.48	
			SW	0.30	0.64	0.49	
			NW	0.26	0.74	0.44	
	Q2	Location	NE	0.31	0.73	0.42	
			SE	0.34	0.60	0.56	
			SW	0.23	0.66	0.50	
			NW	0.29	0.69	0.52	
	Q3	Location	NE	0.33	0.70	0.53	
			SE	0.22	0.62	0.55	
			SW	0.24	0.67	0.57	
			NW	0.36	0.72	0.43	
	Q4	Location	NE	0.25	0.75	0.40	
			SE	0.35	0.63	0.54	
			SW	0.28	0.65	0.56	
			NW	0.27	0.71	0.45	

Figure 8.4   Part of a 3-D view of Walton Stores' sales data showing total revenue from product sales for 2000 according to the dimensions of *time*, *location* and *product*

For an *n*-dimensional space there will be 2^n different views, or aggregations, of the same data. For example, the 2-dimensional view of Walton Stores' sales data shown in Figure 8.3 has $2^2 = 4$ views of the same data: *time* (as shown by Figure 8.1), *location* (as shown by Figure 8.2), *time* by *location* (as shown by Figure 8.3), and the grand total of the measure.

Figure 8.5 shows all these four views of the 2-dimensional view of Walton Stores' sales data shown in Figure 8.3 as a single spreadsheet.

Sales (£ billions)		Location				
		NE	SE	SW	NW	total
Time	Q1	2.02	2.35	1.08	2.07	7.52
	Q2	2.14	2.64	2.05	2.10	8.93
	Q3	2.13	2.51	2.03	2.07	8.74
	Q4	2.04	3.03	2.15	2.04	9.26
	total	8.33	10.53	7.31	8.28	34.45

Figure 8.5   A 2-D view of Walton Stores' sales data showing total revenue from product sales for 2000 according to the dimensions of *time* and *location*

Figure 8.5 is composed from Figures 8.1, 8.2 and 8.3, plus the grand total of the measure: the rightmost column of the spreadsheet contains totals for the *location* dimension (i.e. totals for the indicated time across all regions – Figure 8.1), and the bottom row contains totals for the *time* dimension (i.e. totals for the indicated region across all times – Figure 8.2), and the cell at the bottom right-hand side contains the grand total, the column total of all the row totals.

When analysing data from particular perspectives, the decision maker will typically require the totals of the measures along each dimension.

EXERCISE 8.1

What are the possible views of the data presented in Figure 8.4, a 3-D view of Walton Stores' sales data according to the dimensions of *time*, *location* and *product*?

Dimensions

As we have noted, dimensions provide the context for facts about data. Dimensions are used for two purposes: *selection* of data and *grouping* of data at the desired level of detail.

The combination of dimension values defines the cells of the *n*-dimensional view of the data, and each dimension is defined over a specific domain. That is, each cell in an *n*-dimensional view can be defined by a set of **dimension–value pairs**, for example, *<time = Q1, region = SE>*. A non-empty cell records a fact. For example, the fact recorded by the above dimension–value pair is the total revenue from product sales for Q1 of 2000 in SE of £2.35 billion (see Figure 8.5).

The cells along each dimension of an *n*-D space may be partitioned at a particular level of abstraction or granularity. A **concept** (or **dimensional**) **hierarchy** describes how a dimension may be partitioned into different levels of granularity from a set of low-level concepts to higher-level, more general concepts. The concept hierarchies for the *product*, *location* and *time* dimensions are shown in Figure 8.6.

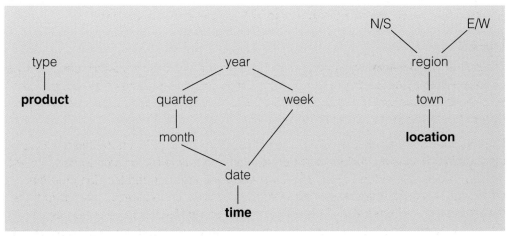

Figure 8.6   Concept hierarchies for the *product*, *location* and *time* dimensions. (Note that as a week could span two consecutive months, weeks are not contained in months.)

Consider the concept hierarchy for the dimension *location*. The locations of stores can be grouped by town, a low-level concept, and towns can be grouped by regions, a higher-level, more general concept. Regions may be grouped according to a north/south division of the country, or an east/west division.

There may be more than one concept hierarchy for a given dimension, based on different decision-maker viewpoints. For example, the *time* dimension has hierarchies for both fiscal year and calendar year.

We can denote the granularity of a dimension by including the name of the concept in parenthesis after the name of the dimension. For example, *time (month)* denotes that facts about the data are partitioned along the *time* by month.

EXERCISE 8.2

Give a concept hierarchy for the *customer* dimension for Walton Stores' sales data by considering the definition of the **Customer** entity type (see solution to Exercise 3.41).

Measures

A measure has two components: a numerical *property* of a fact and a *formula*, usually a numerical function, which can be evaluated at each point in an *n*-D space to combine several measure values into one. A measure value is computed for a given point by aggregating the data corresponding to the respective dimension–value pairs defining the given point. The formula is usually a simple aggregation function which performs a summation.

Measures take on different values for different combinations of dimension values. The property and formula are chosen such that the value of a measure is meaningful for all combinations of aggregation levels.

Manipulating the multidimensional data model

We now consider how the multidimensional data model can be manipulated to visualise and materialise these different views allowing querying and analysis of the data. The operations supported by the model, and provided by both statistical databases and OLAP systems, are strongly influenced by end-user tools such as spreadsheets.

We will consider three operators that act on a multidimensional view of data producing another view (or views) of the same data: roll-up, drill-down and cube.

Roll-up

The **roll-up** (or **drill-up**) operation performs an aggregation on a multidimensional view of data, either by ascending a concept hierarchy for a dimension, or by reducing the number of dimensions. The result of the operation is to produce summary data from detailed data along one or more dimensions.

For example, if we apply the roll-up operator to the data displayed in Figure 8.3 along the *location* dimension, reducing the dimensions from *time* by *location* to *time*, we will get the data displayed in Figure 8.1. If we apply the roll-up operator along the *time* dimension, reducing the dimensions from *time* by *location* to *location*, we will get the data displayed in Figure 8.2. If we apply the roll-up operator along the *location* dimension ascending the concept hierarchy for that dimension from *location (region)* to *location (N/S)*, we will get the data displayed in Figure 8.7.

Sales (£ billions)		Location	
		N	S
Time	Q1	4.09	3.43
	Q2	4.24	4.69
	Q3	4.20	4.54
	Q4	4.08	5.18

Figure 8.7   A 2-D view of Walton Stores' sales data showing total revenue from product sales for 2000 according to the dimensions of *time* and *location (N/S)*

Drill-down

The **drill-down** operation is the reverse of the roll-up operation. The aim of the operation is to move to a more detailed view of the data along one or more dimensions. The drill-down operation performs a distribution on a multidimensional view of data, either by descending a concept hierarchy for a dimension or by increasing the number of dimensions.

For example, if we apply the drill-down operator to the data displayed in Figure 8.1, increasing the number of dimensions by adding *location*, we will get the data displayed in Figure 8.3. If we apply the drill-down operator to the data displayed in Figure 8.2, increasing the number of dimensions by adding *time*, we will also get the data displayed in Figure 8.3. If we apply the drill-down operator to the data displayed in Figure 8.7 along the *location* dimensions descending the concept hierarchy for that dimension from *location (N/S)* to *location (region)*, we will again get the data described in Figure 8.3.

Cube

The **cube** operation takes an *n*-dimensional view of data and produces the other $2^n - 1$ different views, or aggregations, of the same data. For example, if we apply the cube operator to the data displayed in Figure 8.3, it will produce the data displayed in Figures 8.1 and 8.2, and the grand total of the measure. That is, it produces all the data required to generate Figure 8.5 from Figure 8.3: the totals of the measures along each dimension.

EXERCISE 8.3

Describe the essential difference between the way the *drill-down* operation works and the *roll-up* and *cube* operations.

OLAP systems

We now consider how online analytical processing (OLAP) systems implement the structural and manipulative parts of the multidimensional data model.

OLAP is a category of software technology that enables analysts and decision makers to gain an insight into decision support data by allowing them to view and analyse data across multiple dimensions. OLAP systems provide access to historical and summarised data, which are derived from an organisation's operational data, often consolidated from the many applications the organisation may use. The data is typically stored in a data warehouse.

OLAP systems merge multidimensional data analysis tools and database technology into an integrated client–server system. The architecture for OLAP systems is illustrated in Figure 8.8. It is a three-tier architecture where the OLAP system is partitioned into subsystems comprising three tiers responsible for the presentation, processing and storage of multidimensional data. The tiers correspond to a layered architectural style, with the presentation layer relying on services provided by the processing layer that, in turn, relies upon the storage layer.

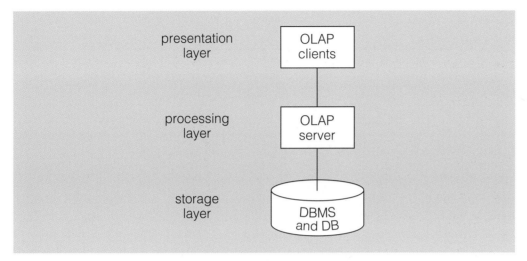

Figure 8.8   An architecture for OLAP systems

OLAP clients (presentation layer) provide tools for multidimensional data analysis, reporting, visualisation and data mining, and also provide interfaces to other software applications, such as spreadsheets and statistical analysis software packages. An OLAP server (processing layer) provides an interface between OLAP clients and the DBMS (storage layer) that is used to manage the database. An OLAP server satisfies requests from OLAP clients by fetching data from the database at the required level of aggregation, and passing it to the OLAP clients as a multidimensional array. As we noted earlier, there are two different approaches to implementing OLAP systems, depending on the nature of the underlying database technology that is used to store the data: *relational OLAP* (*ROLAP*) and *multidimensional OLAP* (*MOLAP*). ROLAP systems employ a relational database system to store the data as *fact tables* and *dimension tables*. MOLAP systems implement the multidimensional data model directly using a multidimensional database system.

In terms of the OLAP architecture shown in Figure 8.8, the differences between ROLAP and MOLAP systems are reflected by differences in the processing and storage layers, and the interface between them. For example, in ROLAP systems the ROLAP server will satisfy requests from OLAP clients by issuing SQL statements to the relational DBMS, and formatting the resultant tables as a multidimensional array.

In the following sections we will describe how ROLAP and MOLAP systems implement the structural and manipulative parts of the multidimensional data model. We conclude with a description of **hybrid OLAP** (**HOLAP**) systems which attempt to integrate the advantages of ROLAP and MOLAP systems.

Relational OLAP (ROLAP)

In ROLAP systems, the structural part of the multidimensional model is represented by a special database schema diagram known as a **star schema**, where an *n*-dimensional view is represented as a **fact table**, and *n* **dimension tables**. The *fact table* is at the centre of the 'star', whose 'points' are the *dimension tables*, which have one-to-many relationships with the fact table. Figure 8.9 shows a star schema for Walton Stores' sales data for the dimensions of *time*, *location* and *product*.

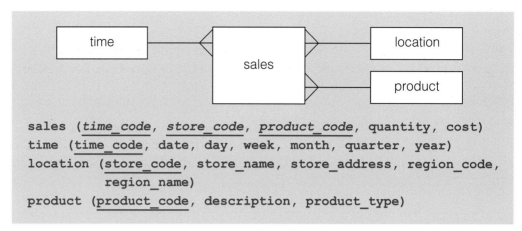

```
sales (time_code, store_code, product_code, quantity, cost)
time (time_code, date, day, week, month, quarter, year)
location (store_code, store_name, store_address, region_code,
         region_name)
product (product_code, description, product_type)
```

Figure 8.9   A star schema diagram for Walton Stores' sales data

The fact table contains unaggregated data. Each row of the fact table represents a fact about the subject of interest: sales data. In Figure 8.9, each row of the **sales** table records the purchase of a certain quantity of a particular product line, at a particular store, at a particular time, and for a certain cost.

A fact table has one or more dependent columns that record the numerical measures of the subject of interest. These are the *real facts* of the fact table, which OLAP operations on the data will aggregate. In Figure 8.9, the dependent columns are **quantity** and **cost**, which respectively record the quantity of a particular product line purchased and the total cost of the purchase. A fact table has several columns that represent the dimensions. They are foreign keys referencing the primary keys of the corresponding dimension tables. In Figure 8.9, the dimensions of *time*, *location* and *product* are represented by the **time_code**, **store_code**, and **product_code** columns, respectively. The primary key of the fact table is usually, though not always, a combination of the primary keys of the dimension tables.

A dimension table describes the values along that dimension. They are used to select rows from the fact table and define possible aggregations of the fact table. For example, in Figure 8.9 the **region_code** column of the **location** dimension table could be used to select data from the **sales** table pertaining to a particular region, and to aggregate the data by region. In a star schema, each level of the concept hierarchy for a dimension is represented by the columns of that dimension table.

As time is an essential dimension for historical data, every star schema will include a dimension table for the *time* dimension. As access to the fact table is driven from the dimension tables, the *time* dimension table should allow analysts to summarise data over different time periods, such as weeks, months, quarters and years, as required. In the **time** table shown in Figure 8.9, there is a certain amount of redundancy, since a week is calculable from the other attributes. However, weeks do not exactly align with months, so we cannot obtain a grouping of data by months from a grouping of weeks, or vice versa. Thus both weeks and months are represented in this dimension table. A business typically has a different financial year from the normal calendar year and will use their financial year to determine their accounting periods. Thus both financial and calendar years are often represented in the *time* dimension table.

EXERCISE 8.4

Revise the star schema for Walton Stores' sales data given in Figure 8.9 to include the *customer* dimension.

The primary key of the **customer** table corresponds to the customers' Frequent Shopper Card numbers. As a customer is identifiable only if they present their Frequent Shopper Card when purchasing goods, **customer_code** cannot be part of the primary key of the **sales** table.

The fact table stores the bulk of the data, while dimension tables will have a smaller number of rows. The advantage of this distribution of data is that a join of the fact table with a dimension table is relatively efficient since the performance of a join is improved when one large table is joined with a small table.

EXERCISE 8.5

The figure below shows the star schema for Walton Stores' sales data given in Figure 8.9 plus the *supplier* dimension. Explain why the **sales** table will include duplicated data (facts).

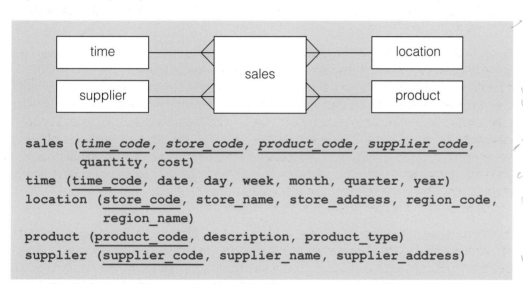

```
sales (time_code, store_code, product_code, supplier_code,
       quantity, cost)
time (time_code, date, day, week, month, quarter, year)
location (store_code, store_name, store_address, region_code,
         region_name)
product (product_code, description, product_type)
supplier (supplier_code, supplier_name, supplier_address)
```

The fact table may also contain duplicated data by including non-primary key columns of the dimension tables. This will make queries on the fact table quicker by avoiding performing joins between the fact table and those dimension tables.

In a star schema, dimension tables may include duplicated data since a concept (dimensional) hierarchy is represented as a single dimension table. For example, the data in the **location** table shown in Figure 8.9 represents the concept hierarchy for the *location* dimension (see Figure 8.6). It includes duplicated data since the **region_name** column is dependent on the **region_code** column rather than the primary key of the **location** table.

EXERCISE 8.6

What are the problems associated with duplicated data? Why would these problems not be likely to occur with decision support data?

A variant of the star schema, called a **snowflake schema**, represents concept hierarchies using several dimension tables, one table for each level of the concept hierarchy. Figure 8.10 shows a snowflake schema representation of the star schema given in Figure 8.9.

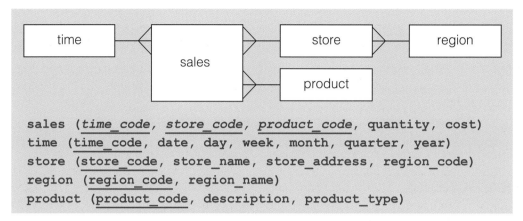

```
sales (time_code, store_code, product_code, quantity, cost)
time (time_code, date, day, week, month, quarter, year)
store (store_code, store_name, store_address, region_code)
region (region_code, region_name)
product (product_code, description, product_type)
```

Figure 8.10   A snowflake schema diagram for Walton Store' sales data

If there are several subject areas of interest in an organisation's decision support data, then multiple fact tables may be required. These may share one or more of the same dimension tables. The collection of star schemas that each represent a subject area of interest are known as a **galaxy schema** or a **fact constellation**. An example of a fact constellation is shown in Figure 8.11.

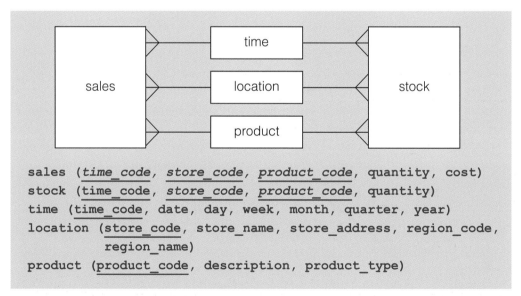

```
sales (time_code, store_code, product_code, quantity, cost)
stock (time_code, store_code, product_code, quantity)
time (time_code, date, day, week, month, quarter, year)
location (store_code, store_name, store_address, region_code,
          region_name)
product (product_code, description, product_type)
```

Figure 8.11   A fact constellation diagram for Walton Stores' sales and inventory data

Figure 8.11 shows Walton Stores' sales and inventory data for the dimensions of *time*, *location* and *product*. This schema specifies two fact tables, **sales** and **stock**. The **sales** fact table definition is identical to that of the star schema given in Figure 8.9. The **stock** fact table has the same three dimensions as the **sales** table, and records an inventory of products stocked at stores. Each row of the **stock** fact table records the quantity of a particular product line, stocked at a particular store, at a particular time.

A fact constellation is used to represent multiple subject areas of interest that are interrelated. The fact constellation given in Figure 8.11 could be used to ask questions about flow of product lines from distribution centre to store to customer, such as the supply and demand of certain product lines.

SQL/OLAP

As we noted earlier, OLAP servers provide an interface between OLAP clients and the DBMS used to manage the database. In a ROLAP system the OLAP server satisfies requests from OLAP clients by fetching data from a relational database by issuing SQL statements to the relational DBMS. We now describe how the manipulative part of the multidimensional model is implemented in ROLAP systems through SQL capabilities that facilitate the interaction between a ROLAP server and a relational database.

Support for the *roll-up* and *cube* OLAP operations are provided by extensions to the **GROUP BY** clause, which allows the use of the **aggregate functions** to summarise the raw data in the fact table.

Roll-up

The *roll-up* operation performs an aggregation on a multidimensional view of data, either by ascending a concept hierarchy for a dimension or by reducing the number of dimensions. A *roll-up* operation is effected by the **GROUP BY** clause, where the grouping columns specify the dimensions and the aggregate function(s) specified in the **SELECT** clause performing the aggregation.

The following SQL query (Figure 8.12), when run against the database described by the star schema given in Figure 8.9, will produce the 1-D view of Walton Stores' sales data according to the dimension of *location* as shown in Figure 8.2.

```
SELECT location.region_code, SUM(cost)/1000000000 AS total_revenue
  FROM sales, time, location
  WHERE sales.time_code = time.time_code
   AND sales.store_code = location.store_code
   AND time.year = 2000
  GROUP BY location.region_code
```

location.region_code	total_revenue
NE	8.33
SE	10.53
SW	7.31
NW	8.28

Figure 8.12   A 1-D view of Walton Stores' sales data according to the dimension of *location* as shown in Figure 8.2

The resultant table given in Figure 8.12 shows the same data as the column totals in Figure 8.5. The effect of the **GROUP BY** clause is equivalent to that of the OLAP roll-up operation

In the logical processing model for an SQL query, the **GROUP BY** clause takes as input the intermediate table resulting from the processing of the **WHERE** clause (or if there is no **WHERE** clause, the **FROM** clause), and creates another intermediate table by partitioning the rows according to the values of the columns specified in the **GROUP BY** clause. These columns are called **grouping columns**, and the resulting intermediate table the **grouped table**. In the grouped table, all the rows belonging to each group, that is, the rows having equal values in the grouping columns, are effectively collected together. The effect is as though an ordering of the rows of the grouped table by the grouping columns had been performed. After the set functions have been applied to each group, a new intermediate table is formed from the grouped table that has one row for each grouping, containing the value of each grouping column and the result of the set function computation over the rows of that group. These rows are called **aggregate rows**, since they aggregate the values in each grouping within the grouped table.

The following SQL query (Figure 8.13) when run against the database described by the star schema given in Figure 8.9 will produce the 2-D view of Walton Stores' sales data according to the dimensions of *time* and *location*, as shown in Figure 8.3.

```
SELECT location.region_code, time.quarter,
    SUM(cost)/1000000000 AS total_revenue
  FROM sales, time, location
  WHERE sales.time_code = time.time_code
    AND sales.store_code = location.store_code
    AND time.year = 2000
  GROUP BY location.region_code, time.quarter
```

location.region_code	time.quarter	total_revenue
NE	Q1	2.02
NE	Q2	2.14
NE	Q3	2.13
NE	Q4	2.04
SE	Q1	2.35
SE	Q2	2.64
SE	Q3	2.51
SE	Q4	3.03
SW	Q1	1.08
SW	Q2	2.05
SW	Q3	2.03
SW	Q4	2.15
NW	Q1	2.07
NW	Q2	2.10
NW	Q3	2.07
NW	Q4	2.04

Figure 8.13   A 2-D view of Walton Stores' sales data according to the dimensions of *time* and *location*, as shown in Figure 8.3. The resultant table shows the same data as the body of the spreadsheet shown in Figure 8.3

There is a ROLLUP option that can be included with the GROUP BY clause in the SQL query given in Figure 8.13, in which the resultant table includes additional rows, as shown in Figure 8.14. These additional rows are called **super aggregate rows**, since they are further aggregate rows already aggregated by the values in each grouping within the grouped table.

```
SELECT location.region_code, time.quarter,
    SUM(cost)/1000000000 AS total_revenue
  FROM sales, time, location
  WHERE sales.time_code = time.time_code
    AND sales.store_code = location.store_code
    AND time.year = 2000
  GROUP BY ROLLUP (location.region_code, time.quarter)
```

location.region_code	time.quarter	total_revenue
NE	Q1	2.02
NE	Q2	2.14
NE	Q3	2.13
NE	Q4	2.04
NE	NULL	8.33
SE	Q1	2.35
SE	Q2	2.64
SE	Q3	2.51
SE	Q4	3.03
SE	NULL	10.53
SW	Q1	1.08
SW	Q2	2.05
SW	Q3	2.03
SW	Q4	2.15
SW	NULL	7.31
NW	Q1	2.07
NW	Q2	2.10
NW	Q3	2.07
NW	Q4	2.04
NW	NULL	8.28
NULL	NULL	34.45

Figure 8.14 A 2-D view of Walton Stores' sales data according to the dimensions of *time* and *location*, as shown in Figure 8.5, but excluding the row totals

These additional rows are created as follows. The set functions are applied to the aggregate rows, grouping by the grouping columns to the left of the rightmost grouping column specified in the **GROUP BY** clause. The set functions are then applied to the super aggregate rows created by the previous aggregation, grouping by the next grouping column to the left, creating more super aggregate rows. This activity continues until all the grouping columns have been considered, when the set functions are then applied to the super aggregate rows created by the previous aggregation, creating a final single super aggregate row, representing a grand total.

In each super aggregate row, one or more of the grouping columns are **NULL**, and the others have the value of the group from which the group is derived. In Figure 8.14, the effect of the **GROUP BY ROLLUP** clause is to produce progressive subtotals of the revenue from product sales for each grouping column moving from right to left.

Cube

There is also a **CUBE** option that can be included with the **GROUP BY** clause in the SQL query given in Figure 8.13; the resultant table includes additional super aggregate rows as shown in Figure 8.15. These super aggregate rows are created for every combination of the grouping columns. The resultant table in Figure 8.15 provides all the data required for the spreadsheet given in Figure 8.5.

```
SELECT location.region_code, time.quarter,
    SUM(cost)/1000000000 AS total_revenue
FROM sales, time, location
WHERE sales.time_code = time.time_code
   AND sales.store_code = location.store_code
   AND time.year = 2000
   GROUP BY CUBE (location.region_code, time.quarter)
```

location.region_code	time.quarter	total_revenue
NE	Q1	2.02
NE	Q2	2.14
NE	Q3	2.13
NE	Q4	2.04
NE	NULL	8.33
SE	Q1	2.35
SE	Q2	2.64
SE	Q3	2.51
SE	Q4	3.03
SE	NULL	10.53
SW	Q1	1.08
SW	Q2	2.05
SW	Q3	2.03
SW	Q4	2.15
SW	NULL	7.31
NW	Q1	2.07
NW	Q2	2.10
NW	Q3	2.07
NW	Q4	2.04
NW	NULL	8.28
NULL	Q1	7.52
NULL	Q2	8.93
NULL	Q3	8.74
NULL	Q4	9.26
NULL	NULL	34.45

Figure 8.15 The data required for the spreadsheet given in Figure 8.5.

The effect of the **GROUP BY CUBE** clause with n grouping columns is equivalent to the OLAP operation of computing the 2^n views of an n-D multidimensional view of the data.

Drill-down

The *drill-down* operation *moves* to a more detailed view of the data along one or more dimensions. The operation does not *produce* new data since you cannot produce more detailed data from summary data. It requires the data to be already available, otherwise it has to be produced from more detailed data using the *roll-up* operation. Since ROLAP systems only store unaggregated data, this operation has to be effected by performing the appropriate *roll-up* on unaggregated data.

Multidimensional OLAP

MOLAP systems use a multidimensional database system to maintain decision support data. Multidimensional databases are specialised databases designed to facilitate multidimensional data analysis. They have been developed to store and manipulate not only decision support data but also image data (such as that produced by scanning devices used in medicine) and scientific data (such as climate data obtained from satellites).

Conceptually, data in a multidimensional database is stored as a multidimensional array where each cell in the array is formed by the intersection of all the dimensions.

EXERCISE 8.7

Give a disadvantage of the MOLAP approach to representing decision support data.

Multidimensional databases are a relatively new database technology. As such, the DBMS functions that should be provided by any DBMS are still absent or partially realised in the multidimensional DBMSs currently available. In particular, limited data types, transaction support, concurrency support and database recovery. Another key issue with multidimensional databases is lack of any standardisation. Each multidimensional database has its own proprietary query language, and so there is a tight coupling between the storage and processing layers of the MOLAP architecture.

The approach to storing decision support data in MOLAP systems is to precompute some or all possible aggregates in a systematic way rather than store unaggregated data. The precomputed data aggregates allow OLAP queries to be satisfied simply by retrieving the required data rather than having to access more detailed data and aggregating the data.

Hybrid OLAP

Both ROLAP and MOLAP systems have specific advantages and drawbacks. This has led to the development of **hybrid OLAP** (**HOLAP**) systems, which attempt to integrate the advantages of ROLAP and MOLAP systems, but at the cost of a more complex system architecture. The approach to maintaining decision support data in HOLAP systems is to use both relational and multidimensional database technologies. A relational database is used to store unaggregated data, while multidimensional databases are used to give access to selected precomputed aggregated data. This precomputed aggregated data is often referred to as a **materialised view** (of the data). The HOLAP server responds to a request from an OLAP client by accessing the multidimensional databases first, and if the data at the required level of aggregation is not available, the request is satisfied by accessing the relational database and aggregating the data.

Clearly, a response to a query will be faster if the data at the required level of aggregation is available from a multidimensional database. An issue in speeding up OLAP queries is which aggregates should be computed (which views should be materialised). Of course, there will be a trade-off between retrieval time and space utilisation. The more precomputed aggregates that are stored, the more likely the HOLAP server will find the appropriate aggregate for answering a query.

The *cube* operator can be used to compute all possible aggregations of the data. As we have noted, for data of n dimensions there are 2^n possible aggregations of that data. However, the number of aggregations is higher when the various dimension levels for each dimension are considered. So, unless the number of dimensions is small, storing all the possible aggregations of the data is not practical.

An empirical approach to precomputed aggregation is to compute an aggregate when it is needed by a query and is not already stored in a multidimensional database. When the space available to store multidimensional databases is full, the next aggregate to be computed will replace the least frequently used aggregate stored.

Summary of Subsection 8.2

In this subsection, we have described the structural and manipulative parts of the multidimensional data model, and the approaches to implementing the model in OLAP systems. The multidimensional data model enables decision makers to view data from different, and multiple, perspectives.

The structural part of the model is based on *facts* and *dimensions*, each fact depending on a set of dimensions, which provides the context for the fact. The *n*-dimensional view of data can be visualised in two dimensions as a spreadsheet (cross tabulation).

The manipulative part of the model is concerned with the operators that present different perspectives of the data and perform statistical summarisation over the dimensions.

There are two different approaches to implementing the model, depending on the nature of the underlying database technology used to store the data: ROLAP systems employ a relational database system to store the data as *fact tables* and *dimension tables,* and MOLAP systems implement the multidimensional data model directly using a multidimensional database system, a database system where data is conceptually stored in cells of a multidimensional array.

8.3   Data warehouses

Data warehousing is the process of constructing, maintaining and using a data warehouse for decision support purposes. The topic encompasses architectures, procedures, and the tools for bringing together selected operational data from multiple heterogeneous information sources maintained by an organisation into a single repository, the data warehouse, suitable for direct querying or analysis by decision makers.

In this subsection, we will:

- ▶ describe the characteristics of a data warehouse;
- ▶ describe the types of data warehouses;
- ▶ consider data warehousing as an approach to information integration;
- ▶ outline an architecture for a data warehousing system.

Data warehouses

In the introduction to this section, we described a data warehouse as a component of a decision support system. It facilitates decision support by providing a repository of consolidated historical data with a logical structure that enables decision makers to view and analyse the data in different, and multiple, dimensions.

EXERCISE 8.8

Why is a data warehouse usually maintained separately from an organisation's operational database systems?

[handwritten margin notes: So accessing does not affect performance. The extra data may increase workload for regular operational tasks]

Many organisations maintain corporate data warehouses to support business decision-making activities, which include:

▶ increasing customer focus by analysing customers' buying patterns (such as buying preference, buying time, budget cycles, and appetites for spending);

▶ repositioning products and managing product portfolios by comparing the performance of sales by quarter, by year, and by geographic region, in order to fine-tune production strategies;

▶ analysing operations to identify sources of profit;

▶ managing customer relationships.

A data warehouse may be characterised as a database that is *subject-oriented*, *integrated, time-variant* and *non-volatile*.

▶ *Subject-oriented* means that the data is organised around subjects (such as sales) rather than operational applications (such as order processing). Operational databases are organised around business applications; they are application-oriented. A data warehouse focuses on the modelling and analysis of data for decision makers and hence typically provides a simple and concise view around particular subjects by excluding data that is not relevant in the decision support process.

▶ *Integrated* means that the same data extracted from different sources is consistent, and hence comparable. This means that values intended to be comparable to each other must always be stored in the same format. Integration is a problem for most organisations, particularly in a distributed heterogeneous computing environment where there may be many different types of technology in use. Some differences are quite fundamental; for example, the representation of data types, such as **INTEGER**, **REAL** or **CHARACTER**, is an issue that must be addressed whenever two or more computer systems are required to exchange data.

Other differences such as dates are more subtle. Most DBMSs have a **DATE** data type (although the storage format may be different from one DBMS to another) whereas file-based systems may have no **DATE** data type and use the **STRING** data type to record dates.

Differences may occur within different applications even within the same technology. This occurs where, for instance, one database designer decides to hold addresses as five columns defined as twenty-five characters each, whereas another might use a single column defined as two hundred characters.

Integration involves recognising incompatibilities between data from different sources, and eliminating these incompatibilities to allow comparisons and aggregations.

▶ *Time-variant* means that historical data is recorded. Data is stored to provide information from a historical perspective. Every key structure in the data warehouse contains, either implicitly or explicitly, an element of time. Almost all queries executed against a data warehouse have some element of time associated with them.

We have established that operational systems do not usually retain historical information, yet to predict what will happen in the future we need historical data. A data warehouse helps to address this fundamental issue by adding a historical dimension to the data taken from the operational databases.

▶ *Non-volatile* means that the data, once placed in the warehouse, is not usually subject to change. Anyone who is using the database has confidence that a query will produce a very similar result no matter how often it is run. (The gradual accumulation of data in the warehouse will change results, but not very quickly.) Operational databases are extremely volatile: they are constantly changing. A query is unlikely to produce the same result twice if it is accessing tables which are frequently updated.

From an architectural point of view, there are three types of data warehouse that an organisation may choose to adopt to maintain its decision support data: the *enterprise data warehouse*, the *data mart*, and the *virtual data warehouse*.

An **enterprise data warehouse** is a collection of information about all subjects of interest to an organisation. It is constructed by integrating all the relevant data from an organisation's operational information systems. It typically contains detailed (raw) data as well as summarised (aggregated) data, and can range in size from a few gigabytes to many terabytes. It requires extensive business modelling in its design and may take months or even years to build. Although the development of an enterprise data warehouse is a major commitment for an organisation in terms of financial and human resources, there are significant long term benefits to the organisation in the enhancement of its ability to make strategic decisions using the data warehouse.

A **data mart** is a collection of information that is of value to a specific group of users within an organisation, or to support specific products. The scope is confined to specific selected subject(s) of interest.

EXERCISE 8.9

What subjects would you consider to be the scope of a marketing data mart?

A data mart typically contains summarised data, and can range in size from a few gigabytes to a terabyte. It will normally take less time to design and build than an enterprise data warehouse because it only deals with a few subject areas and information sources.

Depending on the source of the data, data marts can be categorised as dependent or independent. A **dependent data mart** is sourced directly from an enterprise data warehouse. An **independent data mart** is sourced from data captured from one or more operational systems or external information providers, or from data generated locally within a particular department or geographic area. An organisation may maintain many data marts.

An enterprise data warehouse may exist as a **distributed data warehouse** where the information is distributed over several independent data marts that collectively cover all subjects of interest to an organisation.

EXERCISE 8.10

What problems might an organisation encounter when developing a distributed data warehouse from departmental data marts that they would not necessarily experience with an enterprise data warehouse?

(handwritten margin notes) - 2-step transactions could slow system - update, deletion anomalies Also, possible semantic differences between depts

Enterprise data warehouses and data marts are examples of a **physical data warehouse** since the data extracted from operational information sources is stored in a separate database. In a **virtual data warehouse**, decision makers have direct access to operational information sources through a collection of views over the operational data that are appropriate for decision support purposes. There is no separate database.

EXERCISE 8.11

Although a virtual data warehouse is an attractive type of data warehouse for an organisation to adopt as it has no separate database and it is relatively easy to build, why in most cases can it make only a limited contribution to an organisation's strategic decision making?

(handwritten margin note) no historical data is stored

Because of the limitations described in the solution to Exercise 8.11, a virtual data warehouse is considered by many practitioners not to be a true data warehouse. However, a virtual data warehouse approach is often employed to determine if and how decision makers might use operational data as a part of a feasibility study and/or to prototype the development of an enterprise data warehouse. Furthermore, as we shall discuss below, a virtual data warehouse represents an important approach to information integration.

Information integration

As we have noted, it is highly desirable for organisations that maintain multiple heterogeneous information sources to be able to integrate the data for the purpose of strategic decision making.

(handwritten margin note) running analyses on information stored in different ways different systems

EXERCISE 8.12

What does integrating information involve? Why is it an important issue in data warehousing?

Information integration is the process where data that is maintained in two or more information sources is extracted to build a single repository, possibly virtual, containing information from all sources, so the data can be queried as a unit, easily and efficiently. Information sources may include not only relational databases but also diverse sources such as flat files, legacy systems, news wires, SGML, HTML and XML documents, object-oriented databases, knowledge bases, and so on.

Information integration involves the following tasks:

▶ the extraction of the data from each information source;

▶ the translation of the data, which resolves any incompatibilities between the same data from different information sources so that the data can be integrated;

▶ the cleaning of the data, which deals with the detection and removal of errors and inconsistencies in the data from each information source;

▶ the integration of the data, which combines the extracted, translated and cleaned data from all the information sources.

There are two approaches to providing integrated access to data from multiple, heterogeneous information sources that are relevant to data warehousing: eager (in-advance) and lazy (on-demand). Both follow a very general two-step process.

In an **eager** (**in-advance**) **approach**:

1   Information from each source is extracted, translated and cleaned as appropriate, merged with the relevant information from the other sources, and stored in a centralised repository.

2   When a query is posed, it is evaluated directly at the repository, without the need to access the original information sources.

We refer to this process as an *eager* or *in-advance* approach to information integration, since all the information is extracted from the information sources in advance of queries being posed. It is also commonly referred to as a **warehousing approach** since the repository serves as a warehouse storing the data of interest.

In contrast, in a **lazy** (**on-demand**) **approach**:

1   When a query is posed, the appropriate set of information sources to answer the query is determined, and the appropriate queries or commands for each information source are generated to extract the data.

2   The results obtained from the information sources are translated and cleaned as appropriate, and merged to return the final answer to the user (or application).

We refer to this process as a *lazy* or *on-demand* approach to information integration, since information is extracted from the information sources only when queries are posed. It is also referred to as a **mediated approach** since the module that decomposes queries and combines the results is known as a **mediator**.

In the *eager* approach, the data from several information sources is extracted and combined into a unified schema. The data is then stored at the warehouse database. Figure 8.16 shows a data warehouse populated by several information sources. The user issues a query to the DBMS that maintains the warehouse database, which returns the result without accessing the information sources. In Figure 8.16, a **wrapper** is a module that is responsible for translating data from the native format of the information source into the format and data model used by the warehouse database; the **integrator** module is responsible for installing the data from the different information sources into the warehouse database. Later in this subsection, we will discuss the function of the wrapper and integrator modules in more detail.

EXERCISE 8.13

Physical data warehouses (enterprise data warehouses and data marts) adopt the *eager* approach to information integration. What would you consider are the advantages and disadvantages of adopting this approach?

In the *lazy* approach, the data is extracted from one or more information sources only on demand. Figure 8.17 shows a mediator and wrappers integrating several information sources. A mediator supports a virtual view of the integrated data by having a schema that describes the information source(s) from which each data item can be obtained. The user issues a query to the mediator. In response, the mediator decomposes the query and sends a query to its wrappers, which in turn send queries to their corresponding information sources. The mediator may have to send several queries to a wrapper, and may not query all the wrappers. The results returned by the information sources via their wrappers are combined at the mediator.

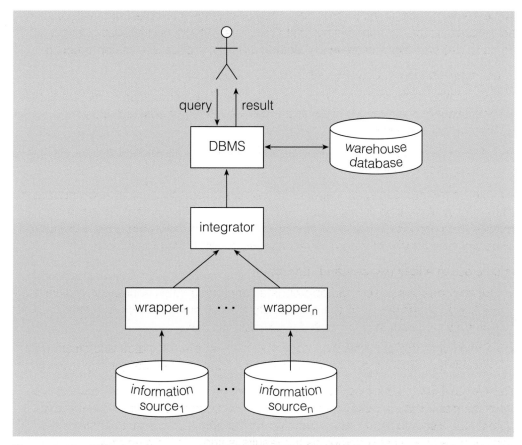

Figure 8.16   The eager approach to information integration where the warehouse database stores the integrated information

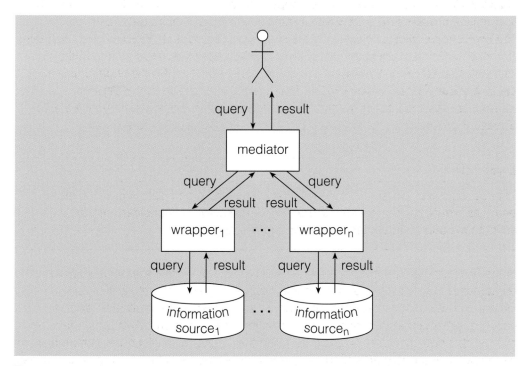

Figure 8.17   The lazy approach to information integration where a mediator and wrappers translate queries into the terms of the sources and combine the results

EXERCISE 8.14

Virtual data warehouses adopt the *lazy* approach to information integration. What would you consider are the advantages and disadvantages in adopting this approach?

EXERCISE 8.15

What issues have to be addressed that are common to development of both physical and virtual data warehouses?

Data warehousing architecture

An architecture for a physical data warehousing system must support the integration of data from multiple heterogeneous distributed information sources to form a repository of consolidated historical data. This database should be capable of being analysed and viewed in different, and multiple, dimensions by decision makers. An architecture for a physical data warehousing system that meets these requirements is shown in Figure 8.18. Since a data warehouse is a component of an OLAP system, the architecture shown in Figure 8.18 is a combination of an OLAP system architecture shown in Figure 8.8 and the components for the *eager* approach to information integration shown in Figure 8.16.

The architecture is an integrated client–server system with a three-tier architecture: the data warehousing system is partitioned into subsystems comprising three tiers responsible for the presentation, processing and storage of decision support data. OLAP clients (presentation layer) provide tools for multidimensional data analysis, reporting, visualisation and data mining, and interfaces to other software applications, such as spreadsheets and statistical analysis software packages. An OLAP server (processing layer) provides an interface between OLAP clients and the DBMS(s) (storage layer) used to manage the warehouse database. (The DBMS(s) are not shown in Figure 8.18.)

The architecture also provides tools for: extracting and translating the operational data from the information sources (**extraction component**); cleaning and integrating this data (**integration component**); loading the integrated data into the warehouse database; periodically refreshing the data warehouse to reflect additions and updates at the information sources; purging data from the data warehouse to archival storage.

The architecture includes a metadata repository for storing and maintaining metadata that describes all the data associated with the data warehousing system. In particular, it describes the structure of the operational data in the information sources, the structure of the decision support data in the warehouse database, and the mappings between them.

Though not shown in Figure 8.18, there are also tools for monitoring and administering the data warehousing system.

We shall now describe in more detail each of the components of the data warehousing architecture shown in Figure 8.18.

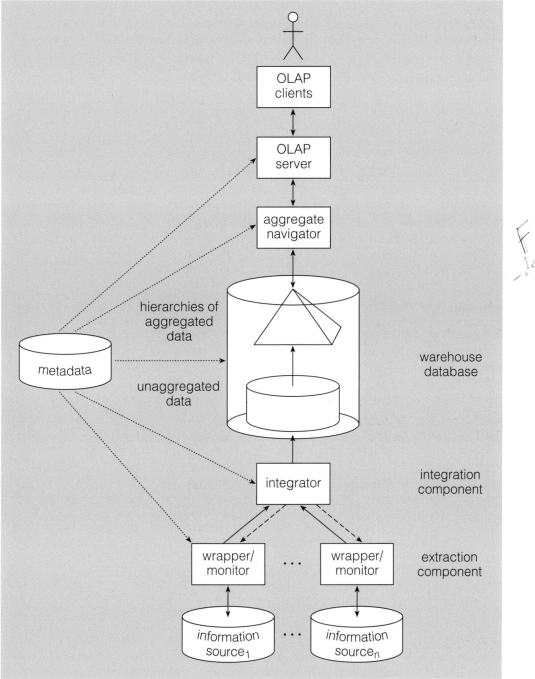

Figure 8.18   An architecture for a physical data warehousing system

Extraction component

The **extraction component** copies operational data from the various information
sources, translates it, and passes it to the integrator. As we have noted, these
information sources may be not only relational databases but also diverse sources
such as flat files, legacy systems, news wires, SGML, HTML and XML documents,
object-oriented databases, knowledge bases, and so on. For each disparate
information source, the data warehousing system must establish:

1   a process by which selected data can be extracted from the information source;

2   a mechanism to detect significant changes and additions to this data so that they
    can be propagated to the data warehousing system to update (refresh) the
    warehouse database.

Data from operational systems and other external information sources is usually (ideally) extracted using application program interfaces (APIs) called gateways. A **gateway** provides a standard or proprietary interface between an external information source (server) and an application process (client), which allows the client to generate commands, possibly SQL statements, to be executed at the information source (server) to retrieve the required data. Examples of gateways include Open Database Connectivity (ODBC), Object Linking and Embedding for Databases (OLE-DB), and Java Database Connectivity (JDBC).

Connected to each information source is a wrapper/monitor module. The wrapper component is responsible for translating data from the native format of the information source into the format and data model used by the warehouse database. For example, if the information source is a set of flat files but the data warehouse model is relational, then the wrapper must support an interface that presents the data from the information source as if it were relational. The wrapper is the client requesting data (held in flat files) from the gateway server and, on receipt of the data, it translates the data into the required format (relational). The translation problem is inherent in all approaches to information integration, both lazy and eager, and not specific to data warehousing.

The **monitor** component is responsible for automatically detecting changes of interest to the data warehouse in the source data, and propagating those changes to the integrator.

EXERCISE 8.16

Why does the monitor need to interact with its associated wrapper?

The importance of change detection to a data warehousing system is dependent on the frequency and the degree of automation required in the updating (refreshing) of the warehouse database. There are two approaches to updating a warehouse database:

1 Periodically detect and propagate changes from each information source to the data warehouse. This approach may be acceptable if the data changes infrequently or the warehouse data needs only to be updated periodically, for example, weekly or monthly.

2 Continually detect and propagate changes from each information source to the data warehouse. This approach is appropriate if the data changes frequently and it is important for the warehouse data to be up to date.

The nature of the information source determines the mechanism to detect changes to its data. We can classify information sources as *cooperative*, *logged*, *queryable* and *snapshot*.

Cooperative sources are databases that support triggers, so that notifications of changes of interest can be recorded automatically.

Logged sources maintain a change (transaction) log that can be inspected, so that changes of interest can be extracted from the log.

Queryable sources allow the wrapper/monitors to query the data at the information source, so that periodic polling can be used to detect changes of interest.

Snapshot sources do not provide triggers, or change logs, and are not queryable. Instead, periodic dumps (snapshots) of the data at the information source must be performed, and changes of interest detected by the comparison of successive snapshots.

A different wrapper/monitor module is needed for each information source, since the functionality of the wrapper/monitor is dependent on the type of the source and the nature of the data provided by that source. Rather than writing a wrapper/monitor for each particular information source participating in a data warehousing system, a **wrapper generator** (software that creates a wrapper) can be used to automate (or semi-automate) the process of implementing wrapper/monitor modules. This is especially useful if operational information sources change frequently, or new sources become available. A wrapper generator uses the specification for an information source to build a wrapper tailored for that source.

Integration component

The **integration component** cleans all the data selected from the different information sources, and combines the data, resolving any incompatibilities between the same types of data from different sources, and brings the data into a consistent format ready for loading into the warehouse database.

When a new information source is attached to the data warehousing system, or when relevant data at an information source changes, the new or modified data is propagated to the integrator. In order to integrate new information properly into the warehouse database, it may be necessary for the integrator to obtain further information from the same or other information sources. The downward dashed arrows in Figure 8.18 indicate this behaviour.

Data cleaning

Data cleaning, also called **data cleansing** or **scrubbing**, deals with the detection and removal of errors and inconsistencies in the data from a single information source in order to improve the quality of the data. (Inconsistencies between information sources are dealt with when the data from the different information sources is combined.) Data warehousing systems require and provide extensive support for data cleaning to guarantee the quality of strategic decision making.

Erroneous data may be classified as *incomplete*, *noisy* or *inconsistent*.

▶ *Incomplete:* missing data, lacking attribute values or certain attributes of interest.

▶ *Noisy:* data values that deviate from the expected.

▶ *Inconsistent:* contradictions between data in one part of the database and data in another. Also data that violates domain, uniqueness, referential or general constraints.

The data quality of an information source largely depends on the degree to which it is governed by schema and integrity constraints controlling permissible data values. For sources without a schema, such as file-based systems, there are usually few restrictions on what data can be entered and stored, giving rise to a high probability of errors and inconsistencies. Database systems, on the other hand, enforce restrictions of a specific data model as well as application-specific integrity constraints.

In general, approaches to data cleaning involve two steps:

1 Data analysis: In order to detect which kinds of errors and inconsistencies are to be corrected or removed, a detailed analysis of the data is required to gain metadata about the data properties. This metadata helps to find data quality problems.

2 Defining data transformation rules: In order to correct errors whenever possible, or remove erroneous data, it is necessary to define rules for handling erroneous data. The removal of erroneous data may also require the removal of any associated data. The data transformation rules are held in the metadata repository.

Handwritten margin notes: reduce the number of heterogeneous data sources if draws data from ✓ ensure constraints are properly used to guarantee data type at source

EXERCISE 8.17

Cleaning data sources is an expensive process. How can an organisation reduce the cost of data cleaning?

Data integration

There are two main aspects of data integration: *format integration* and *semantic integration*.

Format integration is concerned mainly with ensuring domain consistency. In most organisations, there are usually many cases where attributes in one system have different formats from the formats of the same or similar attributes in other systems. Some examples are as follows:

▶ Bank account numbers or telephone numbers might be stored as type `character` or `char` in one system and type `integer` in others.

▶ Sex might be stored as 'male', 'female' or 'm', 'f', or 'M', 'F' or even 1, 0.

▶ Dates can be held in many formats including 'ddmmyy', 'ddmmyyyy', 'yymmdd', 'yyyymmdd', 'dd mon yy', 'dd mon yyyy'. Some systems store dates as a time stamp which is accurate to thousandths of a second. Others use an integer which is the number of seconds since a particular time, for example 1 January 1900.

▶ Monetary attributes are also a problem. Some systems store money as integer values and expect the application to insert the decimal points; others have embedded decimal places.

▶ In different systems, differing lengths are used for string values such as names, addresses and product descriptions.

▶ Different units of measurement might be used. Some systems may use metric units, others imperial.

Format mismatches are very common and this is especially true when data is extracted from systems where the underlying hardware, operating system or application software is different.

The integration procedure consists of a set of rules designed to ensure that the data which is loaded into a data warehouse is in the same format, so all the dates are of the same format, monetary values are always represented the same way, and so on. The integration rule set specifies how data extracted from multiple, heterogeneous information sources must be transformed before it is allowed into the warehouse database. The integration rule set is stored in the metadata repository.

Semantic integration is concerned with the consistent meaning of data extracted from different operational systems. Typically, different types of people in an organisation use different operational systems. For example, financial systems are most likely to be used by the accounts department whereas warehouse staff will use stock control systems. We can illustrate the problem by considering how different people working for the same company can view a sale.

▶ A salesman will normally consider that a sale has occurred when an order has been received from a customer.

▶ A stock manager will record a sale when she receives a notice to dispatch an order.

▶ An accountant does not usually recognise a sale until an invoice has been raised against an order.

This kind of ambiguity exists in all organisations and can be very confusing to a database analyst trying to understand the kinds of data being held. The problem is compounded because the users of the data are often unaware of the problem. In everyday conversations, the fact that they are unknowingly discussing different things may not be obvious to them, and most of the time there are no serious repercussions.

In building a data warehouse, we do not have the luxury of being able to ignore these, usually subtle, differences in semantics because the information produced by the queries run against the data warehouse will be used to support strategic decision making.

It is vital, therefore, that each item of data inserted into the warehouse database has a single meaning that is understood by everyone. A precise description of each attribute in the warehouse database is stored in the metadata repository.

Warehouse database

Once the data from the information sources has been extracted, cleaned and integrated, the data is loaded into the warehouse database. Since many queries posed to a data warehousing system require summary data, whose processing could thus be accelerated by using aggregated data, the warehouse database will typically store both the unaggregated (raw) data extracted from the information sources and selected precomputed aggregated data.

EXERCISE 8.18

Consider the possible aggregations of an organisation's operational data that you would expect the administrator of a data warehousing system might typically choose to precompute in order to facilitate the work of decision makers employed by that organisation.

We noted that for a data warehousing system based on a HOLAP system, the unaggregated data would be maintained by a relational database system, and the aggregated data by a multidimensional database system. The schema for the relational database is created from the star (or snowflake) schema that represents the data requirements of the data warehousing system.

In a data warehousing system based on a ROLAP system, both the unaggregated and aggregated data would be maintained by a (the same) relational database system. An aggregation of raw data can be expressed by a relational view; this can be stored as a physical table in order to accelerate the processing of queries run against the view. Such precomputed aggregates are generally referred to as **materialised views** (in the context of a relational database system).

To exploit effectively the use of materialised views we need to address the following issues.

▶ View selection: which views (aggregates) should be materialised (precomputed and stored).

▶ View maintenance: how materialised views can be efficiently refreshed when the warehouse database is updated.

▶ View use: which views are available to satisfy requests posed to the data warehousing system, and how they can be used effectively by the query processor.

We have already discussed the approaches to **view selection** when we described the architecture of HOLAP systems earlier.

EXERCISE 8.19

Describe an empirical approach to view selection that is used when there is a limited amount of storage space to hold precomputed aggregates.

One of the major performance issues with data warehouse systems is warehouse maintenance. When new or modified data is added to the warehouse, the aggregated data must be refreshed. The process of updating materialised views in response to changes to the underlying unaggregated data is called **view maintenance**.

EXERCISE 8.20

Consider the possible approaches to view maintenance that might be employed by a data warehousing system.

Users of a data warehousing system should not need to be aware of the existence of materialised views in the warehouse database. The **aggregate navigator** shown in Figure 8.18 is an additional layer of software which sits between the OLAP server and the DBMS(s) that manage the warehouse database. The role of the aggregate navigator is to ensure the effective and transparent use of these materialised views. The aggregate navigator receives a query from the OLAP server, examines it to establish which data is required and the level of aggregation needed so that it can determine whether aggregated data can be used to satisfy the request. The aggregate navigator rewrites queries to use materialised views whenever possible.

Aggregate navigators hold their own metadata in the metadata repository, which they use to provide a mapping between queries formulated by the OLAP server, in response to user requests, and the unaggregated and aggregated data content of the warehouse database.

EXERCISE 8.21

How could the aggregate navigator be employed to help the administrator of a data warehousing system in the task of view selection?

Metadata repository

Throughout this section, we have made several references to the use of metadata by data warehousing systems to integrate the functionality of the various components of the system. Metadata is data that describes the data in a data warehouse. It is required not only to maintain the currency and integrity of a data warehouse system, but also to control and monitor access to the data by the users of the system. Without quality metadata, the decision makers cannot perform useful data analyses, and hence cannot make strategic decisions with confidence.

The many different kinds of metadata that have to be managed by a data warehousing system may be stored in a single metadata repository. Metadata in the repository is stored for use both by the decision makers and by the data warehousing system itself.

For the decision makers, the repository should provide a comprehensive guide to the data resource, and such metadata should include:

- a lexicon of common words used in formal data names and data name abbreviation schemes;
- a description of the logical data structure of the data warehouse database, and the data integrity rules;
- an inventory of the operational data maintained by the system and sources of that data;
- a glossary of business words, terms, and abbreviations that support use of the data.

EXERCISE 8.22

Who do you think should be responsible for providing the metadata in the repository that will be used by the decision makers?

Metadata, which will be used by the decision makers, need not be in any particular format. Each of the above items may be stored as character strings. The data warehousing system should provide a search facility so that any desired item can be located easily by the decision makers using the system.

The metadata repository should contain the following details that will be used by the data warehousing system itself:

- the warehouse database schema, the schema of each information source and their mappings to the warehouse database schema which provides the rules for extracting, cleaning and integrating data from the information sources;
- view definition, maintenance and use;
- user identifiers, user authorisation and access control policies;
- the currency of the data in the warehouse database (active, archived or purged).

8.4 Summary

Decision Support Systems (DSSs) are computer-based systems that incorporate data warehouses and employ data mining techniques to facilitate and improve decision making by providing decision makers with relevant information.

A multidimensional data model is a conceptual data model that enables decision makers to view decision support data from different, and multiple, perspectives. A multidimensional view of data allows decision makers to consolidate or aggregate decision support data at different levels of detail.

The multidimensional data model characterises data as *facts*, which are numerical *measures* of the subject of interest, and *dimensions*, which provide a context for the facts. For example, in a supermarket chain, products are sold to customers at certain times in certain amounts at certain prices from certain stores. A typical fact would be the purchase of a product by a customer at a certain time. Typical measures would be the amount and price of each purchase. Typical dimensions would be the location of the store, the type of product being purchased, and the time of the purchase.

A data warehouse is characterised as a *subject-oriented*, *integrated*, *time-variant* and *non-volatile* collection of data built to support strategic decision making. We discussed the three types of data warehouse that an organisation may choose to adopt to maintain its decision support data: the *enterprise data warehouse*, the *data mart* and the *virtual data warehouse*. We considered two approaches to information integration:

the *eager approach* and the *lazy approach* employed by physical data warehouses and virtual data warehouses respectively. We have outlined the architecture for a data warehousing system, and described the extraction component, integration component, warehouse database and metadata repository in detail.

LEARNING OUTCOMES

Having completed your study of this section of the course, you will be able to:

▶ Explain how decision support systems, the multidimensional data model, data warehouses and data warehousing, can each facilitate and improve strategic decision making by organisations who employ databases to manage their day-to-day operations.

▶ Develop a simple design for a data warehouse using a relational database, which facilitates strategic decision making.

Block summary

The purpose of this block has been to enable you to develop the practical skills you will need to undertake the development of a database, from the analysis of the information requirements of an enterprise through to the implementation of a database that satisfies those requirements, using the database management system (DBMS) supplied with the course, SQL Anywhere.

Section 1 provided an overview of the tasks associated with each stage of the database life cycle – establishing requirements, data analysis, database design, implementation, testing and maintenance.

To illustrate tasks associated with each stage of the database life cycle we have used not only the case studies employed by Blocks 1 to 3, the *Hospital* and *University* scenarios, but also a more complex case study – a supermarket chain, which uses databases to facilitate the day-to-day running of its business. The information requirements of this supermarket chain, *Walton Stores*, were introduced in Section 2.

Sections 3 to 6 respectively described in detail the practical tasks associated with data analysis, database design, implementation and maintenance. *Block 5* will consider further one aspect of database implementation: application development.

Our main focus has been on the development of a database to facilitate the day-to-day running of an enterprise where the data is located on a single computer system shared by its many users. But in Sections 7 and 8, respectively, we have considered requirements to distribute and manage data over several computer systems – distributed data management – and the requirement to integrate this distributed data to maintain summarised historical data for strategic decision-making – data warehousing.

Solutions to Exercises

SOLUTION 1.1

Although users could use SQL or tools to define, populate, manipulate and display tables, the uncontrolled ad hoc creation of tables by users would lead to an unmanageable and unusable database environment. Users would inevitably create islands of data under their own control, would be unable to find the data they want or would include multiple copies of potentially inconsistent data. A database is not just a collection of tables that is created at the whim of a user, but should be seen as a coordinated set of tables that are designed to satisfy some specified requirements.

SOLUTION 1.2

(a) The desirable properties of a database are as follows.

Completeness:	Ensures that users can access the data they want. Note that this includes ad hoc queries, which would not be explicitly given as part of a statement of data requirements.
Integrity:	Ensures that the data is both consistent (no contradictory data) and correct (no invalid data), and that users trust the database.
Flexibility:	Ensures that a database can evolve (without requiring excessive effort) to satisfy changing user requirements.
Efficiency:	Ensures that users do not have unduly long response times when accessing data.
Usability (ease of use):	Ensures that the data can be accessed and manipulated in ways which match user requirements.

(b) If a database did not have these properties, then it might: not satisfy all user requirements; contain inconsistent and invalid data; require excessive effort to change; be slow and clumsy to use in order to achieve a desired outcome.

(c) The key task in database development that avoids these problems is data analysis, which results in a detailed understanding of the meaning of the data and its relationships.

SOLUTION 1.3

(a) The data requirements are represented by the logical schema.

(b) The operational requirements are represented by the user processes (application software) and associated external schemas.

SOLUTION 1.4

Task	Purpose	Output
Establishing requirements	To elicit the stakeholders' information requirements through consultation and agreement.	Information requirements
Data analysis	To describe the data, and relationships between the data.	Conceptual data model
Database design	To produce a relational representation of the conceptual data model.	Logical schema
Implementation	To produce a working database that is intended to satisfy the information requirements.	Initial schema and database
Testing	To demonstrate that the database satisfies the information requirements, and then install the database.	Released schema and database
Maintenance	To ensure that the database continues to satisfy the information requirements after it has been installed, and adapt the database to meet new and changing requirements.	Revised schema and database

SOLUTION 1.5

Validation attempts to confirm that the right database has been constructed with the right characteristics to meet the specified requirements. Validation answers the question 'Has the right database been developed to meet the requirements?'

Verification ensures that the processing steps, constraints and other 'programmed' components (security, backup, recovery, audit trails, etc.) of the database have been correctly implemented and contain no errors in program logic or execution sequences. Verification answers the question 'Has the database design been implemented correctly?'

SOLUTION 1.6

Although the M359 student's database probably has a simple structure, and the developer and the sole user are the same person, we would still advocate that the student should follow a formal approach, albeit with a 'light touch', because this would ensure that the database was fit for purpose and well-documented.

SOLUTION 1.7

You would expect most refinement and feedback to occur between the 'initial schema and database' and 'released schema and database' stages. If the released schema and database do not satisfy all the information requirements of the enterprise, then the database design would be flexed (again) and implemented. This is illustrated in *Block 1* by Figure 4.6, which summarises the iterated (repeated) steps involved in database design.

SOLUTION 1.8

Online Analytical Processing (OLAP) could be employed; see *Block 1*, Subsection 1.7. Data warehousing could be employed to integrate the large quantities of historical data on customer purchases, and data mining to identify buying patterns for typical customers to enable targeted marketing.

SOLUTION 1.9

The information requirements could be obtained by:

▶ examining product labelling, till receipts and orders for products from their suppliers;

▶ using questionnaires to gather information from store staff;

▶ observing customers purchasing products, checkout staff processing customer purchases, and staff stocking shelves;

▶ interviewing store managers, warehouse staff and checkout staff.

SOLUTION 1.10

A conceptual data model provides a shared, formal, representation of what is being communicated between clients and developers during database development – it is focused on the data in a database irrespective of the eventual use of that data in user processes or implementation of the data in specific computer environments. That is, a conceptual data model is concerned with the meaning and structure of data, but not with the details affecting how it is implemented.

SOLUTION 1.11

A table that is not normalised is liable to include duplicate information that may result in insertion, amendment and deletion anomalies. See *Block 2*, Section 5.

SOLUTION 1.12

The required tasks are as follows.

Implementation of the first-cut database design for the database using the relational DBMS chosen to manage that database.

Population of the database with sufficient data to facilitate the development of application software.

Development of user schemas (views) and application software (user processes) to satisfy the different information requirements of the users of the database. This will usually include the design and development of appropriate user interfaces, and often interfaces to specialist hardware and other computer systems.

Acceptance testing – demonstrating that the database system will satisfy the information requirements of the enterprise, and is acceptable to both the client who commissioned the database development and the users of the database system.

Integrating the database system into the client's existing hardware and software systems. If the database system replaces an existing system, then ensuring a smooth transition between the old and new systems will be required.

Documenting the database development and the implementation of the database system – providing the appropriate documentation and user guides for the client, database administrators and users of the database system.

Training the client, database administrators and users of the database system to use, maintain and adapt the database system, as appropriate.

SOLUTION 1.13

(a) Database reorganisation involves a change to the storage schema, which involves the implementation task.

(b) Database restructuring involves a change to the logical schema, which necessarily involves the database design task to produce a revised logical schema. If restructuring is required to satisfy new or changing information requirements, it additionally involves the data analysis task.

SOLUTION 3.1

In Section 2, we noted that Walton Stores will need to develop and install several different databases, each facilitating the day-to-day operations of a particular area of the business. Each database will support just those information requirements associated with a particular business area. For example, databases located at individual stores will need to record details of the products stocked at the store, their provision by the store's regional distribution centre, and their purchase by the store's customers. Whereas databases located at the regional distribution centres will need to record details of the products stocked at a distribution centre, their provision by Walton Stores' suppliers, and their distribution to stores within the region. It is important in such situations to establish the scope of each system by determining which information requirements should be satisfied by a particular database, to ensure that there is no unnecessary duplication of data.

SOLUTION 3.2

A conceptual data model represents just the data requirements component of the information requirements of an enterprise; it does not represent the operational requirements component. It describes the data items, the relationships between those data items, and the constraints on those data items that need to be recorded by the database. However, it does not explain how these data items, relationships and constraints need to be processed to meet the operational requirements of the enterprise, nor does it describe how these data items, relationships and constraints will be implemented.

SOLUTION 3.3

The principal difference is that a conceptual data model describes *what* the data requirements are, whereas the relational representation of the conceptual data model describes *how* the data requirements may be represented by a particular database approach. For example, the conceptual data model describes *what* relationships exist between the data, whereas the relational representation of the conceptual data model describes *how* these relationships could be implemented using foreign keys.

SOLUTION 3.4

To avoid any misinterpretation of the data requirements, a description written in English would be necessarily very long, and hence be a less effective means of communication between the clients and developers during a database development.

It is relatively easy to introduce ambiguity into the meaning of English sentences. For example, consider the phrase 'deep blue sea'. Does 'deep' refer to the shade of blue or the depth of the sea? To avoid any misinterpretation of this phrase we would need to express the meaning unambiguously but, as a consequence, more verbosely: 'the sea was a deep shade of blue' or 'the deep sea was blue'.

SOLUTION 3.5

Establishing the domain of discourse will ensure that the client's and developer's staff have a common understanding of the enterprise and its data. The client's and developer's staff are likely initially to have different views of the enterprise. For example, in the context of the case study, the developer's staff may view the supermarket chain initially from the customer's perspective if they have not worked on developing software for similar enterprises. It is important that the developer's staff also view the enterprise from the client's perspective, understanding the client's terminology and data.

SOLUTION 3.6

The *Additional constraints* section records any conditions that cannot be represented explicitly by the *Entity–relationship diagram* and the *Entity types* sections of the entity–relationship model which, if not enforced, would permit the existence of inconsistent data. For example, if we consider the *Hospital entity–relationship diagram*, the relationship between the **Ward** and **Patient** entity types, **OccupiedBy**, may be read from **Ward** to **Patient** as: 'Each ward is occupied by zero, one or more patients'. However, the meaning of the word 'more' is unbounded; it could represent an infinite number of patients, which is clearly inappropriate as there will always be a finite number of beds in each ward. So the *Additional constraints* section of the model includes the condition c.11: 'The number of patients in a ward cannot exceed the number of beds in that ward'.

The *Assumptions* section records the working assumptions the analyst has made while developing the model. When working with clients, these assumptions would be resolved, but in the academic environment we use the assumptions to record any specific decisions we have made about places where there may be ambiguity in the requirements.

The *Limitations* section records the scope of the model. The list of limitations represents a description of expectations about the 'reality' of the situation being modelled that indicates the limits under which the entire model is meaningful. It is intended to ensure that the model is used only for purposes that are compatible with the context for which it was produced. A common limitation of an entity–relationship model is that it may only represent the current situation and does not record historical data or historical relationships between the data.

SOLUTION 3.7

In the entity–relationship model, by definition, the value of an attribute for a given entity occurrence must be a single value and not a collection of several values. Thus, an attribute can only represent a single-valued property of its entity type.

This limitation is not shared by all notations for conceptual data models. However, you might argue that this limitation is not a significant drawback because as the attributes of relations must have atomic values (see *Block 2*, Subsection 2.1), the development of the relational representation of an entity–relationship model during database design will be made easier.

SOLUTION 3.8

Property	SVF/MVF	Represented by
Each consultant is responsible for a number of patients.	MVF	**IsResponsibleFor** relationship where the **Patient** end is :*n*
... junior doctors ... have a position of either registrar or house officer ...	SVF	**Position** attribute
Consultants must have a specialism, but registrars and house officers are not specialists and do not have a specialism.	SVF	**IsA** relationship where the **Specialist** end is :1
Each doctor ... has a staff number ...	SVF	**StaffNo** attribute
Each doctor ... has a ... name ...	SVF	**DoctorName** attribute
Each consultant must head a single group, known as a team ...	SVF	**HeadedBy** relationship where the **Team** end is :1
A house officer or registrar [junior doctors] ... must be a member of one team ...	SVF	**ConsistsOf** relationship where the **Team** end is :1
Each doctor may provide treatment for several patients ...	MVF	**Provides** relationship where the **Treatment** end is :*n*

SOLUTION 3.9

Property	SVF/ MVF	Mandatory/ optional	Represented by
... a team, consisting of one or more house officers and registrars.	MVF	mandatory	**ConsistsOf** relationship where the **Doctor** end is :*n* and the **Team** end has mandatory participation
A team must be headed by a consultant.	SVF	mandatory	**HeadedBy** relationship where the **Doctor** end is :1 and the **Team** end has mandatory participation
Each team has a team code ...	SVF	mandatory	**TeamCode** attribute
Each team has ... a telephone number ...	SVF	mandatory	**TelephoneNo** attribute

SOLUTION 3.10

As the properties of treatments are more complex than the properties of doctors that we considered in Exercise 3.8, we need to analyse this extract from the *Hospital scenario* carefully, line by line.

Consider the first sentence of the scenario:

> **Each doctor may provide treatment for several patients and each patient may receive treatment from a number of doctors.**

This sentence describes a many-to-many (*m:n*) relationship between doctors and patients, where each occurrence of that relationship represents a treatment provided by a particular doctor to a particular patient. (In the *Hospital conceptual data model* this relationship is decomposed into two 1:*n* relationships, **Provides** and **Receives**, and an intersection entity type, **Treatment**, which represents occurrences of this relationship.)

The second sentence states:

> **A patient may receive more than one treatment from each doctor, for which the start date and the reason (e.g. a chest infection) for the treatment are recorded.**

This sentence extends the notion of a relationship between doctors and patients so that each occurrence of that relationship now represents a treatment provided by a particular doctor to a particular patient, on a particular start date, for a particular reason.

The final sentence states:

> **Such a treatment may require several prescriptions, each of which has a prescription number and specifies a total quantity and daily dosage of some drug.**

This sentence describes the fact that a treatment (provided by a particular doctor to a particular patient, on a particular date, for a particular reason) may require several prescriptions.

So the properties of treatments are as follows:

> Each treatment is provided by a particular doctor ...
> ... to a particular patient ...
> ... on a particular start date ...
> ... for a particular reason.

> Such a treatment may require several prescriptions ...

The following table denotes whether the properties are single-valued or multi-valued, and describes how they are represented by the *Hospital conceptual data model*.

Property	SVF/ MVF	Mandatory/ optional	Represented by
Each treatment is provided by a particular doctor ...	SVF	mandatory	**Provides** relationship where the **Doctor** end is :1 and the **Treatment** end has mandatory participation
... to a particular patient ...	SVF	mandatory	**Receives** relationship where the **Patient** end is :1 and the **Treatment** end has mandatory participation
... on a particular start date ...	SVF	mandatory	**StartDate** attribute
... for a particular reason.	SVF	mandatory	**Reason** attribute
Such a treatment may require several prescriptions ...	MVF	optional	**Requires** relationship where the **Prescription** end is :*n* and the **Treatment** end has optional participation

SOLUTION 3.11

In the entity–relationship model this uniqueness property is conveyed by the identifier of an entity type, which comprises one or more attributes of that entity type with values such that no two occurrences of the entity type can have the same values. The identifier of an entity type is denoted by underlining those attributes.

If you have answered that a primary key conveys this uniqueness property, then you are wrong because this term is associated (but not solely) with relational databases,and an entity–relationship model is independent of any particular database approach.

SOLUTION 3.12

Apart from including the corresponding attribute, or combination of attributes, that represents each single-valued property as a non-identifying attribute in the definition of that entity type, a uniqueness constraint needs to be declared on such attribute(s) in the Additional Constraints section of the model.

SOLUTION 3.13

Treatment is a weak entity type because it has mandatory participation with respect to the n:1 relationships with the **Doctor** and **Patient** entity types, **Provides** and **Receives** respectively, and the identifiers of the **Doctor** and **Patient** entity types are subsets of the identifier of the **Treatment** entity type.

SOLUTION 3.14

For each occurrence of a weak entity type, an attribute of the identifier that matches the identifier of the entity type on which the weak entity type is dependent, must have a value that is the same as the identifier of some occurrence of that entity type. For example, for the weak entity type **Treatment**, the additional constraints c.8 and c.9 are needed.

The constraint c.8 states that as **Treatment** is dependent on **Doctor**, each value of **StaffNo** in entity type **Treatment** must be the same value as the **StaffNo** of the **Doctor** instance to which the **Treatment** is related by the relationship **Provides**.

The constraint c.9 states that as **Treatment** is dependent on **Patient**, each value of **PatientId** in entity type **Treatment** must be the same value as the **PatientId** of the **Patient** instance to which the **Treatment** is related by the relationship **Receives**.

SOLUTION 3.15

The figure overleaf shows a subset of the *Hospital conceptual data model* that just represents properties of doctors generally, and those of consultants and junior doctors specifically.

Entity–relationship diagram

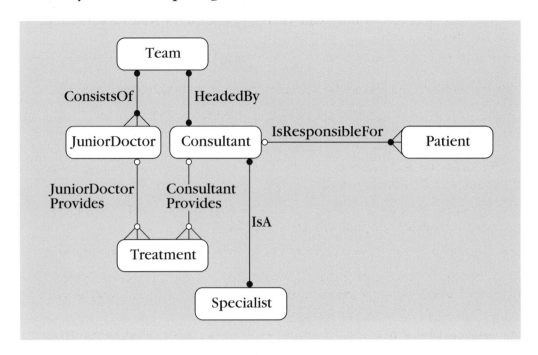

Entity types

Team (<u>TeamCode</u>, TelephoneNo)

JuniorDoctor (<u>StaffNo</u>, DoctorName, Position)

Consultant (<u>StaffNo</u>, DoctorName)

Patient (<u>PatientId</u>, PatientName, Gender, Height, Weight)

Specialist (<u>StaffNo</u>, Specialism)

Treatment (<u>StaffNo</u>, <u>PatientId</u>, <u>StartDate</u>, Reason)

Additional constraints

c.6   Junior doctors can be either registrars or house officers. That is, the attribute Position (of entity type JuniorDoctor) may have a value of Registrar or House Officer.

c.8   Treatment is a weak entity type dependent on JuniorDoctor or Consultant. So, each value of StaffNo in the entity type Treatment must be the same value as the StaffNo attribute of either the JuniorDoctor or the Consultant instance to which the Treatment entity type is related by the relationship JuniorDoctorProvides or ConsultantProvides (a consequence of weak–strong entity types).

c.10   Specialist is a weak entity type dependent on the entity type Consultant. So, each value of the StaffNo attribute in the entity type Specialist must be the same value as the StaffNo attribute of the Consultant instance to which the entity type Specialist is related by the relationship IsA (a consequence of weak–strong entity types).

c.14   A consultant cannot have the same staff number as a junior doctor. That is, the value of the StaffNo attribute for each occurrence of the Consultant entity type cannot be the same as the value of the StaffNo attribute for any occurrence of the JuniorDoctor entity type.

c.15 An occurrence of Treatment is associated either with an occurrence of JuniorDoctor via the JuniorDoctorProvides relationship, or with an occurrence of Consultant via the ConsultantProvides relationship, but not both.

Note the following changes to the *Additional constraints* section of the model:

The condition c.6 has been revised because the **Position** attribute of the **JuniorDoctor** entity type takes only two values – Registrar or House Officer – as all instances of the **Consultant** entity type represent consultants, and each instance of the **JuniorDoctor** entity type represents either a registrar or house officer according to the value of the **Position** attribute.

The condition c.8 has been revised because we have split the original **Doctor** entity type into **Consultant** and **JuniorDoctor** entity types.

The condition c.10 has been revised to reference the new **Consultant** entity type.

The new condition c.14 is required because as we have split the original **Doctor** entity type into **Consultant** and **JuniorDoctor** entity types, we still have to ensure the uniqueness of the values of the **StaffNo** attribute.

The new condition c.15 makes **JuniorDoctorProvides** and **ConsultantProvides** exclusive relationships for the **Treatment** entity type, which means that an occurrence of **Treatment** may participate in one of these relationships but not in both.

SOLUTION 3.16

Entity–relationship diagram

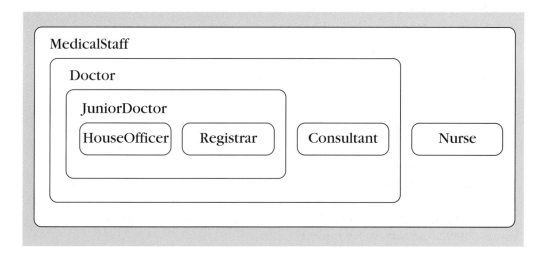

Entity types

MedicalStaff (<u>StaffNo</u>, Name)

    Doctor ( )

        JuniorDoctor ( )

            HouseOfficer ( )

            Registrar ( )

        Consultant (Specialism)

    Nurse ( )

In the above entity–relationship model for **MedicalStaff**, **Doctor** and **JuniorDoctor** are the entity supertypes and hence have no occurrences. **HouseOfficer**, **Registrar**, **Consultant** and **Nurse** are mutually exclusive entity subtypes that may have occurrences representing doctors (house officers, registrars and consultants) and nurses.

Since the subtypes have mutually exclusive occurrences, it will enforce the condition that a doctor and nurse cannot have the same staff number. So the following condition in the additional constraints section of the *Hospital conceptual data model* is no longer required:

> c.13 **A nurse cannot have the same staff number as a doctor. That is, the value of the StaffNo attribute for each occurrence of the Nurse entity type cannot be the same as the value of the StaffNo attribute for any occurrence of the Doctor entity subtypes, Consultant and JuniorDoctor.**

SOLUTION 3.17

A role description (or role name) provides a name to identify the role that a particular entity type plays in a particular relationship. For example, in the *Hospital conceptual data model* the recursive 1:n relationship **Supervises** on the **Nurse** entity type is labelled on the *Hospital entity–relationship diagram* with the **Supervisee** and **Supervisor** role descriptions, which are intended to clarify the meaning of the relationship:

> **Each Nurse-supervisor supervises zero, one or more Nurse-supervisees (:n end), and each Nurse-supervisee is supervised by zero or one Nurse-supervisors (1: end).**

Although we have used role descriptions to clarify the meanings of recursive relationships, they may be used to label any type of relationship where the meaning may not be self-explanatory.

SOLUTION 3.18

Exclusive relationships are two or more relationships connecting a single entity type with two or more other (possibly the same) entity types where each occurrence of the single entity type participates in *exactly one* (or possibly none) of the relationships.

Inclusive relationships are two or more relationships connecting a single entity type with two or more other (possibly the same) entity types where each occurrence of the single entity type participates in *all* (or possibly none) of the relationships.

SOLUTION 3.19

Each occurrence of the **StaffedBy** relationship represents a particular nurse assigned to a particular ward, which is identified by the combination of **WardNo** and **StaffNo** values of the corresponding occurrences of the **Ward** and **Nurse** entity types involved in that occurrence of the **StaffedBy** relationship.

SOLUTION 3.20

The change in requirements whereby nurses could be assigned to more than one ward can be accommodated by making the **StaffedBy** relationship *m:n* (many-to-many). As before, the requirement to record the date that a particular nurse was assigned to a particular ward is a single-valued property of the **StaffedBy** relationship, which we can record by a non-identifying attribute of the intersection entity type that results from the decomposition of the *m:n* **StaffedBy** relationship. The revised entity–relationship model is as shown below. Compare this model with that in Figure 3.9.

Entity–relationship diagram

Entity types

Ward (<u>WardNo</u>, WardName, NumberOfBeds)

WardStaff (<u>WardNo</u>, <u>StaffNo</u>, StartDate)

Nurse (<u>StaffNo</u>, NurseName)

Additional constraints

c.16 WardStaff is a weak entity type dependent on Ward. So, each value of WardNo in the entity type WardStaff must be the same value as the WardNo of the Ward instance to which the WardStaff entity type is related by the relationship StaffedBy (a consequence of weak–strong entity types).

c.19 WardStaff is a weak entity type dependent on Nurse. So, each value of StaffNo in the entity type WardStaff must be the same value as the StaffNo of the Nurse instance to which the WardStaff entity type is related by the relationship IsA (a consequence of weak–strong entity types).

SOLUTION 3.21

Entity–relationship diagram

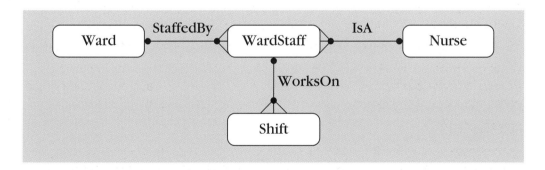

Entity types

Ward (<u>WardNo</u>, WardName, NumberOfBeds)

WardStaff (<u>WardNo</u>, <u>StaffNo</u>, StartDate)

Shift (<u>StaffNo</u>, <u>WeekDay</u>, ShiftTime)

Nurse (<u>StaffNo</u>, NurseName)

Additional constraints

c.16 WardStaff is a weak entity type dependent on Ward. So, each value of WardNo in the entity type WardStaff must be the same value as the WardNo of the Ward instance to which the WardStaff entity type is related by the relationship StaffedBy (a consequence of weak–strong entity types).

c.17 Nurses are assigned to work the morning, afternoon or night shift on a particular day of the week. That is, the attribute ShiftTime (of the entity type Shift) may have a value of morning, afternoon or night.

c.18 Shift is a weak entity type dependent on WardStaff. So, each value of StaffNo in the entity type Shift must be the same value as the StaffNo of the WardStaff instance to which the Shift entity type is related by the relationship WorksOn (a consequence of weak–strong entity types).

c.19 WardStaff is a weak entity type dependent on Nurse. So, each value of StaffNo in the entity type WardStaff must be the same value as the StaffNo of the Nurse instance to which the WardStaff entity type is related by the relationship IsA (a consequence of weak–strong entity types).

The following definition for the **Shift** entity type would be incorrect because its identifier would allow a nurse to work on several wards each day, which is inconsistent with the stated assumption:

Shift (<u>WardNo</u>, <u>StaffNo</u>, <u>WeekDay</u>, Shift)

SOLUTION 3.22

For a particular patient (the occurrence of the **Patient** entity type), the patient identification number (the attribute **PatientId**) should not change as this property is used to distinguish one patient from another. If a patient were to be assigned a new patient identification number each time they were admitted to the hospital, it would be difficult to find details about their previous admissions, or even determine whether the patient had ever been admitted previously.

A patient's name (the attribute **PatientName**) could change over time, particularly if the patient was female and was married (or divorced) between admissions and chose to take her husband's surname (or revert to her maiden name).

A patient's gender (the attribute **Gender**) is unlikely to change over time.

A patient's height (the attribute **Height**) could change over time, particularly if the patient was first admitted as a child.

A patient's weight (the attribute **Weight**) could change over time, particularly during an illness and its treatment.

SOLUTION 3.23

Since we are representing a multi-valued property, according to our guidelines this should be conveyed by a :n relationship with another entity type that records the series of historical heights and weights for each patient. Because it is a temporal property, the identifier of this entity type will include an attribute that specifies the dates that particular patients' heights and weights were measured. Below is a fragment of a revised *Hospital conceptual data model* that records changes to the patients' heights and weights.

Entity–relationship diagram

Entity types

Patient (<u>PatientId</u>, PatientName, Gender)

Height&Weight (<u>PatientId</u>, <u>Date</u>, Height, Weight)

Additional constraint

c.21 Height&Weight is a weak entity type dependent on Patient. So, each value of PatientId in the entity type Height&Weight must be the same value as the PatientId of the Patient instance to which the Height&Weight entity type is related by the relationship HasAHistoryOf (a consequence of weak–strong entity types).

If you also include the patients' heights and weights in the definition for the **Patient** entity type as:

Patient (<u>PatientId</u>, PatientName, Gender, Height, Weight)

where the intention is to record the patients' current (last measured) heights and weights by the **Height** and **Weight** attributes, respectively, then this is an acceptable alternative representation.

SOLUTION 3.24

The semantics of the relationship between wards and patients as defined by the $m{:}n$ relationship **OccupiedBy** shown on the entity–relationship diagram are 'Each ward may be occupied by several (none, one or more) patients, and each patient occupies several (one or more) wards'. These semantics do not meet the actual requirements for two reasons. First, they allow a particular patient to occupy two or more wards simultaneously (whereas the requirement is to record the fact that a patient may occupy several wards at different times). Second, they do not allow a patient to occupy the same ward at different times, because each occupancy cannot be represented by a distinct occurrence of the **OccupiedBy** relationship as its identity is determined by the pair of **WardNo** and **PatientId** values of the corresponding occurrences of the **Ward** and **Patient** entity types involved in the occurrence.

SOLUTION 3.25

The following additional constraint is required to ensure that the different periods that a particular patient occupies a bed on different (or the same) wards do not overlap.

c.24 When instances of the WardPatient intersection entity type for each value of PatientId are ordered chronologically by the values of StartDate, the value of EndDate for each instance should be less than or equal to (<=) the value of StartDate of the succeeding instance.

SOLUTION 3.26

Entity–relationship diagram

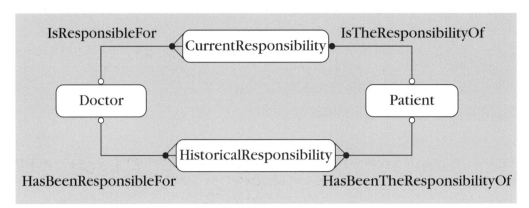

Entity types

Doctor (<u>StaffNo</u>, DoctorName, Position)

CurrentResponsibility (<u>PatientId</u>, StartDate, EndDate)

HistoricalResponsibility (<u>PatientId</u>, <u>StartDate</u>, EndDate)

Patient (<u>PatientId</u>, PatientName, Gender, Height, Weight)

Additional constraints

c.31 CurrentResponsibility is a weak entity type dependent on Patient. So, each value of PatientId in the entity type CurrentResponsibility must be the same value as the PatientId of the Patient instance to which the CurrentResponsibility entity type is related by the relationship IsTheResponsibilityOf (a consequence of weak–strong entity types).

c.32 HistoricalResponsibility is a weak entity type dependent on Patient. So, each value of PatientId in the entity type HistoricalResponsibility must be the same value as the PatientId of the Patient instance to which the HistoricalResponsibility entity type is related by the relationship HasBeenTheResponsibilityOf (a consequence of weak–strong entity types).

c.33 For each instance of the CurrentResponsibility intersection entity type, the value of StartDate should be less than or equal to (<=) the value of EndDate.

c.34 For each instance of the HistoricalResponsibility intersection entity type, the value of StartDate should be less than or equal to (<=) the value of EndDate.

c.35 When instances of the HistoricalResponsibility intersection entity type for each value of PatientId are ordered chronologically by the values of StartDate, the value of EndDate for each instance should be less than or equal to (<=) the value of StartDate of the succeeding instance.

c.36 Each instance of Patient must participate in the IsTheResponsibilityOf relationship, or the HasBeenTheResponsibilityOf relationship, or both.

SOLUTION 3.27

Establishing the characteristics of the data values associated with the attributes of the entity types during the data analysis stage of a database development leads to a better understanding of the enterprise and its data. This will help us develop an entity–relationship model and the accompanying domain of discourse summary that accurately and completely represents the data requirements of that enterprise.

When we develop a relational representation of the entity–relationship model during the database design stage, the characteristics of the data values are used to help us define the domains and other constraints on the data.

SOLUTION 3.28

Patient entity type

Attribute	Value set
PatientId	{p01...p99}
PatientName	{family names}
Gender	{M, F}
Height	{ddd.d cm}
Weight	{dd.d kg}

The value set for the **PatientId** attribute is {p01...p99} as the hospital uses patient identifiers in the range p01 to p99. For the **PatientName** attribute, it is {family names} as a patient's name is recorded as just their family name. For the **Gender** attribute, it is {M, F} as a patient's gender is recorded as either F for female or M for male. For the **Height** attribute, it is {ddd.d cm} as a patient's height is recorded in centimetres to the nearest millimetre, and for the **Weight** attribute, it is {dd.d kg} as their weight is recorded in kilograms to the nearest 1/10 of a kilogram.

The value sets for the **Height** and **Weight** attributes are only preliminary. The upper and lower bounds of these numerical value sets will need to be determined, as value sets {ddd.d cm} and {dd.d kg} are equivalent to {0.0...999.9 cm} and {0.0...99.9 kg}, respectively, which are clearly ranges larger than the expected values for people's heights and weights. Currently, there is insufficient sample data available to determine the appropriate upper and lower bounds of these numerical value sets. For example, there appears to be no data for young children but there is no indication in the *Hospital scenario* that they will not be admitted to the hospital for treatment.

Team entity type

Attribute	Value set
TeamCode	{t01...t99}
TelephoneNumber	{dddd}

The value set for the **TeamCode** attribute is {t01...t99} as each team is identified by a team code in the range t01 to t99. For the **TelephoneNumber** attribute, the value set is {dddd} as each team has a dedicated answerphone service accessible via the internal hospital phone system which uses 4-digit numbers.

Treatment entity type

Attribute	Value set	Characteristics
StaffNo	{001...999}	Dependency: those doctors giving treatment must be known doctors who are on the same team as the consultant who is responsible for the patient specified by the **PatientId** attribute.
PatientId	{p01...p99}	Dependency: those patients receiving treatment must be known patients.
StartDate	{dates}	
Reason	{character strings}	

The **StaffNo** attribute of the **Treatment** entity type takes a continuous range of values, 001...999, but the values must correspond to known doctors. That is, the values must be the same as the values assigned to the **StaffNo** attribute of occurrences of the **Doctor** entity type. This dependency is expressed by the following condition in the *Additional constraints* section of the *Hospital conceptual data model*:

> c.8   Treatment is a weak entity type dependent on the entity type Doctor. So, each value of the StaffNo attribute in entity type Treatment must be the same value as the StaffNo attribute of the Doctor instance to which the Treatment entity type is related by the relationship Provides (a consequence of weak–strong entity types).

Values of the **StaffNo** attribute are restricted further because as the *Hospital scenario* states that

> Any doctor treating a patient must be a member of the same team as the consultant responsible for that patient.

the **StaffNo** attribute is dependent on the **PatientId** attribute. This dependency is expressed by the following condition in the *Additional constraints* section of the *Hospital conceptual data model*:

> c.4   A doctor who treats a patient must be in the same team as the consultant who is responsible for that patient. That is, an instance of the entity type Doctor that provides treatment for a patient must be from the same team as the consultant who is responsible for that patient.

The **PatientId** attribute of the **Treatment** entity type takes a continuous range of values, p01...p99, but the values must correspond to the values that are assigned to the **PatientId** attribute of occurrences of the **Patient** entity type. This dependency is expressed by the following condition in the *Additional constraints* section of the *Hospital conceptual data model*:

> c.9   Treatment is a weak entity type dependent on the entity type Patient. So, each value of the PatientId attribute in entity type Treatment must be the same value as the PatientId attribute of the Patient instance to which the entity type Treatment is related by the relationship Receives (a consequence of weak–strong entity types).

SOLUTION 3.29

First, the **Nurse** entity supertype has only one subtype, **Supervisor**. Entity supertypes must have at least two subtypes. An entity supertype represents a generic form of an entity, whereas a subtype is a specific form. As only subtypes have occurrences, a single subtype is meaningless.

As the *Hospital scenario* states that:

> **Some nurses are designated to supervise one or more other nurses on the same ward.**

only nurses who are supervisors are represented in the entity–relationship model as shown in Figure 3.13.

Let us establish a simple working assumption that those nurses who are not supervisors would be those who are supervised. Then this problem is resolved by including a subtype to represent supervisees, as in the definition shown below

Entity types

Nurse (StaffNo, NurseName)

    Supervisor ( )

    Supervisee ( )

Second, according to the additional constraint, the values that the **Position** attribute, defined in the **Doctor** entity supertype and inherited by the **Consultant** and **JuniorDoctor** subtypes, can take are *Consultant*, *Registrar* and *House Officer*. But as for every occurrence of the **Consultant** entity subtype **Position** will take the value *Consultant*, **Position** should be defined in the **JuniorDoctor** subtype.

Entity types

Doctor (StaffNo, DoctorName)

    Consultant (Specialism)

    JuniorDoctor (Position)

Additional constraint

> Junior doctors can be registrars or house officers. That is, the attribute Position (of entity subtype JuniorDoctor) may have a value of Registrar or House Officer.

SOLUTION 3.30

Weak entity types are those entity types that have a mandatory relationship with another entity type where the identifier of that entity type is the same as, or a subset of, the weak entity type, and that entity type is at the :1 end of this relationship.

In Figure 3.13, **Treatment** is a weak entity type with respect to the **Patient** and **Doctor** entity types.

SOLUTION 3.31

Recording a history of product prices and special offers means that price and special offer become multi-valued properties of the **Product** entity type, where each value is dependent on time.

SOLUTION 3.32

We have not indicated a dependency on the **Price** attribute in Table 3.13 because we are developing an entity–relationship model that represents the data requirements of an individual store and not those of the entire supermarket chain.

SOLUTION 3.33

PriceHistory is a weak entity type because the dependency that is given in Table 3.21 states that values of the **ProductCode** attribute must be those of known products, that is, have the same values as those of the **ProductCode** attribute of the **Product** entity type.

SOLUTION 3.34

The property that differs between those products that are sold by fixed quantities and those sold by varying quantities is the **Quantity** property. **Quantity** is a property of the former because it has a fixed value for each of those products that are sold by specific amounts, but it is not a property of the latter because it varies for each of those products sold by varying amounts.

In the following entity–relationship model we have chosen to name the entity subtypes that represent products sold by the same (fixed) quantities and products sold by varying quantities as **ProductSoldByAFixedQuantity** and **ProductSoldByAVariableQuantity**, respectively. Properties, common to both products sold by fixed quantities and products sold by varying quantities, are represented by the **Product** entity supertype by its attributes and via relationships with the **ProductInformation** and **SpecialOffer** entity types.

The quantity of a product is a single-valued property of those products sold by fixed quantities and is recorded by the **Quantity** attribute of the **ProductSoldByAFixedQuantity** entity subtype. As the quantities of products shown in Figure 2.4 are given in different units of measurement, imperial or metric, by weight or by volume of product, they are considered to be complex data values, comprising two data fields – the numeric quantity and the unit of measurement.

Entity–relationship diagram

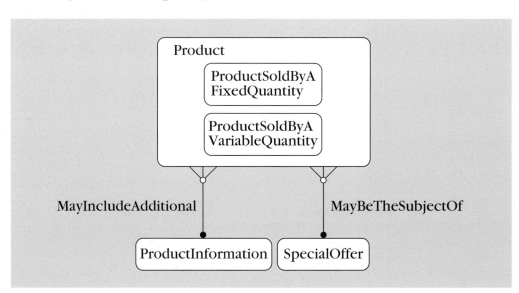

Entity types

Product (<u>ProductCode</u>, Description, Price)

      ProductSoldByAFixedQuantity (Quantity)

      ProductSoldByAVariableQuantity ( )

ProductInformation (<u>Information</u>)

SpecialOffer (<u>SpecialOfferCode</u>, Details, StartDate, EndDate)

Additional constraint

c.1   For each instance of the SpecialOffer entity type, the value of StartDate should be less than or equal to the value of EndDate.

Working assumptions

The data values held by the ProductCode attribute can comprise all possible permutations of eight digits, 00000000...99999999.

A particular special offer will only run for a finite period, having definite start and end dates. Hence there is justification for including the StartDate and EndDate attributes in the SpecialOffer entity type.

Limitation

None

Entity type catalogue

Entity name:	**Product** (supertype)
Description:	A representation of the properties of the products sold by Walton Stores.
Attribute details:	Each product has an identifying product code, a description and a price. Product codes are in the range 00000000 to 99999999. Descriptions of products are character strings. Prices are complex data values, comprising either one data field – money, for products sold by a specific quantity – or two data fields – money and the unit of measurement, for products sold by variable weights.

Entity name:	**ProductSoldByAVariableQuantity** (subtype)		
Description:	A representation of the properties of those products sold by varying quantities: prepacked goods, and goods packaged and weighed by the customers themselves. Each occurrence represents a particular product sold by varying quantities.		
Attribute details:			
Sample data (from Figure 2.4):	ProductCode	Description	Price (£)
	06002669	Gorgonzola	10.99 per kg
	02524730	Carrots (Class 1)	0.31 per kg

Entity name:	**ProductSoldByAFixedQuantity** (subtype)
Description:	A representation of the properties of those products sold by fixed quantities. Each occurrence represents a particular product sold by a fixed quantity.
Attribute details:	Quantities are complex data values comprising two data fields – the numeric quantity and the unit of measurement.

Sample data (from Figure 2.4):	ProductCode	Description	Price (£)	Quantity
	01015277	Pasteurised skimmed milk	0.26	568ml
	01015279	Pasteurised skimmed milk	0.50	1.136 litres
	04789217	Goats' milk yoghurt	0.89	250g
	08562411	Vegetable fat spread	2.49	250g
	07214781	Château Haut d'Allard 1996	5.45	75cl
	02348126	Prunes in syrup	0.62	420g
	02348187	Prunes in apple juice	0.65	410g

The catalogue entries for the **ProductInformation** and **SpecialOffer** entity types, and the **MayIncludeAdditional** and **MayBeTheSubjectOf** relationships from Figure 3.22 are unchanged.

SOLUTION 3.35

By looking at the contents of the standing orders in Figure 2.1, from top to bottom, we can see that each records the following information provided by the store that requests regular deliveries of packs of products from its distribution centre:

> Each standing order names the store (Ramsgard) that requests regular deliveries of the packs of products listed, the distribution centre (South-West) that fulfils the order by supplying those packs of products, an order number and an order date. Each request for the delivery of the packs of a product is identified by the item number, and gives details of the product code, a description of the product, the pack size ((72 × 568ml), (72 × 1.136 litres), (36 × 250g), (144 × 250g), etc.), the number of packs to be delivered (10, 20, 50, 1000, 2000, 5000, 8000), the delivery day(s) (Monday–Saturday) and frequency of delivery (weekly, monthly).

SOLUTION 3.36

At the start of this subsection, we stated that we are focusing just on the data requirements of individual stores. Therefore, the data recorded about standing orders will pertain only to a single store, which obtains all the products it sells from the same distribution centre.

SOLUTION 3.37

In Figure 2.1, each standing order is identified by its order number, so the **OrderNumber** attribute should be the identifier of the **StandingOrder** entity type. Within each standing order, each request is distinguished by its item number. So a combination of the **OrderNumber** and **ItemNumber** attributes should be the identifier of the **StandingOrderItem** entity type.

As **DeliveryDay** is the only attribute of the **DeliveryDay** entity type, then this attribute will be the identifier for the entity type.

SOLUTION 3.38

StandingOrder entity type

Attribute	Value set	Characteristics
OrderNumber	{0000000...9999999}	identifier
OrderDate	{dates}	

StandingOrderItem entity type

Attribute	Value set	Characteristics
OrderNumber	{0000000...9999999}	identifier dependency: must be a known order number
ItemNumber	{1...n}	identifier
NumberOfPacks	{n}	
DeliveryFrequency	{weekly, monthly}	

DeliveryDay entity type

Attribute	Value set	Characteristics
DeliveryDay	{Monday...Saturday}	identifier

Evidence from Figures 2.1 and 2.2 suggests that deliveries will not be made on Sundays, but we will need to confirm this with the client.

SOLUTION 3.39

If we represent products sold by fixed amounts and those sold by varying amounts, as in the solution to Exercise 3.34, by the entity subtypes **ProductSoldByAFixedQuantity** and **ProductSoldByAVariableQuantity** respectively, then by including attributes to represent the pack size property in both subtypes we can achieve our objective. The value set for the attribute of the **ProductSoldByAFixedQuantity** entity subtype would be {n}, which is the number of items of the product in a pack, whereas that for the **ProductSoldByAVariableQuantity** entity subtype would be {pack sizes}, which has complex values, comprising two data fields – the number of items of the product in a pack and the weight or volume of each item. In Figure 3.25 we name these attributes **NumberInPack** and **PackSize**, respectively.

SOLUTION 3.40

A comparison of the contents of the special orders with those of the standing orders reveals that they differ only by the delivery times: with the standing orders, packs of a product are delivered to a store periodically on specified days of the week with a frequency of either weekly or monthly; with special orders, packs of a product are delivered once on the specified date. As a consequence, the properties of the entity types corresponding to standing orders and special orders are identical, except standing orders have the properties of delivery days and delivery frequencies, whereas special orders have delivery dates.

The properties of the **SpecialOrder** and **SpecialOrderItem** entity types, which respectively record details about special orders and each request for the special delivery of packs of a product, are shown in the following tables. Compare these tables with Tables 3.27 and 3.28 respectively.

SpecialOrder entity type

Property	SVF/MVF	Mandatory/ optional	Representation
order number	SVF	mandatory	by an attribute that records order numbers, **OrderNumber**
order date	SVF	mandatory	by an attribute that records the dates of the orders, **OrderDate**
requests for packs of products	MVF	mandatory	via a :*n* relationship, **Comprises**, with an entity type that records details about requests for packs of products, **SpecialOrderItem**, where the **SpecialOrder** end has mandatory participation

SpecialOrderItem entity type

Property	SVF/MVF	Mandatory/ optional	Representation
order number	SVF	mandatory	by an attribute that records order numbers, **OrderNumber**
item number	SVF	mandatory	by an attribute that records item numbers, **ItemNumber**
number of packs	SVF	mandatory	by an attribute that records the number of packs, **NumberOfPacks**
delivery date	SVF	mandatory	by an attribute that records the date of delivery, **DeliveryDate**
special order	SVF	mandatory	via a :1 relationship, **Comprises**, with an entity type that records details about special orders, **SpecialOrder**, where the **SpecialOrderItem** end has mandatory participation
product	SVF	mandatory	via a :1 relationship, **RequestsSpecialDeliveryOfA**, with an entity type that records details about products, **Product**, where the **SpecialOrderItem** end has mandatory participation

The following table shows the representation of the additional properties of the **Product** entity type resulting from the analysis of the standing orders and special orders.

Product entity type

Property	SVF/MVF	Mandatory/optional	Representation
pack size	SVF	mandatory	by an attribute that records pack sizes, **PackSize**
standing orders	MVF	optional	via a :*n* relationship, **RequestsRegularDeliveryOfA**, with an entity type that records details about requests for products, **StandingOrderItem**, where the **Product** end has optional participation
special orders	MVF	optional	via a :*n* relationship, **RequestsSpecialDeliveryOfA**, with an entity type that records details about requests for products, **SpecialOrderItem**, where the **Product** end has optional participation

The entity–relationship model that represents the data requirements of special orders that need to be recorded is shown below.

Entity–relationship diagram

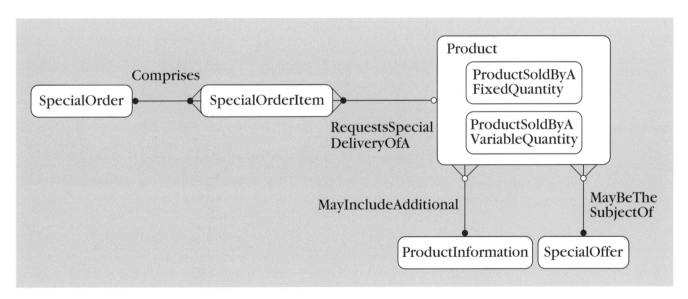

Entity types

SpecialOrder (<u>OrderNumber</u>, OrderDate)

SpecialOrderItem (<u>OrderNumber</u>, <u>ItemNumber</u>, NumberOfPacks,
DeliveryDate)

Product (<u>ProductCode</u>, Description, Price)

      ProductSoldByAFixedQuantity (Quantity, NumberInPack)

      ProductSoldByAVariableQuantity (PackSize)

ProductInformation (<u>Information</u>)

SpecialOffer (<u>SpecialOfferCode</u>, Details, StartDate, EndDate)

Additional constraints

c.1   For each instance of the SpecialOffer entity type, the value of StartDate should be less than or equal to the value of EndDate.

c.3   SpecialOrderItem is a weak entity type dependent on SpecialOrder. So, each value of OrderNumber in the entity type SpecialOrderItem must be the same value as the OrderNumber of the SpecialOrder instance to which the SpecialOrderItem entity type is related by the relationship Comprises (a consequence of weak–strong entity types).

Working assumptions

The data values held by the ProductCode and SpecialOfferCode attributes can comprise all possible permutations of eight digits, 00000000...99999999.

A description of a product found on a product label can apply to several products.

A particular special offer will only run for a finite period, having definite start and end dates.

A product may be requested by more than one special order.

Every product is supplied as a pack comprising several items that is the same size for a given product.

Limitation

l.1   Only the details of a product's current price and special offers, if any, are recorded.

SOLUTION 3.41

1   *What exactly does each occurrence of the entity type actually represent?*

Each occurrence of the **Customer** entity type represents a customer of Walton Stores who has been issued with a Frequent Shopper Card.

2   *What are the properties of, or facts about, the entity type?*

From the section of the form that a customer completes, we can see that the properties of **Customer** that are recorded on the completed forms are the customer's title, forename, family name, address (including the postcode), date of birth, gender, occupation, annual income, residence, whether the customer wants to receive any further information, and the date the application form was completed.

The description of the FSC at the head of the application form includes other potential properties of the **Customer** entity type – points earned, credit limit, outstanding balance, payments and interest due on outstanding balances. We can include credit limit in the properties of the **Customer** entity type, but balance and points earned are derivable from the customer's transactions, payments and accrued interest, and there is insufficient information to enable us to determine the data requirements about customer payments. This aspect of the FSC will have to be postponed until we can obtain an example of a FSC customer statement from the client.

The example of a FSC shown in Figure 2.8 reveals another property of the **Customer** entity type – their FSC number. Because we are developing an entity–relationshp model that represents the data requirements of an individual store, a customer's home store is not a property of the **Customer** entity type.

We can conveniently refer to these properties of the **Customer** entity type as customer title, forename, family name, address, date of birth, gender, occupation, annual income, residence, further information, application date, credit limit and FSC number.

3 *What are the characteristics of the properties of the entity type?*

The characteristics of the properties of the **Customer** entity type are shown in the following table.

Customer entity type

Property	SVF/MVF	Mandatory/optional	Temporal/derivable
title	SVF	mandatory	temporal
forename	SVF	mandatory	temporal
family name	SVF	mandatory	temporal
address	SVF	mandatory	temporal
date of birth	SVF	mandatory	
gender	SVF	mandatory	
occupation	SVF	mandatory	temporal
annual income	SVF	mandatory	temporal
residence	SVF	mandatory	temporal
further information?	SVF	mandatory	temporal
application date	SVF	mandatory	
credit limit	SVF	mandatory	temporal
FSC number	SVF	mandatory	

Except for date of birth, gender, application date and FSC number, all other properties are temporal as they can vary over time. If, for example, the customers' financial circumstances change or they fail to keep up with their monthly payments, then it is reasonable to assume that their credit limits will change.

As we have identified temporal properties of an entity type, we need to establish whether there is a requirement to record historical data values associated with these properties: a history of the changes to a customer's details. Because this requirement is not stated explicitly in the description of Walton Stores (Subsection 2.1), we will need to consult the client in order to determine whether or not this is a necessary requirement.

4   *How should each property be represented by an entity–relationship model?*

How each property of the **Customer** entity type should be represented by an entity–relationship model is shown in the following table.

Customer entity type

Property	SVF/MVF	Mandatory/ optional	Representation
title	SVF	mandatory	by an attribute that records the titles of customers, **Title**
forename	SVF	mandatory	by an attribute that records the forenames of customers, **Forenames**
family name	SVF	mandatory	by an attribute that records the family names of customers, **FamilyName**
address	SVF	mandatory	by an attribute that records the addresses of customers, **Address**
date of birth	SVF	mandatory	by an attribute that records the dates of birth of customers, **DateOfBirth**
gender	SVF	mandatory	by an attribute that records the genders of customers, **Gender**
occupation	SVF	mandatory	by an attribute that records the occupations of customers, **Occupation**
annual income	SVF	mandatory	by an attribute that records the annual incomes of customers, **AnnualIncome**
residence	SVF	mandatory	by an attribute that records the residences of customers, **Residence**
further information?	SVF	mandatory	by an attribute that records whether customers want further information, **FurtherInformation?**
application date	SVF	mandatory	by an attribute that records the dates of application for an FSC, **ApplicationDate**
credit limit	SVF	mandatory	by an attribute that records customers' credit limits, **CreditLimit**
FSC number	SVF	mandatory	by an attribute that records the FSC number, **FSCNumber**

5   *What is the identifier of the entity type?*

It is reasonable to assume that the FSC number will be unique for each card issued and so the **FSCNumber** attribute will be the identifier of the **Customer** entity type.

6   *What are the value sets and other characteristics of the data values of the attributes?*

The value sets and other characteristics of the data values for each attribute of the **Customer** entity type are shown in the following table.

Customer entity type

Attribute	Value set	Characteristics
Title	{character strings}	
Forename	{character strings}	
FamilyName	{character strings}	
Address	{character strings}	complex
DateOfBirth	{dates}	dependency: the application date should be at least 18 years greater than the date of birth (c.1).
Gender	{Male, Female}	
Occupation	{Professional, Managerial, Clerical, Skilled, Unskilled, Unemployed}	
AnnualIncome	{< £10k, £10k – £20k, £20k – £30k, £30k – £40k, £40k – £50k, > £50k}	
Residence	{Owner, Tenant, Other}	
FurtherInformation?	{Yes, No}	
ApplicationDate	{dates}	dependency: the application date should be at least 18 years greater than the date of birth (c.1).
CreditLimit	{money}	
FSCNumber	{dddd-dddd-dddd}	identifier

Addresses are considered to be complex data values, comprising several data fields – house number/name, street name, district, town, county, and so on, whose values may be abbreviated, for example, Cl for Close and Bucks for Buckinghamshire.

As the analysis of the application form for a Frequent Shopper Card has resulted in only a single entity type being required to represent the data requirements, we have not drawn an entity–relationship diagram but just give the definition for the **Customer** entity type.

Entity types

Customer (<u>FSCNumber</u>, Title, Forename, FamilyName, Address,
         DateOfBirth, Gender, Occupation, AnnualIncome, Residence,
         FurtherInformation?, ApplicationDate, CreditLimit)

Additional contraints

c.5   The customer should be at least 18 years old when they apply for a
       Frequent Shopper Card. That is, for each instance of the Customer
       entity type, the value of ApplicationDate attribute should be at least
       18 years greater than that of the DateOfBirth attribute.

SOLUTION 3.42

By looking at the contents of the checkout till receipts shown in Figure 2.6, from top
to bottom, we can see that they record the following information about the purchase
of products by a customer on a visit to a particular store in the Walton Stores
supermarket chain:

> Each checkout till receipt names the store where the products
> were purchased (Ramsgard, Oxford); it also names the checkout
> operator who completed the transaction (Jason, Selena,
> Gerda, Anne). It lists the products purchased by the customer,
> giving a description of each product (Gorgonzola, Goats' Milk
> Yoghurt, ...), the quantity (0.242kg, 250g, ...), the unit cost for
> those products sold by variable quantity (£10.99/kg, ...), the
> purchase price (£2.66, £0.89, ...), and any discount or reward
> (points) resulting from special offers (Buy 2 and save £1, Buy 2 and
> receive 2 extra points, ...). The checkout till receipt also shows
> the total purchase price (£4.14, £10.16, ...), the method of
> payment (cash, cheque, Frequent Shopper Card, debit card),
> the amount tendered (£10.00, ...), and when cash is tendered in
> payment for the products purchased (see till receipt 4), the
> change given. It will include the customer's Frequent Shopper
> Card (FSC) number if the customer presents their card to the
> checkout operator (see till receipts 3 and 4), together with the
> points earned from their purchases (10, 6), and the total points
> accrued if the card is used at a customer's home store
> (e.g. 345). Finally, each checkout till receipt records the date
> and time the transaction took place (25-May-2006 16:04,
> 27-May-2006 11:24, ...).

SOLUTION 3.43

The characteristics of the properties of the **CheckoutTillReceipt** entity type are shown in the table below.

CheckoutTillReceipt entity type

Property	SVF/MVF	Mandatory/ optional	Temporal/ derivable
checkout operator	SVF	mandatory	
products purchased:			
- descriptions	MVF	mandatory	
- quantities	MVF	mandatory	
- unit costs	MVF	optional	
- purchase prices	MVF	mandatory	
- discounts/rewards (special offers)	MVF	optional	
total purchase price	SVF	mandatory	derivable
method of payment	SVF	mandatory	
amount tendered	SVF	mandatory	
change given	SVF	optional	derivable
FSC number	SVF	optional	
points earned	SVF	optional	derivable
total points accrued	SVF	optional	derivable
transaction time	SVF	mandatory	

We have assumed that a transaction will include the purchase of at least one product, but this product (or any product purchased) may not attract any discount or reward. Therefore product descriptions, quantities and purchase prices are mandatory properties, and discounts/rewards is optional.

Unit cost is an optional property because it applies only to products sold by variable quantities, and for such products the purchase price is derivable from the quantity and the unit cost.

The total purchase price is derivable by summing the prices of all the products purchased, the change given is derivable from the total purchase price and the amount tendered, the points earned is derivable from the total purchase price and rewards gained from special offers, and the total points accrued is derivable by totalling the points earned from this and previous transactions associated with the customer who is identified by the Frequent Shopper Card number.

As the total purchase price, the change given, the points earned and the total points accrued are derivable from other properties of the **CheckoutTillReceipt** entity type, we can remove them from the list of properties of that entity type.

SOLUTION 3.44

The representation of the properties of the **CheckoutTillReceipt** entity type by the entity–relationship model we are developing to represent the data requirements of individual stores in the supermarket chain is summarised in the table below.

CheckoutTillReceipt entity type

Property	SVF/MVF	mandatory/ optional	representation
checkout operator	SVF	mandatory	by an attribute that records the name of the checkout operator, **CheckoutOperator**
products purchased:			
- sold by fixed quantities			via a :n relationship, **MayPurchase**, with an entity type that records details about products sold by fixed quantities, **ProductSoldByAFixedQuantity**, where the **CheckoutTillReceipt** end has optional participation
- descriptions	MVF	mandatory	
- quantities	MVF	mandatory	
- purchase prices	MVF	mandatory	
- discounts/rewards	MVF	optional	
- sold by variable quantities			via a :n relationship, **AndOrMayPurchase**, with an entity type that records details about products sold by variable quantities, **ProductSoldByAVariableQuantity**, where the **CheckoutTillReceipt** end has optional participation
- descriptions	MVF	mandatory	
- quantities	MVF	mandatory	
- unit costs	MVF	mandatory	
- discounts/rewards	MVF	optional	
method of payment	SVF	mandatory	by an attribute that records the method of payment, **MethodOfPayment**
amount tendered	SVF	mandatory	by an attribute that records the amount tendered, **AmountTendered**
FSC number	SVF	optional	via a :1 relationship, **MayUseA**, with an entity type that records details about Frequent Shopper Cards, **Customer**, where the **CheckoutTillReceipt** end has optional participation
transaction time	SVF	mandatory	by an attribute that records the date and time of the transaction, **Time**

The participation conditions of the **MayPurchase** and **AndOrMayPurchase** relationships with respect to the **CheckoutTillReceipt** entity type are optional because although in the solution to Exercise 3.43 we assume that a transaction will include the purchase of at least one product, a transaction can comprise either solely products that are sold by fixed quantities or solely products that are sold by variable quantities. The **MayPurchase** and **AndOrMayPurchase** relationships are inclusive/ exclusive: an occurrence of the **CheckoutTillReceipt** entity type must participate in at least one relationship but can participate in both.

Additional properties of the **ProductSoldByAFixedQuantity**, **ProductSoldByAVariableQuantity** and **Customer** entity types that result from their relationships with the **CheckoutTillReceipt** entity type are described in the following tables.

ProductSoldByAFixedQuantity entity type

Property	SVF/MVF	Mandatory/ optional	Representation
products purchased	MVF	optional	via a :*n* relationship, **MayPurchase**, with an entity type that records details about transactions, **CheckoutTillReceipt**, where the **ProductSoldByAFixedQuantity** end has optional participation

ProductSoldByAFixedQuantity has optional participation with respect to the **MayPurchase** relationship because a particular (new) product sold by fixed quantities may not, as yet, have been purchased by any customers.

ProductSoldByAVariableQuantity entity type

Property	SVF/MVF	Mandatory/ optional	Representation
products purchased	MVF	optional	via a :*n* relationship, **AndOrMayPurchase**, with an entity type that records details about transactions, **CheckoutTillReceipt**, where the **ProductSoldByAVariableQuantity** end has optional participation

ProductSoldByAVariableQuantity has optional participation with respect to the **MayPurchase** relationship because a particular (new) product sold by variable quantities may not, as yet, have been purchased by any customers.

Customer entity type

Property	SVF/MVF	Mandatory/ optional	Representation
transactions	MVF	optional	via a :*n* relationship, **MayUseA**, with an entity type that records details about transactions, **CheckoutTillReceipt**, where the **Customer** end has optional participation

Customer has optional participation with respect to the **MayUseA** relationship because a particular customer may not, as yet, have used their (new) Frequent Shopper Card in the purchase of goods from a store in the supermarket chain.

SOLUTION 3.45

Looking at the examples of checkout till receipts in Figure 2.6, a combination of the **CheckoutOperator** and **Time** attributes can fulfil these three roles. An alternative is to include the checkout till number (see Figure 2.3) where the checkout till operator handled the customer's purchases as a property of the **CheckoutTillReceipt** entity type, represented by an attribute named **CheckoutTillNumber**, and use this in place of the **CheckoutOperator** attribute. Thus the identifier of the **CheckoutTillReceipt** entity type is (**CheckoutTillNumber, Time**). We will use the latter identifier.

However, as the checkout till number is not included on checkout till receipts we will need to obtain this information from the client.

SOLUTION 3.46

Each occurrence of the **MayPurchase** relationship represents the purchase of a particular product sold by a fixed quantity in a particular transaction. Similarly, the **AndOrMayPurchase** relationship represents the purchase of a particular product in a transaction, where the product is sold by a variable quantity. However, as a transaction may involve the purchase of several of the same products of either type (as shown in Figure 2.6), the number purchased will be a property of the **MayPurchase** and **AndOrMayPurchase** relationships. Furthermore, in the case of products sold by variable quantities, the quantity of the product purchased is a property of the **AndOrMayPurchase** relationship.

SOLUTION 4.1

In the table below we have shown suggested underlying SQL data types for the columns of the outline definition of the **customer** table as shown in Figure 4.3.

customer table

Column	Value set	SQL data type	Notes
fsc_number	{dddd-dddd-dddd}	CHAR(14)	
title	{character strings}	VARCHAR(4)	1
forename	{character strings}	VARCHAR(20)	1
family_name	{character strings}	VARCHAR(20)	1
address	{character strings}	VARCHAR(100)	1
date_of_birth	{dates}	DATE	
gender	{Male, Female}	VARCHAR(6)	2
occupation	{Professional, Managerial, Clerical, Skilled, Unskilled, Unemployed}	VARCHAR(12)	2
annual_income	{< £10k, £10k – £20k, £20k – £30k, £30k – £40k, £40k – £50k, > £50k}	VARCHAR(11)	2
residence	{Owner, Tenant, Other}	VARCHAR(6)	2
further_information	{Yes, No}	VARCHAR(3)	2
application_date	{dates}	DATE	
credit_limit	{money}	SMALLINT	3

Notes:

1   The length of a character string was determined simply by counting the number of boxes provided on the Frequent Shopper Card application form (Figure 2.7) for applicants to write down their personal details.

2   The length of a character string was selected to accommodate the category with the most number of characters.

3   SQL Anywhere provides the **MONEY** and **SMALLMONEY** data types as vendor extensions to the standard SQL data types. However, as these correspond to **NUMERIC(19,4)** and **NUMERIC(10,4)**, respectively, they are both inappropriate for the subdivision of pounds sterling (£) into pence. Also, we would expect a customer's credit limit to be expressed as a whole number of pounds (£).

SOLUTION 4.2

The table below shows the suggested restrictions on the underlying SQL data types for the columns of the outline definition of the **customer** table as given in Figure 4.3.

customer table

Column	Value set	Restriction	Notes
fsc_number	{dddd-dddd-dddd}	particular format	
title	{character strings}	none	1
forename	{character strings}	none	
family_name	{character strings}	none	
address	{character strings}	none	
date_of_birth	{dates}	none	2
gender	{Male, Female}	specified values	
occupation	{Professional, Managerial, Clerical, Skilled, Unskilled, Unemployed}	specified values	
annual_income	{< £10k, £10k – £20k, £20k – £30k, £30k – £40k, £40k – £50k, > £50k}	specified values	
residence	{Owner, Tenant, Other}	specified values	
further_information	{Yes, No}	specified values	
application_date	{dates}	none	2
credit_limit	{money}	specified range	3

Notes:

1   Since the application form does not use check boxes for applicants to indicate their title, then we will choose not to restrict the **title** column to any particular values.

2   The condition c.5, specified in the *Additional constraint* section of the entity–relationship model for the **Customer** entity type shown in Figure 4.1, does not restrict the values of either the **date_of_birth** or the **application_date** columns *per se*, but determines the validity of an application for a Frequent Shopper Card. That is, it is a general constraint rather than a domain constraint. We will consider the options we have for the representation of the condition c.1 in Subsection 4.4.

3   The upper and lower bounds of the customers' credit limits need to be established with the client.

SOLUTION 4.3

The definition of the domains for all the columns of the **customer** table that could be implemented with SQL Anywhere is presented below. As we discussed in *Block 3*, Subsection 5.5, in SQL Anywhere we need to use the **@VALUE** keyword rather than just **VALUE** in the **CHECK** clauses of the **CREATE DOMAIN** statements. The standard SQL functions **CHAR_LENGTH** and **SUBSTRING** have been replaced by **LENGTH** and **SUBSTR** respectively. See the following Sybase online book: *ASA SQL Reference, Part I SQL, Chapter 3, SQL Functions.*

```
CREATE DOMAIN fsc_numbers AS VARCHAR(14)
   CHECK ((LENGTH(@VALUE) = 14) AND
           ((CAST(SUBSTR(@VALUE, 1, 4))
              AS INTEGER) BETWEEN 0 AND 9999) AND
           (SUBSTR(@VALUE, 5, 1) = '-') AND
           ((CAST(SUBSTR(@VALUE, 6, 4))
              AS INTEGER) BETWEEN 0 AND 9999) AND
           (SUBSTR(@VALUE, 10, 1) = '-') AND
           ((CAST(SUBSTR(@VALUE, 11, 4))
              AS INTEGER) BETWEEN 0 AND 9999)
         )
CREATE DOMAIN titles AS VARCHAR(4)
CREATE DOMAIN forenames AS VARCHAR(20)
CREATE DOMAIN family_names AS VARCHAR(20)
CREATE DOMAIN addresses AS VARCHAR(100)
CREATE DOMAIN dates AS DATE
CREATE DOMAIN genders AS VARCHAR(6)
   CHECK (@VALUE IN ('Male', 'Female'))
CREATE DOMAIN occupations AS VARCHAR(12)
   CHECK (@VALUE IN ('Professional', 'Managerial',
                     'Clerical', 'Skilled',
                     'Unskilled', 'Unemployed'))
CREATE DOMAIN annual_incomes AS VARCHAR(11)
   CHECK (@VALUE IN ('< £10k', '£10k - £20k', '£20k - £30k',
                     '£30k - £40k', '£40k - £50k', '> £50k'))
CREATE DOMAIN residences AS VARCHAR(6)
   CHECK (@VALUE IN ('Owner', 'Tenant', 'Other'))
CREATE DOMAIN yes_no AS VARCHAR(3)
   CHECK (@VALUE IN ('Yes', 'No'))
CREATE DOMAIN credit_limits AS SMALLINT
   CHECK (@VALUE BETWEEN 1000 AND 10000)
CREATE TABLE customer
   (fsc_number fsc_numbers NOT NULL,
    title titles NOT NULL,
    forename forenames NOT NULL,
    family_name family_names NOT NULL,
    address addresses NOT NULL,
    date_of_birth dates NOT NULL,
    gender genders NOT NULL,
    occupation occupations NOT NULL,
    annual_income annual_incomes NOT NULL,
    residence residences NOT NULL,
    further_information yes_no NOT NULL,
    application_date dates NOT NULL,
    credit_limit credit_limits NOT NULL,
   PRIMARY KEY (fsc_number),
   ...
   )
```

SOLUTION 4.4

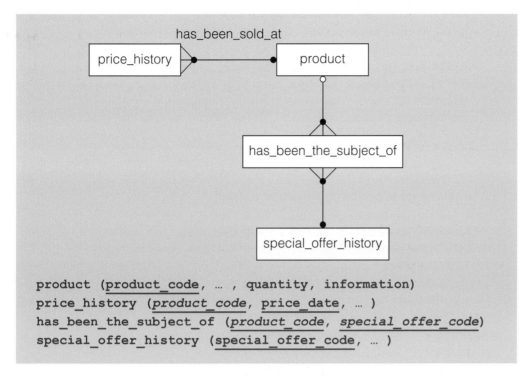

```
product (product_code, … , quantity, information)
price_history (product_code, price_date, … )
has_been_the_subject_of (product_code, special_offer_code)
special_offer_history (special_offer_code, … )
```

The above database schema diagram represents the relationships shown in the entity–relationship model as follows.

As in Figure 4.18, the **SoldByAFixed** and **MayIncludeAdditional** relationships are represented by including **quantity** and **information** as columns of the **product** table.

The *m:n* **HasBeenTheSubjectOf** relationship is represented using the *relation for relationship approach* by decomposing the **HasBeenTheSubjectOf** relationship into two 1:*n* relationships and an intersection table, **has_been_the_subject_of**, which represents the **HasBeenTheSubjectOf** relationship and whose primary key is a composite of the primary keys of the **product** and **special_offer_history** tables. The primary key columns of the **has_been_the_subject_of** table, **product_code** and **special_offer_code**, are also foreign keys that reference the **product** and **special_offer_history** tables, respectively, and being part of the primary key means that the **has_been_the_subject_of** table has mandatory participation with respect to the relationships with those tables.

The 1:*n* **HasBeenSoldAt** relationship is represented using the *foreign key alone approach* by making the primary key of the table at the :1 end of the relationship, **product.product_code**, a foreign key; **product.product_code** is already present in the table at the :*n* end of the relationship, **price_history.product_code**. As this foreign key is part of the primary key, the **price_history** table has mandatory participation with respect to the **HasBeenSoldAt** relationship.

SOLUTION 4.5

```
CREATE TABLE price_history
  (product_code product_codes NOT NULL,
   price_date dates NOT NULL
   ... ,
  PRIMARY KEY (product_code, price_date),
  CONSTRAINT has_been_sold_at
    FOREIGN KEY (product_code)
    REFERENCES product,
  ... ,
  )

CREATE TABLE product
  (product_code product_codes NOT NULL,
   ... ,
  PRIMARY KEY (product_code),
  CONSTRAINT mandatory_participation_in_has_been_sold_at
    CHECK (EXISTS
      (SELECT *
       FROM price_history
       WHERE product.product_code =
             price_history.product_code)),
  ...
  )

CREATE TABLE has_been_the_subject_of
  (product_code product_codes NOT NULL,
   special_offer_code special_offer_codes NOT NULL
   ... ,
  PRIMARY KEY (product_code, special_offer_code),
  CONSTRAINT product_in_has_been_the_subject_of
    FOREIGN KEY (product_code)
    REFERENCES product,
  CONSTRAINT special_offer_history_in_has_been_the_subject_of
    FOREIGN KEY (special_offer_code)
    REFERENCES special_offer_history
  ... ,
  )

CREATE TABLE special_offer_history
  (special_offer_code special_offer_codes NOT NULL,
   ... ,
  PRIMARY KEY (special_offer_code),
  CONSTRAINT mandatory_participation_in_has_been_the_subject_of
    CHECK (EXISTS
      (SELECT *
       FROM has_been_the_subject_of
       WHERE special_offer_history.special_offer_code =
             has_been_the_subject_of.special_offer_code)),
  ...
  )
```

SOLUTION 4.6

In *Block 3*, Subsection 2.7, we noted that the specific order of rows in a table resulting from any query is undefined, and that the rows are in a sequence determined by the SQL implementation, often related to how the data is stored. In particular, there is no guarantee that a particular ordering will remain the same after rows have been inserted into and deleted from a base table that the query accesses.

One of the properties of tables that is shared with its theoretical counterpart, relations, is that the ordering of rows in a table is not significant.

SOLUTION 4.7

One criterion that could be used to select a database design is the relative efficiency of the designs with respect to how the data needs to be processed in order to extract the information in the required format. Another criterion that could be used to select a design is whether this processing is effected primarily using SQL statements rather than by the application process of post-processing the data retrieved from the database.

The first design (Figure 4.21) requires the application process to unpack the address lines and postcode recorded by the single **address** column of each row of the resultant table into the address lines ready for printing. The second design (Figure 4.22) requires the application process simply to print the **address_line_1** to **address_line_6** columns of each row of the resultant table on separate lines. The third design (Figure 4.23) has the advantage that an address will be retrieved in the format that is required to facilitate the printing of an address label by an application process, but has the disadvantage of employing an additional table, which as a consequence, requires a join to be performed between the **customer** and **address_line** tables in order to satisfy the operational requirement specified.

According to the above criteria we would probably choose the design presented in Figure 4.22.

SOLUTION 4.8

As each property in the UK can be identified uniquely by the combination of its property number or name, and its postcode, in order to ensure that each household (property) has only one Frequent Shopper Card we can declare a **UNIQUE** constraint on the combination of the **property** and **postcode** columns of the **customer** table.

SOLUTION 4.9

A separate **address** table in a database design would be appropriate if more than one entity type in an entity–relationship model had an address as a property. For example, suppose that the database located at each store of the Walton Stores' supermarket chain also records details of its employees, including their addresses. Since an employee of Walton Stores could also be a customer of the supermarket chain and have a Frequent Shopper Card, the use of an **address** table would avoid duplication of the employee's/customer's address in separate **customer** and **employee** tables.

The following database schema diagram gives an outline database design for this situation.

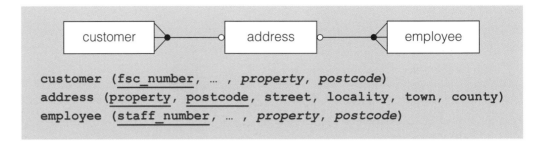

```
customer (fsc_number, ... , property, postcode)
address (property, postcode, street, locality, town, county)
employee (staff_number, ... , property, postcode)
```

In the above database design, we have assumed that Walton Stores does not restrict its Frequent Shopper Card to one per household (property) (as in Exercise 4.8) and its employees may be cohabiting. Hence, the relationship between the **address** and **customer** tables is 1:*n*, and the relationship between the **address** and **employee** tables is also 1:*n*. These relationships are represented by foreign keys, the **property** and **postcode** columns, being posted to the **customer** and **employee** tables. We have also assumed that each member of staff is identified by their staff number.

SOLUTION 4.10

```
CREATE TABLE ward
  (ward_no ... ,
   ...
  PRIMARY KEY (ward_no),
  CONSTRAINT mandatory_participation_in_staffed_by
    CHECK (ward_no IN (SELECT ward_no FROM nurse))
  )

CREATE TABLE nurse
  (staff_no ... ,
   ...
   ward_no ... NOT NULL,
   supervisor_no ... ,
  PRIMARY KEY (staff_no),
  CONSTRAINT staffed_by_relationship
    FOREIGN KEY (ward_no) REFERENCES ward,
  CONSTRAINT supervises_relationship
    FOREIGN KEY (supervisor_no) REFERENCES nurse,
  CONSTRAINT c5
    CHECK (NOT EXISTS
      (SELECT *
       FROM nurse n1, nurse n2
       WHERE n1.staff_no = n2.supervisor_no
         AND n1.ward_no <> n2.ward_no))
```

The check clause representing the condition c.5 realises the **Supervises** relationship and for each supervisee (n2) checks that their supervisor (n1) is not assigned to a different ward.

SOLUTION 4.11

```
CREATE TRIGGER insert_dates
  BEFORE INSERT ON customer
  REFERENCING NEW AS new_customer
  FOR EACH ROW
    WHEN (DATEDIFF(year, new_customer.date_of_birth),
          new_customer.application_date < 18)
    BEGIN ATOMIC
      DECLARE invalid_dates_value
        EXCEPTION FOR SQLSTATE '99999';
      SIGNAL invalid_dates_value;
    END
CREATE TRIGGER update_dates
  BEFORE UPDATE OF application_date, date_of_birth
    ON customer
  REFERENCING NEW AS new_customer
  FOR EACH ROW
    WHEN (DATEDIFF(year, new_customer.date_of_birth,
          new_customer.application_date) < 18)
    BEGIN ATOMIC
      DECLARE invalid_dates_value
        EXCEPTION FOR SQLSTATE '99999';
      SIGNAL invalid_dates_value;
    END
```

SOLUTION 4.12

```
CREATE TRIGGER update_patient
  AFTER UPDATE OF ward_no ON patient
  REFERENCING NEW AS new_patient
  FOR EACH ROW
    WHEN (
      (SELECT COUNT(*)
       FROM patient
       WHERE new_patient.ward_no = patient.ward_no)>
      (SELECT number_of_beds
        FROM ward
          WHERE new_patient.ward_no = patient.ward_no))
    BEGIN ATOMIC
      DECLARE too_many_patients
        EXCEPTION FOR SQLSTATE '99999';
      SIGNAL too_many_patients;
    END
CREATE TRIGGER update_ward
  AFTER UPDATE OF number_of_beds ON ward
  REFERENCING NEW AS new_ward
  FOR EACH ROW
    WHEN (new_ward.number_of_beds <
      (SELECT COUNT(*)
       FROM patient
       WHERE new_ward.ward_no = patient.ward_no))
    BEGIN ATOMIC
      DECLARE too_few_beds
        EXCEPTION FOR SQLSTATE '99999';
      SIGNAL too_few_beds;
    END
```

The above trigger ensures that when we update the **number_of_beds** column of a particular row (ward) of the **ward** table, its new value is not less than the number of patients currently on that ward.

```
CREATE TRIGGER insert_patient
  AFTER INSERT ON patient
  REFERENCING NEW AS new_patient
  FOR EACH ROW
    WHEN (
      (SELECT COUNT(*)
       FROM patient
       WHERE new_patient.ward_no = patient.ward_no) >
      (SELECT number_of_beds
       FROM ward
       WHERE new_patient.ward_no = ward.ward_no))
    BEGIN ATOMIC
      DECLARE too_many_patients
        EXCEPTION FOR SQLSTATE '99999';
      SIGNAL too_many_patients;
    END
```

The above trigger ensures that we cannot insert a row into the **patient** table if the total number of patients on the same ward as that patient is greater than the number of beds available on that ward.

SOLUTION 4.13

Entity subtypes enable us to distinguish between generic and specific forms of an entity type. In the *Hospital scenario*, for example, entity subtypes can be used to distinguish between the properties associated with doctors in general, and those specific to either consultants or junior doctors. The advantage of employing entity subtypes is that they enable us to represent the generic and specific properties of entity types explicitly by the entity–relationship diagram and the entity type definitions.

SOLUTION 4.14

The first approach, that represents all subtypes by a single table, is shown below.

The database schema diagram for the first approach is as follows.

```
customer (fsc_number, ... )
checkout_till_receipt (checkout_till_number, checkout_time, ... ,
                       fsc_number)
checkout_till_receipt_item (checkout_till_number, checkout_time,
                            item_number, ... )
```

The SQL database definition for the first approach is as follows.

```
CREATE TABLE customer
  (fsc_number fsc_numbers NOT NULL,
   ... ,
   PRIMARY KEY (fsc_number),
   ...
   )
CREATE TABLE checkout_till_receipt
  (checkout_till_number checkout_till_numbers NOT NULL,
   checkout_time checkout_times NOT NULL,
   fsc_number fsc_numbers,
   ... ,
   PRIMARY KEY (checkout_till_number, checkout_time),
   CONSTRAINT relationship_uses_fsc
     FOREIGN KEY (fsc_number) REFERENCES customer,
   CONSTRAINT mandatory_participation_in_comprises
     CHECK (EXISTS
       (SELECT *
        FROM checkout_till_receipt_item
        WHERE checkout_till_receipt.checkout_till_number =
              checkout_till_receipt_item.checkout_till_number
          AND checkout_till_receipt.checkout_time =
              checkout_till_receipt_item.checkout_time))
   )
CREATE TABLE checkout_till_receipt_item
  (checkout_till_number checkout_till_numbers NOT NULL,
   checkout_time checkout_times NOT NULL,
   item_number item_numbers NOT NULL,
   ... ,
   PRIMARY KEY (checkout_till_number, checkout_time, item_number),
   CONSTRAINT relationship_comprises
     FOREIGN KEY (checkout_till_number, checkout_time)
     REFERENCES checkout_till_receipt
   )
```

The second approach, that represents each subtype by a separate table, is shown below.

The database schema diagram for the second approach is as follows.

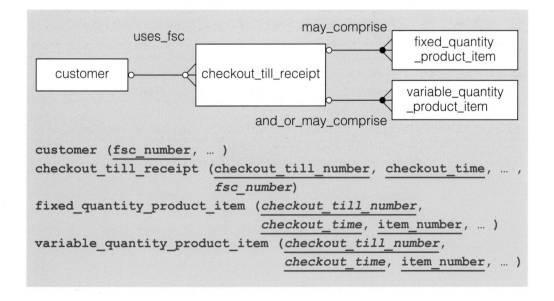

The SQL database definition for the second approach is as follows.

```
CREATE TABLE customer
  (fsc_number fsc_numbers NOT NULL,
   ... ,
   PRIMARY KEY (fsc_number),
   ...
   )
CREATE TABLE checkout_till_receipt
  (checkout_till_number checkout_till_numbers NOT NULL,
   checkout_time checkout_times NOT NULL,
   fsc_number fsc_numbers,
   ... ,
   PRIMARY KEY (checkout_till_number, checkout_time),
   CONSTRAINT relationship_uses_fsc
     FOREIGN KEY (fsc_number) REFERENCES customer
   CONSTRAINT c2
     CHECK ((EXISTS
       (SELECT *
        FROM fixed_quantity_product_item
        WHERE checkout_till_receipt.checkout_till_number =
             checkout_till_receipt_item.checkout_till_number
          AND checkout_till_receipt.checkout_time =
             checkout_till_receipt_item.checkout_time))
     )
     OR
       (EXISTS
         (SELECT *
           FROM variable_quantity_product_item
           WHERE checkout_till_receipt.checkout_till_number =
                checkout_till_receipt_item.checkout_till_number
             AND checkout_till_receipt.checkout_time =
                checkout_till_receipt_item.checkout_time))
     ))

CREATE TABLE fixed_quantity_product_item
  (checkout_till_number checkout_till_numbers NOT NULL,
   checkout_time checkout_times NOT NULL,
   item_number item_numbers NOT NULL,
   ... ,
   PRIMARY KEY (checkout_till_number, checkout_time, item_number),
   CONSTRAINT relationship_may_comprise
     FOREIGN KEY (checkout_till_number, checkout_time)
     REFERENCES checkout_till_receipt,
   CONSTRAINT no_overlapping_primary_keys
     CHECK (NOT EXISTS
       SELECT *
       FROM fixed_quantity_product_item,
            variable_quantity_product_item
       WHERE fixed_quantity_product_item.checkout_till_number =
            variable_quantity_product_item.checkout_till_number
         AND fixed_quantity_product_item.checkout_time =
            variable_quantity_product_item.checkout_time
         AND fixed_quantity_product_item.item_number =
            variable_quantity_product_item.item_number))
   )
```

```
CREATE TABLE variable_quantity_product_item
  (checkout_till_number checkout_till_numbers NOT NULL,
   checkout_time checkout_times NOT NULL,
   item_number item_numbers NOT NULL,
   ... ,
  PRIMARY KEY (checkout_till_number, checkout_time, item_number),
  CONSTRAINT relationship_and_or_may_comprise
    FOREIGN KEY (checkout_till_number, checkout_time)
    REFERENCES checkout_till_receipt
  )
```

SOLUTION 5.1

Specialist hardware: checkout tills that incorporate barcode scanners.

Other computer systems: the store's distribution centre; credit/debit card authorisation.

SOLUTION 5.2

```
// 1 Define all of the domains using
// CREATE DOMAIN statements.
CREATE DOMAIN team_codes AS CHAR(3)
  CHECK ((SUBSTRING(@VALUE, 1, 1) = 't')
    AND (CAST(SUBSTRING(@VALUE, 2, 2) AS SMALLINT)
                                  BETWEEN 1 AND 99))
CREATE DOMAIN telephone_nos AS VARCHAR(4)
CREATE DOMAIN staff_nos AS CHAR(3)
  CHECK (CAST(@VALUE AS INTEGER) BETWEEN 100 AND 999)
CREATE DOMAIN doctors_names AS VARCHAR(20)
CREATE DOMAIN positions AS VARCHAR(20)
  CHECK (@VALUE IN ('Consultant', 'Registrar', 'House Officer'))
CREATE DOMAIN specialisms AS VARCHAR(20)
  CHECK (@value IN ('Cardiac', 'Orthopaedic', 'Paediatric'))

// 2 Define all the columns of all the tables using
// CREATE TABLE statements and include all the column,
// primary key and uniqueness constraints.
CREATE TABLE team
  (team_code team_codes,
   telephone_no telephone_nos NOT NULL,
   staff_no staff_nos UNIQUE NOT NULL,
  PRIMARY KEY (team_code)
  )

CREATE TABLE doctor
  (staff_no staff_nos,
   doctor_name doctors_names NOT NULL,
   position positions NOT NULL,
   specialism specialisms,
   team_code team_codes,
  PRIMARY KEY (staff_no)
  )
```

```
// 3 Define all of the foreign keys using ALTER TABLE statements.
ALTER TABLE team
   ADD CONSTRAINT relationship_headed_by
      FOREIGN KEY (staff_no) REFERENCES doctor

ALTER TABLE doctor
   ADD CONSTRAINT relationship_consists_of
      FOREIGN KEY (team_code) REFERENCES team

// 4 Define table constraints by using either check constraints
// or triggers; check constraints are added to a table
// using ALTER TABLE statements, and triggers
// using CREATE TRIGGER statements.
ALTER TABLE team
   // mandatory participation in relationship consists_of
   ADD CONSTRAINT team_in_consists_of
      CHECK (team_code IN
        (SELECT team_code
         FROM doctor))

ALTER TABLE team
   // constraint c2 "A doctor that is the head of a team
   // must be a consultant"
   ADD CONSTRAINT C2
      CHECK (staff_no IN
        (SELECT staff_no
         FROM doctor
         WHERE position = 'Consultant'))

ALTER TABLE doctor
   // constraint c3 "A consultant must head a team.
   // Doctors who are not consultants must be members of a team"
   ADD CONSTRAINT C3
      CHECK ((position = 'Consultant' AND team_code IS NULL) OR
             (position <> 'Consultant' AND team_code IS NOT NULL))
```

SOLUTION 5.3

With newly created tables containing no rows it is not possible to add rows to either table because both the `checkout_till_receipt` and `checkout_till_receipt_item` tables have mandatory participation with respect to the relationship `comprises` between them.

For a row to be inserted into the `checkout_till_receipt` table it must satisfy the following constraint defined in that table:

```
CONSTRAINT mandatory_participation_in_comprises
   CHECK (EXISTS
     (SELECT *
      FROM  checkout_till_receipt_item
      WHERE checkout_till_receipt.checkout_till_number =
            checkout_till_receipt_item.checkout_till_number
        AND checkout_till_receipt.checkout_time =
            checkout_till_receipt_item.checkout_time)
     )
```

This constraint requires that the primary key value of the row being inserted into the **checkout_till_receipt** table is matched by the foreign key value present in at least one row of the **checkout_till_receipt_item** table, but this is not possible since the **checkout_till_receipt_item** table is empty, so the insertion fails.

For a row to be inserted into the **checkout_till_receipt_item** table it must satisfy the following constraint defined in that table:

```
CONSTRAINT relationship_comprises
    FOREIGN KEY (checkout_till_number, checkout_time)
    REFERENCES checkout_till_receipt
```

This constraint requires that the foreign key value of the row being inserted into the **checkout_till_receipt_item** table is matched by the primary key value of a row of the **checkout_till_receipt** table, but this is not possible since the **checkout_till_receipt** table is empty, so the insertion fails.

SOLUTION 5.4

The approach to populating database tables using the SQL Anywhere database option **WAIT_FOR_COMMIT** will only allow us to populate a table where it has a foreign key declaration referencing another table but no other constraint referencing that table. In the solution to Exercise 5.2, the **team** table has a foreign key referencing the **doctor** table, **staff_no**, and two constraints that reference the **doctor** table. Due to these constraints we cannot add a row to the **team** table without a corresponding row being present in the **doctor** table. The **doctor** table likewise has a foreign key **team_code** referencing the **team** table, and a constraint (**C3**) that references the **team** table. Due to this constraint we cannot add a row to the **doctor** table without a corresponding row being present in the **team** table.

SOLUTION 6.1

Both phases ensure that the database satisfies the information requirements of an enterprise. The activities associated with the database development phase ensure that the database built and installed satisfies these requirements. The activities associated with the database maintenance phase ensure that the database continues to satisfy those requirements after it has been installed, and enable the adaption of the database to meet new and changing requirements.

SOLUTION 6.2

The **checkout_till_receipt_item** table now contains duplicated information as a result of including data recorded by the **checkout_till_receipt** table.

SOLUTION 6.3

Denormalisation results in duplicated data that may result in insertion, amendment and deletion anomalies if the table needs to be updated.

SOLUTION 6.4

The **product** table records *all* products sold by Walton Stores. As the **product** table has optional participation with respect to the **purchases_a** relationship with the **checkout_till_receipt_item** table, the merged table would record just those products that have been purchased by customers. To facilitate the management of standing and special orders, however, we would need to make provision somehow to include products that have not been purchased by customers in the merged table.

SOLUTION 6.5

Optimising retrieval performance can be achieved also by:

▶ Storing derived data – this optimises retrieval performance by pre-computing derived values, which also simplifies the queries.

▶ Creating indexes on the columns that are included in the search conditions of **WHERE** clauses – indexes can optimise access to the rows that satisfy the search conditions. Defining and using indexes was described in *Block 3*, Subsection 5.8.

SOLUTION 7.1

We can get the same result in the University database with the following single update:

```
UPDATE student
   SET region_number = '4'
   WHERE student_id = 's38'
```

SOLUTION 7.2

The coordinator must maintain its log entries until it receives the final OK message from all the participating systems in a transaction. It needs to defer until then any decision to commit or rollback in order to recover from the cases of failure.

SOLUTION 7.3

As we discussed in *Block 1*, Subsection 3.5, we would want a DDBMS to take full advantage of the distributed nature of data, yet still have the general capabilities of a localised database, and so we expect the following characteristics:

▶ A DDBMS should present a single view of all data, since users should not have to worry where the data is actually stored, i.e. there is location independence. As long as a user has the necessary privileges, there should be no difference detected whether a table is local to the user or on one or more remote systems.

▶ A DDBMS should support transactions across system boundaries and maintain the integrity of the distributed database. A DDBMS must be able to recover from the failure of any particular computer participating in the transaction or a failure in the communication network.

▶ There must be a security process that can protect the distributed database from unauthorised access, yet provide uniform access to it for authorised users.

▶ A DDBMS should work consistently over the broadest possible variety of both computer platforms and networks. This means that, with the exception of performance variations, the DDBMS should work the same way whether it uses a mainframe or PC and independently of the characteristics of the interconnecting network.

SOLUTION 7.4

The benefits and drawbacks of the complete replication of the schemas are as follows.

Benefits:	One copy of the schemas at every site, so no need to search for one.
Drawbacks:	Need to keep the multiplicity of replicates consistent and up to date.

The benefits and drawbacks of the distribution of parts of the schemas are as follows.

Benefits:	Reduces the bottleneck of only one schema, improving access.
Drawbacks:	Need to decide where to place each part; some query processing involves two or more parts.

SOLUTION 7.5

(a) The same SQL statement as posed in the question should be executed at each location.

(b) The results of part (a) should be combined by union operations.

SOLUTION 7.6

Plan 1 data to be transferred: $(112 \times 5000) + (18 \times 100) = 560\,000 + 1800 = 561\,800$ bytes.

Plan 2 data to be transferred: $(112 \times 5000) + (50 \times 100) = 560\,000 + 5000 = 565\,000$ bytes.

Plan 3 data to be transferred: $(18 \times 100) + (50 \times 100) = 1800 + 5000 = 6800$ bytes.

Note: the SQL query to produce a list of the names of the departments and their managers results in 100 rows, each of $(10 + 20 + 20)$ 50 Bytes.

SOLUTION 7.7

Plan 1 data to be transferred: $(8 \times 100) + (18 \times 100) = 2600$ bytes.

Plan 2 data to be transferred: $(18 \times 100) + (18 \times 100) = 3600$ bytes.

Plan 3 data to be transferred: $(8 \times 100) + (18 \times 100) = 2600$ bytes.

SOLUTION 7.8

This distribution requires two tables in the global schema: one to include the columns **student_id**, **name**, **address**, **email_address** and **registration_date**, and the other to include the columns **student_id** and **region_number**. Note that **student_id** is required in both tables, so that they may be joined together again.

SOLUTION 7.9

(a) At each regional database, whenever there is a change to a student's email address, a copy is taken and posted to the consolidated table. The DBA at each region must arrange to push changes to the student's email address over to the database containing the consolidated table.

(b) The replication server associated with the headquarters database sends a request to each regional database, asking for changes to be made to the student's email address and then collecting a copy of each change. The DBA at each region must allow changes to the student's email address to be pulled over to the consolidated table.

The disadvantage of the pull mechanism is that the data in the headquarters database will be out of date between the time that the regional databases are updated and the time that the pull is activated.

SOLUTION 7.10

There is now a potential for an update conflict and hence an inconsistency in the data. There would need to be some policy on what to do in such circumstances, which is likely to be defined by the owners of the primary data. Within a database, stored procedures may be used to implement the constraints expressed in the design for such policies.

SOLUTION 8.1

There are $2^3 = 8$ views of the same data as follows:

time;

location;

product;

time by *location*;

time by *product*;

location by *product*;

time by *location* by *product*;

the grand total of the measure.

SOLUTION 8.2

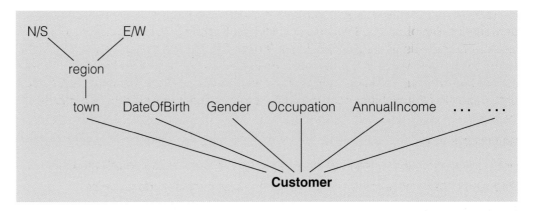

The customers' addresses have been given the same concept hierarchy as the *location* dimension (see Figure 8.6) in order to locate customers in Walton Stores' regions.

Each of the following attributes of the **Customer** entity type can be used to classify customers: **Address, DateOfBirth, Gender, Occupation, AnnualIncome, Residence** and **CreditLimit**.

SOLUTION 8.3

The *drill-down* operation *moves* to a more detailed view of the data along one or more dimensions. The operation does not *produce* new data since you cannot produce more detailed data from summary data. For example, monthly summaries of Walton Stores' sales data cannot be obtained from quarterly summary data but only by summarising (aggregating) more detailed (raw) data. The *roll-up* and *cube* operations produce new views of the data by aggregating the same data.

SOLUTION 8.4

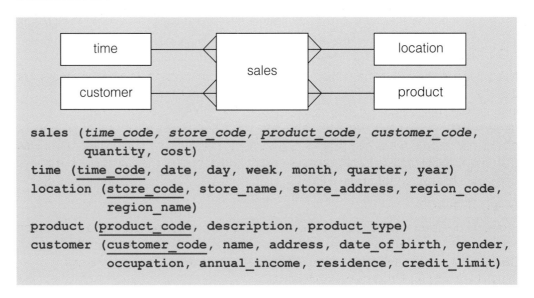

SOLUTION 8.5

In the entity–relationship diagram for Walton Stores, the degree of the relationship between the **Supplier** and **Product** entity types, **Supplies**, is one-to-many. That is, each product line is only ever supplied to Walton Stores by a single supplier. So in the `sales` table, each value of the `product_code` column will have the same corresponding value for `supplier_code`. Hence the `sales` table contains duplicated data, repeating the fact that each particular product line is supplied by a particular supplier.

SOLUTION 8.6

Update, insertion and deletion anomalies can occur when data is duplicated.

Since the data in these tables is not updated, these problems do not arise.

SOLUTION 8.7

Using this approach not every cell may have a value. Depending on the specific application, a varying proportion of cells will be empty. For example, with Walton Stores' sales data, if the *product* and *supplier* dimensions are included, the data will be sparse because suppliers do not necessarily supply all types of product. If the data is sparse and many cells are empty, storage utilisation and query processing may be poor.

SOLUTION 8.8

A data warehouse is usually maintained separately from an organisation's operational database systems because the content, functional and performance requirements of the two kinds of system are different. Decision support requires summarised historical data, whereas operational databases usually store only raw current data. Decision support involves analytical processing, whereas operational database systems support transaction processing workloads.

SOLUTION 8.9

A marketing data mart would probably confine its subjects to *customers*, *products* and *sales*.

SOLUTION 8.10

If the departmental data marts have been developed in isolation, there is the possibility that the format and semantics of related data in different data marts will be inconsistent, hence making integration difficult. Therefore, although individual departmental data marts might serve the departments' decision support requirements effectively, serving the organisation's requirements using a distributed data warehouse may be less effective. We shall discuss format and semantic integration later when we consider *Data warehousing architecture*.

SOLUTION 8.11

Strategic decision making requires access to historical data but operational information sources usually store only current data. A virtual data warehouse also has the disadvantage that queries are made against the operational information systems, which may degrade their performance.

SOLUTION 8.12

Integration involves recognising incompatibilities between data from different sources, and eliminating these incompatibilities to allow comparisons and aggregations.

It is an important issue in data warehousing since a data warehouse is usually constructed by integrating multiple heterogeneous information sources, which may be maintained on many different computer systems using different types of technology. Before operational data can be loaded into the data warehouse, it must be integrated to ensure consistency in naming conventions, encoding structures, attribute values, and so on, to allow comparisons and aggregations.

SOLUTION 8.13

In the eager approach, integrated information is available for immediate querying and analysis by users, which is appropriate for:

- ▶ users requiring specific, predictable selections of the available information;
- ▶ users requiring high query performance (the data is available locally at the data warehouse);
- ▶ users wanting access to information that is no longer maintained at the information sources.

However, if the data maintained at the various information sources changes frequently, the integrated information available becomes out of date, and possibly less useful.

SOLUTION 8.14

The lazy approach is appropriate for:

- ▶ users who require the most up-to-date version of data from information sources that change rapidly;
- ▶ users with unpredictable needs for information.

The lazy approach, however, may incur inefficiency and delay in query processing, especially when different users pose the same queries, when information sources are slow, or periodically unavailable, and when significant processing is required for the translation, cleaning, and merging steps. In cases where the information sources do not permit ad hoc queries, the lazy approach is simply not feasible.

SOLUTION 8.15

The issues associated with the integration of data from multiple heterogeneous distributed information sources will need to be addressed. This involves recognising inconsistencies between the data from different sources, and for each inconsistency providing a form of translation before the data from different sources can be integrated.

SOLUTION 8.16

Changes to the data must be translated from the format and model of the information source into the format and model used by the warehouse database. When the monitor detects changes, it requests the wrapper to translate the data before sending it to the integrator.

SOLUTION 8.17

An organisation should ensure, whenever possible, that the appropriate constraints are enforced by the existing schemas of the information sources to guarantee the quality of data at source, or application processes if not enforced by a schema.

SOLUTION 8.18

Typically, hierarchies of aggregated data along some dimensions are precomputed and stored in the warehouse database, mainly summarising over time; for example, yearly, quarterly, monthly, weekly and daily sales data. The aggregations of an organisation's operational data that the administrator actually chooses to precompute will depend on the requirements of the decision makers to analyse and view the data in order to meet the decision support needs of that organisation. There is a trade-off between the gain in efficiency of query execution using aggregated data, and the cost of keeping the aggregated data up to date. This will need to be taken into consideration by the administrator when choosing data aggregates to precompute.

SOLUTION 8.19

An empirical approach to precomputed aggregation is to compute an aggregate when it is needed by a query and is not already stored in the warehouse database. When the space available to store aggregates is full, the next aggregate to be computed will replace the least frequently used aggregate stored.

SOLUTION 8.20

1   Re-compute all the views whenever the unaggregated data is modified. This approach will be prohibitive if a data warehousing system has many materialised views and requires frequent updating. However, the performance can be improved if the maintenance is coupled with change detection so that only those views that are affected by an update to the unaggregated data are re-computed.

2   Re-compute those views that are affected by an update to the unaggregated data only when a view is queried. This leads to faster warehouse maintenance at the expense of the efficiency of query processing.

3   Update views (rather than re-computing them) by applying the changes to the unaggregated data to the current version of the views. Although such an approach is attractive, it is feasible only for certain types of updates to the unaggregated data.

SOLUTION 8.21

Since the aggregate navigator intercepts all queries, it could also record statistics about execution of each query, including the frequency of use of each materialised view. This statistical data would be stored in the metadata repository, and the administrator could then use the data to determine how effectively their current view selection strategy is working, and maybe improve their strategy.

SOLUTION 8.22

Most of the metadata in the repository that will be used by the decision makers is readily available as a data warehousing system is developed. It is only necessary for the data warehouse developers to have a place to record this information as they encounter it, to recognise the need to do so, and to carry out the process. It is considered good practice for data warehouse developers to store this descriptive data in the repository as the system is being built.

Index

A

acceptance testing 8, 12

adaptive maintenance 12

aggregate functions 245

aggregate navigator 262

aggregate rows 246

aggregation 236

B

Boyce–Codd Normal Form
(BCNF) 150

C

check constraints 143, 171

client 210

client multiserver 209

client–multiserver 209–210

concept hierarchy 238

conceptual data model 25–27

connection management 210

consolidation 227

cooperative sources 258

cube operation 240

current connection 211

D

data cleaning 259

data mart 252

data mining 231

data requirements 7, 24

data warehouse 231

data warehousing 13

database development 6–7

database life cycle 6–7

database maintenance 6–7

database properties 6

database reorganisation 12

database restructuring 12

database schema 141

database schema diagram 146

database server 209

decision making 232

decision support systems 13, 231

dependent data mart 252

derivable property 53

dimension tables 241

dimension–value pairs 238

dimensions 235

dissemination 227

distributed data management 13

distributed data warehouse 252

distributed database 209

distributed database management
system 215

distribution optimisation 219

distribution schema 215

domain of discourse 26, 28

drill-down operation 240

drill-up operation 239

E

eager (in-advance) approach 254

enterprise data warehouse 252

entity subtype 40

entity supertype 40

entity–relationship model 27

extraction component 256

F

fact constellation 244

fact table 241

facts 235

first-cut design 141

flexed first-cut design 141

foreign key alone approach 152

format integration 260

fragmentation 217

G

galaxy schema 244

global logical schema 215

global schema 215

grouped table 245

grouping columns 245

H

horizontal fragmentation 217

hybrid OLAP (HOLAP) 241

I

independent data mart 252

information integration 253

information requirements 7, 24

integration component 256, 259

integrator 254

L

lazy (on-demand) approach 254

local autonomy 217

location independence 215

logged sources 258

M

materialised views 261

measures 235

mediated approach 254

mediator 254

multi-valued fact 29

multi-valued property 29, 31, 33,
48

multidimensional data model 13,
231

multidimensional OLAP
(MOLAP) 235

N

naming problem 224

natural join 147

normalised database tables 11,
13

O

online analytical processing (OLAP) 233

online transaction processing (OLTP) 233

operational maintenance 12

operational requirements 7, 24

P

physical data warehouse 253

primary copy 222

Q

queryable sources 258

R

relation for relationship approach 152

relational OLAP (ROLAP) 235

replication server 226

replication systems 209

roll-up operation 239

S

second-cut design 141

semantic integration 260

server 209

single-valued fact 29

single-valued property 29, 31, 33, 48

site autonomy 217

snapshot sources 258

snowflake schema 244

star schema 241

statement of requirements 7

summarisation 236

surrogate keys 167

T

testing 8

three-schema architecture 7

triggers 143, 171

two-phase commit 212

V

validation 8

value set 53

verification 8

vertical fragmentation 217

view maintenance 262

view selection 262

virtual data warehouse 253

W

waterfall model 7

wrapper 254

wrapper generator 259